Acclaim for Max Hastings's

WARRIORS

"This collective biography addresses the deeper mystery of the wellsprings of exceptional bravery.... Hastings is a skilled and innovative narrator who has a deft touch in sketching the tactical situation of each engagement."

—*The Philadelphia Inquirer*

"A fascinating and surprisingly entertaining study of sixteen warriors, not all of them heroes." —*Scotland on Sunday*

"*Warriors* is indeed the proverbial rattling good read, carried off by a master of his art." —*Literary Review*

"Enthralling and exciting.... [A] fascinating and well-written book." —*The Tennessean*

"His brisk prose has the qualities of his warriors: clear, decisive, forceful." —*The Daily Telegraph* (London)

"Hastings combines his consummate skill as a writer with passages of descriptive brilliance to provide a book for the ordinary citizen. He captures the commitment of the fighting servicemen and women, loyally executing the policy of the government of the day, in language that is powerful yet eminently comprehensible. This is a book to entertain."

—*The Sunday Times* (London)

"Brimming with great anecdotes.... [Hastings's] wonderfully readable book is going to make a lot of armchair soldiers very, very happy." —*Mail on Sunday*

MAX HASTINGS
WARRIORS

Max Hastings was a foreign correspondent and editor-in-chief of Britain's *Evening Standard* and *Daily Telegraph*. He has presented historical documentaries for BBC TV, and is the author of nineteen books, including *Bomber Command*, which earned the Somerset Maugham Award for nonfiction, *The Korean War*, and *Armageddon*. He lives in the countryside west of London.

WARRIORS

WARRIORS

PORTRAITS FROM THE BATTLEFIELD

MAX HASTINGS

VINTAGE BOOKS
A DIVISION OF RANDOM HOUSE, INC.
NEW YORK

FIRST VINTAGE BOOKS EDITION, MARCH 2007

The Library of Congress has cataloged the Knopf edition as follows:
Hastings, Max.
Warriors : portraits from the battlefield / Max Hastings.—1st American ed.
p. cm.
Includes bibliographical references and index.
1. Soldiers—Biography.   2. War.   3. Combat.   I. Title.
U51.H37 2006
355'.0092'2—dc22   2005044302

Vintage ISBN: 978-0-307-27568-4

Book design by Robert C. Olsson
Maps by Hardlines

www.vintagebooks.com

Printed in the United States of America
10 9 8 7 6 5 4 3 2 1

For Professor Sir Michael Howard, OM, CH, MC,
sometime warrior, evergreen teacher.
With affection and admiration, as always.

CONTENTS

INTRODUCTION

This is an old-fashioned book, or at least a book about old-fashioned conflicts, because it concerns people rather than "platforms," that unloveable contemporary synonym for tanks, ships, planes. It addresses the experience of some remarkable characters—variously American, British, Australian, French, German—who made their marks upon the wars of the past two centuries. Like the rest of us, they are a mix of good, bad, ugly, charming and disagreeable. This study will be of no interest to such modern warlords as U.S. Defense Secretary Donald Rumsfeld, because it addresses aspects of conflict they do not comprehend, creatures of flesh and blood rather than systems of steel and electronics. As Admiral Daniel V. Gallery observed about an earlier defense secretary back in 1965: "I doubt if Mr. McNamara and his crew have any morale settings on their computers."

In civil life, people with a penchant for fighting are deemed at best an embarrassment, at worst a menace. Warriors are unfashionable people in democratic societies during periods of peace. Major-General John Pope of the Army of the Tennessee asserted: "The well-being of the people equally with the well-being of the Army requires a common sympathy and a common interest between them." Yet this proposition is far more often honoured in the breach than the observance. "Much more could be done if the women of America would praise their heroes," said George Patton. Nelson liked to quote Thomas Jordan's epigram:

Our God and sailor we adore,
In time of danger, not before;
The danger past, both are alike requited,
God is forgotten, and the sailor slighted.

Yet all nations need warriors to pursue their national interests in conflict, to create disciplined violence within the harness of uniform. In times of war, fighting men are suddenly cherished and become celebrities—or at least did so until very recently. Few of those who experience battle emerge as heroes. Most, even if they have volunteered for military service, discover amid mortal peril that they prefer to act in a fashion likely to enable them to see home again, rather than to perform the sort of feats which win medals. This does not mean they are cowards. The majority do their duty conscientiously. They are reluctant, however, to take those strides beyond duty which mark out the men who win battles for their countries.

One of my favourite stories of World War II concerns a British sergeant-major named Stan Hollis. On D-Day, 6 June 1944, and in the battles that followed, three times Hollis attacked German positions which were holding up his battalion's advance. He charged them alone, with Sten gun and grenades, and killed or took prisoner the defenders. Many years later, his commanding officer reflected in my hearing upon the sergeant-major, who, miraculously, lived to receive a Victoria Cross and keep a pub in his old age. The colonel said: "I think Hollis was the only man I met between 1939 and 1945 who felt that winning the war was his personal responsibility. Everybody else, when they heard there was a bloody awful job on, used to mutter: 'Please God some other poor sod can be found to do it!' " Sherman noted a hundred years earlier: "All men naturally shrink from pain and danger, and only incur their risk from some higher motive, or from habit."

Every army, in order to prevail on the battlefield, needs a certain number of people capable of courage, initiative or leadership beyond the norm. What is the norm? It has changed through the course of history, dramatically so since the mid-twentieth century, with the advance of what passes for civilisation. Western democracies have not become more merciful towards enemies. Indeed, they use ever more terrible weapons to encompass their destruction. Western warriors, however, have become progressively more sensitive to risk and hardship, in a fashion which reflects sentiment in the societies from which they are drawn. A Greek or Roman soldier was required to engage in hours of close-quarter combat with edged weapons which hacked through flesh, muscle, bone and entrails. Modern firearms inflict equally terrible wounds, but by a much less intimate process. "Was this fighting?" mused a World War I fighter pilot, V. M. Yeates. "There was no anger, no red lust, no struggle, no straining muscles and sobbing breath; only the slight movement of levers and rattle of machine-guns."

The absence of physical exertion in the business of killing, which Yeates remarked as a novelty in 1918, has become more emphatic, indeed almost universal, for twenty-first-century warriors, barring only some combat infantrymen. In the past, a soldier's belief in the nobility of his calling stemmed in part from his acceptance of the risk of losing his own life while taking those of others. It would be wrong to overstate the degree of chivalry involved, for, of course, every warrior aspired to kill his enemy while he himself survived. But the acceptance of possible death—of a multitude of deaths on one's own side, win or lose—was part of the contract, in a fashion that has vanished today. Low-intensity engagement with guerrillas continues to inflict painful losses on Western armies, conspicuously so in Iraq since 2003. If matters go according to plan in such set-piece operations as the invasions of Afghanistan and Iraq or the bombing of Kosovo, however, military objectives are achieved at negligible cost to the technological master power. Losses are substantial among the vanquished primitives, but questions are only asked in Congress if there are significant casualties among the victors. Any assumption of parity of human risk is long gone. We have returned to the rules of engagement which prevailed in nineteenth-century colonial conflicts: "We have got the Maxim gun and they have not"; or, in a twenty-first-century context, "We possess body armour impervious to small arms and splinters, and tanks invulnerable to low-technology weapons."

In the battles of Bonaparte's era, an infantryman was expected, as a matter of course, to stand firm at his place in the square, line or column, loading and aiming his musket usually without the protection of trench or earthwork, while the enemy fired volleys at him and his comrades from a range of thirty or forty yards. There was seldom any tactical provision for an individual to evade danger. When Wellington ordered his infantry to lie down during enemy bombardments in his battles with Napoleon's armies, this was perceived as a controversial, possibly pernicious innovation. For a combatant to earn from his peers the reputation of a brave man, he was obliged to exceed a norm which modern soldiers would consider intolerable. And since the wars of Bonaparte persisted for the best part of twenty years, many veterans were called upon to display a willingness to defy the terrors of the battlefield thirty, forty, fifty times in separate engagements.

The American Civil War required from combatants the same submission to massed fire as Bonaparte's and Wellington's soldiers experienced, the ordeals of Gettysburg and the Wilderness being rendered more terrible by improvements in weapon technology. Although the clash of the states was much shorter in duration than the great European wars earlier in the nineteenth century, it exacted by far the highest casualties of any conflict in the history of the United States, albeit many of them by disease.

The end of the nineteenth century marked the passing of a warrior ethic which had prevailed since earliest history, whereby war was deemed a proper source of amusement for the leisured classes, as well as of employment for the impoverished ones. As a war correspondent, Winston Churchill sounded a last hurrah for the gentleman adventurer in a characteristically exuberant dispatch from Buller's South African army in February 1900.

The soldier, who fares simply, sleeps soundly and rises with the morning star, wakes in an elation of body and spirit without an effort and with scarcely a yawn. There is no more delicious moment in the day than this, while we light the fire and, while the kettle boils, watch the dark shadow of the hills take form, perspective and finally colour, knowing that there is another whole day begun, bright with chance and interest, and free from all cares. All cares are banished—for who can be worried about the little matters of humdrum life when he may be dead before the night? Such a one was with us yesterday—see, there is a spare mug for coffee in the mess—but now gone for ever. And so it may be with us tomorrow. What does it matter that this or that is misunderstood or perverted; that So-and-so is envious and spiteful; that heavy difficulties obstruct the larger schemes of life, clogging nimble aspiration with the mud of matters of fact? Here life itself, life at its best and healthiest, awaits the caprice of a bullet. Let us see the development of the day. All else may stand over, perhaps for ever. Existence is never so sweet as when it is at hazard.

A relatively small number of people enjoyed the conflicts of the twentieth century as much as Churchill had revelled in his adventures with the Malakand Field Force. World wars inflicted such horrors upon mankind that it became unacceptable for even the most enthusiastic warrior to avow them as entertainments, even if professional soldiers, sailors and airmen still welcomed the opportunities which they offered for swift advancement. A career officer whose advancement from lieutenant to colonel might take twenty years of peacetime service could achieve the same leap in a couple of campaigns, given luck and ability. However, the majority of participants were unwilling civilians, conscripted into uniform to endure experiences they found uncongenial, even if they accepted a duty to endure them. Few 1939–45 citizen soldiers wrote home from North Africa or the Pacific with Churchill's exuberant delight.

The most dramatic foreshortening of Western democratic man's assumed quotient of courage, his expected tolerance of the circumstances of conflict, took place between the two world wars. In the 1914–18 encounter, infantrymen of all the combatant powers were required to accept a level of sacrifice Bonaparte's or Grant's soldiers would have acknowledged with respect. A generation later, however, a consensus evolved among Anglo-American commanders that it was impossible again to make such demands upon their men. The manner in which World War II campaigns were conducted, especially in northwest Europe, reflected an Allied preference for firepower rather than human endeavour, an acknowledgement of combat fatigue as a recognised medical condition, and a reluctance to persist with any course of action that entailed heavy loss.

However ghastly were some individual Western Allied experiences of World War II, only in the Japanese, Russian and German armies were demands routinely made upon the soldier comparable with those of earlier centuries. It might be observed that "fanatical" enemy behaviour which roused the dismay, even revulsion, of 1939–45 American and British soldiers was no more than had been asked as a commonplace of their own forebears: a willingness to carry out orders likely to precipitate their own deaths. After 1918, the soldiers of the Western democracies in World War II were deemed to have grown more "civilised," a cause of lamentation among their commanders. Senior officers such as Patton, Brooke and Alexander, not to mention Churchill, bewailed the fact that the men whom they led possessed less capacity for suffering than their fathers who bore arms in the Kaiser's war. The norm had changed.

Yet in every society on earth, the most durable convention, from ancient times until very recently, has held physical courage to be the highest human attribute. For thousands of years, in nations dominated by the warrior ethic, this quality was valued more highly than intellectual achievement or moral worth. A.E.W. Mason's classic adventure story *The Four Feathers*, set in 1898, concerns a sensitive young army officer who resigns his commission because he prefers to stay in England enjoying country life with an adored fiancée, rather than accompany his regiment up the Nile to slaughter Dervishes. His girl joins the other officers in offering him a white feather for his "cowardice." He is obliged to perform extraordinary feats of derring-do in order to recover her esteem. The story has always seemed to me flawed, because it requires the hero eventually to marry this foolish creature, who surely proved her unfitness as a partner for life by placing so high a premium upon brawn over brains, preferring to see her loved one immolate himself on a battlefield, rather than indulge his poetic nature.

Yet *The Four Feathers* vividly reflected the values of its period. One consequence of mankind's exaggerated regard for courage is that some remarkably stupid men, their only virtue a willingness to expose their own persons to risk, have been granted positions of responsibility on the battlefield, where their follies have cost lives. Bonaparte often over-promoted officers of high courage and small intelligence, whose headlong assaults upon the enemy cost the imperial army gratuitous slaughter. General Sir Harold Alexander's bravery, patrician manners and dashing appearance made him Churchill's favourite general. "Alex" looked the ideal of a warrior. The prime minister was content to overlook the hero's notorious laziness and lack of intellect.

A less-exalted officer who showed himself "brave as a lion," to quote a comrade, leading a battalion in northwest Europe in 1944–45 had to be relieved of a brigade command in Korea in 1951. His subordinates formally protested to the divisional commander when this committed warrior proposed to launch his men in a frontal assault upon the Chinese. He failed to comprehend the new terms of limited war. A century ago, Ambrose Bierce advised the ambitious American professional soldier: "Always try to get yourself killed." Many of those who display a willingness to pursue this objective are, however, fools by the normal yardsticks of humanity. Courage is a desirable asset in a commander, but is usually fatal to the interests of his soldiers unless accompanied by some intellectual powers. "Valour without wisdom is insufficient," said Frederick the Great. Cavalry and its senior officers were flawed through most of their history, up to and including World War II, by an instinctive compulsion to charge. No warrior should be promoted to higher command merely because he is brave. Two thousand five hundred years ago, the Chinese warrior Wu Ch'i noted: "When people discuss a general they always pay attention to his courage. As far as a general is concerned, courage is but one quality. A valiant general will be certain to enter an engagement recklessly." A skilled and eager fighter is best rewarded by decorations rather than promotion. He should be retained in a role in which he can make himself useful in personal combat, rather than advanced beyond the merits of the rather limited gift—even for a soldier—of being good at killing people.

Yet it is hard to exaggerate the influence which displays of battlefield prowess have always exercised upon others, especially adolescents who are least equipped to perceive the worth of other virtues. As a schoolboy, I read a book written in the 1920s entitled *Stirring Deeds of the Great War* Works of this nature were published in great numbers from Victorian times until, say, the 1960s. They depicted conflict as an extension of school sports, in which young men possessed of the right stuff could win their colours on a national field. They were designed to inspire new generations of Americans and Englishmen to emulate the feats of their forefathers, and often they succeeded. The illustrations in *Stirring Deeds* left a lasting impression upon the impressionable. I remember one captioned: "Lieutenant Smyth's terrible journey with the bombs." It depicted a young officer lugging a box of grenades across no-man's-land amid a storm of shot and shell. In those days, the public perception of heroism was almost entirely related to feats of military prowess. Until at least the 1960s, warriors who had displayed conspicuous courage in one or other of the twentieth century's notable bouts with the Germans were treated with high respect, even if their checks bounced.

It may be argued that portrayals of war as "the great game" prostituted courage for dubious nationalistic purposes. Yet over the past thirty years or so, the word "hero," surely one of the most precious in the language, has become debased in a different way. Public admiration once reserved for warriors has been transferred to sports stars and celebrities, many of negligible attainment. Martial courage has become far less esteemed in Western societies. In part, happily, this is because the need for it in wars of national survival has vanished. Less happily, however, it is because some people in the twenty-first century recoil from any celebration of military achievement.

In the tranquil times in which we are fortunate enough to live—with or without Al Q'aeda, our ancestors would consider our era uniquely privileged—there is a public yearning to make life safe. A corollary of this is a diminution of enthusiasm for those who embrace risk. Most of the people whose stories feature in this book would find our society's quest for an existence without peril incomprehensible, unmanly, absurd. They would be amazed by the childlike and increasingly widespread belief that if governments do their business properly, even a soldier in war can be protected from harm.

It is welcome that popular perceptions of courage no longer embrace only, or even chiefly, achievement in battle. But it seems dismaying that the public today blurs the distinction between a victim, who suffers terrible experiences, and a hero. John F. Kennedy was once asked by a small boy how he became a war hero, and responded with this not wholly inaccurate self-deprecatory explanation: "It was involuntary. They sank my boat." A true hero must consciously consent to risk his or her life for a higher purpose. The media, for instance, will describe a pilot who safely lands a crippled plane full of passengers as "a hero." A party trapped for hours on a cable car which returns to terra firma without betraying visible moral collapse may well be dubbed heroic. In truth, of course, these people are merely prisoners of misfortune. If they behave well, they are doing so to save their own skins, and only incidentally those of other people. Anyone who has served in a theatre of war, even in a noncombatant capacity and even in as perfunctory an affair—from the Allied viewpoint—as the 2003 invasion of Iraq, may be described in any subsequent media report of a divorce, car crash or fatality as a "war hero." This is a travesty. Such a word as "hero" deserves to be cherished as carefully as any other endangered species.

Physical bravery is found more often than the spiritual variety. Moral courage is rare, and perhaps more common among women than among men. A willingness to defy peril comes remarkably easily to some young people. The warrior deserving of the highest praise is he who demonstrates fortitude alone, without the stimulus of comradeship. C. S. Forester wrote a wry little novel entitled *Brown on Resolution*. It tells the story of a British sailor in World War I, the sole unwounded survivor of a cruiser sunk in the Pacific by a German raider. Brown escapes from captivity with a rifle onto an uninhabited volcanic island, Resolution, where the German ship has put in for repairs. This stolid young man, schooled all his life to a simple concept of duty, knows that the consequence of his actions must be death, but accepts his fate unquestioningly. By harassing the warship from the shore, the lone sailor delays its departure just long enough for a British squadron to engage and sink it with all hands. Brown himself is left mortally wounded, dying alone on his barren rock. For our purposes the key element in Forester's story is that no one afterwards knows what Brown did, or what his lonely sacrifice achieved. This is a cautionary tale for warriors. The highest form of courage is that of a man who surrenders his life for others without hope of recognition. There have been innumerable such instances throughout history, which by their nature are unknown to us.

By contrast many acts of heroism, some recorded in this book, have been committed in the active hope of advancement or glory. Eager warriors, aspiring heroes, "gong chasers," are generally disliked and mistrusted by those of more commonplace disposition who are obliged to serve with them. Many soldiers display a baleful attitude towards officers who are perceived to be excessively aggressive. "It's all right for *him* if he wants to win a Congressional Medal," they mutter, "but what about *us?*" Audie Murphy, that hero of heroes of whom I write in this book, was not well liked by his comrades. General Sir Ian Hamilton wrote: "If a British officer wishes to make his men shy of taking a lead from him, let him stand up under fire whilst they lie in their trenches ... Our fellows are not in the least impressed by such bravado. All they say is: 'This fellow is a fool. If he cares so little for his own life, how much less will he care for ours.' "

The leaders most readily admired by fellow-soldiers are those who seem committed to do their duty, and also to bring every possible man home alive. The rank and file recoil from officers who seem indifferent to the "butcher's bill" for their actions. The British colonel most respected by his men in the 1982 Falklands campaign, for instance, was by no means the most celebrated. Instead, he was an officer who gained his combat objectives by meticulous planning and diversionary fire, followed up by a dashing flank assault, which achieved success with minimal casualties.

Many celebrated warriors are detested by their contemporaries. I grew up to idolise Wing-Commander Guy Gibson, who led the famous 1943 RAF dam-breaking raid. When researching the bomber offensive for a book, it was a shock for me to discover how much Gibson was disliked by some of those who served under him. "He was the sort of little bugger who was always jumping out from behind a hut and telling you your buttons were undone," said a gunner in 1978, his resentment undimmed by the passage of thirty-five years. The courage of Lieutenant-Colonel Herbert Jones, commanding the British 2 Para at Goose Green in June 1982, undoubtedly merited the posthumous Victoria Cross which he received. But more than a few of his comrades argued that his action in charging personally at the Argentine positions was the negation of the role of a battalion commander, and reflected the fact that he had lost control of the battle. "H" Jones was a fiercely emotional man, fired by a heroic vision which he yearned to fulfill. Many soldiers prefer to be led against the enemy by cooler and more cautious spirits.

A cynic might suggest that some eager warriors are exhibitionists of an extreme kind, prepared to risk their lives to gain attention. A cynic would be right. This does not diminish warriors' claims upon our regard, but may make us a trifle more sceptical about their motives. "Adventure has always been a selfish business," author and traveller Peter Fleming once observed. "The desire to benefit the community is never [adventurers'] principal motive... They do it because they want to. It suits them; it is their cup of tea." A relative of an officer who was responsible for an exceptionally brave action in North Africa in World War II once related a story which the family hero possessed enough self-knowledge to tell against himself. Soon after the North African battle took place, the young man went to his colonel and complained that while several fellow officers had received decorations, he himself had got nothing. He felt hard done by. The colonel did not reveal to his young lieutenant that he had been recommended for a Victoria Cross, which was announced shortly afterwards. This anecdote emphasises the fact that some men commit brave acts not spontaneously, but in conscious pursuit of recognition.

All armies seek to create an ethos in which such ambitions prosper. Only where at least a handful of soldiers possess either an exceptional sense of duty—like Sergeant-Major Hollis—or an extravagant hunger for fame—like the VC winner mentioned above—can the cause of their nation in arms flourish. A small minority of natural warriors is almost invariably fighting alongside a majority of other soldiers who threaten their army's prospects of operational success by their eagerness to preserve their own lives. Macaulay's Horatius demanded:

> *How can man die better than facing fearful odds,*
> *For the ashes of his fathers and the temples of his gods?*

From a Western commander's viewpoint, however, a distressingly small number of men share this sanguine view. There is an element of hypocrisy about the manner in which democracies deplore "fanatical" or "suicidal" behaviour in battle by foes such as the wartime Japanese and Germans, even the modern terrorist. Western armies have awarded their highest decorations, often posthumously, in recognition of behaviour in action which was more likely than not to result in the death of the warrior concerned. It is because it is so difficult to persuade sensible Western soldiers to perform acts likely to cause their own deaths that democratic societies become alarmed when they perceive hostile races capable of more aggressive behaviour than their own. This observation is not intended to applaud fanaticism, but merely to recognise our double standard. A modern Islamic suicide bomber might assert that his actions would have won warm Western applause, if it had been performed sixty years ago against the Nazi oppressors of Europe. A host of Allied medal citations in two world wars included the approving words: "With absolute disregard for his own safety."

The currency in which a notable warrior has been rewarded in modern times is, of course, an intrinsically worthless disk or cross of metal, which society has successfully promoted as desirable. The United States and Britain have customarily awarded the Congressional Medal of Honor and Victoria Cross—both mid-nineteenth-century creations—for single acts of bravery, episodes which lasted only a matter of minutes. Remarkably few of these supreme national tokens have been given for displays of courage sustained over months or years, such as were demanded as a commonplace from soldiers of earlier centuries. Indeed, the first VC was awarded for an act many people would consider a mere impulsive gesture of self-preservation: a British sailor picked up a live shell which landed on the deck of his ship, and threw it overboard. In a rash moment, Congress once awarded its Medal of Honor to every member of a Civil War regiment, until wiser counsels prevailed and this largesse was retracted.

"A soldier will fight long and hard for a bit of coloured ribbon," Bonaparte observed wryly. A friend who served as an infantry officer in Italy in World War II once observed to me that, when one is twenty years old, the prospect of a "gong" can incite some men to remarkable exertions. George Patton wrote in 1927: "We must have more decorations and we must give them with no niggard hand . . . War may be hell: but for John Doughboy there is a heaven of suggestion in anticipating what Annie Rooney will say when she sees him in his pink feather and his new medal." The possibility of gaining recognition through medals has indeed prompted many warriors to try harder, and thus caused battles to be won. The warrior's cliché is correct, that "the only one who knows what a medal is worth is the man who won it." All veterans perceive a distinction between a "good" Bronze or Silver Star—gained for courage and leadership—and the other kind, which "comes up with the rations," not infrequently as a gesture to a career officer with influential connections. Patton's personal courage was undisputed, but posterity is entitled to recoil from the shamelessness with which in both world wars he solicited medals from friends in high places—and received them. Likewise, I recall the rancour of an RAF veteran, as he described his 1943 squadron commander. Many aircrew considered this officer a coward. He relaxed sufficiently one night in the mess to avow without embarrassment: "I am a career airman. I intend to survive the war." So he did, taking considerable care of his own safety. But the fellowship of the RAF hierarchy ensured that he got his "gong" when he relinquished his squadron. Few people whom the wing-commander met in later life can have possessed any notion how relatively easily his DSO was earned. In the eyes of a new generation ignorant of the nuances of the warrior culture, the mere fact of an officer's operational service admitted him to the ranks of "war heroes."

Many decorations are awarded for spectacular acts of courage. But others are issued cynically, because commanders deem it morally necessary to console a vanquished army, or to inspire men to try harder by giving awards for feats which are, in truth, no more than many of their comrades perform. For instance, some wartime heavy bomber pilots were decorated—several posthumously—for efforts to keep crippled aircraft aloft at the risk of their own lives, enabling the rest of their crews to bail out. This was a relatively commonplace manifestation of courage, but it was rewarded with decorations, to encourage emulation.

Official recognition of warriors' deeds is always arbitrary, not least because it requires the survival of credible witnesses, almost invariably officers, to submit citations. Here, we are back to *Brown on Resolution*. Every army in modern times has operated a more or less crude rationing system in apportioning decorations between units. This creates injustices both of omission and commission, well understood by fighting men. Air Chief Marshal Sir Arthur Harris of the RAF, who famously despised soldiers and sailors, once scornfully rehearsed to me the extravagant list of "gongs" awarded after the Royal Navy's bloody 1918 Zeebrugge raid, to make survivors feel better. If warriors cannot always be successful, their commanders find it expedient at least to convince them that some of their number have been brave enough to sustain collective honour.

What makes some warriors perform exceptional deeds? Charles Wilson, Churchill's personal doctor during his premiership, served in France as an army doctor in World War I, and afterwards wrote *The Anatomy of Courage*. Wilson, who became Lord Moran, rejected the view that courage is simply a quality possessed by some men and not by others. Nor, he argued, is it a constant income; rather, it is a capital sum of which each man possesses a variable amount. In all cases, such capital is eventually exhausted. There seems considerable evidence to support

Moran's thesis. In World War II, it was accepted that most fighting units advanced from amateur status in their first actions to much greater professionalism after some battle experience; thereafter, however, among the Western Allies at least, the aggressiveness and usefulness of a given formation declined, as it became not "battle-hardened"—an absurd cliché—but tired and wary of risk. A veteran of Normandy once observed to me: "You fight a damn sight better when you don't know where it hurts." In other words, the less battle-experienced soldier, the novice, sometimes performs feats from which a veteran would flinch.

The tales recounted in this book are designed to reflect a variety of manifestations of leadership, courage, heroic folly and the warrior ethic. Some are romantic, others painfully melancholy. Some of those portrayed were notably successful in their undertakings. Others were not. I am fascinated by warriors, but try to perceive their triumphs and tragedies without illusion. A touch of scepticism does these remarkable men—and two women—no disservice, nor does an acknowledgement that few were people with whom one would care to share a desert island. My subjects represent a range of nationalities, but are chiefly Anglo-Saxon, for this is my own culture. Three rose to lead large forces, most did not. This is a study of fighters, not commanders.

When I began writing, I intended to include figures as far back in history as Leonidas, Hannibal, Saladin. Yet sifting the evidence about such people, I came to believe that it was too doubtful and fragmentary to form a basis for convincing character studies. The distinguished historian of the Hundred Years' War, Jonathan Sumption, notes that Walter Mannay, one of the foremost among King Edward III's knights, paid Froissart for a fulsome testimonial in his chronicles. The historical evidence about the stand of the Spartans at Thermopylae may be summarised thus: Leonidas probably existed, and probably died in a battle there. That is all, and not enough for the book which I wanted to write.

My own stories are confined, therefore, to modern times, the nineteenth and twentieth centuries. They concern characters about whom we know enough to construct credible and, I hope, entertaining portraits. The selection is whimsical. The range of personalities is designed to illustrate different aspects of the experience of war on land, at sea and in the air over the past two centuries. Several are national icons, while others have lost their lustre, and fallen into an obscurity from which I hope this book will help to rescue them. Some may seem unsympathetic, and some were failures. The characters and fates of warriors are as diverse as those of people who follow any other calling.

Most of these tales concern soldiers, but I have included one remarkable sailor, and two airmen who seem archetypes of the twentieth-century warrior. My collection—for of course it is only a modest assay of a seam overflowing with riches—also favours those who left behind autobiographies, diaries or other writings, which provide insights into their thoughts as well as their deeds. The balance is thus unjustly loaded towards officers at the expense of those whom they commanded, and towards the articulate at the expense of the illiterate. Aficionados of naval history may justly complain that seamen are underrepresented, but this is a portrait of human behaviour rather than a historical narrative balanced between the three dimensions.

If successful warriors have often been vain and uncultured men, their nations in hours of need have had cause to be profoundly grateful for their virtues, even if they have sometimes been injured by their excesses. Today we recognise that other forms of courage are as worthy of respect as that which is shown on the battlefield. But this should not cause us to steal their due from great warriors of history. This book is designed to amuse as much as to inform. After reading my last book, *Armageddon*, my wife urged me to write something a trifle less relentlessly bleak. I bore her injunction in my mind when I embarked upon *Warriors*. I hope it will divert readers with its tales of the gallant, the tragic and the picaresque, and well as stimulate some reflection upon the behaviour of men—and women—at war. For all his social limitations and professional follies, the warrior is willing to risk everything on the field of battle, and sometimes to lose it, for purposes sometimes selfish or mistaken, but often noble.

MAX HASTINGS
Hungerford, England, and Al Pinquan, Kenya
January 2005

WARRIORS

CHAPTER ONE

BONAPARTE'S
BLESSED FOOL

THE WARS OF NAPOLEON produced a flowering of memoirs, both English and French, of extraordinary quality. Each writer's work reflects in full measure his national characteristics. None but a Frenchman, surely, could have written the following lines about his experience of conflict: "I may, I think, say without boasting that nature has allotted to me a fair share of courage; I will add that there was a time when I enjoyed being in danger, as my thirteen wounds and some distinguished services prove, I think, sufficiently." Baron Marcellin de Marbot was the model for Sir Arthur Conan Doyle's fictional Brigadier Gerard: brave, swashbuckling, incapable of introspection, glorying without inhibition in the experience of campaigning from Portugal to Russia in the service of his emperor. Marbot was the most eager of warriors, who shared with many of his French contemporaries a belief that there could be no higher calling than to follow Bonaparte to glory. Few modern readers could fail to respect the courage of a soldier who so often faced the fire of the enemy, through an active service career spanning more than forty years. And no Anglo-Saxon could withhold laughter at the peacock vanity and chauvinism of the hussar's account of the experience, rich in anecdotage and comedy, the latter often unintended.

Jean-Baptiste-Antoine-Marcellin de Marbot was born in 1782 at Beaulieu in the Corrèze, son of a country gentleman of liberal inclinations who became a general in France's revolutionary army. With his round face and snub nose, the child Marcellin was known to his family as "the kitten," and for some years during the nation's revolutionary disorders attended a local girls' school. He was originally destined for a naval career, but a friend urged his father that life aboard a warship mouldering in some seaport under British blockade was no prospect for an ambitious youth. Instead, in 1799 a vacancy was procured for him in the hussars. The seventeen-year-old boy was delighted, and from the outset gloried in his new uniform. His father, however, was uneasy about his shyness, and for some time was prone to refer to his son in company as "Mademoiselle Marcellin"—rich pickings there for a modern psychologist. In those days when every hussar was expected to display a moustache as part of his service dress, the beardless teenager at first painted whiskers on his face.

Marbot met Bonaparte for the first time when accompanying his father to take up a posting with the army in Italy. They were amazed to encounter the hero of the Pyramids at Lyons, on his way back to Paris from Egypt, having abandoned his army to seek a throne, a quest to which General Marbot, a committed republican, declined to give his assistance. In Italy, young Marcellin won his spurs. Despatched with a patrol to seize Austrian prisoners, the sergeant in command professed sudden illness. The boy seized the opportunity and assumed leadership of the troop: "When...I took command of the fifty men who had come under my orders in such unusual circumstances, a mere trooper as I was and seventeen years old, I resolved to show my comrades that if I had not yet much experience or military talent, I at least possessed pluck. So I resolutely put myself at their head and marched on in what we knew was the direction of the enemy."

Marbot's patrol surprised an Austrian unit, took the necessary prisoners, and returned in triumph to the French lines where their self-appointed commander was rewarded with promotion to sergeant, followed soon afterwards by a commission. He survived the terrible siege of Genoa, where his father died in his arms following a wound received on the battlefield. Soon afterwards the young man was posted to the 25th Chasseurs. In 1801 he was appointed an aide-de-camp to that hoary old hero Marshal Augereau, with whom he travelled for the first time to the Iberian Peninsula.

By 1805, already a veteran, Marbot was an eager young officer with Bonaparte's Grand Army, ready for a summer of campaigning against the Austrians and Russians. "I had three excellent horses," he enthused, adding bathetically, "and a servant of moderate quality." The duties of aides-de-camp were among the most perilous in any army of the time. It was their business to convey their masters' wishes and tidings not only across the battlefield, but from end to end of Europe, often in the teeth of the enemy. In the period that followed, writes Marbot, "constantly sent from north to south, and from south to north, wherever there was fighting going on, I did not pass one of these ten years without coming under fire, or without shedding my blood on the soil of some part of Europe." It is striking to notice that, until the twentieth century, every enthusiastic warrior regarded it as a mark of virility to have been wounded in action, if possible frequently. A soldier who avoided shedding his own blood, far from being congratulated on luck and skill, was more likely to be suspected of shyness.

Marbot began the 1805 campaigning season by carrying despatches from the emperor to Marshal Masséna in Italy, through the Alpine passes. Then he took his place beside Augereau for what became the Austerlitz campaign. "Never had France possessed an army so well-trained," he exulted, "of such good material, so eager for fighting and fame... Bonaparte... accepted the war with joy, so certain was he of victory... He knew how the chivalrous spirit of Frenchmen has in all ages been influenced by the enthusiasm of military glory." Seldom has there been an era of warfare in which officers and soldiers alike strove so ardently for distinction. If there were young blades in Bonaparte's army who confined themselves to doing their duty, history knows nothing of them. In the world of France's marshals and their subordinates, there was a relentless contest for each to outdo the others in braving peril with insouciance. Its spirit was supremely captured by the tale of Ney, after the battle of Lutzen, encountering the emperor. "My dear cousin! But you are covered in blood!" exclaimed Bonaparte in alarm. "It isn't mine, Sire," responded the marshal complacently, "except where that damned bullet passed through my leg!"

Having survived the carnage at Austerlitz, Marbot found himself among a throng of French officers sitting their horses around Bonaparte on the day after the battle, gazing out on the broken ice of the Satschan Lake, strewn with debris and corpses. Amid it all, a hundred yards from the shore they beheld a Russian sergeant, shot through the thigh and clinging to an ice floe deeply stained with his blood. The wounded man, spying the glittering assembly, raised himself and cried out in Russian, "All men become brothers once battle is done." He begged his life from the emperor of the French. The entreaty was translated. Bonaparte, in a characteristic impulse of imperial condescension, told his entourage to do whatever was necessary to save the Russian. A handful of men plunged into the icy water, seized floating baulks of timber, and sought to paddle themselves out to the floe. Within seconds they became clumsy prisoners of their frozen clothing. They abandoned efforts to save the enemy soldier, and struggled ashore to save themselves.

Marbot, a spectator, declared that their error had been to brave the water fully clad. Bonaparte nodded assent. The would-be rescuers had shown more zeal than discretion, observed the emperor dryly. The hussar now felt obliged to put his own counsel into practice. Leaping from his horse, he tore off his clothes and sprang into the lake. He acknowledged the shock of the deadly cold, but "the emperor's presence encouraged me, and I struck out towards the Russian sergeant. At the same time my example, and probably the praise given me by the emperor, determined a lieutenant of artillery . . . to imitate me." As he struggled painfully amid the great daggers of ice, Marbot was dismayed to find his rival catching him up. Yet he was obliged to admit that alone, he could never have succeeded in his attempt. Together, and with immense labour, the two Frenchmen pushed the wounded Russian on his crumbling floe towards the shore, battering a path through the jumble of ice before them. At last they came close enough for onlookers to throw out lifelines. The two swimmers seized the ropes and passed them around the wounded man, enabling him to be dragged to safety. They themselves, at their last gasp, bleeding and torn, staggered ashore to receive their laurels. Bonaparte called his mameluke Roustan to bring them a glass of rum apiece. He gave gold to the wounded soldier, who proved to be Lithuanian. Once recovered, the man became a devoted follower of the emperor, a sergeant in his Polish lancers. Marbot's companion in mercy, the lieutenant of artillery, was so weakened by his experience that after months in hospital, Marbot recorded pityingly that he had to be invalided out of the service. The hussar, of course, was back on duty next day.

Marbot saw as much of Bonaparte as any man of his rank through the years that followed. In July 1806 he carried despatches to the French Embassy in Berlin, and returned to report to the emperor in Paris that he had seen Prussian officers defiantly sharpening sabres on the embassy steps. "The insolent braggarts shall soon learn that our weapons need no sharpening!" exclaimed Bonaparte. We may suspect that the emperor viewed Marbot just as his fictional self viewed Gerard in Conan Doyle's tales—a wonderfully loyal, courageous, unthinking instrument with less guile than a gundog. Marbot himself tells several stories of how he was duped by treacherous foreigners with no understanding of the nobility and dignity of war. Indeed, his contempt for the lack of chivalry displayed by Englishmen, Russians, Austrians and suchlike is matched only by his disdain for their military incompetence. On those freakish occasions when he is forced to acknowledge that lesser breeds prevailed on the battlefield, such misfortunes are invariably attributed either to the enemy's superior numbers or to the folly of some French subordinate commander. Bonaparte's soldiers, in Marbot's eyes, were paragons of courage and honour. We learn little from his narrative of the trail of devastation they wreaked across occupied Europe. To the gallant young officer, as to most of his comrades, Bonaparte was an idol, rather than the ruthless despot who brought misery to millions. Marcellin says nothing in his memoirs of his elder brother Antoine-Adolphe, also a soldier, who was arrested in 1802 for an alleged plot against the ruler of France in favour of a republic.

Marbot fretted about receiving less than his share of glory at Jena in October 1806, but a few months later, at the age of twenty-four, he gained his coveted captaincy. It was in this rank that he served at Eylau in February 1807. The battle prompted one of his most remarkable stories, which sounds more like an experience of Baron Munchausen than that of a French cavalry officer. Marbot was riding a mare named Lisette, whose naturally vicious temperament he had with difficulty suppressed. First his servant, then the captain himself, forced sizzling joints of hot mutton into the horse's mouth when she sought to attack them. Since these salutory experiences, Lisette had been a model mount. In the midst of the great engagement at Eylau, in which Augereau's corps suffered severely, Bonaparte sent word to the marshal that he should try to save the 14th Infantry, whose dwindling band of survivors held a hillock in the path of the Russian advance. Two aides spurred forth, to be swallowed up in the chaos and never seen again. Marbot stood next in line. "Seeing the son of his old friend, and I venture to say his favourite aide-de-camp, come up, the kind marshal's face changed, and his eyes filled with tears, for he could not hide from himself that he was sending me to almost certain death. But the emperor must be obeyed."

Marbot dashed away. Lisette, "lighter than a swallow and flying rather than running, devoured the intervening space, leaping the piles of dead men and horses, the ditches, the broken gun carriages, and the half-extinguished bivouac fires." Cossacks turned to pursue Marbot like beaters driving a hare, yet none could catch his racing steed. He reached the frail square formed by the survivors of the 14th, surrounded by dead Russian dragoons and their horses. Amid a hail of fire, the aide passed the order to withdraw. The commanding major shrugged that retreat was impossible. A fresh Russian column was even now a mere hundred paces away. "I see no means of saving the regiment," said the major. "Return to the emperor, bid him farewell from the 14th of the line, which has faithfully executed his orders, and bear to him the eagle which he gave us and which we can defend no longer."

Here, couched in language worthy of Macaulay, is the very stuff of the legend of Bonaparte's army, which Marbot did as much as any man to enshrine for posterity. A Russian cannonball tore through the aide's hat as he seized the regiment's eagle and strove to break off its staff, the more readily to bear it to safety. He was so badly concussed by the impact that blood poured from his nose and ears. As the enemy's infantry closed upon them, doomed soldiers cried out *"Vive l'empereur!"* Several Frenchmen set their backs against Lisette's flanks, crowding the mare so tightly than Marbot could not spur her away. A wounded French quartermaster-sergeant fell under her legs, and a Russian grenadier sought to bayonet the man where he lay. The attacker, drunk as Russians always were on battlefields depicted by Marbot, missed his aim. One thrust struck the cavalryman's arm, another pierced his mount's flank. Lisette's latent savagery reawakened, "she sprang at the Russian, and at one mouthful tore off his nose, lips, eyebrows and all the skin of his face, making of him a living death's head, dripping with blood." Then the mare surged out of the mêlée, kicking and biting as she went, seizing one Russian officer bodily and eviscerating him. She bolted at full gallop, not checking until she reached Eylau cemetery, where she collapsed from loss of blood. Marbot, himself fainting with pain, slid into unconsciousness.

When the battle was done, he was saved by the merest chance from the mound of snow and corpses in which he lay, incapable of movement. A servant of Augereau's saw a looter carrying a pelisse which he recognised as that of the general's aide, and induced the man to lead him to the spot where he had found it. Both mare and rider survived. Marbot wrote archly: "Nowadays, when promotions and decorations are bestowed so lavishly, some reward would certainly be given to an officer who had braved danger as I had done in reaching the 14th Regiment; but under the Empire, for a devoted act of that kind I did not receive the cross [of the Legion of Honour] nor did it ever occur [to] me to ask for it." Poor man, he was in truth obsessed with promotions and medals. He rejoiced mightily when at last he received the cross from his emperor two years later, at the age of twenty-six.

Marshal Augereau was so badly wounded at Eylau that it was years before he was again fit to take the field. Marbot found himself temporarily unemployed. After two months' convalescence in Paris, however, he was attached to the staff of Marshal Lannes, with whom he served at the battle of Friedland in June 1807. He witnessed the meeting of Bonaparte and the Tsar at Tilsit, and was then sent with the emperor's despatches to Dresden. There and afterwards in Paris he briefly savoured the delights of a full purse, his status as one of the emperor's favoured champions, and the tender care of his mother, whom he adored. The only other female object of affection who earns a brief mention in Marbot's memoirs is the wife whom he married in 1811. Women otherwise have no place in his tale, and perhaps little even in his career as a soldier. Many men such as Marbot became so absorbed in the business of war that they perceived women merely as a source of amusement during leaves, and as childbearers when duty granted an officer leisure to think of such marginal matters as procreation.

The year 1808 found the hussar despatched among the staff of the emperor's brother-in-law Prince Murat to Spain, where Bonaparte was bent upon overturning the monarchy in favour of his own nominee. Murat aspired to the crown for himself. To his chagrin, however, he was obliged to content himself with the throne of Naples, while that of Spain was given to Bonaparte's elder brother Joseph. Even the insensitive

Marbot, billeted in Madrid when the Spaniards rose in revolt against the French despot and his occupying army, recognised the folly of Bonaparte's Spanish adventure: "This war...seemed to me wicked, but I was a soldier and I must march or be charged with cowardice." He was appalled by the savagery of the Spanish *guerrillos*, which bore especially hard on aides, who had to travel far and alone. Once, on a mission bearing despatches, he found the body of a young chasseur officer nailed by his hands and feet to a barn door, under which a fire had been lighted. The Frenchman was still bleeding, and Marbot soon afterwards found himself in a bloody confrontation with the killers, which cost him another wound. The package which he bore was finally carried to Bonaparte by another officer, proudly stained with Marbot's blood.

In the spring of 1809, the French army in Spain was battling to seize Saragossa, which the Spanish were defending stubbornly. Assault after assault was beaten back. Marbot was ordered to lead a fresh attack, and was reconnoitring the ground when he felt himself pushed sharply backwards, and collapsed to the ground. A Spanish bullet had struck him beside the heart. The after-effects of this wound caused him much discomfort in the saddle after the fall of Saragossa, when he had to travel back to Paris with Marshal Lannes, and thence onwards for the next of Bonaparte's German campaigns. At the battle of Eckmuhl, Marbot's worst inconvenience was to have his horse shot under him. A few days later, on 23 April, he was in mortal danger again. At the assault on Ratisbon, Lannes was so frustrated by the failure of his men to scale the walls under heavy fire that he seized a ladder himself, exclaiming: "I will let you see that I was a grenadier before I was a marshal, and still am one." Marbot tore the ladder from his mentor by main force, and with a comrade holding the other end, dashed for the walls. Though scores of French soldiers were falling around them, Marbot and his companion claimed the honour of reaching the summit of the walls first among Bonaparte's army. He then persuaded the Austrian officer defending the gate to surrender.

On the banks of the swollen Danube on 7 May, Bonaparte sent for Marbot. He wanted an officer to cross the flood and take a prisoner. "Take notice," said the emperor, "I am not giving you an order; I am only expressing a wish. I am aware that the enterprise is as dangerous as it can be, and you can decline it without any fear of displeasing me." Here

Marbot, in his own account, almost bursts with righteous conceit: "I had broken out all over in a cold sweat; but at the same moment a feeling...in which a love of glory and of my country was mingled perhaps with a noble pride, raised my ardour to the highest point and I said to myself: 'The emperor has here an army of 150,000 devoted warriors, besides 25,000 men of his guard, all selected from the bravest. He is surrounded with aides-de-camp and orderly officers, and yet when an expedition is on foot, requiring intelligence no less than boldness, it is I whom the Emperor and Marshal Lannes choose.' 'I will go, sir!,' I cried without hesitation; 'I will go; and if I perish, I leave my mother to your Majesty's care.' The emperor pulled my ear to mark his satisfaction. The marshal shook my hand."

This is one of the most enchanting passages in Marbot's narrative, inseparably linked to its time, nation and personalities. Conveyed by local boatmen, he braved the Danube torrent, secured three Austrian prisoners, and returned in triumph. He received the embrace of Lannes, an invitation to breakfast with the emperor, and his coveted promotion to major. A fortnight later, after innumerable adventures at Essling and Aspern, he carried the mortally wounded Lannes off the field. Marbot himself had lost a piece of flesh, torn from his thigh by a grapeshot, but carelessly ignored it. Bonaparte noticed the major's bloody breeches and observed laconically: "Your turn comes around pretty often!" It was a measure of the limitations of nineteenth-century weapons that any man could so often be injured by them, yet survive to fight again.

At Wagram in July 1809, Marbot suffered a serious falling-out with Marshal Masséna, on whose staff he was serving. The corn that covered much of the battlefield was set ablaze by smouldering cannon wadding. Men and horses suffered terribly, fighting amid the fires. Marbot's mount was already scorched and exhausted when Masséna sought an aide to check the rout of a division broken by Austrian cavalry, and to direct the fugitives to the island of Löbau on the Danube. First in line for duty was Prosper, Masséna's own son. Yet the marshal could not bring himself to despatch his offspring into the midst of the slaughter. He appealed to Marbot: "You understand, my friend, why I do not send my son, although it's his turn; I am afraid of getting him killed. You understand? You understand?" Marbot, disgusted, claims to have answered: "Marshal, I was going under the impression that I was about to fulfil a duty; I am sorry that you have corrected my mistake, for now I understand perfectly that, being obliged to send one of your aides-de-camp to almost certain death, you would rather it should be me rather than your son." He set off full-tilt across the murderous plain, only to find after a few minutes that Prosper Masséna, shamed by his father's behaviour, had followed him. The two young men became friends thereafter, but the marshal never again addressed Marbot by the intimate *"tu."*

A few days later, at Znaym, the rival armies were once more deploying for battle when an armistice was agreed between the French and the Austrians. Marbot was among a cluster of aides hastily despatched to intervene between the combatants. He raced in front of the advancing infantry, who were already crying *"Vive l'empereur!"* as their bayonets and those of the Austrians ranged within a hundred paces of each other. A bullet struck the aide's wrist, inflicting an injury that cost him six months in a sling. He charged on, crying "Peace! Peace!" and holding up his uninjured hand to arrest the French advance. An Austrian officer attempting to convey the same message in front of his own ranks was hit in the shoulder before he and Marbot met and embraced, in a gesture unmistakable to both sides.

In April 1810, after more months of convalescence, Marbot set forth from his mother's house in Paris to travel ahead of Masséna and prepare for the marshal's arrival to command the Peninsular army. The major's passage was enlivened by fever and a brush with Spanish guerrillas. Once he was on the battlefield with Masséna, his memoirs provide one of the most vivid, if absurdly prejudiced, French narratives of the Peninsula experience. He tells of actions and skirmishes innumerable, of "Marshal Stockpot," the French deserter who established himself at the head of a band of French, Portuguese, Spanish and English deserters, living as bandits until Masséna disposed of them. He inflates the toll of English casualties in every encounter. He castigates Masséna for his failure to anticipate and frustrate Wellington's retreat behind the lines of Torres Vedras—and for his folly in bringing his mistress on campaign.

One of Marbot's best stories, whether accepted at face value or no, concerns a duel with a British light cavalry officer who trotted forward from Wellington's lines one morning in March 1811 to challenge him: "Stop, Mr. Frenchman; I should like to have a little fight with you!" Marbot professed to have treated this nonsense with disdain until the man shouted: "I can see by your uniform that you are on the staff of a marshal, and I shall put in the London papers that the sight of me was enough to frighten away one of Masséna's or Ney's cowardly aides-de-camp." This roused our hero to fury. He turned and charged towards the British officer, only to hear a rustling from nearby woodland, and perceive two English hussars dashing to cut off his retreat. "Only a most energetic defence could save me from the disgrace of being taken prisoner, through my own fault, in sight of the whole French army."

He flew at the English officer, running him through the throat: "The wretch fell from his horse to the ground, which he bit in his rage." Meanwhile, however, the two hussars were slashing Marbot's shako, wallet and pelisse to ribbons. A thrust from the older soldier pierced the Frenchman's side an inch deep. Marbot countered with a cut through the man's jaw which slit his mouth from side to side, arresting his stricken cry of agony and causing him to decamp. The younger English soldier hesitated for a moment before likewise turning to flee, only to receive a thrust in the shoulder to hasten him on his way. Marbot cantered triumphantly back to the French lines, to receive the congratulations of Masséna and Ney, together with the plaudits of the army. As for the price, "the wound in my cheek was not important; in a month's time it had healed over and you can scarcely see the mark of it alongside my left whisker. But the thrust in my right side was dangerous, especially in the middle of a long retreat, in which I was compelled to travel on horseback … Such, my children, was the result of my fight or, if you like, my prank at Miranda de Corvo. You have still got the shako which I wore, and the numerous notches with which the English sabres have adorned it prove that the two hussars did not let me off. I brought away the wallet also, the sling of which was cut in three places, but it has been mislaid."

Marbot's own account of himself is inimitable. Here was a soldier of the same mettle as the knights of fourteenth-century Europe, men for whom fighting was both their business and their pleasure. They cared little for softer pleasures or gentler virtues. A prig might say—and many prigs did—that they were a menace to civilisation, for peace was anathema to them. The major returned to France in July 1811, when Masséna was recalled by Bonaparte after his Peninsula disasters. Marbot himself attributed Bonaparte's fall to his failure to finish the Spanish war before he set forth for Russia. He also acknowledged the quality and marksmanship of British infantry, even if he could never bring himself to think much of Wellington.

Marbot passed the summer and autumn in Paris, and finds a few words in his own tale to mention his marriage, to a certain Mademoiselle Desbrières, of whose character and appearance he says less than about those of his favourite chargers. He was now appointed senior major—and in his own eyes effective commander, given the age and infirmity of his colonel—in the 23rd Chasseurs, a light cavalry regiment. It was at the head of the 23rd, about whose prowess he writes with glowing pride, that he advanced across the Niemen in June 1812, amid the Grand Army bound for Moscow. His regiment served in the corps of Oudinot, for whose incompetence Marbot nursed a hearty contempt. Through the weeks that followed he led his men in action after action, until a brush with Russian infantry on the last day of July cost him a bullet in the shoulder. He frankly admits that he would have accepted evacuation to the rear had not he yearned so desperately for his colonelcy. Bonaparte promoted no man in his absence from the field.

Thus Marbot soldiered on despite the pain of his wound, which was so great that when he led his regiment into action at Polotsk two weeks later he was unable to draw a sword. The 23rd Chasseurs were left at Polotsk with St. Cyr's corps through the two months that followed, while the rest of the Grand Army advanced to Moscow and disaster. To his immense joy, on 15 November Marbot received news of his colonelcy, the letter marked with a scribbled line from Bonaparte: "I am discharging an old debt."

Marbot proudly describes the ingenuity with which he equipped his own regiment to play its part when it was at last summoned to join the Grand Army on the retreat from Moscow. He ensured that the men of the 23rd were provided with winter clothing. Those whose horses died were sent back to Germany, to remove useless mouths. A regimental cattle herd was established and mills commandeered to grind corn for the men, when other units were starving.

In the last days of November, the chasseurs found themselves committed to the terrible action at the crossing of the Beresina, which made an end of so many Frenchmen. On 2 December, in twenty-five degrees of frost, Marbot received a lance thrust in the knee during a mêlée with cossacks, as he strove to turn aside their points with his bare hand in order to reach them with his sabre. Here, indeed, was the bloody intimacy of war as it had been waged since earliest times. The Frenchman was enraged a moment later to feel the pressure of a muzzle against his cheek, and to hear a double report as a cossack fired "treacherously" upon him from behind with a double-barrelled pistol. One bullet passed through the colonel's cloak, the other killed a French officer. Marbot turned on the Russian in a rage as he took aim with a second pistol. The man suddenly cried out in good French: "Oh God! I see death in your eyes! I see death in your eyes!" Marbot responded furiously: "Ay, scoundrel, and you see right!"

Curiously enough, such dialogues were not uncommon in the midst of combat, in an age when many of Bonaparte's foes spoke French. The Russian fell to his sabre. Marbot then turned on another young Russian, and was raising his weapon when an elderly cossack threw himself across the Frenchman's horse's neck, beseeching him: "For your mother's sake spare this one, who has done nothing!" Marbot claims that on hearing his revered parent invoked, he thought he heard her own voice cry out *"Pardon! Pardon!"* and stayed his hand. His sword point dropped.

Marbot came out of Russia in terrible pain from his wound, icicles hanging from his horse's bit, most of his troopers dismounted by the starvation of their mounts, the wounded borne on sledges. Yet his regiment fared vastly better than most. In the 23rd, 698 men returned out of 1,048 who had crossed the Niemen eastwards a few months earlier. Bonaparte complimented Marbot on his achievement in saving so many, though his troopers had missed the worst of the campaign.

The colonel was occupied at the regimental depot at Mons, training replacements, until June 1813 when he resumed command of his active squadrons on the Oder. The highlight of his service at Leipzig was an attempt to encircle and capture the Tsar of Russia and the King of Prussia as they reconnoitred the French positions on 13 October before battle was joined. Marbot had almost completed a manoeuvre to cut off the glittering array of majesties from their own lines when a careless Frenchman dropped his carbine, which went off, betraying the presence of the chasseurs. The throng of enemy commanders and their staffs hastily turned and galloped away. If only his ploy had succeeded, lamented the colonel, "the destinies of Europe would have been changed." As it was, he could only withdraw his men to the French line and share the army's fate—decisive defeat. He himself was wounded, bizarrely, by an arrow in the thigh, fired by a Bashkir tribesman in the ranks of the Russians.

Marbot fought on with his regiment through the last bitter battles of the war. At Hanau, the regiment charged five times. Again and again it fought fierce actions to cover the retreat of the shrinking French army. In the winter of 1814, back at his depot in Belgium, which Bonaparte had claimed as French soil, Marbot found local people increasingly hostile and alienated. He fought one of his last little clashes in Mons itself, against Prussian cossacks.

After Bonaparte's first abdication, Marbot was retained in the Bourbon army, and appointed to command the 7th Hussars. Inevitably, on the return of his idol from Elba he led his regiment to join the emperor's colours. In the first surge of enthusiasm in April 1815 he perceived a chance that the English, and the rest of Europe, might acquiesce peacefully in the restoration of Bonaparte's rule. He was swiftly disabused. On 17 June, after the action at Quatre Bras, Marbot was promoted major-general, though his appointment never took effect. He spent most of the day of Waterloo fuming in frustration on the French right wing, waiting to take to Bonaparte news of Grouchy's arrival with his corps, which was expected hourly.

"I cannot get over our defeat," he wrote in a letter shortly afterwards. "We were manoeuvred like so many pumpkins." He spent much of the afternoon pushing pickets forward in search of Grouchy. These men instead found themselves skirmishing with Blücher's vanguard on the Wavre road. When Marbot sent gallopers to inform Bonaparte that strong Prussian columns were advancing upon Mont St. Jean, the reply came back that he must be mistaken, these were surely Grouchy's regiments. Marbot's few hundred horsemen were driven relentlessly back upon the crumbling imperial army, and soon found themselves receiving the attentions of the British left. The colonel of the 7th Hussars received yet another wound—an English lance thrust in the side. He wrote in a letter soon afterwards: "It is pretty severe, but I thought I would stay to set a good example. If everyone had done the same, we might yet get along…No food is sent to us, and so the soldiers pillage our poor France as if they were in Russia. I am at the outposts, before

Laon; we have been made to promise not to fire, and all is quiet." For Marbot, Bonaparte's final exile to St. Helena prompted despair, and political ruin. He himself, one among so many traitors to the Bourbons, was obliged to quit France for three years of exile in Germany.

To the end of his days, the proud veteran used his pen to defend his beloved emperor and the soldiers of the imperial army against all criticism of their strategy and tactics, and to celebrate their chivalry and courage. Bonaparte read one of Marbot's works in the last year of his life on St. Helena. In appreciation, he added to his will a legacy of 100,000 francs for his former officer, writing: "I bid Colonel Marbot continue to write in defence of the glories of the French armies, and to the confusion of calumniators and apostates." So indeed the colonel did. On his return from exile he became once more a serving soldier, in 1829 taking command of the 8th Chasseurs. He served as aide-de-camp to the Duke of Orléans in the following year, and at the age of nearly sixty received yet one more wound, as a general during the Medeah expedition in Algiers. A bullet struck him in the left knee. As he was being carried to the rear, he remarked to the Duke with a smile: "This is your fault, sir." The Duke demanded: "How so?" Marbot answered: "Did I not hear you say, before the fighting began, that if any of your staff got wounded, you could bet it would be Marbot?" He finally retired in 1848, and died in 1854.

Few warriors in history have taken part in so many of the great battles of their age as did Marbot. Even if a stiff deduction is made from his own account for Gallic extravagance, his courage seems as remarkable as his survival. He performed fifty deeds which, in the wars of the twentieth century, would have been deemed worthy of the highest decorations. Far more astonishingly, he lived to tell the tale. His gifts as a warrior might be described as those of the blessed fool, of whom every army needs a complement in order to prevail on the battlefield, and with which Bonaparte's armies were exceptionally well-endowed. A century later, Marshal Lyautey declared gaiety to be the most important attribute of a soldier. This Marbot possessed in bountiful measure. He was too humble a servant of the emperor to receive much space in the histories of the period, yet his memoirs render him wonderfully accessible to posterity. Without them, he would remain a mere name, a moustache and pelisse among the glittering throng of bold spirits who surrounded the tyrant of France through the years of his wars. As it is, Marbot created one of the most enchanting contemporary portraits of the life of an officer under Bonaparte. If an Anglo-Saxon cannot suppress laughter at the Frenchman's awesome conceit, nor can most of us withhold admiration from his boundless appetite for glory. He and his kind perceived the wars which ravaged Europe through their lifetimes merely as wondrous adventures.

CHAPTER TWO

HARRY AND JUANA

AMONG VISITORS TO SOUTH AFRICA who pass the Natal towns of Harrismith and Ladysmith, or at least glimpse them on the map, a diminishing number possess an inkling of the origins of their names. Yet these modest townships deserve to be remembered by Englishmen at least, for they commemorate one of the great love stories of history. Born in 1787, Harry Smith, fifth of eleven children of a Cambridgeshire surgeon, was in many respects an English counterpart of Marcellin Marbot, and by no means devoid of the Frenchman's exuberance and bounce. He was bluff, brave, passionate, feckless and devoted to his calling as a soldier. Unlike Marbot, he rose from being an eager young swashbuckler to command armies in the field. In his later years, Smith was merely one among many competent British colonial generals. His real claim to fame is shared in equal parts with his wife, who showed herself one of the most remarkable women ever to serve—for serve she surely did—in the ranks of an army.

Smith was a slightly built seventeen-year-old parading with his local Yeomanry when an inspecting general asked: "Young gentleman, would you like to be an officer?" Smith answered eagerly: "Of all things." The general said: "Well, I will make you a rifleman, a greenjacket and very smart." One day in August 1805 the boy sat stiffly through a last dinner at home in Whittlesey, then ran to the stables to embrace his favourite hunter Jack and shed childish tears. His mother, too, sobbed when she kissed him for the last time. Then she suddenly composed herself, held

Harry at arm's length and offered him parting counsel. He should never enter a public billiard room, she said, "and if ever you meet your enemy, remember you are born a true Englishman ... Now God bless you and preserve you." Smith claimed in old age that he never forgot his mother's words during any one of the scores of great battles and skirmishes in which he pitted himself against the foe. He proudly quoted them to the end of his days, when he had become a famous general.

His first military experience was British folly. The young lieutenant and his regiment, the 95th Rifles, were sent to fight the Spanish with Brigadier-General Sir Samuel Auchmuty's 1806 expedition to South America, which ended in devastating casualties and humiliating surrender at Buenos Aires. Smith and other survivors were repatriated by their captors. It was an inauspicious introduction to soldiering. In 1808 he sailed to Gothenburg for another rackety amphibious operation which was mercifully aborted before the troops could land. In August that year he ventured for the first time to the Iberian Peninsula, which was to play a central role in his life. He was posted as a brigade-major with Sir John Moore's army, sent to expel the French governor-general Junot from Portugal following Bonaparte's march into Spain. The function of brigade-major carried no field rank, but at the age of twenty-three Lieutenant Smith acted as executive officer of a force of some 1,500 men, much assisted by a command of the Spanish language which he had acquired in South America.

The British reached Salamanca before being obliged to turn back in what became the retreat to Corunna. Moore's Riflemen played a vital, perhaps decisive, role in covering the withdrawal of the starving army through the snows, day after day fighting off French columns pressing the British rear, buying time for the long column of shuffling men and groaning carts making their way to the coast and safety. Smith was appalled by the behaviour of some of his compatriots, made of less staunch stuff than the Riflemen: "The scenes of drunkenness, riot and disorder we ... witnessed ... are not to be described; it was truly awful and heart-rending to see that army which had been so brilliant at Salamanca so totally disorganised." He excepted only the Rifles and Guards from these charges, and admitted his astonishment that on 16 January 1809 "these very fellows licked the French at Corunna like men." The British stand at the coast, which cost Moore his life, secured the evacuation of the shattered army by the Royal Navy. By Smith's own account, he got home to Whittlesey "a skeleton," racked with ague and dysentery, plagued with lice, bereft of clothing and equipment.

Two months later, he sailed once more with his brigade for Portugal, accompanied by his brother Tom, who had also secured a commission in the Rifles. They reached Sir Arthur Wellesley's army on the morning after its successful defence of Talavera, less a victory than a frustration of French ambitions. Over the months of marching and counter-marching that followed, Smith, like many British officers, spent every hour away from his duties shooting and coursing hares with his beloved greyhounds, in which he took great pride. Throughout the Spanish campaign his dogs often fed his mess on their quarry. Like every prudent officer, Smith loved and cherished his horses in a fashion that was essential when each man's life depended upon the mettle of his mounts. For the Rifle regiments especially, bearing chief responsibility for reconnaissance, outpost duty and skirmishing, almost every day brought action of some kind, either against French vedettes (pickets) or against the enemy's main forces. In the bloody encounter at the Coa crossing in July 1810, both Smith brothers were wounded. Harry was sent back to Lisbon with a ball lodged in his ankle joint. A panel of surgeons debated whether to leave the lead in place or extract it. One of them said, "If it were my leg, out should come the ball." Smith cried out: "Hurrah, Brownrigg, you are the doctor for me," held up his leg and demanded cheerfully: "There it is; slash away." Marcellin Marbot would have applauded. After five terrible minutes, during which the extracting forceps broke, the ball was removed. Here, indeed, were the Roman virtues demanded from every soldier of that era.

After two months in Lisbon, Smith returned to his regiment in the field early in 1811, briefly as a company commander, then once more as brigade-major. On arrival at the headquarters of Colonel Drummond, the benign old Guardsman who commanded the 2nd Brigade, Smith asked: "Have you any orders for the picquets, sir?" The colonel responded amiably: "Mr. Smith, are you my brigade-major?"

"I believe so, sir."

"Then let me tell you, it is your duty to post the picquets and mine to have a d——d good dinner for you every day." Smith wrote: "We soon understood each other. He cooked the dinner often himself, and I *com-*

manded the Brigade." This remark possesses at least partial credibility, for many commanders of the period did not much trouble themselves about the stewardship of their formations, save on the occasion of a battle.

Having pursued Masséna out of Portugal, in January 1812 the British stood at the gates of Ciudad Rodrigo. Smith volunteered to lead the forlorn hope at the storming, but his divisional commander insisted that a younger—and frankly, more expendable—officer must take this post of utmost danger. Yet Smith endured peril enough that night. He was foremost among the Riflemen who mounted the ramparts amid shocking losses. In the madness of close-quarter fighting, with many of his comrades already shot down, he was pressing forward through the darkness amid a heaving throng of friends and foes beside a Grenadier officer when "one of his men seized me by the throat as if I was a kitten, crying out, 'you French ———.' Luckily he left me room in the windpipe to d—— his eyes, or the bayonet would have been through me in a moment." Following the losses at Ciudad Rodrigo, Smith received his captaincy. He remarks that his most notable task during several weeks of idleness that followed was to preside at the execution of British deserters captured in the French ranks. The firing squad botched the shooting, and the brigade-major was appalled to hear himself entreated by a desperately wounded former Rifleman: "Oh, Mr. Smith, put me out of my misery." He was obliged to order the firing squad to reload, close in, and finish off the survivors. Desertion was a besetting problem for every army, in an age when despair rather than patriotism had caused many volunteers to enlist, and most of Bonaparte's soldiers were unwilling conscripts. Only savage discipline held together regiments in which disease and semi-starvation were chronic conditions, even before the enemy entered the reckoning.

In March 1812 the British began besieging Badajoz, an experience that was to prove the turning point of Harry Smith's life. He spent the night of 6 April, one of the bloodiest of the Peninsular campaign, among the Light Division struggling to win through the great breach amid overwhelming enemy fire. Every hand- and foothold in the walls had been studded with French nails and sword blades, sharp as razors. Every officer in the storming party save one was killed or wounded. A third of the Light Division died that night, as French fire tore into each successive party that dared the breach. As the attackers crossed the dry moat of the Santa Maria bastion, the French ignited a mass of combustible material beneath their feet, engulfing the British infantrymen in flames. Still the survivors pressed on, and still they fell. "Oh, Smith," a colonel cried out to the brigade-major, clutching his breast, "I am mortally wounded. Help me up the ladder." Smith said: "Oh no, dear fellow!" "I am," said the colonel. "Be quick." And so Smith heaved the doomed man onto a ladder. Hour after hour through the darkness, the tumult of musketry and artillery fire persisted. Men fought amid rival screams of exhortation, exultation and agony. The hellish scene was lit by torches, burning fascines, gun flashes. At last the British survivors recoiled, acknowledging failure. They had sustained 2,200 casualties. Within its compass, this was an action as terrible as anything endured by attacking infantrymen in the First World War.

Shortly before dawn, Smith was horrified to receive orders from Lord Fitzroy Somerset: Lord Wellington, as Wellesley now was, insisted that the assault must be renewed. Yet even as the two men discussed the ghastly prospect, they heard British bugles beyond the city walls. They had received a miraculous deliverance. While the French threw everything into repelling the 4th and Light Divisions, elsewhere the British had forced the Citadel and Olivenca gate. Picton's diversionary attack succeeded where the main assault failed. Badajoz was won. "There was no battle, day or night, I would not willingly re-enact except this," wrote Smith. Early in the morning, his tunic slashed by musketballs, his body stiff with bruises and cuts sustained in the assault, the Rifleman wandered among the great heaps of British dead before the breach. He met a forlorn colonel of the Guards searching for the body of a brother, who was known to be lost. "There he lies," the colonel said at last. He produced a pair of scissors and turned to Smith: "Go and cut a lock of his hair for my mother. I came for the purpose, but I am not equal to it."

In the wake of the city's capture, maddened by their losses, Wellington's soldiers gave way to a debauch of a kind common among survivors of such a battle, yet shameful to the history of the British army. For two days, ten thousand men of the victorious army indulged in an orgy of drunkenness, looting and rape in the hapless city of Badajoz, in which Spanish allies suffered as grievously as vanquished Frenchmen. Until the fever of violence abated, for twenty-nine hours British officers were powerless to restore any semblance of discipline. Never was the contrast more vivid between the officer class of that era, dedicated to an extravagantly formal code of manners which it cherished even in war, and the brutes upon whom such gentlemen depended to fight their battles. An extraordinary capacity for endurance and sacrifice was demanded of them. They assuaged their sufferings with excesses matching those of Henry V's foot soldiers after Agincourt.

On the morning following the storm, while the rampage was at its height, two Spanish women approached the lines of the 95th Rifles. The elder, throwing back her mantilla, addressed Captain Johnny Kincaid and another officer. She was the wife of a Spanish officer absent on duty, she said. She did not know whether her husband was alive or dead. The home of herself and her young sister had been pillaged by British looters. Blood still trickled down the women's necks from their ears, out of which the rings had been torn. In despair, and for the salvation of the fourteen-year-old sister who stood beside her, she threw herself on the mercy of the British officers. Kincaid wrote: "She stood by the side of an angel! A being more transcendently lovely I had never before seen—one more amiable I have never known!"

The younger girl's name was Juana Maria de Los Dolores de Leon, daughter of an old Spanish family now impoverished by the devastation of war. The romantics of the Rifle Brigade, among whom she became known simply as Juana, took her to their hearts. Kincaid wrote: "To look at her was to love her; and I did love her, but I never told my love, and in the mean time another and more impudent fellow stepped in and won her!" The "more impudent fellow" was, of course, Harry Smith. In truth, Kincaid bore his friend no ill-will. In one of the most enchanting passages of Kincaid's own memoirs, he says of Juana Smith: "Guided by a just sense of rectitude, an innate purity of mind, a singleness of purpose which defied malice, and a soul that soared above circumstances, she became alike the adored of the camp and of the drawing-room, and eventually the admired associate of princes. She yet lives, in the affections of her gallant husband, in an elevated situation in life, a pattern to her sex, and everybody's *beau idéal* of what a wife should be."

Smith was obliged to seek the commander-in-chief's permission to marry. It is hard to believe that Wellington regarded this impulsive alliance of one of his young officers with much enthusiasm. Yet he consented, and even gave away the bride. Though Harry was a staunch Protestant the couple were married a few weeks later by a Catholic chaplain of the Connaught Rangers. Juana's sister, curiously enough, having played her part in creating the romance, faded from the story. Nothing further is known of her, and nowhere in his own writing does Smith allude to her again. As for Juana's feelings, it is hard to escape an assumption that only despair, an absolute need for a protector, could have driven her to accept the hand of a heretic, a grave and terrible step for a Spanish woman of her time.

The subsequent triumph of Harry and Juana's union should not mask the fact that at the outset it was inauspicious. Rankers in Wellington's army often had a woman companion in the field, with whom they might or might not go through some formal ceremony of marriage. Many such camp followers lived with two, three, even four "husbands" before a campaign was over, as each in turn was killed. Yet officers, gentlemen, rarely emulated their men's behaviour. They might somewhere maintain a Spanish or Portuguese mistress, but seldom took her on campaign. It is hard to believe that, outside the tightly knit family of the Rifles, Wellington's officers thought well of Smith's misalliance.

Yet as a breed, soldiers are sentimental men. The presence of a young woman, a child bride, beside the campfires of the Rifle Brigade moved Harry Smith's brother officers to ecstasies. A cynic might suggest that their enthusiasm was reflexive, when from one month to the next they enjoyed the company of no other woman with the attributes of a lady. Objective observers asserted that young Mrs. Smith was not conventionally pretty as Johnny Kincaid suggested, nor even handsome, being possessed of a dark, severe countenance. But all who met her testified to Juana's remarkable personal grace; and to the brilliancy of her devotion to her husband and everything which pertained to him.

As the army marched once more, and Smith with it, his new bride spent what passed for a honeymoon learning to ride a side-saddle made for her by a horse artilleryman. Her mount was an Andalusian thoroughbred named Tiny, which carried her to the end of the war and beyond. Her first battle as a soldier's wife was that of Salamanca on 22 July 1812. Before the great clash began, much to Juana's dismay, Smith's groom West led her to the rear. That night, thanking God for Harry's safe deliverance, she slept on the battlefield amid the groans of the wounded. Next morning she accompanied her husband once more on the victorious British line of march. Each evening she joined him by the fireside, entrancing the Rifles' little mess by dancing and singing to her own guitar. She lay down to sleep in a tiny tent specially made for her, beside her husband when he was not doing duty, anyway sharing the hardships of bare ground and bitter weather, hunger and thirst, without complaint save that she could not bear to see "Enrique," as she always called Harry, suffer likewise. She talked freely to officers and men alike, which won their hearts, though she learned scarcely a word of English during the campaign. "Blackguards as many of the poor gallant fellows were," wrote Smith, in words that echoed his beloved Wellington's view of his own soldiers, "there was not a man who would not have laid down his life to defend her."

The couple enjoyed a brief interlude of comfort during the British stay at Madrid in August and September. But the approach of a superior French army made retreat to Portugal inevitable. Smith's little personal train, which included thirteen greyhounds, was swelled by the addition of a local priest who threw himself on the Rifleman's mercy, asserting that he feared French retribution. The Rifles dubbed the man "Harry Smith's confessor," though in fact Smith's poor Catholic wife suffered many snubs from her fellow countryman for having wedded herself to a heretic.

In those months, Juana and Harry Smith forged a partnership which remained undiminished in passion and mutual respect for almost half a century. Her prudent management of their slender purse and rickety little travelling household won his admiration. She seemed to care only for his survival and professional advancement. By the time they reached Cuidad Rodrigo on 19 November, after weeks of skirmishing with the French in their rear, at last they knew that they were safe for the winter. Many men were sick as well as hungry and weary. An existence exposed to the elements by day and night, without effective protective clothing, caused a host of combatants in the wars of Bonaparte to succumb to death without an enemy in sight. To be continually cold and wet was a soldier's natural predicament. Only the hardiest prospered, Harry Smith with his relentless good cheer prominent among them.

The priest—"the padre," as Smith called him—took over the cooking for their party. They found a billet in a little house, and the gallant captain resumed his habits of hare coursing or duck shooting every day. Thus Harry and Juana passed the army's season in winter quarters, perfectly content in their own society, supporting each other in adversity in a fashion that must have contributed much to the welfare of both. It is realistic rather than cynical to emphasise Juana's dependence upon the fluke of Harry Smith's survival. If a chance bullet carried him away, as there was every prospect that it might, she would be bereft. The couple had no money. Juana's claim upon Harry's distant family was speculative. Her own people considered her an outcast. Her only course if Captain Smith perished would be to seek another protector in the ranks of Wellington's army. And however much his fellow Riflemen loved Juana, it must be questionable whether another of them would have married her. Her entire being, therefore, was subject to her husband's welfare.

Wellington's army set out in high spirits on the 1813 spring march that led to triumph at Vittoria. The weather bloomed, supplies were plentiful. British soldiers shared an absolute confidence that they were now on the verge of decisive victory. Juana's horse Tiny was lame. Instead she rode a strange mare which slipped on a bank, rolled on its rider, and broke a small bone in her foot. Terrified of being left behind, she insisted that a mule should be found to carry her. This prompted half the division's officers to set forth in search of a suitable beast, which was duly found. She was back on her own horse a few days later. Smith passed 21 June, the day of Vittoria, as ever in the thick of the battle, hastening to and fro with orders for his brigade. His wife was horrified to hear that soldiers had seen his horse go down, her husband apparently killed. Ignoring imprecations to remain in the rear, she hastened onto the battlefield, from which the French were now in flight. Amid the chaos of dead and wounded men, shattered and abandoned vehicles, West, the Smiths' groom, urged his mistress to load a horse with plunder, of which Vittoria produced the richest harvest of the campaign. Juana would have none of it: "Oh, West! Never mind money! Let us look for your master." After hours of searching, Smith himself at last heard Juana's loud lamentations. He croaked a greeting to her in a voice stripped hoarse by shouting commands through the bloody day. "Thank God you are not killed, only badly wounded!" his wife exclaimed. Harry growled, "Thank God, I am neither." His only mishap was that his horse had fallen under him, apparently stunned by concussion from the near passage of a can-

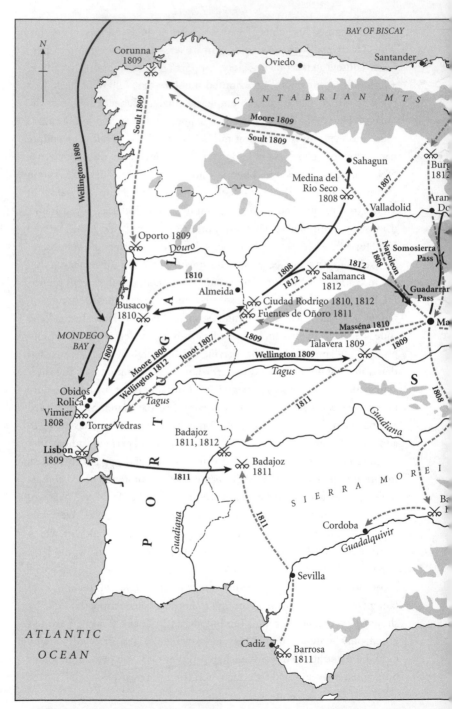

The Peninsular war (1807–1814).

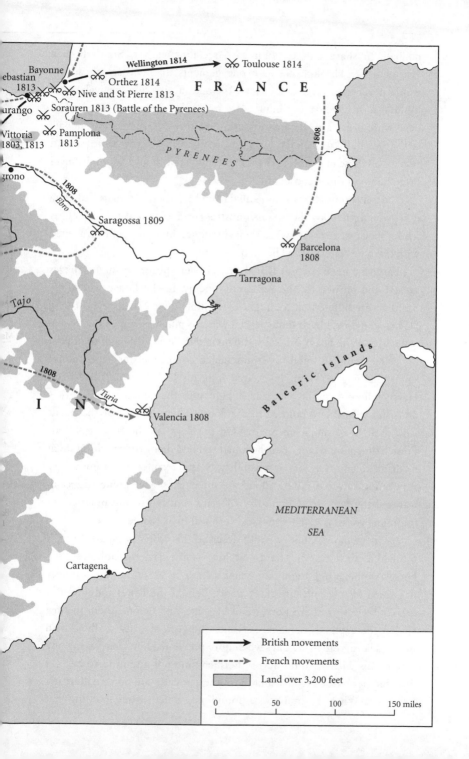

Bayonne
ebastian
1813
urango
Vittoria
1803, 1813
grono

Wellington 1814 ✂ Toulouse 1814
✂✂ Orthez 1814
✂✂ Nive and St Pierre 1813
Sorauren 1813 (Battle of the Pyrenees)
✂ Pamplona
1813

F R A N C E

1808

P Y R E N E E S

1808
Ebro

Saragossa 1809
✂

Tajo

Barcelona
1808 ✂

Tarragona ●

B a l e a r i c   I s l a n d s

1808

Turia
✂ Valencia 1808

S P A I N

MEDITERRANEAN

SEA

Cartagena ●

→ British movements
---→ French movements
■ Land over 3,200 feet

0   50   100   150 miles

nonball. In sharp counterpoint to Marcellin Marbot, Smith bore a charmed life. Through constant engagements in the years ahead, he would never be wounded. Consider the odds against his survival, never mind against his escaping injury: late in life, he computed that he had been within reach of the enemy's fire some three hundred times in battles, sieges and skirmishes. It was no more likely that Harry Smith should survive all these encounters than that a spun coin should fall on its head three hundred times consecutively.

The only booty the Smiths gained from Vittoria was a smart little pug dog given to them by the Spanish mistress of a wounded French officer whom they assisted. "Vitty," as they christened him, thereafter travelled with them to Waterloo and beyond.

The next stages of the British march were bitter, through villages sacked and burned by the retreating enemy. In the house where the Smiths were billeted on the night of 25 June, their Navarese host said: "When you dine, I have some capital wine, as much as you and your servants like." With heavy emphasis, he invited the brigade-major to inspect his cellar. "He had upon his countenance a most sinister expression. I saw something exceedingly excited him; his look became fiend-like." Harry followed his host by candlelight into the cellar, where with a flourish the Spaniard pointed to the floor: "There lie four of the devils who thought to subjugate Spain!" On the flags lay the bodies of four French dragoons, where their host had stabbed them after inciting them to drink themselves into insensibility. Smith recoiled in disgust: "My very frame quivered and my blood was frozen, to see the noble science of war and the honour and chivalry of arms reduced to the practices of midnight assassins... Their horses were still in his stable."

In his memoirs, Smith vividly describes his wife's progress through the fierce rainstorms and hard marching of the days that followed, the horses slipping and stumbling, scant shelter to be found. Each officer possessed his own little flock of goats. Behind the Rifles rode Smith's groom West with spare horses and baggage, and behind them in turn trailed the captain's personal servants and Antonio, his goatboy, with Juana. There were many days when duty prevented him from taking any care of his wife: "I could devote neither time nor attention to her...I directed her to the bivouac and most energetically sought to collect my Brigade...When I got back, I found my wife sitting, holding her umbrella over General Vandaleur (who was suffering dreadfully from rheumatism)." It is a peerless image.

Smith's military career suffered the same frustrations about promotion as did that of Marbot. Neither possessed wealth or influence. While Smith was almost certainly the more intelligent officer, it is unlikely that anyone saw him as a Wellington in the making. The eager young captain thought his majority secure at Vera in October, when before the attack his brigade commander, Colonel Colborne, "who had taken a liking to me as an active fellow," said: "Now, Smith, you see the heights above us?" " 'Well,' I said, 'I wish we were there.' The colonel laughed. 'When we are,' he says, 'and you are not knocked over, you shall be a brevet-major, if my recommendation has any weight.' " The Light Division stormed the heights sure enough, and Colborne submitted his recommendation, but Smith had another year to wait before he got his step.

It was his good fortune, however, to be recognised as a member of an elite of an elite, a Rifleman of General Robert Crauf
ord's legendary Light Division. "Ours," wrote Smith's closest friend, Johnny Kincaid, "was an *esprit de corps,* a buoyancy of feeling animating all which nothing could quell. We were alike ready for the field or the frolic, and, when not engaged in the one, went headlong into the other…In every interval between our active service, we indulged in all manner of childish trick and amusement with an avidity and delight of which it is impossible to convey an adequate idea. We lived united, as men always are who are daily staring death in the face on the same side and who, caring little about it, look upon each new day added to their lives as one more to rejoice in." Kincaid's words represented no romantic flight of fancy. Every man who served with the Light Division in the Peninsula attests to the fact that it was one of the greatest bands of brothers in the history of warfare, and that Harry Smith was among the most celebrated of its young stars.

Whenever the army was in the presence of the enemy, Juana suffered agonies of apprehension about the fate of her Harry. Before every battle they bade a farewell to each other as fond and grave as if they were parting for eternity—as indeed they might have been. One such night in November before her husband met the French at the Nivelle, looking utterly forlorn, Juana suddenly declared: "You or your horse will be killed tomorrow." The irrepressible Harry burst out laughing and said,

"Well, of the two such chances, I hope it may be the horse." Next day as they advanced to storm the French redoubt his cherished hunter "Old Chap" was hit, and fell atop his master, pouring forth a torrent of blood. Some soldiers dragged Smith's gory figure from under the dead animal, exclaiming "Well, d—— my eye if our old Brigade-Major is killed, after all." Smith said: "Come, pull away, I am not even wounded, only squeezed." When he was freed to carry a surrender document to the enemy lines for signature, his French counterpart burst out laughing on beholding his blood-soaked figure. Even Wellington was suitably impressed when Smith reported to him. Juana gasped in horror that evening when first she caught sight of her husband. He assured her that of her tragic prophecy the previous night, only the lesser half had been fulfilled.

Juana courted danger with the lightest of hearts. Once when the French staged a local attack, the Light Division was temporarily hustled into retreat. Smith had to muster with his brigade while his wife struggled into a habit and rode for her life, a few minutes ahead of the enemy. Vitty the pug was left behind with the baggage, but a bugler of the 52nd had the presence of mind to whip the little dog into a haversack and carry him off, as French fire crackled around the retreating regiment. For some hours the enemy held possession of the brigade baggage train. When the British regained the position, the Smiths were crestfallen to discover that a goose which they were fattening for Christmas dinner had vanished.

It is hard to imagine how Juana, a gently reared, convent-educated young Spanish woman, adapted to a life among foreigners whose language she could not speak, and whose customs were wholly alien to her. She was deprived of female society, of a home and any vestige of comfort. Instead, she lived amid an army in which the highest chivalry coexisted with the basest cruelty. She was indefatigable in visiting the sick and wounded, sometimes riding Tiny across empty country in the army's rear, scoured by French dragoons, to reach the hospitals. One night in France the couple were billeted upon an elderly widow who served them with bouillon in a Sèvres bowl which Juana admired. Their hostess remarked that it was one of her wedding presents, never used since her husband's death. Two mornings later on the road to Toulouse, the Smiths were appalled to see their servant enter, carrying the very same bowl full of milk. Juana, mindful of the pillage of her own home in Badajoz, burst into tears. Harry's man shrugged off his master's reproaches: "Lord, sir, why the French soldiers would have carried off the widow an' she had been young, and I thought the bowl would be so nice for the goats' milk in the morning." That night, when Harry returned to the cottage in which they were staying, there was no sign of his wife. At last she entered, weary and mud-stained. She had ridden thirty miles back to Mont de Marsan to return the widow's bowl. Reader, remember: she was barely sixteen.

"When I was first troubled with you," Harry wrote to Juana some years later, "you were a little, wiry, violent, ill-tempered, always faithful little devil, and kept your word to a degree which, at your age, and for your sex, was as remarkable as meritorious, but, please Almighty God, I shall have this old woman with me, until we both dwindle to our mother earth, and when the awful time comes, grant we go together at the same moment." It is not hard to perceive the springs of Harry's devotion.

The Smiths were with the British army at Toulouse in March 1814 when word came of Bonaparte's abdication. Harry's old battalion of the Rifles, which had sailed from England in 1808 numbering 1,050 officers and men, had in the meantime received only one draft of a hundred men, and now returned home just five hundred strong. Those five hundred were recognised, however, as the greatest skirmishing unit in the world. Johnny Kincaid observed wryly that the Rifles sailing from France looked a "well-shot corps . . . Beckwith with a cork leg—Pemberton and Manners with a shot each in the knees, making them as stiff as the other's tree one—Loftus Gray with a gash in the lip and minus a portion of one heel which made him march to the tune of dot and go one—Smith with a shot in the ankle—Eeles minus a thumb—Johnston, in addition to other shot-holes, a stiff elbow, which deprived him of the power of disturbing his friends as scratcher of Scotch reels upon the violin—Percival with a shot through his lungs—Hope with a grapeshot lacerated leg—and George Simmonds with his riddled body held together by a pair of stays, for his was no holiday waist." Smith's survival with so small a loss of his own blood was an extraordinary accident.

The captain was now presented with a painful dilemma, however. His brigade was given immediate orders to sail for America, where the British were committed to a new war. No leave was being granted. He himself might choose to resign his post and go home. But, for all his reputation as one of the boldest and brightest spirits in Wellington's army, he still craved and needed promotion. Amid grief and many tears, he agreed with Juana that they should part. She was to go to London with Harry's brother Tom and all the money the couple could muster, lodge in the capital and learn English while he campaigned. She flatly refused to approach his family in Cambridgeshire until he himself could escort her there. "Many a year has gone by," he wrote in his autobiography about the day of their separation, "still the recollection of that afternoon is as fresh in my memory as it was painful at the moment—oh, how painful!...I never was unmanned until now, and I leaped on my horse by that impulse which guides the soldier to do his duty." Heaven knows what would have befallen Juana if her husband had not returned.

Smith was appalled by the incompetence of the American expedition—a British attempt to escalate on land a struggle with the former colonists that had begun as the naval war of 1812—and by General Robert Ross's handling of his small army at Bladensburg, outside Washington, on 24 August 1814. The brigade-major described the burning of the American capital as "barbarous," though he and his comrades ate eagerly enough the supper which they discovered on the White House table. As the British force withdrew towards the fleet, the soldiers riddled with dysentery, Ross deputed Smith to proceed to London with his despatch, reporting victory of a kind at Washington, together with an exposition of the acute difficulties of proceeding further. Little more than three weeks later, the Rifleman was in England. After seven years' absence from his own country, he revelled in the spectacle of southern England in glorious summer sunshine; and even more, of course, in his reunion with Juana. He delivered his despatch to the prime minister's residence in Downing Street, then hastened to his wife. From the window of the house where she was lodging she glimpsed his hand on the coach door as he peered forth in search of the right number, and shrieked: *"Oh Dios, la mano de mi Enrique!"* He wrote later: "Oh! you who enter into holy wedlock for the sake of connexions—tame, cool, amiable, good, I admit—you cannot feel what we did!" After the joy of their encounter, he was summoned back first to meet the prime minister the Earl of Liverpool, and then to an audience with the Prince Regent. Here was heady stuff for a twenty-seven-year-old soldier without experience of high places. Now at last, he was granted his majority.

Juana for the first time met her father-in-law, who travelled to London for the encounter. Old Mr. Smith burst into tears of "joy, admiration, astonishment and delight" at the spectacle of this passionate young woman in full Spanish costume. She immediately threw herself into his arms. The happy family journeyed together to Whittlesey, where there was a great reunion with Vitty the Pug, with Harry's old hunter Jack, and finally with Tiny the Andalusian, whom the Smith grooms had found hard to manage. Juana, of course, had no such difficulty. "Don't make a noise," she said, "and he will follow me like a dog." And so the horse did—into the family drawing room.

After just three weeks of domestic tranquillity, Major Smith was summoned again to Horse Guards. There was more news from America, all bad. General Ross had attempted to take Baltimore and failed, with the loss of his own life. Sir Edward Pakenham was to replace him, and Smith was appointed to become his assistant adjutant-general, a senior staff post. The commander-in-chief and his large staff set forth across the wintry Atlantic in November 1814, crowded into a frigate. They landed before New Orleans on 26 December, four days after the army had been put ashore. The subsequent battle, disastrous for British arms, cost Pakenham's life. Its conduct shocked Smith. Since the débâcle in South America at the outset of his military career, he had never seen his countrymen so utterly confounded. In Spain, Wellington's army set about its business with a confidence founded upon absolute faith in its leader, which was seldom misplaced. Now, in America, Smith once more stood witness to folly and mismanagement of the most grievous kind. There was only one Wellington. Many lesser British generals were utterly unworthy of their commands.

After the battle of New Orleans, Smith was sent to the enemy's lines to arrange a truce for the burial of the dead. He found his American counterpart, Colonel James Butler, the future president General Andrew Jackson's adjutant-general, "a rough fellow" who carried a drawn sword lacking a scabbard on his belt. Smith apologised for the delay in bringing forward the surgeons. Butler, gazing out upon the heaps of British dead and dying, said: "Why now, I calculate as your doctors are tired; they have plenty to do today." Smith riposted outrageously: "*Do?* Why, this is nothing to us Wellington fellows! The next brush we have with you, you shall see how a Brigade of the Peninsular Army (arrived yesterday) will serve you fellows out with the bayonet." He asked Butler why he carried a drawn sword. The American, matching Smith's spirit, answered boldly: "Because I reckon a scabbard of no use so long as one of you Britishers is on our soil. We don't wish to shoot you, but we must, if you molest our property; we have thrown away the scabbard."

Smith was pleasantly surprised to notice that the Americans had not stripped the dead in the fashion of the French, indeed had taken only British soldiers' boots, of which they were much in want. He and Butler fell out, however. The American seems to have been a grave fellow, unaccustomed to the manners of such insouciant cavaliers as Smith. Butler may have been disconcerted by the bearing of this English professional warrior, who was content to fight almost anyone wherever he was ordered, with scant heed to weighing the merits of the cause. Casualties that seemed appalling to the Americans gave no pause to such as Smith, who had seen Badajoz. In his eyes, losses were merely the price soldiers paid for practising their trade. Wellington seldom grieved for long over the casualties of his battles, and indeed he could not afford to.

At New Orleans Smith told Jackson's man that he hoped next time they met, it would be Butler's turn to ask leave to bury American dead. Yet after a few more weeks of desultory skirmishing, the invaders acknowledged failure. Smith, appointed military secretary to Pakenham's successor Sir John Lambert, was one of the few men of the army in America who returned to England with an enhanced reputation. His courage on the battlefield was no more than that expected of any officer of those days, but his eager fellowship, zeal and efficiency marked him out for future advancement. He remained unfailingly popular with his comrades. The latter point should not be taken for granted among successful warriors. Many of those depicted in these pages were disliked or resented by their peers. Yet few men failed to warm to bluff, plain, eager, guileless Harry Smith.

As his ship entered the Bristol Channel on the homeward voyage, its passengers, eager for news, lined the side when it passed an outbound merchantman. A voice cried out from the deck: "Ho! Bonaparter's back again on the throne of France!" Smith, ever the career soldier, tossed his hat to the sky and cried out in exultation: "I'll be a lieutenant-colonel yet, before the year's out!" Arrived at Whittlesey in a chaise, he found Juana, emotional as ever, fainting with fear that the vehicle brought some stranger bearing bad news for her. She recovered soon enough, of course, and Smith observed happily that never again in their marriage did they face a long separation. He himself embarked upon buying horses for the new campaign with the enthusiasm of a schoolboy off to play in a great match. One of his younger siblings, Charles, was to join the Rifle Brigade as a volunteer, and brother Tom was already in the field. There was one alarm before the Smiths departed. The whole family rode out together on the last evening. As they approached home, Harry glimpsed a fence and ditch at the edge of the town, and could not resist an exuberant flourish: "I'll have one more leap on my war horse." He set his old mare at it. To the horror of them all, she came down. Her rider found himself with a leg trapped between the fence and his struggling mount. For a few terrible seconds he was sure that his leg must be broken, "and there was an end to my brigade majorship!" Instead, to everyone's relief horse and rider scrambled to their feet unscathed.

Major Smith set out next day for Harwich with Charles, Juana, assorted servants and West the groom, reaching Sir John Lambert and his brigade at Ghent on 5 June. Once again he was to fill his old post as brigade-major. A few days later, on 15 June 1815, the force was abruptly summoned to march for Brussels. Next afternoon, as they approached the Belgian capital, they were given fresh orders for Quatre Bras. Bonaparte and his army were closing upon the city from the west. A great battle was plainly imminent. As the column passed through Brussels, they were appalled by the scenes of confusion, haste, muddle and civilian flight which met their eyes. They encountered a mob of Hanoverians galloping for the coast, proclaiming that the French had already turned their rear. Smith went to report to Lambert, whom he found sitting down to dinner with Juana and his ADC. That cool commander contemptuously dismissed the Hanoverian rumour, and urged his brigade-major to enjoy a magnificent turbot which his butler had brought up from Brussels.

That evening came a thunderstorm which drenched the armies and reduced the ground to a quagmire. During the night Lambert's brigade was ordered forward, a movement which the regiments found hard to execute amid the mud and the milling throng of panic-stricken camp followers and baggage carts. The troops were further disgusted when

orders arrived instructing them to clear and hold open the road for further reinforcements, rather than join the main army which was expecting at any moment to receive Bonaparte's assault. Early next morning,
the day of Waterloo, Lambert sent Smith cantering forward to petition
the Duke of Wellington for more congenial orders. He found the great
man near Hougoumont, riding the ridge of Mont St. Jean among his
staff, deploying his divisions. Smith reported. The commander-in-chief
directed Lambert's brigade forthwith to move forward to occupy a position on the left of the British line.

Sometimes, the witnesses of great events do not perceive their mag-
nitude until afterwards. On the morning of Waterloo, almost every man
on the field understood that he was a part of history being made. Smith
was sublimely conscious of beholding his idol the Duke at the summit of
his powers, concise and assured as ever in his vision of the day ahead.
Wellington showed the Rifleman exactly where Lambert's brigade must
deploy. Finally he said: "Do you understand?" "Perfectly, my lord." Then
Smith turned his horse and hastened back to Lambert.

As the brigade formed column for its advance to the field of Waterloo, Harry found time to instruct Juana to ride Tiny back into Brussels
to await the outcome of the battle. Mrs. Smith reached the great square
of the city to encounter West the groom presiding over a heap of the
family's possessions. Orders had just come for the army's baggage train to
move to a village five miles further back. There, like Thackeray's Becky
Sharp with Jos Sedley in *Vanity Fair*, Juana and West spent an interminable afternoon, waiting upon news amid a torrent of rumour and
alarms. Vitty the pug, infected by the excitement around him, leapt
hither and thither, rejecting repose. Tiny the Andalusian would scarcely
stand still. Word suddenly came that the French were upon them. Juana
mounted and took Vitty in her arms. At that moment, the little horse
bolted. For eight frightening miles he would not check until suddenly he
gathered himself to leap a wagon, changed his mind and stopped. Juana
was thrown over his head. She had just remounted and was gathering her
breath when over the hill came a party of fast-riding horsemen. These
proved to be British officers and troopers, together with one of her own
servants, all bent on flight. "Pray, sir, is there any danger?" she demanded
of a hussar. "Danger, mum! When I left Brussels, the French were in pursuit down the hill." Unwillingly, she was persuaded to follow the party

down the road. She sensed that she was in the company of scoundrels, however, when one man urged that she should throw away Vitty to hasten their flight. She arrived at Antwerp emotionally and physically exhausted, her face streaked with mud and tears. She took refuge in the care of the British commandant of the citadel and his wife, with whom she spent the long hours that followed, awaiting news of the outcome of the great clash of armies beyond Brussels.

Lambert's brigade came late to the field, yet in time to share with the rest of the British army the terrible blood price of the day. Wellington's sixty-seven thousand men held the ridge of Mont St. Jean against French bombardment and relentless assault, at the cost of fifteen thousand casualties. By nightfall, some British infantry squares still occupied the ground they had defended all day, but they were heaped regiments of the dead. One of Lambert's units, the 27th, was reduced to two officers, both wounded, and 120 men. Smith himself, plunging to and fro through flame and smoke hour after hour, must by late afternoon have been within a few hundred paces of Marcellin Marbot. Two horses were badly wounded under the Englishman. There was an extraordinary moment late that afternoon, when firing died away across the battlefield. Out on the left flank Smith felt sure the outcome of the battle had been decided, yet could not judge which side was victorious. The fog of war, so literal a term in the age of black powder, obscured the rest of the army from his gaze. Only when the smoke drifted away from the ridge of Mont St. Jean could he see redcoats still standing firm along its length, amid the wreckage of Bonaparte's hopes. It was the supreme triumph of Wellington's generalship against that of the Corsican, a victory gained by the stubborn defiance of the British infantryman. Smith saw that it was safe to surrender to rejoicing.

At the end of that June day, "to my wonder, my astonishment, and to my gratitude to Almighty God," the Smith brothers found that all three survived. Charles had suffered a slight neck wound. Harry, physically and emotionally exhausted, sat down to make tea in a soldier's mess tin for Sir James Kempt, Sir John Lambert and himself. Gazing upon the victorious field, he observed that never in his career had he seen such slaughter. Everywhere stood men weeping for dead comrades or relatives, for this was an age when soldiers felt no shame to vent their emotions. As Charles Smith helped to gather the dead of his regiment, he

glimpsed the corpse of a French officer of delicate mould and appearance, and was astonished on closer examination to discover that this was
a young and beautiful woman. Harry Smith mused: "What were the circumstances of devotion, passion or patriotism which led to such heroism
is, and ever will be, to me a mystery. Love, depend upon it."

It was late in the afternoon of 19 June, the day following the battle,
before the suspense of Juana Smith and thousands of other British camp
followers at Antwerp was ended and they were assured that Boney was
beaten. Yet still Juana knew nothing about the fate of her Harry. At three
o'clock on the morning of the twentieth, against all the pleadings of her
companions, she set out with West in quest of him. Arrived at Brussels at
seven, she fell in with a party of Riflemen who, to her horror, dolefully
declared that Brigade-Major Smith was killed. She hastened towards the
battlefield, expecting every cart which passed laden with corpses to con-
tain that of her beloved Harry. Reaching the field of Waterloo, she began
to run distraught among fast-decaying bodies and newly dug graves.
Suddenly she met Charlie Gore, ADC to Sir James Kempt. "Oh, where is
he?" she cried. "Where is my Enrique?" Gore replied easily: "Dearest
Juana, believe me; it is poor Charles Smyth, Pack's Brigade-Major [who
is dead]. I swear to you, on my honour, I left Harry riding Lochinvar in
perfect health, but very anxious about you."

"Oh, may I believe you, Charlie! My heart will burst."

"Why should you doubt me?"

"Then God has heard my prayer!"

She rode on to Mons, arriving at midnight to snatch a few hours'
sleep. At dawn next morning, 21 June, she hurried on to Harry's brigade
bivouac at Bavay, where "soon, O gracious God, I sank into his embrace."

Smith was made brevet lieutenant-colonel and a Companion of the
Bath for his part at Waterloo. He was not yet thirty. The Duke of Wellington presented Juana to the Tsar of Russia, explaining: *"Voila, Sire, ma
petite guerrière espagnole qui a fait la guerre avec son mari comme la héroïne de
Saragosse."*

So she had indeed. Many years of active service and glory lay before
Harry, always with Juana at his side. He led armies to war against the
Mahrattas in India and against the Kaffirs in South Africa, rose to the
rank of lieutenant-general, and received a knighthood for his contribu-

tion to victory at Maharajpore in 1845. He was later elevated to a baronetcy, though sadly the couple bore no child to inherit the title, for his triumph at the 1846 battle of Aliwal in the Sikh Wars. In 1847 he was posted as governor and commander-in-chief at the Cape. In the highest commands, his superiors in London did not deem him a success, and he was eventually recalled from the Cape in 1852. Bluff, eager, hearty little Harry Smith lacked subtlety or political judgement, just as all his life he was reckless with money. In 1854, when Lord Raglan died in the Crimea, Harry was briefly considered a possible successor as commander-in-chief. He himself still chafed for action, and chronic indigence made him desperate for paid employment. But he was sixty-five years old. Lord Panmure, as secretary at war, wrote to Queen Victoria explaining that the most ardent of her lieutenant-generals had been passed over "from the circumstances of impaired health and liability to excitement."

Poor Sir Harry died broke. All his solicitations failed to gain him the peerage he craved. Yet, perhaps more than any other man described in these pages, his life was happy and fulfilled, thanks to his peerless partnership with Juana. There must have been a tinge of melancholy about their childlessness, but to the end of his days, his letters to his wife whenever they found themselves apart were those of a young lover. It is hard to improve upon Smith's own epitaph for himself, composed in 1844:

> I have now served my country nearly forty years. I have fought in every quarter of the globe, I have driven four-in-hand in every quarter, I have never had a sick certificate, and only once received leave of absence, which I did for eight months to study mathematics. I have filled *every* staff situation of a regiment and of the General Staff. I have commanded a regiment in peace, and have often had a great voice in war. I entered the army perfectly unknown to the world, and in ten years by force of circumstances I was lieutenant-colonel, and I have been present in as many battles and sieges as any officer of my standing in the army. I never fought a duel, and only once made a man an apology, although I am as hot a fellow as the world produces; and I may without vanity say, the friendship I have experienced equals the love I bear my comrade, officer or soldier. My wife has

accompanied me throughout the world; she has ever met with kind friends and never has had controversy or dispute with man or woman.

HARRY SMITH.

If his words were not lacking in conceit, they were nothing less than the truth. Here indeed was the happy warrior, who enjoyed the rare good fortune to share his many campaigns with a perfect companion. For years, the old man celebrated the anniversary of his greatest battlefield triumph with a dinner, at which he caused his charger Aliwal to be led into the hall to share the feast. When the old horse was finally ailing, with many tears Sir Harry led him out to be shot.

Smith wrote in his autobiography of the soldier's lot: "Fear for himself he never knows, though the loss of his comrade pierces his heart." In this, he spoke only for himself. He was indeed personally fearless, but many soldiers even of that era were made of softer metal. The record suggests that, like Marbot, Smith carried courage to the point of foolhardiness. Yet unlike some of his brother officers, he was prudent and humane in his stewardship of the lives of others under his command. He was not the stuff of which great captains are made, but he was the kind of British soldier who wins affection and respect as a great comrade. At a glittering soirée in London, he was once asked with wonderful naïvety whether he had often faced great risk. "My horse did, sometimes," he answered lightly. Consider the answer Marcellin Marbot would have made to such a question!

Sir Harry Smith Bart., KCB, died at the age of seventy-three in his London home, 1 Eaton Place West, on 12 October 1860. Juana survived for a further twelve years, almost to the day, living quietly in Cadogan Place, her existence devoted to keeping bright the flame of her husband's memory and reputation. She was buried beside him at Whittlesey. Few couples have achieved such harmony and understanding in times of peace; perhaps none amid the thunder of war.

CHAPTER THREE

PROFESSOR OF ARMS

THROUGHOUT THE REIGN of Queen Victoria, Europe remained the focus of the civilised world. The memory of the wars of Bonaparte dominated the culture of warriors. This was a folly. If British and continental soldiers of the later nineteenth century had paid less attention to the memories of 1815, and rather more to the experience of the armies of Ulysses S. Grant and Robert E. Lee in the New World's decisive conflict, it would have profited them greatly. The American Civil War taught dramatic and important lessons about the nature of future confrontations in arms between industrial societies, for anyone willing to heed them. Yet many European soldiers were foolish enough to suppose that nothing that happened within the mongrel, adolescent society of the United States could be relevant to their own affairs. They paid the price for their lack of interest in the American experience again and again between 1862 and 1914.

For the inhabitants of the North American continent, the Civil War was the most important event in their domestic experience, and produced the greatest soldiers in their history. No American general of the Second World War matched the gifts of Lee, nor perhaps even of Grant; few subordinate commanders showed the brilliance of Thomas "Stonewall" Jackson, Philip Sheridan, James Longstreet and some of their peers. It is sometimes forgotten, even by Americans, that the nation lost twice as many dead in the conflict between 1861 and 1865 as it did in that between 1941 and 1945, when the U.S. population was vastly larger.

While the rival armies were manned first by citizen volunteers and later by conscripts, most higher commands were held by professional soldiers, many of them West Pointers or graduates of the Virginia Military Institute. Some two thousand alumni of these institutions provided the senior leadership of both sides during a conflict which at one time or another involved four million men. Necessity placed many regiments in the hands of amateurs—in the early days, elected by their men—often with tragic consequences for those they led. Yet a few of those thrust into uniform proved uncommonly talented leaders. None more so than Joshua Lawrence Chamberlain, at the outbreak of war a thirty-two-year-old professor of modern languages at Bowdoin College in Maine. The conflict ended before Chamberlain was tested in higher commands, but he had already shown himself one of the Union's finest officers, a model of courage, intelligence and inspirational leadership. When to these qualities were added charity, humanity and generosity of spirit, a knight emerges who might be deemed worthy of a place at an Arthurian Round Table. There have been more distinguished commanders in American history than Professor Chamberlain, but few seem so deserving of admiration as a human being.

He was born in 1828, into a family of stern Maine farmers. His father proposed an army career for Joshua as a teenager, and sent him to be schooled at a local military academy. Yet Chamberlain's ambitions were at that time scholarly and artistic. He was devoted to music, and played the bass viol. While still a schoolboy he gained a little experience of teaching, and liked the work. He crammed assiduously for a college place with a view to entering the ministry and becoming a missionary overseas. He was finally admitted to Bowdoin College in 1848, after a struggle to learn the necessary classical Greek. His college record was exemplary. He emerged garlanded with prizes and honours, led the choir at the local Congregational church, and fell deeply in love with Fannie Adams, the ward of its minister, a girl two years older than himself. It was often later remarked that Chamberlain could well have been singing in the choir on the day the wife of a Bowdoin professor experienced her vision of the death of Uncle Tom while sitting in Pew 23, which caused Harriet Beecher Stowe to write *Uncle Tom's Cabin* (1852), vastly influential in mobilising Northern opinion against slavery.

Still anticipating a career as a missionary, and too poor to marry Fannie Adams, whose family anyway opposed the match, Chamberlain enrolled at Bangor Theological Seminary. He spent the next three years studying—Hebrew, German, Arabic and Latin as well as theology—and preaching, to growing local acclaim. In 1855 he became an instructor in logic and natural theology at Bowdoin, and was soon promoted to professor of rhetoric and oratory. Having at last achieved some financial security, he was able to marry Fannie, evidently a moody and sometimes irascible girl, whose enthusiasm for her husband later waned, as his for her never seemed to do. They began to raise a family. By 1861 Joshua Chamberlain had become a significant local figure, respected for his cleverness, integrity and commitment to everything he undertook. Though he had abandoned ideas of a career in the ministry, in a God-fearing age he was a sombrely upright, God-fearing man, not much given to jesting, direct to the edge of naïvety. His deep-set eyes reflected remarkable powers of concentration. By a notable feat of will he had overcome an early liability to stammer, to such effect that he gained a reputation as a formidable speaker, as well as a writer. On his salary of $1,100 a year, he and Fannie were able to acquire for $2,500 a pleasant house just off the college campus in which to rear their two surviving children. He found himself increasingly impatient with what he considered the restrictive regime of Bowdoin, with its emphasis on the ancient languages and its unwillingness to give students freedoms he thought they deserved. In 1862 he was granted a two-year leave of absence from the college to travel and study in Europe. This was partly, no doubt, to assuage the restlessness of a teacher whom the college admired and wanted to keep.

Yet already the Civil War was a year old. At the outset it had been perceived as the business of soldiers, no concern of such as Joshua Chamberlain. Now, however, every citizen was conscious of both sides' desperate need for men. The Bowdoin professor was hostile to slavery, and wholly unsympathetic to secession. In August 1862 he travelled to the state capital, Augusta, to meet the governor and discuss whether his services might be of value to the Union cause. Maine was raising thirteen regiments, and the governor was at his wits' end how to officer them. At once he offered Chamberlain a colonelcy and a command. The professor declined. Without military experience, he said, he was quite unfit to lead a thousand men. He would, however, consider a lieutenant-colonelcy, in which role he might learn to be a soldier.

On that note he returned to Bowdoin, to face a chorus of recrimination. Colleagues urged his unfitness for military life, the faculty's need of him, and no doubt also the threatened waste of a clever man's life, doing a job best left to coarser material. A Bowdoin teacher told the governor that Chamberlain was "no fighter, but only a mild-mannered common student." Brunswick's town doctor, however, wrote in contradiction, testifying that Chamberlain was a man of "energy and sense, as capable of commanding a Reg't as any man out of... West Point." The latter view prevailed. When the 20th Maine sailed from Portland for the theatre of war on 3 September, Lieutenant-Colonel Chamberlain was with them, along with a magnificent grey warhorse presented to him as a parting gift by the people of Brunswick. His father, who cared little for the Union cause, offered a somewhat qualified farewell blessing, muttering that his son was "in for good, so distinguish yourself and be out of it... Come home with honor, as I know you will if that lucky star will serve you in this war. We hope to be spared, as 'tis not *our war*."

The men of the 20th Maine were volunteers aged between eighteen and forty-five, enlisted for three years, and now commanded by Colonel Adelbert Ames, an ambitious twenty-six-year-old not long out of West Point, who had earned promotion by his courage during the Union defeat at First Bull Run, the earliest major battle of the war, where he won the Congressional Medal of Honor. Arrived at the encampment of his new command, instead of a sentry's salute Ames received an outstretched hand and the greeting, "How d'ye do, Colonel." He took one horrified look at the shambling crowd of recruits for whom he had become responsible, and said: "This is a hell of a regiment." In one of his gloomier moments, he urged the Maine men that the biggest favour they could do the Union was to desert. They had no more notion of soldiering than Professor Chamberlain, and precious little time in which to acquire one.

They joined McClellan's Army of the Potomac in September 1862, a few days before Antietam, the bloodiest single day's fighting of the war, at which their own 5th Corps was fortunately left in reserve. From high ground they were shocked spectators of the slaughter. The battle ended in stalemate, but checked Lee's advance. The 20th Maine could not even march in step. Its officers and men dedicated themselves to mastering the disciplines of war, none more energetically than Chamberlain. He had told the governor of Maine that his greatest advantage in becoming a soldier was that he knew how to learn. So it proved. He also possessed notable self-discipline. When his regiment came under fire for the first time on 20 September, retreating across the Potomac River at Shepherdstown, its lieutenant-colonel impressed all who saw him by the coolness with which he sat his horse in midstream, while Confederate bullets splashed into the water. One of these caused his mount to collapse under him, precipitating Chamberlain into the flood alongside his men. It might be argued that this performance reflected only a green officer's innocence of peril, save that Chamberlain would behave in the same fashion through the twenty battles that followed.

For the next month, the regiment trained hard. Chamberlain wrote to Fannie: "I believe that no other New Regt. will *ever* have the discipline we have now. We all *work*." It was a revelation to this college professor, no longer in the first flush of youth, to discover that he loved the military life: "I have my cares and vexations, but let me say that no danger and no hardship ever makes me wish to get back to that college life again...My experience here and the habit of command...will break in upon the notion that certain persons are the natural authorities over me." By upbringing he was a country boy, for whom the wilderness held no terrors by day or night. He discovered a natural gift for leadership by example, stripping his jacket to wield a spade beside men digging trenches, sharing every hazard of battle. If his regiment slept on open ground, he shared it with them rather than commandeer a house. He possessed a natural authority, tempered by consideration for those he commanded, which earned more than respect. One of his soldiers wrote: "Lieutenant Colonel Chamberlain is almost idolised by the whole regiment...If I wanted any favors, I should apply to him at once, knowing that I should get them if it were in his power to confer them."

Chamberlain himself wrote to Fannie: "Picture to yourself a stout-looking fellow—face covered with beard—with a pair of cavalry pants on—sky blue—big enough for Goliath, and coarse as a sheep's back... enveloped in a huge cavalry overcoat...and...cap with an immense rent in it...A shawl and rubber talma strapped on behind the saddle... 2 pistols in holsters. Sword about three feet long at side—a piece of blue beef and some hard bread in the saddlebags. This figure seated on a magnificent horse gives that particular point and quality of incongruity which constitutes the ludicrous."

Chamberlain and his regiment suffered their first experience of heavy action on 13 December at Fredericksburg, Virginia. Under fire, and cut off from their own right wing by a fence they were ordered to tear down, most of the men hesitated to expose themselves. Their lieutenant-colonel sprang angrily forward and began to tear the palings apart, shouting to his soldiers: "Do you want me to do it?" They rushed the fence. He wrote later: "An officer is so absorbed by the sense of responsibility for his men, his cause, or for the fight that the thought of personal peril has no place whatever in governing his actions. The instinct to seek safety is overcome by the instinct of honour." His regiment's discipline on that battlefield, advancing as if in parade order, roused the admiration of all who witnessed it. That night, Chamberlain slept uneasily between two corpses, with his head on a third. In the days of fighting that followed the regiment was conspicuous for its steadiness in ghastly circumstances. One night, visiting pickets, Chamberlain strayed into the Confederate lines and was challenged. A vision of inglorious captivity flashed before him. Improvising brilliantly, he began inspecting the trenches Confederate soldiers were digging, offering a word of encouragement and caution here and there. In the darkness, his uniform was invisible. "Keep a right sharp lookout!" he urged, then strode back to his own men.

After losing Fredericksburg, the Union army retired to winter quarters for six weeks. Its men were dismayed and indeed enraged by the incompetence of its generals. Chamberlain and the 20th Maine were unusually fortunate in their colonel, Ames, an officer of energy and intelligence. They could not have learned from an abler tutor. Ames sacked some officers whom he considered incorrigible, and formed a close relationship with Chamberlain, with whom he shared a tent. An outbreak of smallpox caused the regiment to be employed on rear area guard duties, in quarantine, through the Confederate victory at Chancellorsville, during which Stonewall Jackson was mortally wounded, though Chamberlain contrived to have another horse shot under him on 4 May as he watched the army's advance. Two weeks later, Ames was promoted to command a brigade. On his strong recommendation and that of his divisional general, the 20th Maine's fighting professor took over the regiment.

It was a strange business, that such a man as Chamberlain should discover himself to be one of the rare breed who enjoys war, even while recoiling from its barbarity. He chose to perceive much of what befell him in Homeric terms, as an epic in which he thrilled to play a role. He was growing to realise that he might excel as a warrior. Such men are initially surprised to discover that they possess greater powers to endure than others, that their susceptibility to fear is overcome by strength of will and the need to exercise responsibility. Chamberlain always took pains to brief his men, possessing the rare skill of ensuring that those charged with a duty understood it. He knew that he possessed the bearing of a soldier, and was proud of this. The clean-shaven academic now boasted a great shaggy moustache. He possessed no false modesty about the gifts he had discovered in himself. More than anything, he was lucky—though heaven knows, not invulnerable: his head had already been grazed by a minié ball, and much worse would come later. Yet while a host of other officers of comparable courage and ability found their graves in Maryland, Virginia, Pennsylvania, Chamberlain survived. This was due to no special skill of his, but rather to the fluke which throughout history has dictated which men survive to become legends and which are cut short, to form a legion of forgotten warriors.

Just six weeks after assuming command, on 1 July 1863, Chamberlain was hastening his men up a Pennsylvania road, amid applauding, cheering, and even singing Union sympathisers, towards a small town where the vanguard of the Northern army was already heavily engaged with Lee. It was a cloudless summer's afternoon. The dusty men of the 5th Corps covered twenty-six miles—not nearly as far as the 2nd Corps hiked that day, but enough. At last they halted to bivouac, and set about finding those indispensables for marching soldiers, water and fence rails for firewood. A galloper burst among them from the front. There was to be no bivouac: the 5th Corps must keep marching. The army faced crisis. After the previous day's heavy action, only the fall of darkness had prevented a Confederate triumph. Union forces had been obliged to fall back to new positions south of Gettysburg. It was plain that the action would be renewed at daybreak, and that a ridge between two eminences known as Culp's Hill and Round Top must be held against Lee's assault.

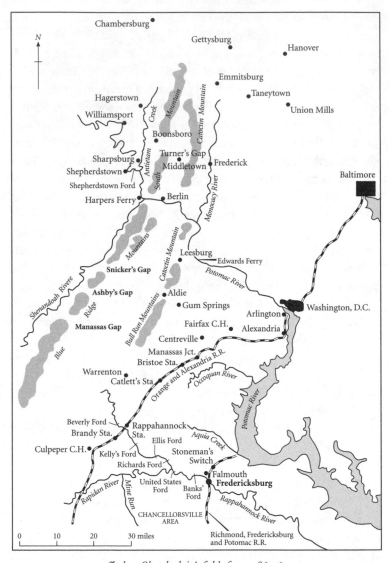

Joshua Chamberlain's field of war, 1862–63.

As the 5th Corps trudged on under moonlight, a rumour spread through the ranks that the ghost of George Washington had been seen riding across the battlefield on a white horse. Chamberlain wrote later: "Let no one smile at me! I half believed it myself."

An hour after midnight, the regiment halted to rest for three hours, then set forth again without breaking its fast. Arriving early in the morning at the edge of the battlefield, at last they halted. A statement was read to them from General George Meade, now commanding the army, about the gravity of their task. Sporadic fire was already audible, yet for reasons that have baffled posterity, Lee was slow to launch his great assault. For some hours the 5th Corps lingered in the rear, before at last it was committed to join the five-mile front along Cemetery Ridge, where the Army of the Potomac was to stand. Its commanders were granted vastly greater licence than they might have expected to deploy their eighty-eight thousand men, regiments still hastening forward piecemeal. Only late in the afternoon did Meade's chief engineer, Gouverneur Warren, perceive to his horror that the key elevations of Round Top and Little Round Top, on the left flank of the line, were undefended and indeed unoccupied, save for a signal corps outpost stationed on the latter. He rushed the 5th Corps forward from reserve, even as Longstreet's corps was making its laborious eight-mile detour in order to reach the start line for the Confederate assault unobserved by the Union army. The 15th Alabama Regiment, commanded by Colonel William C. Oates, together with elements of the 47th Alabama, was able to advance up Round Top, scattering the few Union skirmishers in the area, and occupy that hill without resistance.

Disaster threatened the Union. The way seemed open for Lee's army to turn Meade's flank and roll up his line. Oates called for Confederate cannon to be hustled up Round Top to sweep the blue-uniformed Union divisions. He himself proposed holding the dominant summit rather than pressing onwards, but his brigadier insisted on renewing the advance. After giving his men ten minutes' rest following their exertions on the climb, Oates began to align them once more to assault Little Round Top, immediately to the north. He afterwards asserted that his decision to give his men a brief respite cost the Confederacy victory at Gettysburg. He may have been right.

At the last moment, Union commanders perceived the mass of Lee's men closing on their left flank, preparing to seize Little Round Top. They recognised that if the few hundred yards' frontage of this steep, wooded rock outcrop were lost, so was the battle. Colonel Strong Vincent, twenty-six-year-old commander of the 3rd Brigade which included the 20th Maine, doubled his men towards the crest, shells already falling upon them. Chamberlain's was the last of Vincent's four regiments to fall into line at the southern extremity, with his brigadier's order "You are to hold this ground at all costs." Another officer, Colonel James Rice, observed sonorously: "Colonel, we are making world history today." Chamberlain detached one company to cover his left flank from a distance, down the valley east of Round Top. This left him with 358 men to hold the summit. For a brief moment, three Chamberlain brothers were together on the field, for in addition to Tom, who was serving as Joshua's adjutant, John had appeared as a civilian spectator. Then a shell exploded close by, and the colonel bade the little family group disperse: "Another such shot might make it hard for Mother."

Below him, Chamberlain beheld chaos, with Confederate troops crowding the Devil's Den and Plum Run gorge. Longstreet's sharpshooters had a good view of the summit of Little Round Top, and brought a galling fire to bear on its defenders, which cost a stream of casualties. There could be no more convincing proof of the increased effectiveness of rifled weapons during the half century since the campaigns Marcellin Marbot and Harry Smith knew. The whole of Vincent's brigade was soon exchanging fire with dense masses of advancing Confederates. Both sides were equally weary with long marching. The Union's only advantage was that the Confederate artillerymen were obliged to cease fire as their own infantry closed on the objective.

Chamberlain had been a soldier barely nine months, yet his grasp of tactics was already remarkable. Seeing that his rear was critically exposed, under fire he ordered his officers to shuffle the regiment's entire line leftwards, curling back among the boulders along the southeast face of the hill. He thus doubled the 20th Maine's front, at the cost of thinning its ranks. His new disposition formed an arrowhead with the regiment's colours on a rock at the tip. The companies just had time to complete their difficult manoeuvre before a storm of shouting and musketry signalled the assault of five Confederate regiments. There were now two Union brigades on Little Round Top, under heavy attack and losing leaders fast—a brigadier and a colonel fell dead within minutes, and more officers soon followed.

Oates's 15th Alabama had supposed the rear of the Union position to be undefended. As they sprang forward the last yards to the summit, they were shocked to meet a frenzy of fire from the left wing of Chamberlain's positions. "Again and again was this mad rush repeated," wrote one of the Maine officers, "each time to be beaten off by the ever-thinning line that desperately clung to its ledge of rocks." Chamberlain said: "At times I saw around me more of the enemy than of my own men; gaps opening, swallowing, closing again with sharp, convulsive energy ... All around, strain, mingled roars—shouts of defiance, rally and desperation." The Maine men were pushed back in places, yet somehow summoned the energy to recover their ground. Soldiers were tearing open cartridges with their teeth, ramming and firing like madmen. Some wrestled hand-to-hand with attackers. Chamberlain had thrown into the line every man he possessed, including the sick, cooks, bandsmen and even two former mutineers from the 2nd Maine who had been held as prisoners. He sent the adjutant, his brother Tom, to reinforce the depleted colour guard.

The Confederates, exhausted after twenty-five miles of marching followed by this terrible encounter, fell back to regroup. Chamberlain walked among his men, supervising the gathering of dead and wounded, closing ranks and offering the reassurance of his calm presence. A shell fragment had gashed his right foot, while his left leg was bruised where a ball had smashed his scabbard against it. As the grey ranks of the 15th Alabama stumbled uphill once more through the trees, the colonel almost despaired of holding his ground. He begged for reinforcements, but succeeded only in persuading his neighbours of the 83rd Pennsylvania to take over a portion of the 20th Maine's right flank frontage.

A new crisis came as men began to cry "Ammunition!" They had started the action with sixty rounds apiece. Almost all were gone, even after emptying the cartridge boxes of the dead and wounded. Seeing some of his soldiers preparing to resist the Alabama's charge with clubbed muskets, Chamberlain made the greatest tactical decision of his life. Calling "Bayonet! Forward!" he ordered Captain Ellis Spear to lead the entire left wing of the regiment in a sweeping, wheeling charge downhill. The right wing held its ground until the regiment was aligned, then sprang forth also. The astounded Confederates checked, recoiled,

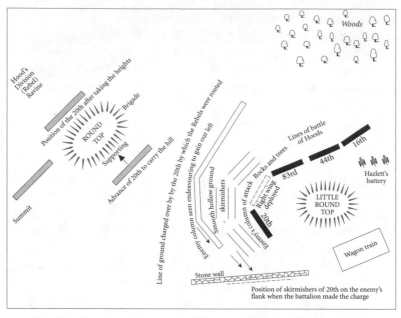

*The 20th Maine's positions on Round Top and Little Round Top, 2 July 1863,
adapted from Joshua Chamberlain's sketch.*

then broke. One of the Alabaman officers fired his Colt at Chamberlain's
face before surrendering when he found the colonel's sword at his throat.
Many of the erstwhile attackers threw down their weapons and raised
their hands. A Confederate attempt to make a stand before a field wall
collapsed when from behind the stonework emerged Chamberlain's
detached B Company, firing on their rear. "We ran like a herd of wild
cattle," a crestfallen Colonel Oates acknowledged. Two Confederate
colonels, one badly wounded, surrendered. Chamberlain described how
his regiment, "swinging like a great gate on its hinges" down the lower
slopes of Little Round Top, "swept the front clean of assailants." Crossing the Union line at the base of the hill, the men of the 20th Maine
were eager to press on, but Chamberlain checked them beneath the
frontage of the 44th New York. After two hours in action he had only
some two hundred men left, and he could see the Texas and Alabama
survivors rallying. It is a remarkable tribute to his powers of command

that he was able to muster his soldiers and redeploy them on the summit of Little Round Top. Having commenced the action 358 strong, they had lost 40 killed and 90 wounded. In addition to the casualties inflicted on Lee's men, they had taken 400 prisoners.

Both friend and foe paid handsome tribute to Chamberlain's achievement, which each perceived as the decisive action of Gettysburg. Colonel Oates of the 15th Alabama said: "There never were harder fighters than the 20th Maine men and their gallant colonel. His skill and persistency and the great bravery of his men saved Little Round Top and the Army of the Potomac from defeat."

And the day was not yet done. Early in the long summer evening, Chamberlain and his new brigade commander—Strong Vincent had been mortally wounded—discussed the chances of regaining Big Round Top while the Confederates were reeling. They were fearful that the enemy might yet regain the advantage by deploying artillery on its height. A newly arrived brigade of Pennsylvania reservists was invited to undertake the recapture of the hill. Its commander declined, and Chamberlain was given the job. Contemplating his exhausted band of survivors, he recalled, "I had not the heart to order the poor fellows up." Instead, he said simply: "I am going, the colors will follow me. As many of my men as feel able to do so can follow us." Drawing his sword, he set off, and of course the 20th Maine went after him.

Still lacking ammunition, they deployed in a single line, bayonets forward. Around 9 p.m., in deepening darkness, they scrambled wearily, silently uphill through the trees, fearful of premature detection. As they approached the crest, however, they met only desultory fire. The Confederates fled. With a handful of casualties, the 20th Maine secured the position and called for ammunition. The Pennsylvania reserve brigade was now sent up to provide support. Yet when its regiments encountered Confederate fire, they turned and fled. Further reinforcements eventually arrived during the night. At noon next day, Chamberlain's little force was relieved and sent into reserve. As the Maine men marched back, the brigade commander seized their leader's hand: "Colonel Chamberlain," he said, "your gallantry was magnificent, and your coolness and skill saved us." On 3 July, while the regiment endured some heavy shellfire, it was not engaged. Meade's victory rendered almost a third of both sides' combatants casualties, but Confederate losses were proportionately higher—twenty-eight thousand dead, wounded and missing, to the Union's twenty-three thousand. Lee's daring invasion of the North had failed, and could never be renewed.

Soldiers, like the rest of us, are sometimes ungenerous about the achievements of their peers. Yet from highest to lowest, the Union's men applauded the achievement of Chamberlain and the 20th Maine, which made up a fraction of 1 per cent of Meade's army. Ames, the regiment's old commander, swelled with proprietary pride, and wrote to Chamberlain to say so. What Chamberlain had done reflected not merely courage, but imagination, leadership and tactical gifts of the highest order. A professional soldier, steeped in the craft of war, might have been proud to display such speed of thought on a battlefield. Instead, this was the achievement of a rank amateur, a man who had known nothing of soldiering a year before, indeed had intended himself for a cultural pilgrimage among the cathedrals and monuments of Europe. For his deeds at Little Round Top, Chamberlain was later awarded the Congressional Medal of Honor. "We are fighting gloriously," he wrote to Fannie. "Our loss is terrible, but we are beating the Rebels as they were never beaten before. The 20th has immortalised itself." On 4 July he led his regiment back to the battlefield to bury their dead, each man's place signified by a marker formed from an ammunition box. He also visited the wounded, some of whom he was distressed to find suffering in the open, beneath rain now falling heavily. Then Meade led his divisions away, on a deplorably leisurely pursuit of Lee's beaten army.

For some soldiers, that July day in Pennsylvania would have represented the summit of military achievement, a supreme exertion never to be repeated. Several of the men portrayed in this book achieved their reputations in a single brush with glory. Even if Joshua Lawrence Chamberlain had never again done anything of note as a soldier, he would be remembered for Little Round Top. Yet this proved only the first notable experience of an extraordinary Civil War career.

In August he succumbed to malaria, which caused him to be sent home for a fortnight's sick leave and a rousing reception from his hometown of Brunswick. He returned to the army to find himself assigned to command of a brigade, the 3rd, to which the 20th Maine belonged, though his formal elevation to brigadier-general's rank was delayed for a time. One of his own soldiers wrote proudly: "Colonel Chamberlain had, by his uniform kindness and courtesy, his skill and brilliant courage, endeared himself to all his men." In Chamberlain's first action with his new command, at Rappahannock Station in Virginia, though he played no significant role his horse was again shot under him. In November, sleeping with his men in the snows, he succumbed again to malaria, which turned to pneumonia. For a time, as he lay in a Washington hospital, his survival was despaired of. He never forgot the army nurse who tended him to recovery: years later when she was widowed he helped her to secure a pension. By January 1864 he was well enough to perform light administrative duties, and in April he conducted Fannie around the Gettysburg battlefield. In mid-May, after relentless pleading with a medical board, he rejoined the army in Virginia. His sickness may have saved his life, for it caused him to miss the bloody actions at the Wilderness and Spotsylvania Court House.

Through late May and June, sometimes commanding his brigade and sometimes relegated—perfectly contentedly—to leading the 20th Maine, Chamberlain fought through battles at Pole Cat Creek and Bethesda Church, together with some lesser skirmishes. His regiment now ranked as veterans. When withdrawing on 3 June, his brigadier asked earnestly if he could fight the 20th Maine by the rear rank, a difficult and delicate manoeuvre that required the unit to reverse its front. Chamberlain answered insouciantly that he could do it any way that was wanted. A few days later he was posted to command the 1st Brigade of General Charles Griffin's division, which comprised six Pennsylvania regiments. Griffin soon remarked admiringly that the spectacle of Chamberlain dashing from flank to flank in action, leading his men forward from the front, was "a magnificent sight." In the battles of the nineteenth century, a man on a horse was always a prominent target. The horse was essential not, as is sometimes supposed, as a privileged mode of transport, but rather as an officer's only means of swift movement in an age when command and communication depended entirely upon personal contact.

Early on 18 June at Petersburg, Virginia, Chamberlain led a dashing attack to seize one of the strongest Confederate positions, "Fort Hell," which he then hastened to emplace for artillery. Yet even as he did so— with yet another horse shot under him—a galloper brought orders from Griffin to attack the main Confederate positions three hundred yards further forward, which had been fortified through months of labour.

Chamberlain was too intelligent a man to execute any order blindly, or out of fear of being thought timid. He despatched a vigorous written protest: "I have just carried an advanced position...I am advanced a mile beyond our own lines, and in an isolated position. On my right is a deep railroad cut; my left flank is in the air...Fully aware of the responsibility I take, I beg to be assured that the order to attack with my single Brigade is with the General's full understanding...From what I can see of the enemy's lines, it is my opinion that if an assault is to be made, it should be by nothing less than the whole army."

Chamberlain's moral courage availed nothing. Ordered to proceed with the attack, "It was a case where I felt it my duty to lead the charge in person, and on foot." A sergeant offered Chamberlain a drink of water from his canteen. He answered: "Keep it, thank you. I would not take a drink from an enlisted man going into battle. You may need it. My officers can get me a drink." If his words reflected a soldier self-consciously acting a hero's part, no one did it better. As the brigade swept forward, the colour bearer was shot at his side. Chamberlain himself seized the flag. Suddenly he found himself floundering in marshy ground at the foot of a slope below the Confederate position. He turned to urge his men to angle leftward, and was hit in his right hip joint by a minié ball, which passed through his body and the other hip. He asserted later that his first thought was: "What will my mother say, her boy, shot in the back?" Desperate not to be seen to fall, he stuck his sabre into the ground and leaned upon it. His men rushed past him before being halted by devastating fire a few yards short of the enemy's earthwork. Chamberlain himself collapsed, bleeding profusely. Two of his aides carried him back some distance amid a throng of retiring Union soldiers before he ordered them to leave him and carry orders to his senior colonel to assume command. He also sought infantry support for the gunners, now threatened by a Confederate counterattack.

An artillery officer surveying the corpse-strewn ground through binoculars spotted Chamberlain's prostrate figure and identified his rank by his shoulder straps. A stretcher party was sent to bring him in. At first the colonel remonstrated with the bearers, urging them to turn to others in worse case. But even as they hesitated a shell exploded nearby, showering them with stones. Without further ado they seized the wounded man and took him to the rear. Neither Chamberlain nor anyone else expected him to live. He said his farewells. After the surgeons had laboured for some hours—as well as his hip wounds, the internal damage was severe—they desisted for a time, fearing that they were causing a doomed man needless agony.

Chamberlain surprised them, however, by keeping breathing. They renewed their efforts. He survived the surgeons' agonising intrusions, and after a few days was evacuated to the navy hospital at Annapolis, where he was exhibited as a miracle of contemporary medical science— and of human willpower. Ulysses S. Grant, by now commanding the Union army, was so moved by the story of Chamberlain's conduct and wounding—"gallantly leading his brigade at the time, as he had been in the habit of doing in all the engagements in which he had previously been engaged," as Grant wrote—that he made his only field promotion of the war, formally recognising Chamberlain as a brigadier-general. The man himself, in a hospital bed, enjoyed the rare pleasure of reading his own obituary notices, which had been published in the New York papers.

It was 19 November before he resumed command of the 1st Brigade. Still unable to walk far or to ride a horse, he remained determined to take the field. He found the army weary and depleted by losses, his own brigade reduced to just two regiments. A few weeks later he once again succumbed to the pain of his wound, and was despatched to hospital in Philadelphia. His friends implored him to acknowledge the inevitable, and retire from military service. Instead, after a month's sick leave he returned to duty, just in time to participate in the closing actions of the war.

These battles set the seal upon Chamberlain's reputation. On 29 March 1865 he once again found himself in action under heavy fire, as his brigade crossed the Gravelly Run stream to attack the Confederate right flank. He was riding his beloved little chestnut Charlemagne, purchased out of government hands for $150, among stock captured from the Confederates. Chamberlain was leading a charging column when his horse reared, a bullet struck the beast in the neck, passed on through Chamberlain's leather orders case, hit a brass-mounted mirror just below his heart, and glanced off to graze two ribs and exit through his coat. It then smashed the pistol of one of his aides with such force that the man was knocked from his saddle.

Shocked, bleeding and winded, Chamberlain collapsed onto his horse's neck. The divisional commander, Griffin, believing him mortally hit, hastened to his side and said as he put a supporting arm round the reeling man's waist, "My dear general, you are gone." But by an extraordinary effort of will, Chamberlain collected himself and responded:

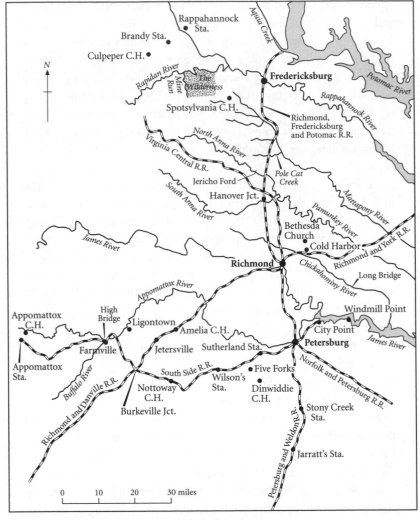

Joshua Chamberlain's field of war, 1864–1865.

"Yes, General, I *am* gone," and spurred away. Capless, liberally smeared in his horse's blood, he looked to all who saw him a man destined for death. Yet his appearance among his own soldiers, who had broken off their assault and were falling back, sufficed to rally them, and they stormed forward once more.

Chamberlain's horse Charlemagne collapsed from loss of blood, and the general caused the poor beast to be led to the rear. He himself was still shocked—"I hardly knew what world I was in"—but plunged forward into the mêlée. He became isolated from his own troops, surrounded by Confederate soldiers who presented their weapons and demanded his surrender. For a second time in his war, he exploited his dishevelled condition to play a brilliant bluff: "Surrender?" he cried. "What's the matter with you? Come along with me and let us break 'em." Flourishing his sword towards the Union line, he hastened the bewildered Confederates forward until they themselves were taken as prisoners.

There was now a lull in the action. A small crowd of spectators gathered around the exhausted Chamberlain, marvelling at this miraculous survivor as they might have gazed upon a Martian. One of the 20th Maine's officers proffered a flask. The general, a teetotaller in early life, drank very deeply indeed. Somebody found him another horse. He hastened away, still covered in mud and blood, to a sector where one of his regiments was pressed. It was plain that this force—the 185th New York—must counterattack. "Once more!" he shouted. "Try the steel! Hell for ten minutes and we are out of it!" Then he led them forward to a hillock where he was bent upon mounting guns, and held the ground until the cannon arrived. He was stirred by the splendour and terror of the scene—"the swift-served bellowing, leaping big guns; the thrashing of the solid shot into the trees; the flying splinters and branches and tree-tops coming down upon the astonished heads."

As Chamberlain sat his horse, swaying with fatigue, Griffin arrived and cried out: "General, you must not leave us. We cannot spare you now." Chamberlain responded dryly: "I had no thought of it, General." Then he led his men, strongly reinforced, to charge the wood harbouring the enemy. The Confederates were thrown back in disarray down the Quaker Road. His own brigade of some seventeen hundred men including gunners had suffered four hundred casualties fighting a Confederate force six thousand strong. Visiting the wounded that night, he came upon old General Sickel, badly hit during the day. Sickel welcomed his tenderness, but thought Chamberlain looked more in need of comfort and succour than himself. He whispered wryly: "General, you have the soul of a lion and the heart of a woman." Chamberlain could scarcely walk from the pain of his wounds old and new, but before he lay down to rest he visited the wounded Charlemagne in a farm building, then sat down by the light of a guttering candle to write a letter to the mother of one of his officers killed that day, to describe the heroic manner of his passing.

Two days later, on 31 March, Chamberlain was resting, very conscious of the pain of his wounds, when a new crisis broke. Lee had attacked the 5th Corps in overwhelming force, driving back many of its regiments in headlong flight. A rabble of disorganised men was pouring through the Union positions. The corps commander, Gouverneur Warren, turned in despair to Chamberlain, the finest battlefield leader of men whom he commanded: "General," he said, "will you save the honour of the 5th Corps? That's all there is about it." Chamberlain replied: "I'll try it, General. Only don't let anybody stop me except the enemy." His arm was still in a sling. Every movement cost him pain from his bruises. Yet he led his men forward across Gravelly Run, scorning to linger for bridging, the infantry carrying cartridge boxes above their heads on bayonets. After Chamberlain's force had swept the far bank, Warren urged a delay to consolidate before trying the strength of the next line of Confederate entrenchments. Chamberlain demurred—speed and momentum were all, he said. He got his way. Instructing his regiments to advance in open order rather than close ranks, and once more mounted on Charlemagne, he cantered forward as the bugle sounded. His force carried the Confederate breastworks and drove the enemy back three hundred yards across the White Oak Road. Although Chamberlain's deeds that day formed a minor part of the Army of the Potomac's battle, they provided a further example of remarkable personal leadership. And before it was all over, there was one more action yet to come.

On the morning of 1 April, a day of Union confusion which cost Gouverneur Warren his command while bringing disaster to the Confederate army, Chamberlain at the van of the 5th Corps met General Sheridan, under whose command the corps had been placed. "By God, that's what I want to see!" exclaimed the irascible cavalry commander. "General officers at the front." Scattered parties of Union infantry were roaming in disarray after suffering an early repulse at Five Forks. Sheridan cantered away, having given Chamberlain a peremptory order to assume command of all infantry in the sector and take them forward. As he rallied groups of men wherever he found them, Chamberlain met a soldier hiding from the crackling rifle fire behind a tree stump. "Look here, my good fellow," cried Chamberlain concernedly, "don't you know you'll be killed here in less than two minutes? This is no place for you. Go forward!"

"But what can I do?" demanded the man. "I can't stand up against all this alone!"

"No, that's just it," said Chamberlain. "We're forming here. I want you for guide center. Up and forward!" Chamberlain gathered two hundred fugitives around him, and watched them advance under command of a staff officer. He wrote afterwards: "My poor fellow only wanted a token of confidence and appreciation to get possession of himself. He was proud of what he did, and so was I for him." Chamberlain spent the rest of the day in his accustomed role, leading forward elements of his command to confront the enemy wherever he stood. The Confederates broke. Lee was obliged to evacuate Richmond and Petersburg. Yet the chief emotions within the 5th Corps that evening were shock and dismay at the news that Sheridan had sacked its commander, Warren, for alleged dereliction of duty.

All through the week that followed, the rival armies conducted their legendary race as Lee and his starving men strove to link up with the Confederate forces led by General Joseph E. Johnston, and Sheridan led the pursuit to cut him off. On the night of 8 April, the exhausted Chamberlain had scarcely fallen asleep when he received a terse message from Sheridan. Rising on his elbow, he read it by match light: "I have cut across the enemy at Appomattox Station, and captured three of his trains. If you can possibly push your infantry up here tonight, we will have great results in the morning." Chamberlain and two brigades reached the station at sunrise. Within minutes he received orders which swung his men into line to support Sheridan's cavalry. The epic drama of America's Civil War was all but finished. The Maine general and his comrades saw before them "a mighty scene, fit cadence of the story of tumultuous years. Encompassed by the cordon of steel that crowned the heights about the Court House, on the slopes of the valley formed by the sources of the Appomattox lay the remnants of…the Army of North Virginia—Lee's army! It was hilly, broken ground, in effect a vast amphitheatre."

As the Union masses prepared to attack, a lone horseman rode out of the Confederate lines and approached Chamberlain. It was an officer carrying a white towel. He saluted Chamberlain and reported: "General Lee desires a cessation of hostilities until he can hear from General Grant as to the proposed surrender." Chamberlain, stunned, said: "Sir, that matter exceeds my authority. I will send to my superior. General Lee is right. He can do no more." Yet even as the South's principal commander acknowledged defeat, so keyed for combat were the men of both sides that their officers were obliged to struggle to restrain them. It took time, and a few lives, before desultory firing could be quelled. At last, as silence fell on the field, a figure appeared between the lines, superbly mounted and accoutred. Chamberlain was awed to perceive Robert E. Lee. Ulysses S. Grant rode out to meet him. The great war between the states was all but over.

That night, 9 April 1865, Longstreet rode over from the Confederate lines and declared wretchedly: "Gentlemen, I must speak plainly; we are starving over there. For God's sake, can you send us something?" They did so, of course. Chamberlain wrote, with his accustomed stately pride: "We were men; and we acted like men." That night also, he was informed that he would have the honour of commanding the representative infantry division of the Union army at the ceremony of surrender. On the morning of 12 April, four years to the day since the attack on Fort Sumter which opened hostilities, as Chamberlain stood at the head of the 1st Division, long, silent grey files began to march past. This was a moment of humiliation for the defeated Confederates, which Grant was determined that they must experience. Yet as they began to pass Chamberlain, the brigadier turned to his bugler. A call sounded. The entire Union division, regiment by regiment, brought its muskets from "order arms" to "carry," in token of salute. It was a magnificent gesture, which went to the hearts of a host of Confederates, who immediately responded in kind. Here was a token of mutual respect and reconciliation which won for Chamberlain the acclaim of the greater part of the American people.

His generosity of spirit in the Union's hour of triumph, reflected in all his dealings with the defeated Confederates, earned him as much regard as his deeds on the battlefield. Though the war was effectively over, on Griffin's strong recommendation Chamberlain received brevet promotion to major-general in recognition of his services of 29 March 1865, on the Quaker Road. He assumed formal command of the 1st Division, which spent the weeks that followed the surrender at Appomattox seeking to maintain order in the countryside amid the chaos accompanying the collapse of the Confederacy.

On 23 May Chamberlain received a final honour when he headed the 5th Corps in the Grand Review of the Armies through Washington. It was one of the most emotional moments of his life. Though he had always deplored the horrors of war, he took deep pride in what he and the soldiers of the Union had accomplished. "Fighting and destruction are terrible," he wrote later, "but are sometimes agencies of heavenly rather than hellish powers. In the privations and sufferings endured as well as in the strenuous action of battle, some of the highest qualities of manhood are called forth—courage, self-command, sacrifice of self for the sake of something held higher—wherein we take it chivalry finds its value."

It is remarkable that a man as humane and intelligent as Joshua Chamberlain emerged from such an experience as the American Civil War with a romantic enthusiasm for the nobility of conflict, despite his uncertainty about the divine view: "Was it God's command we heard, or His forgiveness we must forever implore?" he mused. His own writing about his experiences may jar a modern reader by its unashamed lyricism. Yet it is unsurprising that such a man in such an era perceived his experience in these terms, for he had discovered personal fulfilment as a soldier. Many of the people described in this book possessed courage, charm and professional skill, yet lacked intellect. Chamberlain, by contrast, became celebrated as a hero of the United States whose intelligence and nobility matched his courage.

The Civil War represented a technological and tactical midpoint between the campaigns of Bonaparte and those of the early twentieth century. Railways had transformed mobility, and the telegraph strategic communications. The improved technology of rifled weapons had increased their killing power, but the decisive change wrought by breech-loading and repeating weapons had not yet come. The battles of Grant and Lee were among the last in which formation commanders led from the front, and thus where the personal example of a general officer could exercise a decisive influence "at the sharp end," as did Chamberlain again and again.

The general thoroughly enjoyed his postwar celebrity. He served four terms as Republican governor of Maine, and became president of his old college, Bowdoin. His performance in the latter role was controversial. He introduced military science to the curriculum, including compulsory drilling. This provoked a student revolt which ended in the abandonment of uniformed training. Though Chamberlain's military career spanned less than four years of a long life, he continued to think of himself as a warrior through the decades that followed. Almost seventy when the Spanish-American War broke out in 1898, and suffering recurring pain from his old wounds, he pleaded in vain for a field command. Even in his own family he was always called "General," affectionately abbreviated by his grandchildren to "Gennie." His marriage was tempestuous—in 1868 Fannie demanded a divorce—but somehow survived until her death in 1905. The surgeons who predicted that the terrible wounds Chamberlain received in 1864 would kill him were right—they did so when he was eighty-five, in February 1914. He remains the pattern of American military virtues, one of the most admirable men to wear the uniform of any army, in war or peace.

CHAPTER FOUR

THE LAZY ENGINEER

MOST OF THE CHARACTERS portrayed in this book distinguished themselves through months or years of active service. Yet there is another kind of warrior, who stumbles upon a single moment of glory. Lieutenant John Chard was considered by most of his peers to be one of the least impressive soldiers in the British army. Indeed, there could scarcely be a greater contrast with Joshua Lawrence Chamberlain. Until a January afternoon in 1879, Chard was esteemed only for his good nature and was notorious for his professional indolence. Then, wholly unexpectedly, he found himself thrust onto the centre of a stage where he gave a performance that won the applause of Victorian England. In a few hours of violent action, Chard achieved a celebrity which persisted to his death, though he never again did anything of military worth. Today, Chard would be relegated to the musty archives of imperial history but for the fact that in 1964 his exploit was embroidered into the epic film *Zulu,* which almost everyone susceptible to cinema adventure must at some time have seen and delighted in, and in which he was played by Stanley Baker. Modern readers must judge for themselves how far, in reality, its principal actor deserved the status conferred upon him when he became one of the more honoured officers of the nineteenth-century British army.

John Rouse Merriott Chard was born into a family of minor Devon gentlefolk on 21 December 1847. He was educated partly at Plymouth New Grammar School, partly by tutors. He followed his elder brother

William into the army, entering the Royal Military Academy at Woolwich aged eighteen for the usual thirty-month course of gunnery, fortification and bridging, mathematics, natural and experimental philosophy, landscape drawing, mechanics, French and Hindustani. After passing out of Woolwich eighteenth in a batch of nineteen, he was gazetted lieutenant in the Royal Engineers in July 1868. A subaltern he stubbornly remained through the next eleven years. Until December 1878 he served in a dreary succession of home and foreign garrison postings—Chatham, Bermuda, Malta, Aldershot, Devonport and Chatham again. *"A partir de trente ans, on commence à être moins propre à faire la guerre,"* Napoleon observed incontrovertibly. Even after passing thirty Chard did not marry: in those days his humble rank discouraged family responsibilities. Not merely did he fail to distinguish himself professionally, he irked superior officers by his laziness. The only memory Woolwich contemporaries retained of Chard was that he was always late for breakfast. His chief merit, in the eyes of his peers, was that his West Country affability rendered him an easy companion in the mess, an important consideration when one had to meet a man there for three meals a day, month in and month out, amid a routine of irksome monotony. When Sir Garnet Wolseley, supreme British field commander of his generation, met Chard later he was unimpressed, dismissing him as "a slow, heavy fellow." The engineer, with his big black beard and a manner diffident to the point of ineffectuality, left youth behind without making any mark upon his chosen profession.

It will never be known why Chard was posted to South Africa as war with the Zulus loomed, nor whether he welcomed the opportunity for active service. Most likely, and as usual in these matters, some engineers had to go, and Chard's name chanced to be on a list. His nature was to accept, oxlike, whatever duty the army in its wisdom decreed for him. On 11 January 1879 Chard found himself accompanying Lieutenant-General Lord Chelmsford's army into Zululand, following the expiry of a British ultimatum to King Cetewayo to which that monarch had deigned no reply. Chelmsford's expedition was characteristic of its time and kind. The Zulus displayed less deference and more truculence than the conceit of the neighbouring imperial power would tolerate. The British resolved to impose their will, and despatched four columns to preempt the threat of a Zulu incursion into Natal. The only thing unusual about this venture was that those who knew Cetewayo's people warned that they ranked among the most formidable and disciplined warriors in the continent.

Chelmsford's No. 3 Column reached its intended base at Isandlwana, some ten miles inside Cetewayo's territory, on 20 January, after a single desultory skirmish with the inhabitants. His lordship left a battalion of the 24th Foot to garrison the camp, while he led out his remaining force in search of the enemy. Ten miles south of Isandlwana stood the little mission station of Rorke's Drift, a few hundred yards on the near side of the Buffalo River border from Zululand, and thus inside British Natal. Amid a cluster of stone and wooden kraals stood two single-storey thatched buildings, in one of which the British had established a hospital. The other was stacked almost to the roof with biscuit, mealies and ammunition. In command of the post was Chelmsford's deputy assistant quartermaster-general, Major Henry Spalding.

This officer had been given a company of the 24th Foot and a detachment of Natal Native Levies to guard the supplies, and was also left responsible for thirty-six sick and injured men. The 24th was mostly composed of Englishmen, but around a quarter of its strength was Welsh. Among the ranks of B Company were five men named Jones and another five named Williams. The riflemen at Rorke's Drift were commanded by Lieutenant Gonville Bromhead. He, like Chard, was an unimpressive officer who had served more than a decade without attaining a captaincy, despite being the product of a line of distinguished soldiers. One of his brothers was a rising star of the "Wolseley ring." "Gonny," however, was something of a disappointment. Though two years older than Chard, his lieutenancy was three years younger. His professional career was hampered by the fact that he was deaf, and deemed by his superiors almost as lazy as the engineer. Indeed, the two men shared a reputation for good nature and incompetence. It is almost certain that Bromhead had been left at Rorke's Drift because he was deemed unfit to command a company of the 24th in field operations.

Chard, meanwhile, with four sappers was repairing the broken cables of one of two big iron punts at the ferry built to carry Chelmsford's heavy equipment across the Buffalo. The engineers completed this task on the evening of 21 January. The ferry was then fully occupied moving wagons across the river, for onward passage to Isandlwana. It was heavy work, for rain had churned the crossing approaches into a quagmire. A steady stream of visitors passed through on their way to join Chelmsford's column. On the morning of the twenty-second, young Lieutenant Horace Smith-Dorrien paused for a gossip. He observed that "a big fight was expected," and borrowed a few rounds of revolver ammunition from his friend "Gonny" Bromhead. Then he rode on his way.

Chard's sappers received orders to join the main force at Isandlwana. They boarded a wagon behind a native driver, and bumped their way slowly round the hills, in the wide loop that was necessary for anything but a bird to pass from Rorke's Drift to Chelmsford's base. Chard himself was given Major Spalding's permission to ride over, nominally in search of further orders for himself, but chiefly to indulge a little war tourism. In two hours, Chard reached Isandlwana to find most of the force there roused by glimpses of Zulu movements on the surrounding hills. Seeing some enemy moving towards the Nqutu Plateau, the possibility crossed the engineer's mind that they might "make a dash at the drift"—Rorke's Drift. He himself was told to return to the river, continue supervising the ferry, and build a redoubt to enable riflemen to cover it. The camp's senior officer, Colonel Durnford, asked Chard, on his way, to pass movement orders to some detachments. There was a general expectancy of action at Isandlwana, but little apprehension. Here was a substantial, well-armed British force, preparing to dispense the usual medicine to savages. Chard rode unhurriedly back to the ferry with his batman, Driver Robson, the two men oblivious that they had escaped death by a couple of hours.

At noon, some twenty thousand Zulus stormed Isandlwana, catching the defenders poorly deployed on open ground. After a brisk and costly fight, the warriors overran Durnford's position when the 24th's riflemen ran out of ammunition. Some 1,350 defenders were slaughtered. Only 75 escaped. One of the most scenically beautiful battlefields of history witnessed one of the most deplorable British humiliations. The Zulus were able to exploit their numbers to swamp the redcoats' line, because the defenders manoeuvred clumsily and allowed themselves to be cut off from their ammunition supply. It took Cetewayo's men little time to overcome the British, but rather longer to loot their camp, from which all cattle and mules were driven off to the king's kraal. Horses were killed.

They played no role in Zulu society and, in the disdainful words of a warrior, "they were the feet for the white men."

The garrison at Rorke's Drift heard gunfire over the hills. Of itself, this was neither surprising nor alarming. Lord Chelmsford had gone to find Zulus. The crackle of musketry suggested that he had been successful. Three men—Surgeon Major Reynolds, an army chaplain and the Swedish missionary Otto Witt—rode to the crest of the Oscarberg, a hill behind the post, to see what was happening. Witt had sent his wife and three children away to Pietermaritzburg, but himself remained as an interpreter for the British. The horsemen scanned the horizon in vain. The mountains intervening between Isandlwana and the Drift muffled even sounds of musketry. When they spotted natives in the northern distance, they took them for British levies. Only later did they realise that these were Zulus hunting down fugitives. The sightseers gingerly picked a path back down the Oscarberg to the mission.

Major Spalding, however, remained uneasy. He was conscious of the vulnerability of his position and the weakness of its defenders. Around 2 p.m., he himself mounted a horse and set off briskly towards Helpmakaar, some ten miles southwards, to hurry forward two companies of the 24th that were posted there. Before leaving, he ascertained that Chard's lieutenancy predated that of Bromhead, and went through the formality of assigning command of Rorke's Drift to the sapper. Contrary to cinematic myth, this does not appear to have caused any difficulties with Bromhead, with whom Chard was on easy terms. No one perceived the issue as significant, for Spalding intended to return before darkness fell.

Chard was evidently undisturbed by what he had seen of the enemy milling above Isandlwana. In his little camp by the river he ate a leisurely lunch before retiring to his tent to write letters, unaware that the four sappers who had left him only that morning were lying dead and eviscerated less than ten miles away. Around 3 p.m., however, tranquillity was banished. Two lathered horses scrambled down to the waterside, bearing fugitives from the catastrophe—Lieutenants Adendorff and Vaines of the Natal Native Contingent. They shouted the headlines from the far bank of the Buffalo, before urging their mounts across the Drift. Not only had there been a massacre, they reported that a Zulu *impi* was moving towards Rorke's Drift. Chard at once despatched a sergeant and five men to picket the high ground beyond the river. Vaines hastened the few hundred yards to the mission station to tell his news, then rode for Help-makaar. Adendorff also seized an opportunity to slip away, avoiding the subsequent battle. He was later arrested in Pietermaritzburg as a deserter.

Bromhead, it transpired, had received a note scribbled by an officer of No. 3 Column at the same time and of the same import as the tidings borne by the slouch-hatted fugitives who met Chard. The infantryman sent his own runner to summon the engineer from the river. Chard took one small but important step before complying—he ordered a water cart to be filled and taken up to the station. He then hurried to the cluster of buildings to find Assistant Commissary James Dalton directing fevered efforts to fortify them. Some men were striking the 24th's tents to clear the field of fire, tearing out guy ropes and leaving a tangled mass of can-vas, which subsequently provided a significant impediment to the attack-ing Zulus. Other soldiers and Native Levies were packing wagons with bags and boxes to make solid obstacles, loopholing brick walls and creat-ing new ones with mealie sacks. Bromhead raised with Chard the possi-bility of evacuation, which it seems that the two lieutenants seriously considered. Dalton, a former sergeant-major, insisted that such a course was madness. The only option was to stand and fight. After a hurried consultation between the three men, Chard agreed that the others were doing everything possible, and went back to his picket.

Sergeant Milne and his riflemen, who were from the 3rd Buffs, roused the officer's admiration by volunteering to take up firing positions on the punts in mid-river, to delay the Zulu advance. Chard demurred. When the time came, he would need every man at the station. He and Brom-head, as a survivor later approvingly recorded, now joined their men heaving mealie bags in the sweltering heat. There was no nonsense about class condescension at Rorke's Drift, and indeed no subsequent reports of personal friction between the British defenders. All of them vividly recognised that they faced a struggle for their lives, the outcome of which would be determined solely by their own exertions.

Around 3:30 p.m., Lieutenant Henderson arrived with about a hun-dred men of the locally raised Natal Native Horse, a welcome re-inforcement. Chard directed them to throw out a scouting screen around the position. A few more stragglers from Isandlwana arrived, in a state of hysteria and despair. They urged the men of the garrison to flee for their lives. A stand was hopeless. If an entire battalion, almost a thousand strong, had failed to stop the Zulus that morning, how could a weak company numbering a hundred-odd men do so that afternoon? Yet Chard had made his decision. The seventy-five minutes between the first alert and a sighting of the Zulus—"Here they come, black as hell and thick as grass!" a certain Sergeant Gallagher cried from the south wall—was not long, but just enough time to contrive an effective breastwork. Unlike the victims of the morning, the men at Rorke's Drift were well supplied with ammunition. Now they also possessed the essentials of every effective infantry defence—obstacles covered by fire. The single-shot .45 falling-block Martini-Henry rifle was a deadly tool against tribesmen chiefly armed with assegais, so long as it could be kept fed with bullets. The biggest problem for the defenders was that considerable cover, bush and trees and grass, extended close to the mission station on two sides. There was no time to clear this away and improve the British field of fire.

By far the most experienced soldier at Rorke's Drift was Commissary Dalton. Both Chard and Bromhead later paid tribute to his advice and leadership. He was a forty-nine-year-old former NCO of the 85th Foot who had taken his pension six years earlier and settled in Natal. It was Dalton, veteran of a course in field fortification, who hastily sketched the design for a perimeter at the mission station, which Chard and Bromhead seized upon and executed. It is plain that, before the battle began and perhaps also afterwards, Dalton was the strongest personality among the defenders, a forceful, leathery old soldier who knew exactly what he was doing. Surgeon-Major Reynolds noted the opinion of all the officers that if either hospital building or storehouse fell to the Zulus, the whole British position must collapse. But as the little garrison weighed their chances against those of their comrades at Isandlwana that morning, they told each other that their ramparts vastly improved the odds, compared with those facing the victims of the morning, caught in the open. They were right.

Around 4:15 p.m. the 350 Native Levies on the walls took to their heels, accompanied by their European officers, at the first sighting of the Zulus. Five minutes later, the horsemen of the Natal Carabineers also fled. Their commander, one Lieutenant Vause, shouted to Chard that he could no longer control his men, then put spurs to his own horse and joined the flight. One of Vause's corporals fell to a bullet in the back, fired by a disgusted rifleman of the 24th whom no one inside the perimeter felt minded to reproach. Otto Witt also decamped at this point, announcing as he galloped away that his duty was to his family. The missionary emerges from survivors' accounts as a liar and a charlatan— he later announced himself in England as a veteran of both Isandlwana and Rorke's Drift. Who could blame him for his flight, however? The Swede was no soldier, and no enemy of the Zulus either. He later unsuccessfully sued the Crown for £600 for the destruction of his property in the battle for the mission station.

Chard at once perceived that his drastically shrunken force—8 officers and 131 NCOs and men, of whom 36 were sick—could not hope to hold the existing four-hundred-yard perimeter. Only the 81 men of the 24th's B Company formed a coherent fighting body. The sapper shortened his line, relinquishing a big kraal, and put men to work constructing an inner rampart of biscuit boxes. They erected a further mound of mealie bags, nine feet high, at the centre of the position. From its eminence, men could fire down over the heads of the front rank. One of the most important things Chard got right, probably thanks to the advice of Dalton, was to ensure that his men had a fallback position if they lost a section of their initial perimeter. Paradoxically, the flight of the Native Levies probably saved Rorke's Drift. If a substantial section of front had remained in their hands when the Zulus charged, they would almost certainly have broken and run. Sudden exposure of a gaping hole in the defence must have precipitated a wholesale collapse.

Instead, Chard was given time to reorganise his little garrison, now entirely composed of reliable men, before the storm broke. Yet such deliverances can only be perceived by posterity. At 4:20 on the afternoon of 22 January, morale at Rorke's Drift was low. The men of the 24th Foot who remained on the walls had been forced to witness the flight of all those who possessed the means or the liberty. The defenders had been abandoned to what the fugitives considered certain death. More than a few riflemen must have muttered unsympathetically about Bromhead and Chard—an officer whom they scarcely knew—for committing them to a course of action likely to cost their lives.

The defenders took up firing positions. Bromhead gave the order to fix bayonets. The mission station echoed with a chatter of clicking steel,

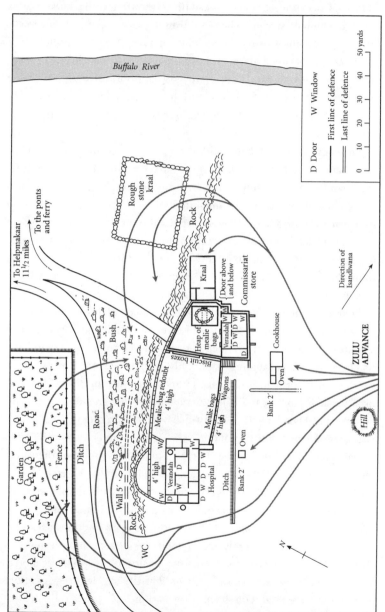

The mission station at Rorke's Drift, 22 January 1879.

as the two-foot swords were locked to rifle barrels. The only task neglected, because every fit man had been labouring at the defences, was the evacuation of sick and wounded from the hospital into the redoubt. It was simply not possible to accomplish everything necessary in the brief interval between alarm and assault. Men lost their lives in consequence of this omission, but Chard got his priorities right. Whatever indolence his superiors had previously observed in him, at the moment of truth he displayed a welcome willingness to act energetically, and to accept advice.

In many respects, Chard's character as sketched by his contemporaries suggests, a little out of time, a character from the pages of P. G. Wodehouse. He was a simple, undemanding, infinitely good-natured fellow, devoid of ambition, who inhabited an exclusively masculine world in which a woman's function was to applaud prettily if some chap holed in one. Yet Chard also possessed virtues implicit in Wodehouse's amiable idiots: loyalty and an absolute sense of duty. If duty now demanded that John Chard sacrifice his life for Queen and Country at Rorke's Drift, then he would do so without complaint.

Three Zulu regiments—the uThulwana, uDloko and inDluyengwe—made up the *impi*, between three thousand and four thousand warriors strong, which descended in two columns upon Rorke's Drift. All had been present at Isandlwana, but only on the edge of the battle. Their principal achievement had been to pursue and kill fugitives. Most had not "washed their spears." They were anxious for greater glory. Their commander, Dabulamanzi, a thirty-five-year-old brother of Cetewayo's, was eager for personal distinction. Apparently impulsively, as his men paused above the Buffalo River to take a pinch of snuff after their long pursuit from the battlefield, Dabulamanzi determined to attack Rorke's Drift. By doing so, he breached his king's direct instructions. Cetewayo had given orders that no one should cross the Buffalo into Natal; he had also directed that there should be no attempt upon any fortified place. The Zulu leader thoroughly understood the Europeans' advantage if they could employ firearms from fixed positions against assegais. Yet Dabulamanzi reasoned that success would justify all. He threw his entire strength into the assault on the mission station.

The shock of the first charge, at around 5 p.m., was marginally diminished by the eagerness of some attackers to loot the tents of the 24th

Foot and the engineer wagon abandoned on the open ground beyond the mission station. Driver Robson, Chard's batman, furiously observed from his position on the perimeter the enemy ransacking "our things." But when the onslaught came, the rush of six hundred chanting Zulu warriors against the south wall of the post presented a terrifying spectacle. Devastating rifle fire checked them fifty yards short. Some Zulus took cover behind ovens, equipment and a cookhouse in the 24th's tent lines. From such shelter, the few who possessed firearms maintained a harassing fire on the British, mostly with old flintlock muzzle-loading rifles. If their marksmanship was poor, it was sufficient to force the defenders to remain behind cover. Chard's men noted the thud of Zulu balls striking mealie bags, rattling noisily against biscuit boxes. Casualties caused by enemy fire from the Oscarberg behind the post caused Chard to order a retirement from the outer wall to the biscuit-box inner rampart.

Repulsed on the south side, hundreds of warriors swarmed in a wide circle round the British position to emerge again at the northwest corner of the hospital, where their approach was sheltered. The Zulus, said Private Henry Hook—a former cook who was now firing from a loophole in the hospital—"took advantage of every bit of cover there was—anthills, a tract of bush we had not time to clear away, a garden or sort of orchard which was near us." British riflemen on the hospital roof were knocking down assailants at long ranges, but an alarming number broke through to close quarters. The lanky figure of Commissary Dalton attracted much admiration among the defenders. He strode up and down the line, exposing himself fearlessly, using his own rifle most effectively until he spun and fell, hit in the shoulder by a Zulu ball. Thereafter, though he could no longer use a weapon, he continued energetically to stride the line, pointing targets for others.

Both Chard and Bromhead had taken up rifles alongside their men. A corporal of the Natal Native Contingent, hit in the shoulder and back, crawled to the engineer and handed him cartridges which he could no longer fire himself. Both sides were using black-powder weapons, and dense gunsmoke eddied around the British position. Some Zulus outside the wall seized with bare hands the protruding bayonets of defenders, striving to wrest the weapons from their grasp. Most were shot for their pains. Attackers had gained a lodgement on the hospital verandah, and were fighting hand-to-hand with defenders behind its doors. Bromhead led a charge to clear the Zulus back.

The hospital, it became plain to both sides, was the weak point of the British defence. Riflemen at its loopholes had a much less useful field of fire than those on the mealie-bag walls. When Zulus broke into the building, almost an hour of fierce fighting followed in its cramped little maze of rooms. For the British, this was the bloodiest phase of the battle. A big, cheerful young man named Cole, fighting in one room beside Hook, lost his nerve and fled. Zulus cut down "old King" Cole when he ran from the hospital door. As flames from the thatched roof set ablaze by the Zulus began to spread through the building, Bromhead's riflemen struggled to help patients crawl to safety through holes hacked in the partition walls. Bayonets and assegais clashed constantly. A small, high window soon offered the only line of retreat for fevered and bleeding men who could squeeze through the aperture into Chard's perimeter. No officer could direct the fierce struggle within the building. Each British soldier simply fought as best he could, face-to-face with the enemy, until he escaped or died. Two-thirds of the defenders' casualties at Rorke's Drift were incurred in and around the hospital. All four of the last soldiers to withdraw from the building—Hook, Williams J., Jones R. and Jones W.— were subsequently awarded Victoria Crosses for holding off attackers with bayonets alone when their ammunition was expended. Fortunately for the defenders, the smoke and flames which finally drove them from the building also rendered its shell untenable by the Zulus. The blaze formed an effective barrier through the critical hours which followed.

The storehouse now became the hub of Chard's shrunken perimeter. It was a mud-brick building some thirty yards by twenty in extent, against which the enemy's spearmen surged and eddied in the darkness. After the fifth or sixth assault, weary defenders standing shoulder to shoulder could scarcely raise their rifles or thrust their bayonets, which the British noted were far more effective in causing attackers to flinch than the threat of a bullet. The mere physical exertion of such a close-quarter struggle was akin to that of some nightmare wrestling match. Rifle barrels were fouled, breeches often jammed. Faces were blackened with powder smoke, mouths parched. Weapons grew so hot that men scorched their hands as they worked the lever actions. There were repeated outbreaks of hand-to-hand fighting at the wall, where a huge, feckless Swiss of the Natal Native Contingent named Corporal Scheiss—already wounded in an earlier skirmish with the Zulus—distinguished himself, continuing to fight even after being hit again. The hospital blaze became a vital aid to the defenders. In the darkness, it provided illumination to guide their aim. Without the light of the flames, weight of numbers would probably have proved decisive for the Zulus.

There were few moments of silence, seldom a complete lull in the firing, at any time before midnight. When Private Brickey rolled down the storehouse roof after being hit by a Zulu shooting from the Oscarberg, one of the men who picked him up muttered: "Poor old Brickey." At this the wounded man opened his eyes and said: "Never mind, lads, better a bullet than an assegai!" Surgeon-Major Reynolds dug out the slug. Brickey lived. Reynolds was now tending wounded on the verandah of the storehouse. His unshakeable calm impressed every man who watched him at work. A spectator had attached himself to the surgeon—Pip, a terrier belonging to an officer of the 24th who had left the little dog at the Drift while he himself departed to meet death at Isandlwana. Pip cavorted beside Reynolds throughout the battle.

As soon as any casualty was bandaged he was sent back to the perimeter, to fire a rifle if he could, to carry ammunition if he could not. Even Reynolds was now "beginning to consider our situation rather hopeless." He, Chard and the other defenders would have felt even gloomier had they known that during the afternoon Major Spalding and two companies of the 24th which he had fetched from Helpmakaar marched within three miles of the mission station before meeting panic-stricken fugitives who assured them that Rorke's Drift had fallen to the Zulus. Spalding quite correctly turned back. Whatever the fate of Chard's command, had the major advanced further on open ground, his little band of 150 men would almost certainly have been wiped out.

At Rorke's Drift, some men's rifles were no longer serviceable. Against Zulu assegais, they relied upon bayonets. Several of these buckled in desperate jousts across the parapet. A little before midnight, the Zulus launched their last big attack, chanting their war cry *"Usutu! Usutu!"* as they came. Once again, murderous British volleys halted and drove them back. Thereafter sporadic enemy rifle fire persisted, but Chard seized the lull to take every second man from the parapet and set a party to work repairing defences, moving wounded and distributing ammunition. The engineer himself, Webley revolver in hand, led three or four men who jumped the barricade and ran fifty yards into the 24th's abandoned tent lines to reach their water cart. They could not hope to drag it inside the perimeter, but fetched desperately needed supplies to quench the thirst of the defenders.

Zulu chanting began again in the darkness. Every fit rifleman returned to the wall. Nothing happened. At around 4:15 a.m., first light, patrols moved cautiously out from Chard's ramparts, and were bemused to encounter only dead and bleeding enemy. Private Hook bayoneted a wounded warrior who reached up to snatch at his rifle barrel. Returning to their positions, fear persisted that another Zulu attack was imminent. Most of the weary defenders were again set to work on the barricades, dragging stones from the ruined hospital to reinforce the walls, stripping thatch from the roof of the storehouse to prevent the Zulus firing it. At 7 a.m. Colour-Sergeant Frank Bourne cried: "Stand to!" A strong party of Zulus had appeared on the hills to the south-west. The enemy made no move. Meanwhile, as the British watched the high ground, a lone black figure advanced along the track towards the mission station. He was recognised as a local Natal native. Chard scribbled a hasty note to Major Spalding, and despatched the man with it to Helpmakaar.

Just as this messenger set off, the Zulu *impi* again appeared in the distance. Once more the British manned their walls. By now their ammunition was reduced to around twenty rounds a man. They felt at the last gasp of exhaustion, and many also must have despaired. What did Chard think? His subsequent report details his actions rather than his sentiments—indeed, he was the least reflective of men—but he possessed the comfort of knowing that no decision was demanded of him. He and his men could only hold their ground until death, which must at that moment have seemed very close.

Around 8:15 a.m., however, both Zulus and British riflemen sighted an approaching column of horsemen. This was too much for Cetewayo's warriors. They were exhausted and very hungry, having eaten little for four days. Their chief knew that he would face bitter recriminations from the king for having disobeyed orders, failed in his attempt on Rorke's Drift, and lost the lives of several hundred men. The Zulus withdrew into the hills. Lieutenant-Colonel Russell led a column of Chelmsford's mounted infantry into the blackened post, where smoke curled thickly from the ruins of the hospital but a union flag still flew from the storehouse roof. Chard's exhausted men gave three cheers. The battle of Rorke's Drift was ended.

The engineer officer, exhausted, wandered among heaps of black corpses to his looted wagon, where he was pleasantly surprised to find an unbroken bottle of beer. He shared it with Bromhead while they gazed upon the debris of the struggle. Colour-Sergeant Bourne issued a rum ration to the men, and was amazed to find Private Hook, a lifelong teetotaller, queueing for his tot. "I feel I want something after that," asserted Hook, not unreasonably. Around the mission post, the British counted 350 dead Zulus. Others were found later in the grass and caves where they had crawled to die. More corpses were thrown into the Buffalo by their own people. Around the mission station lay some twenty thousand cartridge cases. Chard's men had fired almost two hundred rounds apiece, a remarkable expenditure for single-shot weapons. In a close-quarter action, in which the enemy masses had provided the most conspicuous of targets, the defenders had hit something like one Zulu for every twenty-five shots, a vastly better average than infantrymen attained in the wars of the twentieth century.

In any normal military encounter, wounded outnumber the dead by at least three to one. At Rorke's Drift there is no record of prisoners being taken, wounded or otherwise. Those Zulus unable to crawl far from the battlefield—there may have been as many as five hundred—were hunted down and summarily despatched by the victors during the days that followed, with the same ruthlessness the Zulus displayed towards British casualties. Quarter was neither sought nor given in colonial wars. Native enemies were deemed unworthy of humanity. There was a zest for vengeance after Isandlwana. The defenders of Rorke's Drift had lost seventeen killed and eight men seriously wounded. Most of the former were patients burned or speared in the hospital. Only five of Chard's men died while playing an active part in the defence. Although the Zulus were poor hands with firearms, they made more impact upon the garrison with bullets than with assegais.

The amazingly short British casualty list is another characteristic of colonial encounters of the period. The principle of "winner takes all" almost invariably obtained. On rare occasions when courageous warriors such as the Zulus, the Dervishes of the Sudan, the Sioux at Little Big

Horn somehow got close enough to overrun white soldiers or prevent them from using firearms effectively, the outcome was disastrous for what passed for the forces of civilisation. If, however, the white men could maintain continuous rifle fire and an unbroken front, even with relatively primitive breech-loading weapons they could kill attackers more quickly than the most nimble assailants could close with them.

On the same day as the Zulus attacked Rorke's Drift and Isandlwana, another *impi* engaged Chelmsford's No. 1 Column at the Nyezane River. In the subsequent engagement, four white officers and NCOs of the Natal Native Contingent were killed by Zulus when their men abandoned them. Otherwise, this action went entirely the way of the British. A charge made by, improbably enough, a naval landing party from HMS *Active,* together with judicious use of a Gatling gun, secured a casualty list for the morning's work of four hundred Zulus killed against just twelve Europeans.

None of this, though, detracts from the achievement of the defenders of Rorke's Drift. Even if technology was on their side, it required notable coolness and pluck to stand fast and keep firing in the face of assaults by overwhelming numbers of the fiercest tribesmen on earth. Chelmsford himself arrived at the mission station soon after the battle, having led his column back from the hills, past the stricken field of Isandlwana. As he offered his congratulations to the defenders, he was struggling to conceal bitter disappointment. He had hoped to find many survivors of Isandlwana at the post, and there were none. That disaster reflected incompetence throughout the leadership of the British force, and Chelmsford stood at its summit. The British public was appalled. The War Office fumed when a reassuring telegram from Queen Victoria to Chelmsford, asserting her full confidence in his generalship, was not only despatched but published. This precluded the obvious course of sacking the commander-in-chief. There was only one palliative. If gross blunders had caused a massacre, heroes were at hand to ease the pain. Enthusiastically celebrated, the little victory at Rorke's Drift might go far to erase the shame of Isandlwana. Chelmsford hastened to forward Chard's report, admitting that he was "anxious to send that gleam of sunshine home as soon as possible."

His efforts were not in vain. Back at home the prime minister, Benjamin Disraeli, now Lord Beaconsfield, established the tone, speaking to the House of Lords. "The heroism of those eighty men who for twelve hours kept back four thousand of the enemy and in the end repulsed them," he said, "shows that the stamina of the English soldier has not diminished." It is not recorded whether the Welshmen of the 24th took offence at the prime minister's choice of words, but the country followed his lead. His behaviour closely resembled that of another British prime minister 103 years later, after the muddled little battle at Goose Green in the Falklands War. Like Rorke's Drift, Goose Green came at a moment when an embattled government needed good news and heroes. Margaret Thatcher gratefully embraced the 2nd Battalion, Parachute Regiment, and heaped laurels upon them in exactly the same spirit as did Disraeli upon B Company of the 24th Foot. A modest military success was ruthlessly inflated to meet the political demands of the moment.

The award of eleven Victoria Crosses to the 1879 defenders of the mission post was, even by the standards of the day, absurdly generous. Sir Garnet Wolseley thought so. "It is monstrous making heroes of those...who, shut up in buildings at the Drift, could not bolt & fought like rats for their lives, which they could not otherwise save," he wrote contemptuously in his journal. Wolseley was not alone among professional soldiers in deeming the garrison of Rorke's Drift to have been victims fighting to save their own skins, rather than heroes who earned acclaim by initiative or voluntary sacrifice. Never before or since has Britain's supreme military decoration been broadcast with such abandon. Amid the embarrassment of the British army and government about Isandlwana, rich rewards were bestowed upon those who had done something in the afternoon and night of 22 January to redeem the morning's disaster. This should not imply that Chard, Bromhead and their comrades behaved other than well. But they did no more than British soldiers on many remote imperial battlefields who received a great deal less thanks for their pains. Chard stood stolidly at the head of his men in a fixed position while they fought for their lives. No imagination was required of him, and indeed imagination can be a shocking handicap in such circumstances. He simply did his duty at a critical moment.

Chard and Bromhead were foremost among the Rorke's Drift VCs, which Wolseley eventually presented with clenched teeth. He resented his role in what he saw as a politically motivated farce. Beyond sharing the view of Sir Evelyn Wood, head of the British army, that both recipients were charmless incompetents, he also entered the even more damning view that he had seldom met officers "less gentlemanly." Needs must, however. Insiders were in little doubt that Commissary Dalton's part at Rorke's Drift had been more notable than those of Chard and Bromhead. Dalton also, indeed, received a VC, but in the vital propaganda war at home he was deemed less serviceable than the other two. Unlike Chard and Bromhead, he was not voted the thanks of Parliament.

The Queen commissioned the celebrated heroic artist Lady Butler to commemorate on canvas the action at the Natal mission station. Both lieutenants were accorded brevet promotions to major, skipping captaincies. Chard became the first Royal Engineer ever to be distinguished in this way. His comrades were bewildered by the fashion in which he received his laurels, with a passivity that transcended modesty. After expressing thanks in the usual benign, inarticulate English way, he settled back to doing such engineering jobs as his superiors saw fit to offer him. For several weeks he remained at the scene of the battle. This was a mistake. The British shovelled Zulu dead from the mission post into a large, shallow mass grave, which soon began to display symptoms of decay. A fever epidemic followed, to which Chard himself fell victim. The army could scarcely allow its foremost hero to expire so ingloriously. He was sent to convalesce at a doctor's home in Ladysmith. Restored to health, he rejoined Chelmsford's army just in time to stand at the head of an engineer company in the British square at the final battle of the Zulu War, Ulundi, on 4 July 1879. Chard thus shared in the belated triumph of enlightenment and imperial might.

His superior officer in South Africa, Captain Walter Jones, professed himself bemused by the brevet-major's failure to exploit his celebrity. Chard should have returned promptly to England to ride the crest of fame, Jones told his own family with an audible sigh of exasperation: "I advised him, but he placidly smokes his pipe and does nothing. Few men get such opportunities ... As a company officer, he is hopelessly slow and slack." As it was, only in October did Chard, shorn of his huge beard, reach Portsmouth aboard the chartered liner *Egypt,* along with Driver Robson and some other Rorke's Drift men including Surgeon-Major Reynolds, VC. The army's commander-in-chief, the Duke of Cambridge, was at the dockside to greet them. Both Chard and Bromhead were lauded as "young officers," which was stretching a point, but met the requirements of romance. When Chard took the train for his sister's home in Somerset, a crowd of four thousand greeted him at Taunton station, singing "Hail the Conquering Hero Comes!" His sister's village was decorated with banners. A large local party was held in his honour, followed by a succession of receptions up and down the country. Several Zulus attended a Royal Engineers' dinner at Brompton Barracks, Chatham. Like the "Fuzzy-Wuzzies" who broke a British square at the Atbara in 1898, at Isandlwana Cetewayo's men gained house colours in the eyes of their foes. The British felt able to be magnanimous now that they had been victorious in the grand final.

Queen Victoria invited Chard to Balmoral, and was much taken by his economical mode of conversation, which she interpreted as soldierly modesty. She presented him with a diamond ring. A legend grew up, for which there is not a shred of evidence, that Chard formed a passion for one of the monarch's ladies-in-waiting. If so, no business resulted. The engineer never married, though as the hero of Rorke's Drift he must have had plenty of opportunities. The faithful Robson left the army. His officer quietly resumed the usual round of garrison postings: two years at Devonport, a spell in Cyprus, another in Singapore. Finally, in September 1896, he became colonel commanding the Royal Engineers in Perth, Scotland. He was still in that post when he was diagnosed as suffering from cancer of the mouth, which killed him in November the following year. Absolutely nothing of professional interest is known to have happened to Chard in the eighteen years of service which followed his hours of glory at Rorke's Drift. He retained to the end a reputation for amiable indolence, notable even by the standards of the Victorian army.

Chard was certainly extravagantly rewarded for a single night's work, in which an equal burden fell upon those whom he commanded. One such was Private Robert Head of the 24th, who sat down after the battle and wrote with the stump of a pencil to his brother in Cape Town:

> I daresay you will have seen in the paper before you receive this we under Leuit [*sic*] Chard and Bromhead had a nice night of it at Rodke's [*sic*] Drift I call it I never shall forget the same place as long as I live I daresay the old Fool in command will make a great fuss over our two officers commanding our company in keeping the Zulu

Buck back with the private soldier what will he get nothing only he
may get the praise of the public...I am jolly only short of a [pipe]
and bacca, your loving brother Bob Head.

Here, indeed, was the authentic, immortal voice of the British private
soldier. Head's view is unlikely to have been altered by Chard's elevation. Yet it would be more charitable to remark that many soldiers, confronted once in a lifetime by a supreme crisis such as Chard faced, baulk
the jump. More than a few men, offered such a challenge and opportunity, fail to rise to them. Chard did his duty at Rorke's Drift in precisely
the fashion Queen Victoria's army demanded—with resolution on the
field of battle, and without vainglory afterwards. From the moment of
his first report to Lord Chelmsford he paid generous tribute to his com-
rades-in-arms, even though it has been suggested that his lordship's staff
officers were chiefly responsible for composing the document. The
example set by the defenders of the mission post did much to revive the
pride of the army in South Africa, after the trauma of Isandlwana. Many
other soldiers in history have done as much as the sapper lieutenant,
without receiving any portion of his rewards. But that is a part of the
injustice of the lot of the warrior. The quirky little battle fought by the
men of the 24th Foot, with some modern assistance from the celluloid
skills of Stanley Baker and Michael Caine (shorn of the beards both
Chard and Bromhead affected) and a great many twentieth-century
Zulu extras, maintains its claim upon our affection and respect more
than a century after the stand at Rorke's Drift.

CHAPTER FIVE

COLONEL FRED

IN LONDON'S National Portrait Gallery, few of the images of soldiers since the seventeenth century are artistically distinguished. The sort of paintings favoured by regimental messes and respectful contemporaries are seldom blessed with insight or creative merit. There is, however, one brilliant exception. James Tissot's 1870 rendering of a young exquisite of the Household Cavalry has proved irresistible to successive generations of admirers. Captain Frederick Burnaby reclines on a sofa, magnificent in blue patrols, legs nonchalantly crossed, lips slightly parted, a cigarette poised elegantly aloft in one hand. It is a supremely mannered pose, which seems to reflect all the assurance of a Victorian cavalry officer at the high point of empire. Here sits a figure at ease within his own tiny, privileged world, the polished perfection of his boots unsullied by the vulgar blood and dust of war. Here is an archetypal warrior of fashion, whose curiosity ends at the doors of a ballroom and the boundaries of a polo pitch.

Yet any such assumptions about Tissot's subject would be mistaken. Fred Burnaby rejected many, if not most, of the conventions of the cavalry mess. He pursued a career of startling originality, indeed exhibitionism, which incurred the distaste of as many of his contemporaries as it delighted. He never marched in step. He was an adventurer in the fullest sense, forever eager for sensation. Burnaby's relatively short life was characterised by an instinct for mischief, a desire to surprise and an irresistible urge to challenge himself physically, for which war offered the most notable opportunities. If he was not born fearless, he made himself so. Though he spent most of his years in uniform, only latterly did he fulfil his ambition to serve as a warrior, and even then he was obliged to force his way onto the stage. His approach to battle, like that of many imperial soldiers, notably including Winston Churchill, was self-indulgent. He regarded conflict as a means of securing a theatre in which to play out fantasies and also, perhaps, to dispel demons.

Frederick Gustavus Burnaby was born in 1842, elder son of a prosperous Bedford "squarson." His father hunted three days a week, preached in St. Peter's church on Sunday, and was grand enough to entertain the Duke of Bedford. The Reverend Gustavus had a reputation for rigid and outspoken opinions which caused a local farmer to dub him "the biggest nuisance in the parish." An anonymous critic followed up by daubing "Nuisance Hall" on the parson's gates. Fred himself was initially destined for the Church. He made plain his disinclination at an early age, however, and his father did not insist. The boy acquired an early reputation as a venturesome spirit, much indulged by his parents. At the age of thirteen he rowed alone through the river and canal system from Windsor to Shrewsbury and back during his summer holidays.

Burnaby spent two years at Harrow, which were not a success. He failed to distinguish himself academically, and was threatened with expulsion when the headmaster heard that he had written a letter to *Punch* deploring the servitude of the fagging system. Here was an early hint of Burnaby's lifelong zest for exposing himself in the public prints. After a spell in a tutor's hands, he was sent to Oswestry school on the Welsh border. He emerged with a reputation for athleticism and physical prowess, worsting the town boys whenever he encountered them. His delight in combat for its own sake was also to persist.

After school, Burnaby was sent to Dresden to study languages for the army entrance exam. "My dear Governor," wrote this huge, genial young man with adolescent banality,

> I like Dresden very much, the old professor is a capital fellow. I am getting on very well with the cornet, and the German is becoming easier every day. It is awfully hot, but we live almost the whole day in the Elbe, so it is very comfortable. They have got capital bathing places here—large rafts with houses on them and capital places to

spring from so and so feet from the water. The scenery is lovely. Give
my best love to Mamma and Annie, and with best love to all friends,
Believe me, ever your very affectionate son,
F. Burnaby.

After Dresden, the young man passed smoothly into the army. A Household Cavalry officer in the 1860s was unlikely to expire from overwork.
Mounted drill and ceremonial attendance on the Queen allowed for a
dazzling social round of balls and dinners, together with five months'
annual leave. A private income of at least £1,000 a year was essential, and
the purchase of Fred's commission cost his family £1,250. His principal
leisure activity, carried to the point of obsession, was body-building at
the London Fencing Club. He stood six feet four and weighed fifteen
stone, which meant that when he wore full dress uniform his horse was
required to carry twenty-three stone. He cut an ungainly figure, especially in the saddle. Yet before he was twenty Fred was reputed to be the
strongest man in the Queen's service, and he was not bashful about
showing his powers. He trounced professional sparring partners, lifted
great weights, won every wager for athletic feats, and roused the mess to
roars of enthusiasm by twisting a poker round the Prince of Wales's
neck on guest night. When, for a jape, fellow officers shut two small
ponies in his bedroom, Burnaby reputedly marched downstairs carrying
one under each arm.

More controversially, he used his strength to fell lesser mortals who
ventured to differ with him. When he rebuked a Windsor crossing-
sweeper for splashing him with mud, the man riposted contemptuously:
"Go and wash yourself if you like!" Burnaby seized the sweeper by the
collar and dumped him bodily in his own cart of horse manure, observing equally contemptuously: "You needn't go and wash unless you like!"
In 1864, his taste for fisticuffs provoked serious trouble. He found himself
charged in the Exchequer Court with assault and battery against a
farmer whom he had downed after an exchange of abuse while out partridge shooting with a brother officer in Kent. Burnaby lost the case, and
had to pay the plaintiff £150. Still digging his own hole after the hearing
was over, he wrote a long, unconvincing letter to *The Times* justifying his
conduct.

If this sort of behaviour gained him some notoriety, his next exploit

increased it. One evening he was lounging with a cluster of fellow officers in the Cremorne Gardens beside the Thames in Battersea, where
Monsieur Eugène Godard was preparing to launch his huge hot-air balloon the *Eagle* next day. The lieutenant fell into conversation with the
French aeronaut and another officer. "Very good fun, I should think,"
said Burnaby. "Fun indeed," exclaimed Captain Williams-Bulkeley.
"Fun with the chance of being burnt as well as of being smashed. You
would not think it fun if you went up with him." Burnaby said impulsively: "I shall be delighted to ascend if M. Godard will take me." And
for a fee of £5, at a time when there were few volunteer passengers for
balloon flights, Godard agreed to do so.

The following afternoon, watched by an amused throng of Household Cavalry officers, Burnaby stood in readiness as Godard applied a
match to a huge stove fuelled with chopped straw, which fed hot air into
his limp silk bag through a thirteen-foot chimney, all borne within the
balloon basket. Half an hour later the balloon, adorned with the golden
eagles of Godard's Napoleonic mentor, stood ready. Yet, bathetically, the
aeronaut announced that his soldier passenger could not accompany the
flight after all, because the warm weather reduced the *Eagle*'s lifting
power. When Burnaby ruefully reported this to his fellow officers, a
chorus of teasing about "funk" broke out. Just as Godard, carrying only a
correspondent of the *Daily Telegraph*, ordered the moorings cast off, the
nettled cavalryman sprang into the basket. The balloon bumped back to
earth. Godard, unable to see the stowaway from the far side of his big
stove, in some bewilderment threw more straw into the flames. The balloon rose unsteadily into the air as bands played and the crowd roared. A
lurch cast the gasbag against one of its mounting masts, which broke
away and precipitated panic below. Then the balloon drifted slowly
down the Thames in a light breeze, M. Godard delivering exultant blasts
on a trumpet. "The whole expanse of the mighty city was visible," wrote
the *Telegraph* correspondent afterwards; "... the wonderful roar of London rose up through the evening air, like the passionate clamour—impatient, querulous, irresistible—of the sea. And behind each gazer, close to
his head, was the roaring and raging of the furnace."

They drifted as far as East Greenwich, at a height of about three
thousand feet, before Godard determined on descent. As they struck the
earth, the basket bounced violently and dangerously several times before

bystanders seized the craft's mooring ropes and dragged it down. Burnaby returned exultant to the mess, having acquired a taste for ballooning which lasted all his life, and which infected his fellow cavalrymen. One Blues officer bought his own balloon, and made several flights with his huge comrade. One evening, Parson Burnaby was standing in his Bedfordshire garden chatting to the church organist when a balloon passed overhead. "Shouldn't be surprised if my boy were in that car!" the old man observed cheerfully, telling the servants to keep some dinner, in case. Sure enough, at midnight his exuberant son burst in: "Hullo, governor, here we are! Started from the Cavalry Barracks and came down at Risely!"

If Burnaby's enthusiasm for ballooning might be regarded as a fashionable eccentricity, his taste for the society of journalists, and indeed for personal publicity, seemed to the decorous arbiters of London society downright vulgar. He befriended one Tommy Bowles, a former Inland Revenue clerk with ambitions to found a new fashionable journal which would be witty, iconoclastic and imperialist. Burnaby and the diminutive Bowles spent many hours pacing the streets of St. James's as they discussed their brainchild. It was the cavalry officer who conceived the title: *Vanity Fair*. Burnaby invested £100 of his own modest capital in the venture, which was launched in November 1868 and became an immediate success. The French artist James Tissot and the celebrated caricaturist "Spy" were among its early artistic contributors. Burnaby extracted a commission himself to contribute a series of articles from Andalusia, where he had a fancy to travel.

After touring Spain he wanted to visit Paris, which was under Prussian siege, but his military superiors, anxious to preserve British neutrality, vetoed this. He was obliged to travel Russia instead, enjoying the country but complaining bitterly about the climate and his liver, from which he suffered agonies all his life. "However, I am getting very near twenty-seven," he wrote ruefully, "so I suppose it is time to expect some ailments or other, particularly after twelve years racketing about in London." He returned from Odessa on hearing news that his father was close to death. Reaching home, he found the old man resigned to his fate, and conversing weakly with his close friend the family doctor. "I wish I could take you with me, Bullock!" Mr. Burnaby exclaimed emotionally. His witty son said: "I really don't think Bullock wants to go, father. Besides, what would a doctor do there?" Fred finally inherited the family estate on the parson's tardy expiry in July 1872.

In 1873 he returned to Spain amid the Carlist insurgency against the Spanish monarchy, and enjoyed several social brushes with guerrillas, whom he charmed into granting him passage. The following year he returned in the guise of a correspondent for *The Times*—what we should now call a mere "stringer," paid by the great editor John Delane on linage. The army's commander-in-chief, the crusty old Duke of Cambridge, had ordered Burnaby to break with *Vanity Fair*, which was deemed too warm a connection for a serving officer. *The Times*, however, was thought acceptable. Burnaby complained to its readers that the Carlist war was being prosecuted in a lamentably unprofessional spirit, and would never reach a conclusion until one side or the other tried harder. He was somewhat embarrassed when a story appeared in a Spanish paper that he himself had offered to raise and lead a foreign legion in the Carlist cause. Later, in exile, Don Carlos himself—who gave his name to the uprising—testified that he had found Burnaby "a good soldier and a perfect gentleman."

The next year, 1874, Burnaby persuaded Delane to accept a series of articles from the Sudan, where General Charles Gordon had recently accepted the governorship from the Khedive of Egypt. The amateur correspondent sailed by P&O steamer to Suez, and thence down the Red Sea to Suakin, aboard a malodorous pilgrim ship with a party of Foot Guards officers on their way to shoot lion in Abyssinia—Lords Ranfurly, Mayo and Coke Russell, together with Sir William Gordon Cumming. Burnaby busied himself on the journey conversing with Arab passengers, aided by a phrase book. From the cluster of hovels which formed the port of Suakin he set out with a train of twenty camels and a Nubian servant across the desert to Khartoum via Berber. On 4 January 1875 he filed his first *Times* despatch, with the dateline: "Under the Old Tree of Aryah, Tropical Africa." He revelled in the scenery, an encounter with slavers, and even the heat. From Khartoum he reported the economic desolation that had overtaken the place since Gordon destroyed its livelihood as the great slaving capital of the region. When finally he encountered the governor, there was no meeting of minds. Gordon disliked journalists, and insisted that Burnaby should confine his despatches to physical descriptions of the country rather than address its politics or personalities. The correspondent's subsequent reports were thus rich in "colour," and devoid of historical significance.

At Khartoum, Burnaby's eye fell upon an old newspaper which reported that the Russian government had forbidden any foreigner to travel into Russian Asia, where the Tsar was spreading his tentacles in a fashion that alarmed British Tories. Burnaby wrote later: "I have, unfortunately for my own interests, had from my earliest childhood what my nurse used to call a most 'contradictorious spirit,' and it suddenly occurred to me, Why not go to Central Asia?" He returned promptly to London, and spent November 1875 preparing to make a journey to Khiva, the exploit which would make him a celebrity.

In St. Petersburg in the first days of December, English friends urged him to abandon his attempt, because the Russians would never countenance it. The Tsar's war minister advised him that he could not proceed beyond the territories of Russia proper. Burnaby ignored them all, took a train to Sizeran and thence, by troika in temperatures already thirteen degrees below zero, to Samara, on the bank of the Volga. He cared little for the Russians, and even less for the government of the Tsar which, like most Englishmen of his day, he deemed a direct threat to British India. Various officials on his route emphasised the prohibition on travel to Central Asia, and the deep Russian winter posed difficulties which made their own case. After parting with one drunken rogue whom he engaged as a servant, Burnaby set off by sleigh accompanied by Nazar, a repulsive but courageous Tartar dwarf. The captain was rash enough to fall asleep on one stage with his hands exposed, and awoke with severe frostbite. At the next halt he showed the threatened extremities to some cossacks, who shook their heads and warned that he would lose his fingers if he could not restore circulation. On their advice he plunged his arms into icy water, then rubbed them with naphtha. After hours of near-paralysis, his hands recovered.

At Kasala he was fortunate enough to secure not only a billet from the local commandant, but also a guide to the Russian fort beyond the Oxus. Burnaby asked what would happen if he went on to Khiva alone. "That would never do!" expostulated his host. "Why, the Khan would very likely order his executioner to gouge out your eyes, or would keep you in a hole in the ground for five or six days before he admitted you to an audience."

Undeterred, on 12 January 1875 Burnaby set out to cover the four hundred miles to the Oxus with three horses, three camels, a Turkoman camel-driver and supplies—chiefly frozen cabbage soup, cooked meat and bread. Nazar the servant reclined atop a camel, usually asleep, bound to the saddle by a rope. After some days the party fell in with a caravan of merchants who were proceeding direct to Khiva. Burnaby determined to accompany them, and wooed their guide into overcoming fears of official retribution. At Kalenderhana, near the Oxus, the local mullah observed that the Englishman must send warning of his coming to the Khan of Khiva, couched in "words so soft and sweet that they were like the sounds of sheep bleating in the distance." The mullah asked Burnaby his *tchin*—rank. Was he a colonel? No, said Burnaby, he was a mere *kapitan*. Surely they could leave all that out. The mullah dissented. *Tchin* was essential. A letter signed by "Colonel Burnaby" was duly sent, soon followed by the Englishman and his little train. They crossed the great frozen Oxus, which marked the limits of the Tsar's territories, sixty miles from Khiva. Soon afterwards, Burnaby was met with all ceremony by two Khivan nobles who came to escort him to the Khan. In the great garden city, behind its fifty-foot walls, he was installed in a fine house and plied with hospitality. Here, at last, was the exotic Asia he had come to see.

He found the Khan himself a cheerful young man, wholly unthreatening, who plied him with questions about England and Russia, which Burnaby claims to have answered circumspectly. The Englishman explained that he was a mere traveller, not an ambassador. At the conclusion of his audience he presented the potentate with a dressing gown, and returned to the Khan's guesthouse to find two Russians with a letter demanding his immediate return to Petro-Alexandrovsk, where he must accept delivery of a telegram. Surprisingly, Burnaby acceded without demur, and made no attempt to continue his journey beyond Khiva. A man of ardent but transient enthusiasms, he seems now to have tired of Asian travel. He retraced his steps tamely enough in company with the Russians, until at their fort he was handed a wire from the Duke of Cambridge, despatched from Horse Guards under pressure from St. Petersburg, demanding his immediate return.

Yet Burnaby's arrival in London that summer of 1875 was triumphant. The Duke interviewed him and wrote in most flattering terms to the secretary for war: "A more interesting conversation I never remember holding with anybody. He is a remarkable fellow, singular-looking, but of great perseverance and determination. He has gone through a great deal, and the only surprise is how he got through it." The Queen commanded Burnaby to dinner at Windsor, and he was toasted in London society. When his account of his journey, *A Ride to Khiva*, was published shortly afterwards, it became an immediate best-seller. He was a celebrity. Spy's caricature of him for *Vanity Fair* depicts a huge, moustachioed figure almost bursting out of his evening clothes.

Burnaby's name was now seldom out of the papers. Of active service with his regiment he had seen nothing. He had no pretensions to intellect, and even less to conformity with military custom. He seemed unlikely to achieve high command, or indeed to be suited for it. He sought success instead as a big, bold English misfit who loved to travel, and funded his journeys by describing them in print—for, despite his inheritance, he was not a rich man. Of women, nothing is known in Burnaby's life until his marriage, and not much then. It is reasonable to surmise that no man who lived as he chose to do can have cared much for female society. He treated women always with extravagant courtesy but never, so far as we know, with much romantic enthusiasm, despite his status as a minor member of that praetorian guard of adulterers, the Prince of Wales's set.

From the perspective of the twenty-first century, it seems extraordinary that a serving army officer was permitted to pursue a vigorous second career as a journalist-adventurer. In November 1876, financed by a publisher's advance of £2,500 for a new book which became *On Horseback Through Asia Minor*, Burnaby set out across Turkey to report on the Turko-Russian confrontation following the notorious "Bulgarian atrocities" in which the Turkish sultan's forces had massacred twelve thousand Bulgarians, rousing the wrath of both the Tsar and Gladstone. Burnaby's sympathies were with the Turks, chiefly because the Russians had taken up arms in the Bulgarians' support. He was equipped with the usual accoutrements of an Englishman abroad in those days—express rifle, shotgun, quinine, mustard plasters, Cockle's liver pills, and a faithful servant, in the person of one Radford. "Lord, how they kisses each other," observed the disgusted Radford on beholding the familiar embraces of Turkish men, "just like a lot of great girls." Burnaby, passionately hostile to the Russians, refused to accept at face value Gladstone's denunciation of Turkish atrocities against the Slavs, which had provoked Russian intervention in their support. He insisted, dubiously, that the Slav victims were at least as guilty as their Muslim persecutors. At Batum, Burnaby reached the end of his journey. As the forthcoming war was obviously delayed he took a steamer back to Constantinople, and thence to London, where his book sold a first printing of 3,500 copies. "It is a bore being lionised," wrote Burnaby unconvincingly to his sister Annie in November 1877. Admiration for his writing was not, however, universal. Several critics complained of the book's relentless anti-Russianism, careless prose, heavy humour, shameless chauvinism, and preference for prejudices over facts.

Only a few weeks later, Burnaby was back in Turkey. War had started at last. He joined the retinue of Turkey's British mercenary commander Valentine Baker. Baker was a personal friend, a colonel cashiered from the 10th Hussars two years earlier after a bizarre and notorious court case in which he was convicted of assaulting a young woman in a railway carriage between Liphook and Woking. Many people, including Burnaby, thought Baker's sentence to a year's imprisonment and a fine of £500 was unjust. So too, plainly, did the Turks, who hastened to secure the ex-colonel's services. Burnaby chanced upon Baker Pasha at Adrianople railway station, and travelled onward with him via Sofia to the Bulgarian front. The Russians had heard that their huge critic was a tourist in the opposing camp. A senior Russian officer who had last seen Burnaby performing feats of strength in an officers' mess in St. Petersburg on guest night told a correspondent about him, observing: "He is quite mad, of course, and always was; and he hates us."

In Bulgaria Burnaby at last gained a glimpse of battle. On the morning of 31 December at Tashkessan, Baker's Turks rose to cry defiance and invoke the mercy of Allah, as the Russian masses swept forward. "It was a sensation worth feeling," Burnaby wrote later, "a sensation worth ten years of a man's life; and a thrill passed through my heart at the time— that curious sort of thrill—the sensation which you experience when you read of something noble or heroic, or see a gallant action performed. It was grand to hear these two thousand four hundred Mahometans, many of them raw levies at the time, cheering back in defiance of thirty picked battalions, the choicest troops of the Tsar."

The Turks, however, lost their battle against overwhelming numbers. They embarked upon a retreat through the Rhodope Mountains in the snows which became one of the most harrowing experiences of Burnaby's career. The survivors reached the coast after a month of terrible privations, and embarked for Gallipoli. By the time Burnaby reached Constantinople, the Turks had accepted defeat and signed an armistice. The correspondent was disgusted that Britain had not intervened in the Turkish cause. "What a lot of shopkeepers we are!" he wrote to his brother. On his return to England he addressed tempestuous public meetings designed to alert the public to the Russian threat.

These platform appearances whetted his appetite for public life, and indeed for a political career. Characteristically, as an aspiring Tory MP he chose for his battleground the great Radical stronghold of Birmingham, for Burnaby perhaps the least winnable seat in England. In July 1878 he was adopted as a candidate against such Liberal giants as Joseph Chamberlain and John Bright. The Household Cavalry officer's flirtation with politics, which persisted to his death, translated his career from the picaresque to the ridiculous. His tub-thumping rhetoric endeared him to the likes of Lord Randolph Churchill, but made more thoughtful people leery. The Birmingham public mocked his cavalry drawl, and was uneasy about his way with hecklers. He seized two such interlopers in his huge hands and carried them by their collars to separate chairs, in which he dumped them. "You sit *hyah,* little man!" he told one, "And you little man, sit *hyah!*" the other. He descended eagerly into fisticuffs with opponents among his audiences rash enough to solicit confrontation. On election day, Burnaby doubled the 1868 Tory vote, but lost easily to the Liberals. The contest had made him more famous, yet also more absurd in the eyes of all save the bluest of "true blues."

There was only one rash extravagance he had not thus far indulged, and to which he now succumbed—marriage. On 25 June 1879 Burnaby joined his fortunes to those of Elizabeth Hawkins-Whitshed, a Wicklow baronet's eighteen-year-old only daughter who appears to have been seduced by the bridegroom's literary accomplishments and public image before even meeting their thirty-six-year-old begetter in the flesh. The ceremony was graced by a guard of honour from the Blues. One of the bridesmaids was Ottoline Cavendish-Bentinck, later Morrell. Miss Hawkins-Whitshed's Irish tenantry sent a grand silver service, the

Prince of Wales a Benares smoking set. Don Carlos of Spain contributed a pearl-handled revolver. Unsurprisingly, the union was not a success. The bride soon showed symptoms of chronic lung trouble, which had plagued her mother's family. She produced one child, a son and heir named Harry St. Vincent Augustus, but otherwise passed most of her life in Switzerland, where she became the author of a series of gushing and not unprofitable volumes about the joys of the high Alps. Her son was left with his grandmother, while Burnaby resumed life in bachelor chambers in Charles Street, Mayfair. There was never a public breach between the couple, but contemporaries took the view that of all men on earth, Fred Burnaby was the least suited to wedlock. The writer Frank Harris, an unreliable witness, later claimed the big soldier had confessed to him that he was a failure as a lover of women, and improbably attributed this to his youthful excesses as a body-builder.

In 1882, the march of seniority made Burnaby lieutenant-colonel commanding the Blues. Yet he did not allow even this responsibility—and there is no doubt of his unsatisfied ardour for battle—to interfere with his continuing passion for ballooning. He now formed an enthusiasm for making a Channel crossing. This had been done before, but several subsequent attempts had ended in disaster. Burnaby wrote to Wright, a professional balloonist, enquiring if he might hire a suitable craft. Back came the answer: "I have a balloon that will just suit you ... Poor Powell once made an ascent in it." This was clumsy advertising, for the MP for Malmesbury Walter Powell had recently drowned while attempting a Channel passage. Undaunted, early on the morning of 23 March Burnaby stood between two gasometers at Dover, watching the Wright balloon inflating. By 10 a.m. the great gasbag was bulging, seventy feet tall. Burnaby was determined to share the glory with no man, and refused Wright's pleas to accompany him, if only to protect his valuable balloon. On a billhead of the Dover Gas Light Company the colonel scrawled: "I agree to be responsible to Mr. Wright for all damage or loss incurred to him through any accident happening to his balloon in which I ascend today. Fred Burnaby, Royal Horse Guards."

Then, in a striped blazer and pillbox cap, he took his seat and cast off. Clearing a factory chimney by a few feet after hastily jettisoning ballast, he drifted southwards, much troubled by the heat of the morning sun, which was driving gas from the balloon's escape valve at an alarming rate.

At five thousand feet, after an hour in the air, he glimpsed the French coast. His balloon suddenly began to fall rapidly. He hurled out ballast, and checked the descent at 1,500 feet. Yet now the wind changed and he found himself drifting westwards, towards the Atlantic. The crews of two fishing boats signalled him frantically to accept rescue. Burnaby ate a beef sandwich, waited for the wind to change again, and carelessly tossed the Frenchmen a copy of *The Times*. With characteristic insouciance, he lit a cigar. He was becalmed.

Trusting in his long-cherished theory that winds varied at different altitudes, he threw out more ballast. At ten thousand feet he was rewarded by a north-east wind which propelled him once more towards France. Crossing fields near Dieppe, the balloon plunged earthwards. Burnaby encountered new perils. His grapnel would not catch. The craft bounced over the ground in an alarming series of fifty-foot springs and falls. His progress was checked at last by a crowd of local peasants who seized the craft's anchor and enabled the aeronaut to step triumphantly onto Norman soil. "Voyage difficult but very amusing," Burnaby wired to Wright. "Your balloon uninjured." It was Burnaby's last ascent. Though he wrote a book about his experiences aloft—which, oddly enough, did not sell well—the Duke of Cambridge not unreasonably decreed that aeronautics was an unsuitable pastime for the colonel of the Blues.

Yet the source of Burnaby's most bitter frustration was that he seemed doomed never to lead soldiers into action. Four months after his Channel exploit, in July 1882, the Household Cavalry was ordered to join Sir Garnet Wolseley's Egyptian expeditionary force against Arabi Pasha. Instead of Burnaby, however, by seniority the colonel of the Life Guards was deputed to command the composite regiment which sailed for Egypt. The forlorn balloonist was permitted merely to select officers and men for active service. Even this got him into trouble. The regiment's colonel-in-chief, the Prince of Wales, interfered shamelessly with appointments, and there was an angry exchange of letters between the two men about names included and others omitted. Some believed that the Prince's impatience with Burnaby derived from a rash moment of lèse-majesté, when the colonel jested to the heir to the throne that his own family descent from Edward Plantagenet gave him a more convincing claim to a crown than any mere Saxe-Coburg. The Prince turned away in anger. Burnaby became neither the first nor the last British subject to discover that a royal appetite for wit invariably stops short of its own majesty being the target.

There was more trouble when Burnaby threatened an action for defamation against Major-General Owen Williams, a crony of the Prince. The general had accused Burnaby of being responsible for a newspaper report that he was turned down for the post of brigadier of the Household Cavalry. There is little doubt that the colonel had indeed rashly leaked this titbit to his newspaper friends. A truce was patched up before the case came to court, but the squabble did nothing to enhance Burnaby's popularity in court circles. He was a mischief-maker, of the kind who could not help himself. The Blues came home from Egypt richly adorned with laurels. Their colonel's forlorn function was to toast them.

Yet in December 1883 Burnaby perceived another narrow window to glory, or at least to action. The Khedive of Egypt despatched a force to the Sudan, commanded by Burnaby's old friend Valentine Baker, to suppress a troublesome prophet. The Dervishes, followers of this figure, who called himself the Mahdi, had recently inflicted a defeat on another British mercenary, Hicks Pasha, who died along with all his officers. It was Baker's business to avenge this humiliation. "We are all longing for you," Fanny Baker wrote to Burnaby from Shepheard's Hotel in Cairo. She and her husband wanted the famous colonel to stir up the British press so that Baker's expedition against the Dervishes would be reinforced. As constituted, it was composed entirely of Egyptian troops, with a few British officers. "Now he is to go to Suakin with a set of untried people about whom we know only *one* thing—that cowardice is their nature," wrote Mrs. Baker crossly.

Burnaby joined Baker and his wretchedly inadequate little Egyptian army just in time to witness its engagement against the Mahdi's lieutenant Osman Digna at El Teb on 3 February 1884. The colonel wore civilian clothes and carried a pistol and umbrella, as befitted a noncombatant. He watched contemptuously as the Egyptian levies began emptying their weapons into the scrub, where not an enemy was in sight. Finding the role of spectator intolerably passive, he began to act as a galloper for Baker, spurring across the battlefield to arrest the headlong departure of a regiment of cavalry pursuing a few Arab horsemen. Several Egyptian troopers were killed by fire from their own infantry squares. When the small body of Dervishes charged, the Khedive's entire force of four thousand Egyptians broke and fled. Baker and his staff forced an escape through the mêlée, in which the Arabs slaughtered his men with impunity. The Egyptians lost 2,250 men and 112 officers. The survivors escaped only because the Dervishes halted to plunder their baggage.

The hapless Baker was relieved of command. Amid a storm of fury about this débâcle in the Tory press at home, fed by the despatches of such witnesses as Burnaby, an expeditionary force of British troops was ordered forthwith to Suakin, while General Gordon was sent back to Khartoum to evacuate the Egyptian garrison. "It was with a feeling of satisfaction that we learned that no Egyptian troops were to take part in the [Suakin] expedition," wrote Burnaby. "... They were utterly unworthy to serve with English officers." He himself was formally appointed to the intelligence staff of the expedition. Its mission, so reluctantly authorised by Gladstone as prime minister, was to "disperse the enemy" rather than to recapture the country. On 29 March Sir Gerald Graham led out his square into the desert towards El Teb, where vultures still wheeled over poor Baker's battlefield. Burnaby, at last in uniform, rode ahead with the mounted infantry. Amid the skirl of pipes from the Black Watch they advanced on the Dervish entrenchments. The Arabs began to use Krupp field guns captured from Baker to considerable effect. Burnaby's horse was killed, and a bullet grazed the colonel high on the left arm. As the British infantry closed in with bayonets fixed, the Dervishes rushed forward to meet them.

At last Burnaby could play the warrior he yearned to be. Irregular as ever, he had armed himself with a double-barrelled shotgun, firing cartridges loaded with heavy balls. He stood in shirtsleeves outside the British square, knocking down Dervishes like driven deer. He later claimed thirteen Arabs for twenty-three shots. He was enchanted by the fashion in which the enemy kept coming: "It was as splendid an exhibition of courage as the world has ever seen." Veterans of the Zulu War asserted that the Mahdi's followers surpassed the performance of Cetewayo's warriors. The outcome, however, was inevitable. Ancient in their "uncivilised" willingness to face death, the Sudanese collided with modern technology in the hands of experts. Disciplined British fire broke the attackers. The Dervishes left 825 bodies on the field, while the British lost 35 killed and 155 wounded, most of these among the cavalry, who conducted a charge of the usual futile and costly kind. "I confess I did envy the people who were in the scrimmage," a British officer wrote home, "and would have given a good deal to have a go at the niggers, but of course that would have been *infra dig*. However, it was very pleasant to look on at, and I had the pleasure of seeing several men behave most uncommonly well, notably Burnaby of Khiva notoriety." Burnaby rode back to Trinkitat to have the wound in his arm dressed, and thence took ship to England. One of the pleasures of late-Victorian campaigning was that steamships and railways made it possible to attend even the empire's remoter battlefields, then return to one's London chambers for a haircut and a visit to one's tailor before the next bout.

Burnaby's participation in the Suakin campaign attracted fierce controversy, especially among his Liberal political enemies. Critics suggested that it was unsporting to pot Dervishes with a shotgun rather than a rifle. The rifle was a soldier's proper armament, and the colonel's choice of weapon somehow seemed to imply the self-indulgent frivolities of the upper classes killing grouse on Scottish moors in August, rather than war in the Sudanese desert out of season. There was something in this. Pleasure, not duty, had drawn the commanding officer of the Household Cavalry to El Teb. Indeed, Burnaby had gone to considerable lengths to avoid accepting delivery of a direct War Office instruction telegraphed to Cairo forbidding him, as a colonel on full pay, to participate in the fighting. His admirers, of course, loved it all. Here was yet another turn in the career of a brilliant adventurer, at last performing under the flag of old England. He appeared in Birmingham, arm in a sling, to storm the political platforms of the city with tales of the Sudan, and to demand that the Liberal government should send an army to finish the Mahdi off.

There was a memorable exchange with one heckler who, after hearing Burnaby speak, declared emotionally: "They paid me to interrupt, but since you spoke of war I wish I hadn't. I apologise." Burnaby held out his hand. The man shook his head: "I'm not a gentleman, sir, I'm a sweep." Burnaby said: "I don't care a damn what you are by trade, the trade doesn't make the man." The penitent heckler cried: "But I only sweep chimneys!" Burnaby: "Do you sweep them well?" Heckler: "I hope

Baron Marcellin de Marbot, one of Bonaparte's most dashing cavalry officers and a raconteur of genius.

Napoleon receives news from a French officer at Austerlitz, one of a host of battlefields on which Marbot served his adored emperor.

The storming of Badajoz in 1812, bloodiest of all the actions in which Harry Smith fought under Wellington's command.

Smith, a young Rifle Brigade officer who fell passionately in love on the battlefield, painted shortly after promotion to colonel for his role at Waterloo.

Juana Smith, who married Harry in Spain at the age fourteen, depicted by a French artist three years lat She accompanied her "Enrique" to war through a c voted relationship that would last almost fifty years.

(Above) Joshua Lawrence Chamberlain as an earnest young college professor and *(right)* as a colonel of the Union army in 1862, the role in which he discovered his vocation as a warrior.

John Chard wearing the Victoria Cross he was awarded for his command of the garrison of Rorke's Drift on January 22, 1879. Much of the British army thought he received more than his share of credit for the battle.

Lady Butler's famous depiction of the struggle against the Zulus assaulting the mission station at Rorke's Drift, where a small British victory was exploited by the British government to ease the pain of the shocking defeat at nearby Isandlwana on the same day.

(Above) Fred Burnaby, captured by Tissot as a young exquisite of the Household Cavalry in 1870. Burnaby's lust for adventure and publicity did not endear him to most of his superiors, including the Prince of Wales.

(Right) Burnaby's huge figure, as familiar on political hustings as on Horse Guards, proved irresistible to such caricaturists as Spy of *Vanity Fair.*

(Below) The battle of Abu Klea in January 1885, where Burnaby died fighting the Dervishes on the ill-fated expedition to rescue General Gordon.

Captain Karl Friedrich Max von Müller, whose chivalrous conduct as commander of the raiding cruiser *Emden* in the Indian Ocean in 1914 won the admiration of the world. Müller's ship *(below)* was already obsolescent, and obviously doomed when she sailed for her last voyage, yet the German wreaked havoc on British trade routes before *Emden* met her nemesis.

Frederic Manning, Australian intellectual who penned one of the greatest of all novels of the soldier's experience on the Western Front in World War I, sketched by his friend William Rothenstein in 1921, when he was thirty-nine.

Captain Eddie Rickenbacker *(left)* became the leading American fighter "ace" of the First World War, after forging an earlier career as one of the star drivers *(below)* of pre-1914 auto racing.

(Below) John Masters with the tiger he shot near his Gurkha regiment's depot at Bakloh, northern India, in 1938. Masters became one of the most vivid British chroniclers of his nation's great Indian romance. When World War II came, he commanded a brigade in the 1943 Chindit operation, far behind the Japanese lines in Burma.

so." Burnaby: "Then do your duty and no man can do more, and the man that does his duty is a gentleman."

The issue of Gordon, besieged in Khartoum, had by now roused national feeling to fever pitch. Burnaby himself cared nothing for the man, whom he disliked, but much for British prestige. Critics such as the poet and adventurer Wilfrid Scawen Blunt deplored Burnaby's enthusiasm for fighting, and despised his boorish politics. "He is a dull, heavy fellow in my opinion," Blunt wrote after the two men lunched uncomfortably together, "with a dash of cunning and more than a dash of brutality." Here spoke the authentic voice of fastidious, cultured, liberal England, disdaining the rougher stuff which serviced her empire.

In this last phase of his life Burnaby had also become an unpopular figure within his own aristocratic circle. His eagerness for self-publicity, his indiscretions—which included gossiping to journalists about the personal lives of brother officers—were weighed in the balance against his spectacular courage, a virtue which most Victorian soldiers took for granted in each other. Social opinion found against the colonel. He had quarrelled with some important people. He was publicly at loggerheads with the government of the day. After his death, his old friend Tommy Bowles of *Vanity Fair* lamented the fact that Britain had never offered Burnaby title, ribbon, decoration or honour. Yet why should his country have done so? He had shown himself a considerable troublemaker. All his life he suited himself. There was precious little selflessness or sacrifice in anything he did; rather there was the sense of a huge, naughty child translating wilfulness and perversity into a career. Frank Harris claims that before Burnaby left England for the last time, his brother officers of the Blues had sent him to Coventry. Whether or not this was true, there is no doubt that many of his own kind had had enough of him. He was trying to write a novel. The passages which survive vividly convey its awfulness: " 'Men of the 21st,' said Sir Titus Mulligan, 'our ship is going down. Die like men. Save the women if you can.' " For all his fame, at forty-two Burnaby had become a lonely and desolate figure, increasingly troubled by melancholy and digestive illnesses. He perceived himself, by no means wrongly, as a failure.

On 26 August 1884, Lord Wolseley—as he now ranked—was officially, reluctantly, belatedly authorised to launch an expedition up the Nile to rescue Gordon. Burnaby wrote to beg a place on the general's staff.

Wolseley answered kindly that if he asked for the colonel's services in London the War Office would certainly block the appointment, but if Burnaby would wait until his lordship reached Cairo, he was sure something could be arranged. Meanwhile, two officers and forty men of the Blues, led by Major Lord Arthur Somerset and Lieutenant Lord Binning, sailed to join an elite volunteer camel corps which was to take a short cut across the Bayuda Desert, missing the great easterly bend of the Nile, to hasten Gordon's relief.

When Wolseley reached Cairo, as promised he asked the War Office to send Burnaby to join his intelligence staff. The request was summarily rejected. The fretting colonel returned to rhetorical battle amid the mobs and political riots of Birmingham, alongside Lord Randolph Churchill. Yet all through October he was making farewells. He told Birmingham political comrades that he doubted he would return to the city. He gave a dinner for his local villagers at which an old farmer said: "I suppose you'll be agoing to the Soudan, colonel? Be advised and don't go! If an Arab could hit a haystack he couldn't very well miss you." He went to Bedford and visited old friends to whom he dropped hints that he did not expect to see them again. With characteristic lack of judgement, he appointed Valentine Baker as guardian of his four-year-old son. He said to a footman at his home: "Goodbye, Robert, I shan't come back." He told Tommy Bowles: "I am very unhappy, and I can't imagine why you care about life. I do not mean to come back."

Burnaby possessed self-knowledge enough to confront his own failure as a soldier. He would never achieve a significant command. He had forfeited the confidence of many of those among whom he lived. For whatever reasons, his marriage had not come to much. His celebrity had tipped over into notoriety. On 10 November 1884 this disappointed, lonely man set out from Victoria Station for Egypt "on spec"—hoping that if he could smuggle himself to the scene of war, Wolseley would find some way to give him employment. That very day, the general wrote to his wife about his friend: "There will be the devil's own row if I give him anything to do, and yet I should like to do so, as he is clever and brave as a lion. I shall let him come to the front at any rate, and if there is fighting he shall have a place at the forefront of the battle, which will please him and confound his enemies." Burnaby was coming to Egypt to seek death. Wolseley, whose reputation conferred latitude, was not unwilling to indulge him.

The colonel hastened through Cairo, lest a telegram from the War Office demanding his recall should already have been despatched. Arrived at Wadi Halfa on 4 December, he was given the post of inspecting staff officer on a stretch of the Nile. From Dal a week later he wrote to his wife: "I have been very busy... Our work is to spur on all officers and men... it will be very difficult to get more out of them... A strong north wind is blowing today, which helps us much with the boats. I do hope it will continue, as some four hundred and fifty more have to pass through the cataracts very shortly."

By now they knew that Gordon's plight must be desperate. Yet the army could not advance without its long riverborne train of supplies. Burnaby was grateful to have a role, but he yearned above all things to command troops in an engagement with the enemy. However unsatisfactory might be his relationship with his wife, from deep in the desert he wrote to "my darling Lizzie" and lamented the absence of any letter from her for many weeks. He described his gratitude for his Arab bedstead, "which keeps my middle-aged bones off the ground," and exulted in his success in buying from a passing trader a dozen pots of jam at three shillings apiece, five times the Brompton Road price. "Believe me, my darling wife, your very affectionate husband, FRED." This was addressed to her at Davos, the envelope marked "On Active service. No stamps. Pay at other end. F. Burnaby. Col."

Wolseley, at last displaying urgency, had despatched his Camel Corps 150 miles across the Bayuda Desert, shortcutting the great eastern bend of the Nile. Burnaby followed the advance guard with a grain convoy to Jakdul Wells, which he reached on 14 January 1885. His first question on arrival at the craggy heights overlooking the deep green pools was: "Am I in time for the fighting?" Yes, he was. As soon as he had reported to the commanding general, Sir Herbert Stewart, he visited the Blues' contingent. They rewarded his appearance with a rousing cheer. Past dissensions were forgotten. Late that afternoon, led by cavalry scouts, the three-thousand-strong British force set out across the undulating wasteland of dunes towards the next wells at Abu Klea, marching in square to protect eight hundred baggage camels. There were bluejackets pulling a

Gardner gun, three seven-pounders of the Royal Artillery, grenadiers, Coldstream and Scots Guards, lancers, dragoons and Life Guards. It was a bizarre, even preposterous Victorian colonial expedition, relying upon pluck and firepower to compensate for the absence of almost everything else, notably including intelligent command. Burnaby rode a little grey polo pony named Moses, on which he looked even more disproportionate than usual. He carried a four-barrelled Lancaster pistol. When Bennet Burleigh of the *Daily Telegraph* wryly asked the whereabouts of his shotgun, the colonel replied that he had given it to his servant, following Liberal allegations after El Teb that it was somehow a dishonourable weapon.

That day the British covered only ten miles, each step causing a man's boot to sink deep in the soft sand underfoot, then halted for a few hours of darkness. Before the sun rose they made a breakfast of bully beef and biscuits, then set forth once more. Their overladen camels, which found the going little easier than the foot soldiers, struggled against hunger and exhaustion. Stewart did not expect to meet Dervishes in force before reaching the Nile at Metemmeh. He said that he would then ask Burnaby to assume the role of governor of the town. This must have been unwelcome news. The great adventurer would find it intolerable to be left behind while others advanced upriver to deliver Gordon. There must be a suspicion that Stewart did not share Wolseley's enthusiasm for Burnaby, and had no intention of sharing Khartoum laurels with the glory-hungry colonel.

That night of the fifteenth, Burnaby messed with the correspondents, also inviting Lord Binning of the Blues to join them. "Tell the men," said their colonel, "I shall be disappointed if each of them does not account for at least six of the enemy tomorrow." Here was familiar Burnaby bombast. The force set off next morning up a wide valley, halting for a meal at eleven o'clock some three miles short of the wells at Abu Klea. Scouts cantered in to report enemy forces occupying high ground on both flanks, and apparently preparing to attack. Stewart and his staff, Burnaby among them, rode ahead to reconnoitre. They saw white-robed Arab figures leaping among the rocks. Drums were beating. Banners could be glimpsed in the distance. Stewart decided to delay a further advance until next day. His men built a zareba of thorns around their position, and all through the cold, windy, moonless night they stood to

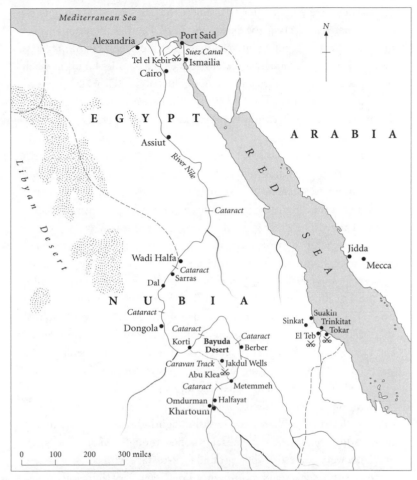

The route of the Gordon relief expedition, January 1885.

their arms as sporadic Arab rifle fire fell among them. British pickets glimpsed the glow of a cigar approaching through the darkness, and Burnaby rode in from a solo reconnaissance. The colonel passed the rest of the night arguing politics with Bennet Burleigh, which thoroughly annoyed Sir Herbert Stewart, who had ordered silence throughout the British position.

At first light the Arabs began firing on the British with disturbing accuracy from behind stone breastworks they had built during the hours of darkness. Stewart's bugler fell, shot as he accompanied the general and Burnaby inspecting the positions. Lord Charles Beresford, commanding the naval contingent, in vain begged the general's group to dismount. Burnaby was finally forced to do so when a bullet hit his horse in the fetlock and he was thrown. "I'm not in luck today, Charlie!" observed the winded colonel ruefully. What else did he expect? He was inviting death every moment. He now urged Stewart to attack, rather than maintain an exposed position in which the British were suffering a steady stream of casualties. Still the general delayed, "to give the niggers a chance to come on." Only when it became plain that the Dervishes were well content to maintain a harassing fire did the general reluctantly order an advance. Burnaby, back on his wounded horse, was given command of the square's rear face, which included the Blues.

Minutes after the British began to move, from the low hills around them fifteen thousand yelling Dervishes swarmed down. Stewart's skirmishers and scouts fled hastily for the safety of the main body. Burnaby, for the first time commanding troops in battle, gave a wildly ill-judged order. He told the dragoons to break square and wheel outwards, so that their rifles could bear on the enemy approaching the front of the square. But Dervishes on the higher ground at once perceived the opening at the rear of the British formation, and rushed towards it. Too late, Burnaby perceived his error and ordered the dragoons back. Arabs swarmed through the gap, crying defiance with wild yells. A lethal scrum developed, with British soldiers and Dervishes fighting wherever they met. A naval rating received seventeen stab wounds, though he survived. Stewart's men were contesting their ground face-to-face with rifles, bayonets, sabres against spears and swords in a great tangle of humanity, steel, sand and blood. Circumstances, assisted by Burnaby's folly, had temporarily deprived the British of their huge advantage of firepower. At Abu Klea, for a few minutes "savages" were able to fight the representatives of the world's great imperial power on something like equal terms. They inflicted a bitter toll.

Burnaby spurred forward in an apparent attempt to help a skirmisher regain the safety of the square. Caught in the open by the surging mob of Arabs, he parried a spear thrust with his sabre, only to catch another point in his shoulder. Corporal Macintosh of the Blues ran out to support his colonel but was immediately cut down. Another spearpoint took

Burnaby in the throat as he glanced backwards. He fell to the ground amid a dozen Dervishes, tried to rise again to use his sword, and finally fell wounded in a dozen places, blood pouring from his jugular.

British discipline and rifle fire turned the battle. The Dervishes were thrown back, leaving scores of dead. Lord Binning ran to the spot thirty yards beyond the square where Burnaby lay, his life's blood draining away, in the arms of a young soldier of the Bays: "Oh! sir," cried the trooper, "here is the bravest man in England dying, and no one to help him." Binning took his colonel's hands, felt a feeble pressure and saw a faint look of recognition, before Burnaby was gone. Both the spear thrust in his throat and a sword slash through his skull were mortal wounds. "His face," wrote Binning, "bore the composed and placid smile of one who had been suddenly called away in the midst of a congenial and favourite occupation; as undoubtedly was the case." The pony Moses lay dead beside his rider, also hacked to pieces.

The colonel was among nine officers and sixty-five British soldiers killed, nine officers and eighty-five wounded. The dead were buried beneath a stone cairn. Many men of the Blues sat down and wept at the loss of their commanding officer. A few days later, after the death at Dervish hands of Sir Herbert Stewart, the expedition faltered, then fell back in failure. Gordon himself, of course, died at Khartoum. Wolseley lamented the fact that Burnaby had not survived Stewart. The colonel had been nominated to succeed to the command if the general was killed. Wolseley believed, surely wrongly, that Burnaby's dash and energy might have turned the scale and pushed the Camel Corps through to Khartoum in time. More likely, the small relief force would simply have perished with Gordon.

The British press and Burnaby's admirers celebrated the colonel after his passing, though Gladstone omitted him from the list of senior officers lost in the Sudan whom he eulogised by name to the House of Commons. The Duke of Cambridge wrote to Wolseley: "Burnaby was certainly a most gallant man, and courted death. He had peculiarities which I could not appreciate, but I am deeply grieved at his being killed." Burnaby's was a clumsy life. He was a size too large in everything save judgement. The difficulty with such men who, as the Duke justly observed, court death, is that they often carry with them others who have no urge to travel to the same destination. Burnaby provided his contemporaries, and posterity, with much entertainment. He commands the attention of any student of Victorian eccentricity. He was an inimitably British figure, tinged with pathos. Yet his brief experience of battlefield responsibility suggests that it was fortunate he never achieved the position of command for which he yearned. He was too reckless and self-indulgent to be fitted for it. The troopers who sobbed for their colonel at Abu Klea might better have lamented the men whose lives he caused to be lost by so rashly opening the British square. Like many romantic warriors, Frederick Burnaby was not a voyager in whose wake it was wise to follow, unless a man was eager to venture a passage across the Styx.

CHAPTER SIX

GENTLEMAN-OF-WAR

THE FIRST WORLD WAR shattered the illusions of European societies about the nature of conflict in general, and of war with the Germans in particular. In August 1914, the Kaiser's nation set about its purposes with a ruthlessness that shocked its foes. German atrocities towards civilians in Belgium and France were exaggerated by propaganda, yet were bloody enough in reality, involving the authorised murder of several hundred unarmed people. Later came Germany's introduction of poison gas, air bombardment of civilians and a U-boat campaign against unarmed merchant shipping. Germans, in their turn, argued that the Allied naval blockade imposed greater suffering upon civilians than any policy initiated by Berlin. Compassion for the foe was among early casualties of the conflict, together with scruples about methods of destroying him. In a war of national survival, almost every old ideal about humanity in warfare was snuffed out. Though the Franco-Prussian and Boer wars had scarcely been notable for chivalry, the twentieth century set a new pattern for the behaviour of combatants, from which surviving warriors of the old era recoiled.

Yet in the early months of the First World War one man, a German naval officer, for a short season kept alive the conventions and manners of former times. Captain Karl Friedrich Max von Müller of the light cruiser *Emden* waged a lone war in the eastern oceans which won him the attention of the world, and the ungrudging respect of his enemies. At a time when already the British and French peoples were being urged to perceive "the barbarous Hun" as a descendant of Attila, Müller showed himself at all points a gentleman. It may be argued that this was a foolish aspiration in such a struggle. Some other characters depicted in this book would have deemed Müller's fastidiousness absurd, and questioned his credentials as a serious warrior. But Müller's conduct enchanted his enemies. They still possessed generosity enough, in those last days of innocence, to accord laurels to an enemy who played the game.

Müller was born in Hanover in 1873, son of a colonel in the Prussian army and his French wife. He himself was intended for an army career, and became an officer cadet after attending a military academy in Schleswig-Holstein. Shortly before his eighteenth birthday, however, the boy persuaded his father of his enthusiasm for the sea. He was permitted to transfer to the Imperial Navy. In the years that followed he served the usual round of postings, in big ships of the High Seas Fleet and in small ones protecting outposts of the Kaiser's empire such as German East Africa. There Müller contracted malaria, which dogged his health for the rest of his life. Reports on his career progress from higher commanders were glowing. In 1912, after he served a stint at the Imperial Navy office in Berlin, Admiral von Tirpitz himself wrote: "First-class, completely reliable officer. Warmly recommended to future superiors." Yet at thirty-nine, an age at which the future British First Sea Lord David Beatty was already a rear-admiral, Müller had yet to captain a ship. This austere, correct, reserved bachelor could scarcely be described as a high-flier when, in May 1913, he was at last posted to command the light cruiser *Emden* on the China station.

Müller's new command was a graceful, white-painted 3,600-ton vessel commissioned in 1909. Both her propulsion system and her weapons were already obsolescent. Coal-fired piston engines enabled the ship to attain twenty-four knots, but her economical cruising speed was just twelve. *Emden*'s principal armament consisted of ten 4.1-inch guns and two underwater torpedo tubes. She carried a crew of almost four hundred. Within a few weeks of Müller joining the ship at the German treaty port of Tsingtao (now Qingdao), he at last gained an opportunity for distinction when *Emden* found herself in action on the Yangtse against Chinese rebels whose activities were deemed to threaten the interests of the resident foreign powers. The cruiser's bold handling won her captain approving publicity in the German press, and a warm report from the East Asiatic Squadron's commander, Graf Maximilian von Spee. Promotion and a medal followed.

In those palmy days there was considerable fellowship among representatives of the rival imperial powers, united in remoteness from home and belief in their own role as civilising forces on the margin of a continent they regarded as untamed, even if it boasted a culture far older than their own. British and German vessels exchanged punctilious salutes. *Emden*'s crew played football and entered gymnastic contests against their British counterparts. Officers visited each other's ships. The German Imperial Navy was a young service, self-conscious about its short history, and determined not to be outdone by elder brethren in either efficiency or courtesy. Müller possessed a natural authority which quickly earned him the respect of his crew. Despite his personal reserve—indeed, he was a lonely man—a pleasantly collegiate atmosphere prevailed among his officers, who were not in the least afraid of taking initiatives and offering ideas to their commander. The first lieutenant, Kurt Hellmuth von Mücke, was to prove a remarkable personality in his own right. Eight years younger than his captain, he came from a similar social background. Appointment to the *Emden* followed his specific request for an overseas posting. Mücke was extrovert to the point of exuberance, ambitious and personable. Several other officers shared his outspokenness, which must have made the wardroom a noisy place. The ship's efficiency was never in doubt—*Emden* possessed the best gunnery record in Spee's squadron.

On 20 June 1914, the rest of the force sailed on a cruise from Tsingtao intended to last three months, leaving *Emden* as the colony's guardship. Within a few days of the admiral's departure, the crisis in Europe broke, and worsened rapidly. Müller spent many hours with his young adjutant, Sub-Lieutenant Albert von Guerard, war-gaming contingency plans. His principal assumptions, which proved prescient, were that hostilities would commence with Britain, France and Russia on 1 August. He saw no purpose in seeking to protect Tsingtao by sitting in its harbour and waiting for the enemy. Rather, he intended to put to sea and make trouble, forcing his foes to pursue him. On 31 July a picket posted for the purpose at Tsingtao post office brought the news Müller had expected: hostilities with the Triple Alliance were imminent. That evening, *Emden* slipped out of harbour, having stripped for action. Two days later, a wireless message announced Germany's mobilisation. Müller addressed his crew. War, he said, had come in consequence of the enemy's jealousy of their country's economic success, and despite all its own leaders' strivings for peace. The captain expected every man to do his utmost for Germany, and for the honour of the ship. *Emden*'s company, in amazingly good heart, responded by giving three cheers for the Kaiser.

They might have added: *Nos morituri te salutamus.* It is impossible to withhold admiration for the sailors of Spee's squadron on the outbreak of war. They were doomed men, vastly outnumbered by the ships of their enemies. Only a handful of friendly ports were open to them. Before many months had elapsed, they must either be hunted down or accept neutral internment. Winston Churchill wrote later of Spee: "He was a cut flower in a vase, fair to see and yet bound to die." *Emden*'s little guns packed punch enough to cow a merchant ship, but were no match for those of any vessel of the Royal Navy which the light cruiser was likely to meet. The duty of Spee and his commanders was simply to cause as much trouble as possible for Germany's enemies before meeting their fate with dignity. It is a tribute to the spirit of the Kaiser's navy that the East Asiatic Squadron's captains addressed their task with such resolution.

Müller first set about provoking alarm in the steamer lanes between Korea and Japan. In heavy seas and darkness, early on 4 August he sighted and pursued a ship showing no lights. Dawn revealed her as a Russian, which ignored even a blank shot and a signal ordering her to stop and make no wireless signal. The merchantman steamed hard towards neutral Japanese waters until 6 a.m., when after an hour's chase a dozen live 4.1-inch shells persuaded her to heave to. A boarding party led by the jovial, paunchy Lieutenant Julius Lauterbach, a former merchant navy captain who had joined *Emden* for the duration, questioned the master, who at first professed to speak no German. Lauterbach laughed, and reminded the Russian that only a month back the two men had shared a drink in a bar in Tsingtao. The captive was the *Ryazan,* a fast, new, German-built 3,500-ton mail steamer. Müller decided that rather than sink her, he would commandeer her as an auxiliary. Heading back towards Tsingtao with his first prize, the *Emden*'s captain was dismayed suddenly to sight five warships, which he identified as the local French squadron. He turned to run, and ordered preparations to scuttle the

Ryazan. Instead, however, the French fled. Plain-language signal traffic was intercepted, revealing that they believed *Emden* to be scouting for Spee's big cruisers. The Germans, amused and relieved, sailed triumphantly back into Tsingtao, now blacked-out for war.

In haste, the cruiser's crew performed that most nightmarish of all seamen's tasks in the tropics, coaling ship. At 6 p.m. on 5 August, *Emden* left its base for the last time, heading for the German island of Pagan in the Marianas chain, to join Spee along with an accompanying collier and an auxiliary cruiser, both disguised as British merchantmen. With characteristic thoroughness, Müller ordered the name *Nagato Maru* to be painted on his own ship's life rafts. Even if *Emden* should be sunk, her captain wanted the enemy to remain confused about her identity.

Wireless intercepts told the Germans that their presence in the East China Sea was known, which may help to explain why Müller met no further victims on his course to the rendezvous. On 12 August *Emden* anchored alongside Spee's big cruisers in the shadow of Pagan's volcano, together with eight supply ships which had been sent to meet them. That very day, the Royal Navy's Vice-Admiral Sir Thomas Jerram, with two heavy cruisers, was shelling the German radio station on Yap, nine hundred miles south-westwards, whither he had gone in search of Spee. A long game of hide-and-seek across the Pacific had begun, which would end only after many of the ships engaged had gone to the bottom.

At a captains' conference aboard the 11,400-ton armoured cruiser *Scharnhorst* on 13 August, Spee declared his intention of making for the west coast of South America. He had been told that Chile was friendly, and would provide coal. Müller urged an alternative course. He suggested that there was little chance of destroying enemy shipping on a long run across the Pacific. The Indian Ocean offered better pickings, as well as a chance to impress the subjects of Britain's vast Indian empire. At the very least, suggested Müller, his own ship might be detached for this task. Spee asked for an hour or two to consider. He concluded that Müller was right: alone, *Emden* might accomplish far more than as a mere appendage of the squadron. The light cruiser's 4.1-inch guns could not in the smallest degree influence any encounter with major British units. Detached, however, she might create a useful diversion. Early that afternoon, a pinnace from *Scharnhorst* delivered written orders for Müller to enter the Indian Ocean with the task of "waging cruiser war as best you can." Through the three months that followed, this was what Müller did with spectacular success.

Early on the morning of 14 August, at sea once more, *Scharnhorst* signalled *Emden:* "Detached. Wish good luck." Müller answered by semaphore: "Thank your Excellency for trust placed in me. Wish Cruiser Squadron *bon voyage* and good luck." Spee steamed towards the destiny that would bring him victory at Coronel off the coast of Chile, then defeat and death when he went down with his ship at the battle of the Falklands. Müller, accompanied by the collier *Markomannia*, headed southwest, anxious to avoid any sighting by enemy vessels until he burst upon the shipping lanes of the Indian Ocean. By the twenty-fifth he was off Timor. On the twenty-seventh he met the neutral Dutch warship *Tromp* in Dutch East Indies waters. Müller exchanged courtesies with her captain, though he declined an offer to meet for drinks. *Tromp* escorted *Emden* out of Dutch waters, and appears not have revealed the Germans' presence. Next day, the cruiser slipped down the narrow channel north of Bali, having rigged a dummy fourth funnel made of wood and canvas to alter her silhouette. In the safety of Dutch waters off Sumatra the ship profited from a brief pause at anchor to clean boilers and carry out other essential maintenance. The crew coaled again before being chivvied back into international waters by a Dutch official. The Dutchmen who met Müller were punctilious about their neutrality. They did not report his presence, and noted wryly that the Germans had missed the British cruiser *Hampshire* by a mere twenty miles.

On 6 September, amid rain squalls, Müller conducted divine service. Through the three days that followed, his ship prowled the Indian Ocean, searching in vain for prey. Increasingly frustrated and even a little depressed, *Emden*'s lookouts scoured the horizons, seeking smoke, funnels, masts. Day after day, they saw none. Tension mounted in the cruiser. Then at last, after dark on 9 September, the alarm bells summoned the crew to action stations. The stern light of a ship had been spotted. The cruiser closed in, fired two blank shots, and signalled by lamp: "Stop your engines. Don't use wireless." The usual boarding party led by the corpulent Lauterbach chuffed briskly over to the steamer by pinnace. She proved to be a Greek neutral, carrying 6,600 tons of coal for the British government. The ship's engineer was British. Müller decided to keep the coal, and politely invited the captain to accept a German charter contract, which he could scarcely refuse.

Early next morning, now with two consorts in her wake, *Emden* stopped another ship, the 3,393-ton *Indus*, sailing in ballast to Bombay to load troops. There was only one commodity aboard the prize of serious interest to the Germans: soap. For some reason, *Emden* was short of washing materials. A generous consignment was transferred to the cruiser. Two weeks later, the Calcutta newspaper *Empire* carried an advertisement: "There is no doubt that the German cruiser *Emden* had knowledge that the *Indus* was carrying 150 cases of North-West Soap Company's celebrated ELYSIUM soap, and hence the pursuit. The men on the *Emden* and their clothes are now clean and sweet, thanks to ELYSIUM soap. Try it!" This good-natured jollity in the enemy's camp was reported to *Emden*, and recorded in the ship's signal log.

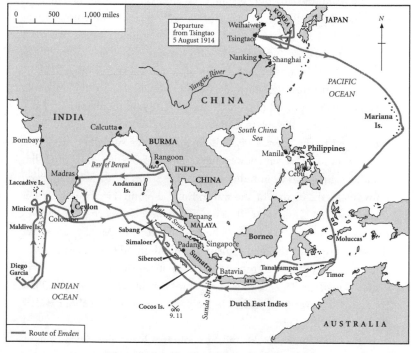

The path of the Emden, *August–November 1914.*

Before *Indus*'s seacocks were opened, the ship was stripped of every luxury that might give pleasure to her captors—beer, towels, chocolates, tobacco, wine. Müller's men deserved anything he could give them. Conditions aboard the cruiser, designed for war in the North Sea, became hideously sultry in the Indian Ocean. Working a coal-fired ship in the tropics was a relentless ordeal, especially for those in the engine room. It proved intolerable to close scuttles to black out the ship at night. Instead, lighting was disconnected in some messdecks. There was no chance that the crew would receive mail from home, the lifeblood of morale. Many men must have brooded or gossiped at their stations about the ship's inevitable final fate, a tiny floating German island on the far side of the world, in the midst of an ocean dominated by enemies. Yet fighting spirit, training and leadership sufficed to sustain the morale of *Emden*'s company in a remarkable fashion. This was, above all, a tribute to her captain.

The *Indus* took an hour to sink, even after the Germans had fired six shells into her hull. The British captain sadly watched his ship's passing from the deck of the *Markomannia*, which now held *Emden*'s prisoners. The victim was not due at Bombay for five days, so it was assumed that she would not be missed before the fifteenth. Next morning, Müller's men were still stowing booty from the prize when more funnel smoke was seen, which proved to come from the 6,102-ton merchantman *Lovat*. The crew were allowed to collect personal belongings before being transferred to the *Markomannia*. Before *Lovat* was sunk, her messdecks were relieved of recent newspapers. These proved useful, providing detailed sailing lists from Indian ports. The *Emden*'s crew were appalled, however, by the picture of the war in Europe painted in the news pages: these reported Germany collapsing, her generals shooting themselves, the Kaiser's armies shattered. The first lieutenant, Mücke, addressed himself to reviving the men's spirits. He highlighted the fantastic stories already being published around the world about the activities of Spee's cruiser squadron. The crew knew these to be rubbish, said Mücke. Thus, they should be ready to acknowledge the same likelihood about tales of their country's eclipse.

On 12 September, *Emden* and her colliers closed the Calcutta light-ship, to await three British ships which prisoners reported due to sail. The first appeared around 11 p.m., fully lit. The 4,657-ton *Kabinga*, loaded with British goods for North America, obeyed a lamp signal to halt, and made no attempt to use her wireless. With characteristic scrupulousness, Müller decided that cargo consigned to neutrals, and thus not belligerent property, could not legitimately be seized. He merely offloaded prisoners into the *Kabinga,* which the Germans decided to use as a *Lumpensammler*—a rubbish dumper. Lauterbach's men also disabled the *Kabinga*'s wireless, in case her captain should have second thoughts and attempt something heroic. Three hours later, at 2 a.m., the lights of the 3,544-ton collier *Killin* were seen. She was duly seized. The little German-led flotilla headed out to sea before first light, where *Killin* was sunk. Müller was unimpressed by the low-grade Bengal coal she carried, and rejected it for *Emden*'s furnaces.

After a night on the deck of *Kabinga,* Lauterbach the prize officer was in his berth that afternoon when he was turned out again to lead a boarding party to the 7,615-ton *Diplomat,* carrying ten thousand tons of tea. The cruiser's men set scuttling charges, then put off again with their prisoners, who included a handful of passengers. While Lauterbach's men were at work, *Emden* raced away to catch a small, dirty Italian steamer spotted by the lookouts. As a neutral, she could not be seized, but with some difficulty Müller persuaded her master to take two hundred prisoners to Calcutta.

The Germans' punctilious behaviour did their warlike purposes no favours. As the Italian steamer closed the Hooghly, she hastened to announce by semaphore her encounter with *Emden.* The news was passed to the Admiralty in London on 14 September. All merchant sailings out of Calcutta were halted, which saved three British ships already proceeding downstream. The cruiser *Hampshire* was despatched from Singapore to give chase, likewise a Japanese warship, for Japan had now joined the Allied cause. *Emden*'s diversionary objectives were being abundantly fulfilled. Admiral Jerram, British Commander-in-Chief of the China station, reported to London that he could not send a squadron to seek Spee at Samoa, because half his ships were pursuing Müller, while the rest were protecting a big troop convoy westbound from Australia and New Zealand.

Müller intercepted another merchantman off Calcutta, which was identified as a neutral Italian and allowed to pass. He was transferring his last prisoners from *Markomannia* when the 4,028-ton *Trabboch* was seen and stopped, her crew sent aboard the *Kabinga*. Coal dust in the collier's hold exploded spectacularly when scuttling charges were fired. The Germans feared that the pillar of flame might be seen, but once again *Emden* was lucky. She escaped undetected, while *Trabboch* disappeared beneath the waves. Müller now sent away *Kabinga* and her cargo of captives. The British master, who was sailing with his wife and two children, made a remarkable gesture. He sent a personal letter to *Emden*'s captain, thanking him for the manner in which he and his family had been treated. Then the entire complement of British crewmen and prisoners gave three cheers for Müller as the two ships parted. Here, indeed, was an unusual reflection of sentiment between enemies, genesis of the legend of the *Emden*. In Karl Friedrich Max von Müller, the British recognised a gentleman. These were the last knockings of an age in which a gentleman was deemed a fine thing, whatever uniform he affected. This indeed was the term the Royal Navy began to use of Müller. British officers called him the "gentleman-of-war."

The *Kabinga*'s crew successfully restored its radio to service even before they reached Calcutta. Warnings about *Emden*'s presence were soon pulsing across the six-hundred-metre waveband. Yet they came too late for one vessel, stopped by a live round after blank fire made no impression. "What ship?" hailed one of *Emden*'s officers by megaphone.

"Clan Matheson."

"English?"

"No, British!"

The crotchety response from the merchantman's Scottish master provoked mirth on *Emden*'s bridge. *Clan Matheson,* laden with cars, locomotives and machinery en route from Britain to India, was sunk after her crew had been transferred to *Markomannia*. A racehorse in the hold was shot to spare it the terrors of drowning. This was *Emden*'s eighth capture. On 16 September off the coast of Burma, the cruiser exploited a flat calm to refill her coal bunkers. As the Germans moved back into the shipping lanes, they had the satisfaction of hearing the ether hum with nervous radio traffic about their doings. Müller paid a passing neutral Norwegian steamer the unlikely sum of a hundred Mexican silver dollars to carry his latest crop of prisoners to Rangoon. The Norwegian master even agreed to slow his passage, to give *Emden* time to get clear. He told Müller that he had seen two French warships and two British auxiliary cruisers nearby. One of *Emden*'s officers suggested a raid on Penang, in the British-controlled Malay States. The captain decided this was the wrong place and moment to advertise their presence. Another day would come for Penang.

Müller was a grave, isolated figure, who seldom left the bridge even when the ship was cruising. His crew held him in deep respect, and cherished his sparse words of approval. Despite the moments of triumph and laughter in the messdecks, for her captain the tension never relaxed. In those days before radar, he knew that at any hour dictated by chance the smoke of an enemy warship might appear, signalling the extinction of his small ship and its crew. Thoughtful subordinates placed a deckchair, property of the self-indulgent Lauterbach, on the bridge where the captain could snatch dozes. Most of Müller's days were spent in silent thought, contemplation of charts and captured newspapers, tidal almanacs and fragments of signal intelligence. During lulls in raiding operations he exercised his men in all manner of emergencies, above all engagement with an enemy warship. Sooner or later, whatever *Emden*'s good fortune, this must come.

The lot of a sailor at war is quite unlike that of a soldier. A man's ship is far more than a mere gun platform—it is his home, the focus of his being, in the midst of the cruel sea. Though seamen engage and destroy the enemy at every opportunity, few withhold a stab of pity at the sight of a sinking ship, whatever its allegiance. There was no hint in Müller of the vanity that characterised many of the men portrayed in these pages, nor of any lust for bloodshed. He was simply a conscientious and superbly competent naval officer, committed to do everything within his power to aid his country's cause. He sought to wage war, however, without broadcasting death or even distress among his foes. Müller was an unwilling killer, one of the last men of his age to seek to prosecute war without much troubling the innocent.

The cruiser coaled again on 19 September, in the midst of the Bay of Bengal. Müller was now heading for the Indian port of Madras, where he intended a noisy demonstration. Though he could not know it, he was again profiting from luck. His most dangerous pursuer, the British cruiser *Hampshire*, had raced away north-eastwards after receiving reports of gunfire heard off the Burmese coast—in reality, probably a thunderstorm. As the Germans approached Madras, Müller briefed his officers about what he could divine of the general war situation, and his own intentions. They prepared the ship for every contingency, and allowed the crew a rare freshwater shower. At 8 p.m. the *Emden* closed the big port at full speed, stopping engines three thousand yards offshore. The cruiser switched on her searchlights, sweeping the coastline until they fixed upon what they sought—a cluster of big white oil storage tanks. The *Emden* opened fire as she got under way again, all five starboard 4.1-inch guns erupting in flame and smoke. She fired twenty-five salvoes in all, and was soon able to douse her own lights, for the blazing tanks provided illumination enough for the gunlayers. The cruiser's shells ignited 346,000 gallons of fuel. This was far less than *The Times* gloomily reported in London, but by now all the exploits of the *Emden* commanded an extravagant press. Thousands of local people lined the Madras waterfront, too fascinated by the spectacle to be frightened as they should have been. Müller took pains to minimise civilian casualties. Five people were killed and twelve injured during the German bombardment. After twenty minutes he ceased fire. His business was done. Long before dawn, the cruiser was far out at sea again, making for a rendezvous with *Markomannia*. Eighty miles offshore, from the bridge officers could still see smoke from the burning tanks of Madras.

This was a remarkable propaganda coup, from which reverberations echoed across India and all the way back to London. It was more than a century since British maritime trade had been exposed to the predations of foreign warships. The Royal Navy had grown rusty in the art of protecting merchantmen. Winston Churchill, first lord of the Admiralty, praised Müller's "enterprise and audacity," but administered blistering rebukes to his senior sailors for their failure to catch this uniquely impudent enemy. "I wish to point out to you most clearly that irritation caused by an indefinite continuance of the *Emden*'s captures will do great damage to Admiralty reputation," he fumed. The raider's activities were becoming a serious embarrassment to the British government. The public was bemused by the inability of the Royal Navy to check this German mischief. Yet the difficulties were immense in finding a single ship in the vast operating area over which Müller was ranging. The material damage done by his activities was small, yet the moral effects were great. The German Foreign Office became so excited by the cruiser's successes that it persuaded the Kaiser's Admiralty to transmit to Müller orders to raid the Andaman Islands penal colony, to liberate some Indian revolutionaries who might make trouble for the British raj. A day or two later, wiser counsels prevailed and the instruction was countermanded.

The *Emden* cruised southwards down the Indian coast, seeking custom, before approaching the coast of Ceylon—modern Sri Lanka. At lunchtime on 25 September, the 3,650-ton *King Lud* was intercepted and sunk. At ten o'clock that night the 3,314-ton *Tymeric*, carrying 4,500 tons of sugar, was stopped. For the first time in the cruiser's campaign its boarding party met a stubborn lack of cooperation from the crew, who folded their arms and refused to help "the damn Germans" in any way. The master and chief engineer were brought aboard *Emden*, where they were dressed down by the first lieutenant for their recalcitrant attitude, reflected not least in the cigarette drooping from the British skipper's lower lip. Lauterbach sank the freighter, and returned aboard *Emden* with a precious batch of newspapers. Only a few hours later, the prize officer was climbing the side of another capture, the 4,437-ton *Gryfevale*, which Müller decided to use for the disposal of his prisoners. Shortly afterwards the Germans intercepted an exchange of radio signals between a British vessel and a Dutch steamer which had crossed the raider's track. In answer to questions about whether he had seen *Emden*, to the Germans' delight the Dutch captain refused to reply, citing his neutrality.

On 27 September Müller seized a collier, the *Buresk*, carrying six thousand tons of top-grade Welsh coal intended for the Royal Navy's China Squadron. The ship's obliging captain offered to continue working his vessel under the prize crew's supervision. The Germans' respect for their foes was somewhat diminished when a drunken riot broke out among prisoners transferred to the *Gryfevale*, with British and Chinese sailors fighting with fists and knives until order was restored by the guards. The most violent culprits were clapped in irons. All alcohol aboard the British ships was collected and thrown overboard.

That afternoon, two more vessels fell victim to *Emden*—the 4,147-ton *Foyle* and the 3,500-ton *Ribera*. In one day, Müller had accounted for three merchantmen. Under searchlights and the eyes of watchful German gunners, the remaining prisoners were put aboard *Gryfevale*. Lauterbach and his boarding party returned to the cruiser. The British ship was then set free to make for Colombo. As it gathered way, the liberated prisoners lining the rail gave three cheers for Müller, three more for his officers, and a final three for his crew. In good part, this gesture must have reflected gratitude for regaining their liberty—but also, surely, respect for the decency of their foes.

Müller coaled ship off the Maldives, at last emptying the faithful *Markomannia*, which now parted company. The *Buresk* could assume its role as collier. For some days the cruiser patrolled the Cape Town to Colombo sea-lane, hoping to catch a troopship, but the horizon remained frustratingly empty. Müller decided to find a sheltered spot in which to make some repairs. On 9 October *Emden* arrived off the British island of Diego Garcia. She had scarcely dropped anchor when a small boat brought aboard the English manager of the local coconut plantation, who cheerfully greeted his visitors. This loneliest of men, lacking a radio, had no inkling that Britain and Germany were at war. Müller and his crew perceived no virtue in disillusioning him. For twenty-four hours, while the Germans worked on their ship, the courtesies of peace were observed.

A voluble French Creole came aboard while Müller's seamen chipped barnacles—the ship's hull was exposed by ballasting each side in turn. His hosts hastily hid recent newspapers before he was indulged with whisky and soda in the wardroom. The Creole was much excited by the encounter, remarking that his last sight of a German warship had been the *Bismarck* in 1899. He expressed some bewilderment that the Germans had not put into a port to coal and to scrape their hull. His puzzlement was disarmed when the captain sent a party to mend the broken engine of his motorboat. They told him the most recent uncontroversial world news, that Pope Pius X was dead. The effusively grateful visitor returned ashore and sent his hosts a live pig and a load of fresh fish, fruit and vegetables. Müller responded by despatching this unknowing foe wine, whisky and a box of cigars.

On 10 October the cruiser sailed from Diego Garcia amid a host of friendly gestures of farewell from the shore. Repairs were complete, the bunkers full of coal. After making north-northwest for a few miles to deceive witnesses, *Emden* set a course which eventually took her west of the Maldives. At that moment, the Royal Navy's questing *Hampshire* was passing the eastern coast of the same islands. On 12 October the auxiliary cruiser *Empress of Russia* put in to Diego Garcia, searching for news of *Emden*, and of course heard the tale of the German visit. Here was a new addition to the raider's legend. Even British newspapers treated the incident as high comedy.

Meanwhile, the interloper again set about ravaging trade. The *Clan Grant* was seized on 15 October, yielding welcome beer and cigarettes for her captors' messdecks. *Buresk* was left to load plunder, while the cruiser chased a new smoke column on the horizon. The Germans were amazed and no doubt disappointed to find that this came from the 478-ton dredger *Ponrabbel*. Its crew proved delighted to become prisoners. They perceived *Emden* as their deliverer. Captain Edwin Gore had been struggling to get his unseaworthy charge to the port of Launceston in Tasmania ever since war broke out. He and his crew had found their voyage a nightmare, at a maximum speed of four knots. They cheerfully packed their personal baggage and climbed aboard the *Buresk*. They then applauded loudly when a couple of shots from *Emden* caused the detested *Ponrabbel* to turn turtle. As darkness fell, the cruiser met the 4,806-ton *Benmohr*, carrying a large and valuable cargo from London to the Far East, and sank her after taking off the crew.

Soon after divine service ended on Sunday the eighteenth, the 7,562-ton *Troilus*, a crack cargo liner on her maiden voyage, was stopped. When Lauterbach went aboard with his riflemen, among the passengers he met a British woman who greeted him as an old friend—she remembered him from his prewar days commanding a merchantman. The German officer remained on the freighter's bridge while *Emden* stopped the 5,596-ton *St. Egbert*, and later that night the collier *Exford*. Müller was still performing a complicated game of musical ships, moving captives and booty between vessels on the morning of the nineteenth, when smoke was sighted to the north. *Emden* hoisted in one of her boats and set off in pursuit, soon afterwards returning with the 5,140-ton *Chilkana*, usefully supplied with provisions and medical supplies. All these captures were swiftly sunk, save the *St. Egbert*, which was despatched to Cochin in south-west India with six hundred prisoners.

The cruiser had now claimed thirteen prizes since bombarding Madras. Müller had performed a remarkable feat merely by ranging the seas and surviving for ten weeks since the outbreak of war. It was a feat possible only at that midpoint of technology, between radio's invention and its coming of age, and before the advent of radar. Just as the chivalry of *Emden*'s behaviour reflected the ethos of earlier centuries, so too did its cruise summon memories of roving corsairs. We know much more about what Müller did than about what he felt during this period, when the exploits of himself and his ship echoed around the world, making headlines from New York to Hong Kong. The strain on the captain was enormous, knowing as he did that his daily decisions about course and target were those of a roulette player who must eventually be confounded by the zero. At every turn he was obliged to act without the smallest knowledge of his foes' whereabouts. He knew only that they were searching desperately for him. *Emden*'s luck had been astonishing, again and again missing pursuers by days or even hours. Somewhere, some time, however, nemesis must be waiting. Müller knew that he could never hope to sail home, or even to reach a friendly port. He must raid until he had to fight, then fight until his ship—and probably most of her crew—had to die. The *Emden*'s captain was always a sombre man. In those days, it would have been remarkable if melancholy did not sometimes assail him.

Müller set a course eastwards again, leaving Ceylon a hundred miles to the north. *Emden* was rust-streaked now, her decks cluttered with a bizarre assortment of captured livestock which recalled the menageries commonplace in sailing ships a century earlier. In the afternoon watches, the ship's band sometimes played. On 22 October there was a formal parade to mark the Kaiserine's birthday, with the crew in dress uniforms and a twenty-one-gun salute. *Exford* and *Buresk*, too slow to accompany the cruiser into action, were detached to await its pleasure at a rendezvous many hundreds of miles southwards.

Just before daybreak on 28 October, wearing her dummy fourth funnel to help her to be mistaken for a British cruiser, *Emden* approached the Malayan port of Penang with gun crews closed up, every man at action stations—and the Royal Navy's White Ensign aloft. The normal marker buoys, illuminated as in peace, guided the Germans' passage inshore. The tension was electric. The attackers had no means of knowing whether a major British warship was in the anchorage. Seconds before *Emden* opened fire, the White Ensign fell and German Imperial Navy colours broke out. Among the dense forest of masts in the harbour, the lookouts identified an obvious target. Just 1,300 yards away, point-blank range, lay the elderly Russian light cruiser *Zhemchug*. The raider first loosed a torpedo, which struck *Zhemchug* amidships, then poured gunfire into her hull. A black comedy was played out aboard the Russian vessel. She was wholly unprepared for action, her captain ashore with his mistress and much of his crew preoccupied below decks with a visiting deputation of some sixty Chinese prostitutes. After firing a few desultory 4.7-inch rounds, her ready-use ammunition was exhausted. The Royal Navy's harbourmaster had warned the Russian cruiser's captain of the risk of German attack and begged him to take proper precautions. Now the British officer closed the *Zhemchug* in a launch. Vainly, he urged the crew to fight in earnest. A second German torpedo intervened, causing a huge explosion which sent the victim to the bottom, just fifteen minutes after the first shot of the action. Of the crew, 89 died and 123 were wounded. The fate of their female guests is not recorded. *Zhemchug*'s captain and first lieutenant were afterwards cashiered and imprisoned by a tsarist naval court.

A French destroyer captain in the harbour, confronted by *Emden*, decided that discretion was the better part of duty, given his much smaller guns. "Under these conditions, could I give the order to fire?" he demanded later. "I did not think so. To open fire would have been for the enemy, already triumphant, but the signal for another easy victory." The French ship survived the bombardment unnoticed. Meanwhile the cruiser opened fire on a vessel speeding across the harbour, but immediately desisted when Müller perceived that it was an unarmed patrol boat. As *Emden* sailed out of Penang, in the channel it met the British steamer *Glenturret*. Lauterbach and his boarding party were sent aboard, to ask her master to pass on Captain Müller's regrets to the British authorities for having mistakenly fired on the patrol craft, and also for not despatching boats to rescue survivors from the *Zhemchug*. *Glenturret* was then sent on its way.

The day's events were not yet ended. Outside the harbour another small French destroyer, the *Mousquet*, displayed more verve than her compatriot in the anchorage. She closed *Emden* at speed, firing fiercely if ineffectually. The Frenchmen fought until their ship sank under them ten minutes after the first shot. The French captain went down with his command. Müller sent boats to recover survivors. Early on 30 October, *Emden* stopped the steamer *Newburn*, put thirty-three French prisoners and wounded aboard her, and gave her master a letter—which was delivered—addressed to the German consul in Batavia, reporting the Penang raid.

The *Emden* now set course southwards for the tiny specks of the Cocos Islands, 2,300 miles west of Darwin. There was an important British cable and wireless station there, linking Britain and Australia. On 31 October, off the Dutch East Indies, she made a scheduled rendezvous with the *Buresk*. Next morning, a Sunday, Müller announced some forty promotions among the crew, and joined his officers in the wardroom after church for a celebratory drink. He intended his next move, against the cable station on Direction Island, to be a feint. He wished to lead his pursuers eastwards, then himself turn west once more towards the Aden-Bombay shipping route. On the night of 7 November, *Emden* reached the appointed rendezvous with *Exford*. There was no sign of her until eight o'clock next morning. A failure to adjust the little ship's chronometers had caused a navigational error, which brought the collier late onto her station. The cruiser's navigating officer, who was in temporary command, must have been vastly relieved at last to sight his own ship. These few hours' delay, apparently unimportant, caused Müller to postpone his planned raid on the cable station until the following day. They also sealed the doom of his ship. Now, at last, *Emden*'s wonderful luck ran out.

The Germans intercepted a British warship's coded signals, the strength of which told them that the vessel was at least two hundred miles distant, and receding fast. Müller correctly divined that it was headed for German South-West Africa, to assist the South African campaign for its seizure. The Royal Navy's messages were not being repeated to any other warship nearer at hand. Fatally, this caused the German captain to deduce that his passage was clear to Direction Island. At 6 a.m. on 10 November, *Emden* stopped to offload the first lieutenant, Mücke, and forty-one armed ratings into a steam pinnace and four cutters, to seize and destroy the cable and wireless station. When the British began insistently demanding the ship's identity, the Germans sought to jam transmissions. They failed. The British sent out the same message again and again: "Strange ship in entrance." Then it became: "SOS, *Emden* here."

The cable station's signals were received by British warships, and acted upon within minutes. The Australian light cruiser *Sydney*, one of the escorts of a big troop convoy carrying Australian and New Zealand soldiers westwards to war, was just fifty-two miles, two hours' steaming, from Direction Island. She was immediately detached by the commodore and ordered to seek out the German raider. Here again, Müller and his men were unlucky. The Japanese battlecruiser *Ibuki* pleaded for the honour of the pursuit, citing her vastly superior armament. But *Emden* could have outrun *Ibuki*. The Australian light cruiser was sent instead, because she could claim a two-knot advantage on the Germans' maximum speed.

The *Sydney*'s crew, and especially seconded Royal Navy personnel who held the ship's key executive posts, were thrilled to be offered this opportunity. Captain John Glossop was an unimaginative officer, but the task now thrust upon him demanded only obedience to fundamental rules of naval warfare, drummed into such a man since adolescence. A few minutes after 9 a.m., when the German landing party had been ashore wrecking the cable station for almost three hours, funnel smoke was sighted, and by 9:15 identified as that of a British warship. There was no time to recover Mücke and his men. Müller issued a string of hasty orders. *Emden* hoisted her anchor and crept out of the lagoon, her stokers pouring on coal to build up speed, while the party stranded ashore were obliged to watch in consternation. The depleted crew hastened to their action stations. The captain was suffering agonies of self-reproach, asking himself how he had so gravely misjudged the situation. He might have guessed that, making a landfall in daylight, the odds were overwhelming that the cable station would signal his arrival before it could be destroyed. Even given his expectation that *Emden*'s presence at Direction Island would be reported to the British before he turned westwards once more, it was disastrous that word had been broadcast this swiftly to an enemy so close at hand. Müller found a moment to notice the young face of his adjutant, Guerard, glowing with excitement at the prospect of action. Yet he himself well knew the disastrous nature of their predicament.

At 9:40, when *Emden*'s rangefinders reported *Sydney* at 10,500 yards, Müller ordered his guns to open fire. Yet this was to be no chivalrous encounter between jousting rivals. Glossop's business was to destroy the enemy with minimal injury to his own ship. The first two German salvoes bracketed the Australian cruiser with remarkable accuracy, followed by a third which scored hits inflicting some damage and casualties—four killed and eight wounded. If those rounds had impacted a few feet differ-ently, the Australian ship's fire control system would have been smashed. As it was, *Sydney* turned away to open the range, running parallel with her adversary as her own bigger guns engaged. It was now Müller who steamed all-out in a futile attempt to close. Again and again his guns scored hits, but at extreme range the tiny shells failed to explode against *Sydney*'s side armour.

By contrast, it was twenty minutes before the Australian ship's indif-ferent gunnery achieved a significant impact on *Emden,* wrecking the wireless cabin and communications between the bridge and gun posi-tions. After that, however, a rain of shells devastated Müller's vessel. The German funnels fell quickly, because their supporting stays had been removed to prepare the ship for coaling. The steering was smashed, tor-pedo positions put out of action. Many men were killed by explosions among ready-use ammunition. At 11:15 *Emden* ceased fire after expending some 1,500 rounds. She no longer possessed a gun that would bear. The experience of those ninety-five minutes under continuous fire, receiving some hundred six-inch hits, was disastrous for the ship and many of its crew. The superstructure, gun positions and messdecks had been repeat-edly ravaged by explosions. Ventilating fans were destroyed, so that tem-peratures below decks soared, leaving stokers and engine-room staff gasping and all but incapable in the tropical heat. Wreckage lay every-where. The ship was listing sharply to port. Müller's men did their cap-tain and their country much honour. Hopelessly outgunned, they fought to the last in a fashion that brought lustre to the Imperial Navy. Müller turned his stricken ship for a nearby reef, and deliberately ran her aground at full speed to save further loss of life. "Everybody on board was demented—that's all you could call it, just fairly demented," said one of *Sydney*'s officers after meeting the German survivors, "by shock, fumes and the roar of shells bursting among them."

In his subsequent report, *Emden*'s captain wrote: "As I no longer had the capacity to damage the enemy, I then decided to put the ship, thor-oughly shot to pieces and burning in many places, on the luff side of North Keeling island in the breakers on the reef, to reduce it completely to a wreck in order not to make a useless sacrifice of the survivors." He was haunted by his own reflections on those who had died, especially Zeidler, his personal servant, and Guerard, his devoted adjutant, who had been so thrilled a few hours earlier by anticipation of battle. Controversially, even after Glossop saw his enemy aground, he poured more fire into the hulk before turning away to seize the collier *Buresk,* which he overtook in a sinking condition after the Germans had scuttled her. He then returned to *Emden,* heaving to just offshore at 4 p.m. Müller and his men had used the interval to destroy documents and equipment. Some German sailors had drowned seeking to reach the island from the reef through heavy surf. Glossop noticed the cruiser's colours still flying. Receiving no reply to a lamp signal demanding surrender, for five minutes he resumed firing. Only when white flags appeared and a German sailor swarmed aloft to lower the cruiser's colours did her tormenters desist. *Sydney* had expended 670 rounds of 6-inch ammunition.

The victor despatched a party of German prisoners to the wreck in one of *Buresk*'s boats, to inform Müller that Glossop had turned away towards Direction Island to investigate what mischief the Germans had wrought at the cable station, before returning next day to recover *Emden*'s survivors. This was scarcely noble behaviour. Glossop might at least have landed a party with his own doctor to aid a hapless and defeated enemy. As it was, *Sydney* reached the cable station to find that the birds had flown. While the battle was raging, Lieutenant Mücke and the German landing party displayed astonishing initiative. After seeing *Emden* depart, they perceived that their fate must lie in their own hands. The only vessel large enough to carry them all was the schooner *Ayesha,* at anchor in the lagoon. Bidding farewell to the British cable station staff who had briefly been their captives, Mücke and his men boarded the schooner and put to sea. They were out of sight before Glossop and his ship put into the anchorage. After an astounding odyssey by sea and overland, in May 1915 the Germans reached Constantinople, and thence returned as heroes to their homeland.

Next day when Glossop returned to North Keeling, he sent one of his officers, Lieutenant Garsia, to insist upon an assurance from Müller that he and his men would make no attempt to interfere with the running of *Sydney,* before the cruiser began to embark prisoners. Garsia approached Müller, saluted, and said: "You fought very well, sir." Müller abruptly responded, "No," and turned away, apparently nursing the bitterness of defeat. The German commander said later that he felt honour demanded that he should have died in the action. Then he collected himself and returned to the young British officer. "Thank you very much for saying that," he said, "but I was not satisfied. We should have done better. You were very lucky in shooting away all my voice pipes at the beginning."

The long, hard business began of getting German wounded aboard boats, and thence from the reef to *Sydney*. Müller himself was the last to leave the hulk of his command. Next day, those survivors who had swum to the island were retrieved. Among Müller's crew, 7 officers, 124 men and 3 Chinese laundrymen were killed in action or died of wounds—around a third of those aboard. Another third were wounded. Only Müller and five others among the commissioned officers were unscathed. Whatever the shortcomings of Glossop's behaviour in action—for *Sydney* had made clumsy work of destroying its much weaker foe—the captain behaved with impeccable sensitivity as his ship approached Colombo on 15 November. He signalled the shore that there should be no cheering or visible celebration, out of deference to Müller and the crewmen of *Emden* whom he carried, the most gravely wounded lying in cots on the quarterdeck.

The German officer was fêted in Colombo. In seventy days he had captured twenty-three vessels. He was visited by Captain Grant of HMS *Hampshire*. They exchanged tales of each other's movements, which revealed how often they had missed an encounter by a hairsbreadth. Churchill wanted the German captives to be brought to England, but the chief of naval staff strongly objected. Müller would be lionised, he said: "All sorts of ill-balanced people will want to write to him and visit him." Kitchener, as secretary for war, instead ordered that the prisoners should be despatched to Malta. On the Mediterranean island Müller languished in confinement with his crew until October 1916. Thereafter, his circumstances underwent an abrupt change. One morning he was ordered aboard the old British battleship *London*, without personal possessions or courtesies. He was held under close guard and incommunicado below decks, escorted even to the bathroom by a sentry, during *London*'s passage to Plymouth. Once ashore, he was held in a military prison cell until being transferred to a grim camp in Derbyshire. On 26 September 1917 he escaped briefly, only to be recaptured and sentenced to fifty-six days' close confinement. In January 1918, following a renewed outbreak of his old malaria, he was sent to neutral

Holland for medical treatment. Two months later, Müller learned that he had been awarded Germany's highest decoration, the Pour le Mérite, for his achievements in command of the *Emden*. He was finally repatriated to Germany near the end of the war in October 1918, and held an administrative post in the Admiralty until he was retired three months later. He served briefly as a liberal member of the Brunswick provincial parliament, but died suddenly on 11 March 1923, aged forty-nine, after a recurrence of malaria. He had devoted his last years to the welfare of survivors from his old ship.

From first to last, Müller was a lonely figure, monastically devoted to his duty, apparently loveless and almost friendless. Luck had played a large part in enabling him to wreak havoc among the wandering sheep of the British merchant fleet in those first days of war, before either combatant came to terms with the ruthless new world in which they were pitted against each other. Thereafter, Germany concluded that only submarines could wage effective trade war in the face of overwhelming British naval power. The cruise of the *Emden* was a unique episode in the war at sea. Müller's meticulous humanity, his desire to spare the innocent and succour the afflicted while doing his utmost to aid the cause of his country in arms, marks him out in the eyes of posterity.

In those first months of a new and terrible age, for a brief season he sought to sustain the manners of other times. Though there is no evidence, it seems probable that the British were prompted to act churlishly towards their prisoner in 1916 in retaliation for the German escalation of the struggle at sea. The mood of the world, and of the conflict, had changed immeasurably since 1914. There seemed little incentive to concede respect to a captive enemy amid gas, zeppelins and U-boats. Europe was engaged in a death struggle in which millions were dead or doomed. Müller's manner of making war seemed not merely outdated, but almost perverse.

Today, all passion spent, it is once more possible to celebrate this grave, courageous, profoundly decent seaman. Müller made the name of the German navy echo to the world's applause. He did his duty to the end like the perfect gentleman he was, and deserved better from his foes.

CHAPTER SEVEN

MOST PRIVATE SOLDIER

MOST OF THE PEOPLE described in this book were successful warriors. Even if they did not embark upon their careers with an intention or desire to fight, when obliged to do so they played their parts well, sometimes brilliantly. Yet any representation of the condition of the warrior in modern times must take heed of the citizen soldier, who dominated the two world wars. Few conscripts felt wholly comfortable about their masquerade in uniform. The majority did their duty well. Some, however, proved unconvincing men at arms.

Prominent among the latter was Frederic Manning, an Australian who had achieved a precarious status on the fringes of the Edwardian world of letters. If he does not loom large in the memoirs of the literary giants, he was at least invited to some of their soirées. In the latter part of 1916, Manning spent four months in France as a private soldier with an infantry battalion. For many years it was assumed that his humble status was a matter of choice. In reality, however, he served in the ranks because he had failed in an attempt to become an officer, even at a time when it was not difficult for any educated man to gain a commission. Manning's military career was a series of small disasters, which ended in disgrace. Twenty-five years later, another notoriously unsuccessful soldier, the novelist Evelyn Waugh, wrote to his friend Frank Pakenham to suggest that the chief use of the Second World War "would be to cure artists of the delusion that they were men of action." This the First World War did for Frederic Manning.

Manning's unsatisfactory life suggests that he was not cut out to achieve much success or happiness. Yet, if he failed as a soldier, he proved himself one of the conflict's finest recorders, portraying with inspirational force the predicament of the conscript amid the hellish circumstances of the Western Front. Although "other ranks" made up the overwhelming proportion of combatants, in the nature of things they wrote far less than did their leaders. British literature of the war is dominated, indeed distorted, by the poetry and prose of a small number of officers steeped in disgust at its futility—Siegfried Sassoon, Wilfred Owen, Robert Graves. Theirs has come to be perceived as the authentic voice of a generation. It was not so. The response of the commissioned poets to the war was valid for some people of a certain kind, but far from universal.

Many men who served in the trenches were angered by the later popular delusion that Sassoon's and Owen's vision was also theirs. It was not that others enjoyed the Western Front more—what sane man could? But they rejected the poets' view that the rival combatants were morally indistinguishable, that no cause including that of democracy and freedom could justify the human sacrifice. Many thoughtful Allied soldiers believed that Europe would have fallen victim to a brutal tyranny if the Central Powers had prevailed, a contemporary judgement endorsed today by some of the best modern historians of the period. A veteran's view has been well expressed by H.E.L. Mellersh, a twice wounded infantry officer. In his book *A Schoolboy Goes to War* (1978) he deplored the delusion that most combatants believed that "the war was one vast useless, futile tragedy, worthy to be remembered only as a pitiable mistake. I and my like entered the war expecting an heroic adventure and believing implicitly in the rightness of our cause; we ended greatly disillusioned as to the nature of the adventure, but still believing that our cause was right and we had not fought in vain."

This view was far more widely held among soldiers than that of Siegfried Sassoon or Wilfred Owen. It is odd that the British public, along with British filmmakers and novelists, remain addicted to the simplistic "futility" school of history where the First World War is concerned. Many veterans of the trenches preferred the vision offered by Frederic Manning—which vividly depicted war's horrors while treating the event almost as a divine judgement upon man—to that advanced by the proponents of futility. Modern novels such as those of Pat Barker may present convincing portraits of some unusual individuals in the Sassoon mould, but they have little valid to tell us about the predicament or sentiments of most British soldiers who fought on the Western Front. To comprehend these, Manning's autobiographical novel *Her Privates We*, first published in 1929, has never been rivalled.

The book offers a brilliant depiction of the unlettered men among whom the author served. While Manning was as appalled as any man by the horrors of the Western Front, his portrait of the experience was less intemperate, more fatalistic, than that of the war poets. The irony of Manning's disappointed life is that his own failure as a soldier is eclipsed in the eyes of posterity by his triumph in recalling its sensations. Though most of his book describes what happened to a group of men out of the line between attacks, rather than steeped in the mud and blood of the trenches, critics perceived from its first appearance that his humble characters assume something close to moral greatness. The author emerged, quite unexpectedly, as one of history's great bards of conflict.

Frederic Manning was born in Sydney in July 1882, sixth of eight children of a successful businessman who became lord mayor of the city. Grandfather Manning had migrated from Ireland in 1840. Frederic's beloved mother, Nora, was born in County Clare, a short, stout woman of staunchly Catholic principles. Frederic was a weak child, indulged in consequence. He played no games, attended no school, and was taught by a Jesuit tutor who came to the family home in Rushcutters Bay. From an early age he displayed a precocity and a literary bent that made him eager to escape from the uncultured world of his Sydney childhood. He was encouraged by a friendship he formed with a self-consciously intellectual young Englishman named Arthur Galton, who was serving as private secretary to the governor of New South Wales.

Manning's family was rich and broad-minded enough to indulge their wheezy, asthmatic boy's wanderlust. At the age of fifteen, in March 1898, he left Australia for England in company with Galton, who had reached the end of his secretaryship. Manning seems to have been imbued with an ambition to follow the educational path of well-heeled young Englishmen, through Winchester and New College, Oxford. For reasons that are unknown, he did not do so. Supported by an allowance from his family, instead he roamed Europe, reading avidly and becoming especially devoted to the classics. His intelligence and striking good looks—his nephew described him, with his piercing brown eyes, as "like a Spaniard"—enabled him to stroll the lower slopes of English literary life while still in his teens. He was sketched, top hat in hand, by young William Rothenstein, a friend who later became important to Manning's story as a recipient of his wartime correspondence. Max Beerbohm took him to see Bernard Shaw's *You Never Can Tell*. He lodged for a time with a parson in Buckinghamshire, but spent much of his time in Italy, devouring Dante and Anatole France. His mannered, studiedly mature style of writing and behaviour seems to have been formed by living in the company of his elders rather than of his contemporaries. Before he was twenty, Manning had published an essay on Ibsen in the Sydney *Daily Telegraph*. Ill-health caused him to return briefly to Australia, but when his parents travelled to England in 1904 for a six-month tour, Frederic accompanied them, and this time he remained.

He had no notions of a career, save as an intellectual. His health was his principal preoccupation, refuge, alibi. If the ailments were real enough, there is little doubt that they were psychologically based. He hated crowds and the cities they inhabited: "I'm not a gregarious animal; and people who move about in herds seem to me no better than shadowers of each other, without any ultimate reality." His nerves suffered agonies whenever he found himself in London, so Manning opted for a rural life in a remote Lincolnshire village. His friend Galton had taken orders, and invited Manning to share the parsonage at Edenham, where he was to spend the next eight years. Heaven knows what the sturdy Lincolnshire villagers made of the newcomer's more exotic practices, such as burning incense in his room, but once established in rural tranquillity, he began to write. He published a book of poems, *The Vigil of Brunhild,* and became a regular reviewer for St. Loe Strachey's *Spectator*. His intellectual ambitions were pretentious. In November 1905 a letter of his was published in *Outlook* discussing "the symmetrical resemblance in the leading ideas of Gobineau and Matthew Arnold." T. E. Lawrence noticed an essay of Manning's in the *Spectator,* "a picture of life seen through the eyes of an organ grinder's ape." Manning began work on a historical romance entitled *The Gilded Coach,* which he intended "to rival [Thackeray's] *Henry Esmond*."

In 1909 he achieved a brief flash of celebrity with the publication by John Murray of *Scenes and Portraits*. This was a collection of imaginary colloquies, each set in a historical period when traditional beliefs were being questioned, which could have found favour only in the precious world of Edwardian letters. In the first piece, titled "At the House of Euripides," Socrates, Protagoras and Euripides discuss whether and how the gods exist. In "At San Coscino," Macchiavelli debates with Thomas Cromwell. A critic wrote with wild hyperbole, unconscious self-parody: "The principal hope for English prose literature lies in the fact that Mr. Manning writes." Manning was awarded the prestigious Edmond de Polignac prize, until it was found that the book's publication date did not fit the terms, and the £100 cheque had to be taken away from him. Some reviewers found *Scenes and Portraits* a trifle laboured, as did the public. Sales were less than a thousand copies, almost as modest as those for a subsequent collection of Manning's poems. He had established himself as a minor literary figure, was invited to house parties by such people as Aubrey Herbert at his famously literate Somerset home, Pixton, and was widely agreed to be full of promise. He professed to be working on a lyrical poem, as well as a narrative poem and a philosophical poem. But the poet Henry Newbolt wondered whether Manning "would ever take hold of the public; at present he does not touch life closely enough for that." This was shrewd.

Women seem to have played no romantic part in Manning's life. It is reasonable to surmise that he was celibate, perhaps one among many unfulfilled homosexuals of the period. There is a strong narcissistic strand in his writing, partly reflected in his preoccupation with his own health. "I have a sort of respect for human endeavour, human vanity and human failure even," he observed archly. When he visited Paris in 1913, he wrote to a French connection introducing himself with embarrassing coyness as *"un petit enfant,"* nervous of venturing *"dans un autre monde."* He was addicted to the ancients in a fashion remarkable even in an era during which classicism ruled. His friendships were marked by strong intimacies and passionate quarrels on the most esoteric issues. He was close to Ezra Pound, but they fell out abominably over Milton.

By 1914, Manning was thirty-two years old. Unkind people were asking whether he would ever fulfil the youthful promise about which so much had been said. He still cherished his ambition to produce a historical novel, but had written only a few pages. His father, Sir William, turned up in London with Frederic's brother Charlie. The Australian man of business seems to have been proud of his literary son, but by now the stolid lord mayor must have begun to wonder why this aspiring prodigy had neither married nor achieved anything of substance. None of Manning's books had sold more than a few hundred copies. Perhaps Sir William's allowance had been a bane and not a boon. Together with a modest interest in an Australian sheep station owned by his brother, it had enabled Frederic year after year to postpone a reckoning with reality. The divide between this no longer youthful writer's ambitions and achievement appeared embarrassingly wide.

Evidence is fragmentary about Manning's initial response to the war. It broke out while he was staying at a country house party. He was deeply moved by the German invasion of France, a country he loved. His friend and mentor Arthur Galton loathed all things Teutonic, including Goethe, to the point of obsession. In December 1914, Manning attempted unsuccessfully to join the Royal Flying Corps. Like many men of his generation, he was fascinated by the idea of flight. There are also hints of several attempts to gain a commission in various regiments. These failed, possibly for medical reasons. For whatever cause, he delayed enlistment in the army until October 1915. It is unknown why he then chose to offer himself at Shrewsbury as a private in the King's Own Shropshire Light Infantry. His medical record shows that he stood only five feet eight inches tall, weighed 127 pounds, and had suffered from pneumonia. For some reason, on his enlistment papers he declared himself a member of the Church of England, though both earlier and later he professed the Catholicism in which he was baptised. He was sent to train at Pembroke Dock in South Wales, an experience which affronted his fastidious nature. Like many educated men, he recoiled from the confiscation of privacy imposed by army life, the babble of mindless conversation, the cramped living conditions. His only release came from an acquaintance he struck up with a local parson, who gave him the freedom of his home at weekends.

"On Saturday and Sunday afternoons," Private 19022 wrote to his friend William Rothenstein in a correspondence that became the most important autobiographical evidence of Manning's war service, "I can escape into its quiet and civil life for a few hours, and remember that I am a civilised man. It is not that I want to escape from the men, because I have honestly come to love them with all their faults and defects, which they carry bravely enough as being their own concern. But I do find it necessary to escape into a silence that is not of sleep. It is like a bath of quiet, one can almost feel its coolness rippling upon the flesh."

Manning asserted that army life "woke up my powers of resistance." This enigmatic remark may help to explain some of his subsequent behaviour. From a literary viewpoint, however, his most important response was one of intense curiosity about the men among whom he served, most of them peasants. He might have experienced a glancing acquaintance with such men in rural Lincolnshire, but he had certainly never shared intimacies with them. Even now, while eager to observe the Shropshiremen, he shrank from situations in which he might be forced into personal revelation. As comrades said of Manning's alter ego, Bourne, in his novel: "'e's a gentleman, all right, an' better educated than we are, but 'e never talks of himself." Manning told his barrack roommates that he was teetotal, to escape their off-duty drinking bouts: "These men are like children," he wrote in a letter. "When drunk their acquired character is all dissolved away, and they are simply traversed by their own emotions. A mixture of discipline and drunkenness is funny enough; it exemplifies Bergson's theory of the comic, the disparity between the ideal and the reality; but perhaps the addition of piety brings it too close to tears... This training develops the brute in us, but at the same time a curious increased reaction from the brute; just as the Middle Ages brought forth the ideal of Galahad as a reaction from the reality of their life. These people have the primitive passions and brave simplicity of an earlier age. 'We be sinful men,' they say, and do not know how close that spirit is to the true heart of religion."

Manning took refuge from his own unhappiness in heavy drinking, probably alone. His behaviour irresistibly echoes Kipling:

> *Gentleman-rankers, out on the spree,*
> *Damned from here to Eternity.*

After six weeks at Pembroke Dock Manning felt that he had endured enough of the doubtful privileges of observing his fellow man in the proximity of a barrack room. He applied for a commission. In April 1916 he was posted to an officer cadet battalion quartered in Balliol College, Oxford. On 13 June he faced a court martial for drunkenness. He was charged with having brought alcohol into the college contrary to Battalion Standing Order 12, and with being drunk. He was sentenced to be admonished and returned to his unit. Manning never wrote about his various disgraces in the army, which were to become progressively more extravagant. There is therefore no further evidence to show how or why he behaved so foolishly, indeed almost masochistically, if he wanted to escape the servitude of life in the ranks. Alcohol played a disastrous role in his life. A later colonel wrote: "Manning is a gentleman but apparently has no strength of will and is quite unsuitable as an officer." Even before the war began, he had shown himself a man more comfortable amid intellectual fantasy than contemporary reality. To have behaved as he did at Oxford, this melancholy misfit must have been very wretched indeed.

The few months following Manning's return from officer cadet training, when he served briefly with a line infantry battalion, were the only period of his life in which he was obliged to perform tasks among others within a disciplined framework. Both his earlier and later years were spent dallying in lonely, largely ineffectual contemplation. It must have been a grim moment when he returned to the barrack hut at Pembroke Dock, having failed ignominiously in an attempt to escape to higher things. Yet unless his novel is entirely deceitful about his own role, in the ranks he achieved an accommodation with the men among whom he experienced war which rendered him a committed spectator of their doings, if not a happy participant.

He was sent with a draft to the Western Front in August 1916. A woman friend, Eve Fowler, came up from the country to London in order to accompany him from Paddington to Waterloo to board the train for France. He became one among a host of heavily burdened men saying stilted farewells on the station platform, though his embraces must have been among the most chaste. He was thirty-four years old, a difficult age both physically and emotionally at which to embark upon the life of a private soldier in the line on the Western Front. He joined the 7th Shropshires just before they moved to Guillemont, and immediately began to write. First there were his letters, mostly to William Rothenstein. He described the sensation of fear "walking behind me like a live thing, alongside an indifference which is not pious enough to be termed resignation."

He called his comrades "the Shropshire lads," and sketched them as they came in from the trenches "weary, plastered with grey clay, in their steel helmets that are like chinese hats and the colour of verdigris." He noted "the music of the guns," and observed: "I can't sort out and analyse my experiences yet—they're too immediate—tedium, and terror, then a kind of intoxication... we really deal not with the experience itself, but with the traces of the experience." He envied his comrades a fortitude which he perceived as much greater than his own: "I think the heroism of these men is in proportion to their humiliations; the severest form of monastic discipline is a less surrender. For myself I can, with an effort, I admit, escape from my immediate surrounding into my own mind; but they are almost entirely physical creatures, to whom actuality is everything."

Here, Manning was recording sentiments echoed by the fighter pilot Cecil Lewis, who joined the war straight from school and had never known anything else: "We lived supremely in the moment. Our preoccupation was the next patrol, our horizon the next leave. Sometimes, jokingly, as one discusses winning the Derby Sweep, we would plan our lives 'after the War.' But it had no substantial significance. It was a dream, conjecturable as heaven, resembling no life we knew. We were trained with one object—to kill. We had one hope—to live."

The likes of Marcellin Marbot or Harry Smith would have recoiled from such a brutal assertion of the nature of their calling. While warriors of an earlier era accepted the need to kill as part of war, they liked to perceive their trade in nobler terms, insofar as they reflected upon it at all. They recorded their experiences almost exclusively in terms of what they did, rather than what they felt. That is the nature of men of action, such as most professional soldiers are. They stood in contrast to thoughtful figures of the stamp of Manning and Lewis, whom the twentieth century's wars of national survival swept into uniforms which they would never otherwise have considered wearing.

A modern myth has grown up that the First World War was a uniquely terrible experience. In reality, many individuals who served in the great struggles of history, whether with Wallenstein's regiments in the Thirty Years' War or in the ranks of Napoleon's Grand Army retreating from Moscow, suffered comparable horrors. The First World War achieved its special place first because of its scale, and second because it was experienced chiefly by citizen soldiers for whom the Somme and Passchendaele formed no part of their acknowledged contract with society, such as professional warriors recognised. In the ranks of all the 1914–18 armies served intellectuals, amateurs affecting a temporary imposture as soldiers, who afterwards described their experience in a wholly new fashion. Fred Burnaby or John Chard would have been baffled by the sort of poetry Frederic Manning sent home from France:

> *These are the damned circles Dante trod,*
> *Terrible in Hopelessness*
> *But even skulls have their humour,*
> *An eyeless and sardonic mockery.*

He watched a transport column in the darkness:

> *The moon swims in milkiness*
> *The road glimmers curving down into the wooded valley*
> *And with a clashing and creaking of tackle and axles*
> *The train of limbers passes us, and the mules*
> *Splash me with mud, thrusting me from the road into puddles,*
> *Straining at the tackle with a bitter patience,*
> *Passing me . . .*

In his novel, Manning wrote in the third person about his sense of remoteness from those among whom he lived in such intimacy: "They were mere automatons, whose only conscious life was still in England. He felt curiously isolated even from them. He was not of their county, he was not even of their country, or their religion, or of their race . . . in the vague kind of home-sickness which troubled him he did not seek company, but solitude." Here was a renewal of the sensations he had described at Pembroke Dock, his profound distaste for being obliged to live among a herd, such as afflicted many sensitive men in military service. In France, Manning's closest human contacts were with the friends in England with whom he corresponded. In April 1917 some of his war

poems were published as part of a wider collection of his work entitled
Eidola.

> *Each man is alone in this multitude:*
> *We know not the world in which we move.*

Musings of this kind proved no more popular with the public than his
earlier work. By the time the book appeared, Manning had already
seized the opportunity of a leave in London to make a further application for a commission, for which he mustered some influential referees,
including his grand Lincolnshire neighbour and acquaintance Lord
Ancaster. In his application, he cut two years off his real age. It is not
clear how or why Manning was able to leave France after only four
months in the line, the last two serving with the battalion signals section,
but he did not return to 7th KSLI after December 1916. He was fortunate
enough to survive service in France unwounded, though he was once
concussed when a shell hit the dugout in which he lay. Ironically his old
friend Galton thought that Manning after his experiences in the trenches
"looked better and stronger than I have ever known him." Manning's
mother was now in England, living in London to be nearer her sons, of
whom three were serving in uniform. It was a reflection of the British
army's dire shortage of officers that Manning's new application for a
commission was accepted despite his earlier court martial. It seems likely
that he had found sufficient favour with his commanding officer during
his brief period in France to get a recommendation from him. He himself
felt enough goodwill for his old regiment to send copies of *Eidola*, when
it was published, to two 7th KSLI officers, one of them the padre.

In July 1917 Manning was posted as a second lieutenant to the Royal
Irish Regiment, stationed at Templemore outside Dublin. Here was a
remarkably safe billet. Yet within ten days of his arrival at the depot, he
was found to be drunk on duty. Once again he faced the grim ritual of a
court martial, which this time issued him with a severe reprimand. He
promptly reported sick and was diagnosed by an indulgent doctor as suffering from delayed shell shock. Sent on leave, he returned to his unit
on 31 August, and somehow managed to quarrel with the colonel. On
17 October he was hospitalised in Cork for treatment for delirium
tremens. A week later he offered to resign his commission, stating in his

application that "owing to nervousness and constant insomnia I feel that I am unable to carry out competently my duties as an officer." These words convey a strong hint of having been drafted at the dictation of a superior.

On 29 October, while his future was still under consideration, Manning was found drunk again. The battalion MO reported: "I have seen 2nd Lieutenant Manning. This officer is in a stupor, quite unfit for any duty evidently as a result of a drinking bout." Manning's colonel wrote to the War Office, suggesting that yet another court martial would be redundant: "2nd Lieutenant Manning has submitted his resignation, and if this is to be accepted I cannot see any useful purpose will be served by again trying this officer." In response, the War Office asked crossly why Manning had not been court martialled already. Correspondence about his future shuttled to and fro across the Irish Sea for a further two months, while the delinquent presumably remained under open arrest. In January 1918, by a decision surprising for its common sense at a time when the British army faced a manpower crisis, Manning was indeed allowed to resign. His file recorded the reason not given in the *London Gazette*'s brief announcement of the termination of his military service: "ill health brought on by intemperance."

It is plain that at least some fellow officers in the Royal Irish regarded Manning's fate as a matter for pity rather than animosity. To recover his health, the discharged officer was invited for a prolonged stay at the country home outside Dublin of Sir John Lynch, a prominent Irish solicitor whose son-in-law had served with Manning at Templemore. There he met some ardent nationalists, including Constance Markiewicz, who helped to convince him before he left Ireland that the union with England was a dead letter. There was a bizarre new twist to his dealings with the army when he proposed himself once more for a commission. Unsurprisingly, his application was rejected by the War Office, which informed him curtly that the only possible route by which he could again become an officer lay through service with an infantry battalion, and a subsequent recommendation by its commanding officer. That was in October 1918. The war was over a few days later. Manning wrote to Rothenstein: "It will always be a regret that I wasn't in at the finish." He went to stay for a few months in London with his mother, at a flat in Carlisle Place, Westminster. In July 1919, however, he returned to lodge with Arthur Galton in his old sanctuary at Edenham in Lincolnshire.

It is unlikely that further evidence will emerge about Manning's relationship with the British army. He himself seems to have concealed his various disgraces from friends, and perhaps also from his family. All observations are thus based upon surmise. His final attempt to regain a commission, although absurd, suggests that Manning was sincere in his remark to Rothenstein that he regretted having played so small a part in the war. It is tempting to attribute his troubles with alcohol to the effects of his experiences in France. This will scarcely serve, however, when his first court martial took place before he heard a shot fired. Rather, his history suggests a personality disturbed from the moment at which he enlisted. It is interesting that, whatever else troubled him during his army service, he never complained of his old health problems. With more immediate and pressing matters to worry about, his ailments simply fell away, confirming a widespread belief that they were always psychosomatic. Poor Manning obviously carried with him through life a baggage of stresses and complexes which afflicted him in unexpected ways, at unexpected moments. What could have caused him to surrender in the most self-destructive fashion to drunkenness, while anchored in the safe harbour of the Royal Irish depot at Templemore? It is impossible to know, and almost impertinent to guess. Yet the consequence was that he emerged from the war for the first time facing a real rather than an imagined risk to his health, from alcoholism.

Manning's postwar literary career seemed destined to be as ineffectual as his prewar one. He was commissioned to write a section of Sir George Arthur's official biography of Kitchener, no doubt through the influence of friends, but abandoned the attempt after exasperating Sir George by his dilatoriness. He earned a little money by writing a commissioned biography of a naval architect in whom he cannot have felt the smallest interest. His friend and mentor Galton died in 1921, and the homeless Manning eventually found another rural retreat in Surrey. He was always broke, presumably because family subsidies had dried up. He destroyed many of his own literary essays. His drunkenness cost many friends. He made an important new one, however, in T. E. Lawrence. William Rothenstein described an occasion when, in Manning's company, the reticent Lawrence suddenly started to gush about his wartime experiences, "spread his peacock tail, and again and again he began, to be interrupted each time by Manning who broke in, to my amusement, to talk of himself." Each man surely recognised in the other a supreme narcissist, sharing a compelling loneliness.

One day in 1927 a publisher named Peter Davies, who knew Manning and had heard some of his war reminiscences, persuaded him that he should write "some actual experiences of the war in the form of a short story or rather a short novel." For almost a decade since the Armistice, few of those who had lived through the most terrible war in history wanted to read or write about it. Shrewdly, Davies perceived a new time coming, in which there would be a big market for books that told the truth about what the Western Front had been like. Manning began to scribble. "It was wilful and spontaneous," he wrote later, "and took its own way. It came so hurriedly that some things are forgotten." The author's feckless ways constantly interrupted composition. At last, fearing that the book would never be finished, Davies placed Manning in benign confinement in a London flat—not the first or last such treatment deemed needful for a writer—and forbade him society until the novel was finished.

Her Privates We was published in 1929 in a limited edition of 1,500 copies, under the title *The Middle Parts of Fortune.* Its author's identity was concealed by the pseudonym "Private 19022." Manning professed to Davies and others that this reflected his impatience with the prewar celebrity he had achieved, and perhaps even with his entire identity. In truth, it is much more likely that he did not want his authorship known, lest the revelation should provoke some old comrade to expose the truth about his wretched army career. Concealment of the book's authorship proved a brilliant stroke of marketing, prompting a feast of speculation in the press. The book's impersonality seemed to emphasise its universality. The tale of a small group of infantrymen could relate to any such cluster of threatened humanity, anywhere among the four million British soldiers who served in France between 1914 and 1918.

One reader was not deceived by the author's attempted anonymity. Peter Davies received a bizarre telephone call one morning, lauding the new novel to the skies: "It's magnificent, a book in a thousand. You've published a masterpiece." The caller then rattled Davies by asking why he had not named Manning, explaining that he himself immediately recognised the author of *Scenes and Portraits.* Davies confessed himself at a loss, not least because he did not know who he was talking to. "Oh,

Shaw's my name, you probably won't know who I am, but I once wrote a book myself called *Revolt in the Desert*."*

After this dazzlingly disingenuous exchange, Davies persuaded Shaw-Lawrence to provide a quotation about the novel for publication. He responded with: "No praise can be too sheer for this book...Its virtues will be recognised more and more as time goes on." One may suspect that Lawrence identified the book's author not from fading memories of *Scenes and Portraits*, but more likely because he recognised fragments of Manning's drunken reminiscences about military service. Lawrence's endorsement helped to secure *The Middle Parts of Fortune* a brilliant reception from press and public. It was felt necessary by the publishers to bowdlerise the book for a wider audience, removing the obscenities inseparable from any authentic record of soldiers' speech, and to change the title to that which made it famous. The popular edition of *Her Privates We* first appeared in 1930, and was reprinted many times thereafter.

The title of the original, limited edition paraphrases a bitter sexual pun from Hamlet's exchange with Rosencrantz and Guildenstern, "heroes who achieve moral greatness despite the degeneration of the world around them," in the words of American critic Judith Lynn Johnstone, and the title of the popular edition is taken from the same scene.[†] The book centres upon three soldiers of the Westshire Regiment, identified only as Bourne, Shem and Martlow, and a supporting cast of officers and NCOs. At the outset they are resting behind the line after one of the Somme attacks; then preparing for the next offensive; and finally

---

Revolt in the Desert (1927) was a shorter version of T. E. Lawrence's *Seven Pillars of Wisdom*, which was not publicly printed until 1935. Lawrence legally adopted the name T. E. Shaw in 1927.

†HAMLET: My excellent good friends! How dost thou, Guildenstern? Ah, Rosencrantz! Good lads, how do you both?
ROSENCRANTZ: As the indifferent children of the earth.
GUILDENSTERN: Happy, in that we are not over-happy;
     On Fortune's cap we are not the very button.
HAMLET: Nor the soles of her shoe?
ROSENCRANTZ: Neither, my lord.
HAMLET: Then you live about her waist, or in the middle of her favours?
GUILDENSTERN: Faith, her privates we.
HAMLET: In the secret parts of fortune? O, most true; she is a strumpet.
     (*Hamlet*, Act II, scene ii)

carrying this out. Bourne, the central character, is readily identifiable as Manning, to those familiar with his story, in small matters of personal biography such as his Australian connection. He is recognised by his fellow soldiers as a man set apart by education and social background, wise about wine and able to cash a check for £5 in an army in which men were paid in shillings, and hardly any ranker possessed a bank account. His officers want to see him commissioned, and Bourne reluctantly accepts that he will have to leave his mates—no hint here of Manning's familiarity with courts martial. Bourne also displays a lively interest in women.

Where the writings of the most celebrated British war poets are dominated by anger, compassion is the foremost emotion in Manning's novel. Bourne is the outsider amid a battalion of peasants in khaki. In one passage, a soldier mentions tearing up some French pornographic pictures he found in a dead comrade's kit, before sending it home: "'e were a decent enough lad, but boys are curious about such things; don't mean no 'arm, but think 'em funny. 'Tis all in human nature. An' I'll write a letter to 'is mother. Swales is decent folk, farmin' a bit o' land, an' I'm only a labourin' man, but they always treated me fair when I worked for 'em."

If the fictional Bourne cuts a more impressive figure in uniform than ever poor Manning did, the author's portrait of the love between men at war is wholly convincing, even unto the moment of Martlow's death in the final attack.

In the light, the fog was coppery and charged with fumes. They heard in front of them the terrific battering of their own barrage and the drumming of the German guns. They had only moved a couple of yards from the trench when there was a crackle of musketry. Martlow was perhaps a couple of yards in front of Bourne, when he swayed a little, his knees collapsed under him, and he pitched forward onto to his face, his feet kicking and his whole body convulsive for a moment. Bourne flung himself down beside him, and, putting his arms round his body, lifted him, calling him.

"Kid! You're all right, kid?" he cried eagerly.

He was all right. As Bourne lifted the limp body, the boy's hat came off, showing half the back of his skull shattered where the bul-

let had come through it; and a little blood welled out onto Bourne's
sleeve and the knee of his trousers. He was all right; and Bourne let
him settle to earth again.

A few days later, Bourne himself dies in a paltry night raid. Manning
chose for his fictional persona a tidier termination than he contrived for
his own military career. Yet his book is anything but melodrama. Indeed,
much of its power derives from its understated manner. It casually takes
up a cluster of men emerging from a nightmare beyond the comprehen-
sion of most, follows them for a season, then allows them to fall equally
lightly back to earth again—or, more accurately, to disappear beneath
the earth.

A study of 7th KSLI's war diary for the period between July and
December 1916 makes it easy to identify the episodes upon which Manning based his book. The battalion joined the Somme offensive for the
first time on 14 July 1916, with a strength of 34 officers and 993 other ranks.
At the end of its operations that day, only 5 officers were unwounded,
179 other ranks were dead or missing, while 263 were wounded. Reinforcements from England, among whom was Manning, replaced the
casualties. The colonel did not think much of these new men: "training
very frustrating," he wrote, "owing to poor quality of draft." Evidence
suggests that the battalion was not regarded by higher commanders as
exceptional, nor even perhaps as especially competent.

A further attack supporting 10th Royal Welsh Fusiliers on 18 August,
in which Manning probably took part, cost another 130 casualties. By
21 August the battalion was 350 men under strength. It spent many of the
weeks that followed training, resting or providing working parties which
imposed a steady trickle of losses and additions to the sick list. The
record for 20 September, for instance, revealed the following atten-
dances at field hospital: one pyrexia, one crushed finger, one Bright's
disease, one tonsillitis, one broken dentures. The war diary for
17–18 October, when the battalion was in billets behind the line at Mailly-
Maillet, reads like that of a boarding schoolboy: "Nothing of interest
occurred."

On the night of 12–13 November, the Shropshires moved into the line
for a big attack which obviously provided a basis for the climax of Manning's novel. Early on the morning of the thirteenth they were due to

follow the 1st Royal Scots Fusiliers over the top, in an assault directed against Serre. However, when word came back that the Fusiliers were in trouble amid thick fog, the Shropshires' CO ordered his own companies to advance piecemeal in support. The result was a shambles, with fragments of several units entangled and bewildered all over the battlefield. Here was one of the chronic difficulties of war on the Western Front, in which the technology of communication lagged far behind that of destruction. "At 9:45 a.m.," wrote acting Lieutenant-Colonel K.S.L. Arnott, "one of my officers returned to headquarters and informed me that he believed the majority of the battalion were in No Man's Land, but practically all touch had been lost owing to the fog by the time they had arrived at our front line. It appears that several platoons had advanced on the enemy front line, believing that 1st RSF were still in front of them." A B Company runner arrived to report that its officer commanding "wished to inform me that he [if Manning's version is accurate, in company with the novelist] was in the German front line with some men of the Gordons, and was holding on there."

Not for long, alas. The survivors of the seventeen-strong KSLI party finally trickled back to the British line. Coordination of the infantry advance and the supporting bombardment collapsed, so that British shelling did scant damage to the Germans and much to their own foot soldiers. It was a day of chaos and carnage tragically characteristic of the Western Front. By evening, once again only 5 KSLI officers remained unwounded, while 214 other ranks had also been killed or wounded. The events of these twenty-four hours represented a bloody fiasco of a kind familiar to every infantryman of the First World War. The terse phrases of 7th KSLI's war diary reveal the gloom and muted anger which overhung its survivors.

The final episode of Manning's book, a night patrol in which his alter ego dies, seems closely to resemble a local action in the small hours of 1 November, when Second Lieutenant Southwell of 7th KSLI left the junction of Southern Avenue and the British front line soon after midnight, on a raid designed to identify the opposing German troops. Perhaps Southwell's party included Manning. The party found a small gap in the wire in no-man's-land, and crawled within reach of the enemy line around 2:15 a.m. Then they sprang forward. "One German who was at that point on duty as sentry was made prisoner," recorded the battalion intelligence officer, "and was taken out of the enemy trench with considerable difficulty. While this was being done about a dozen of the enemy appeared and opened rifle fire. The prisoner made an attempt to escape, so Second Lieutenant Southwell was compelled to shoot him. It is certain that two other Germans were killed, both being shot at point-blank range, and it is believed others were wounded. It was unfortunately impossible to bring away an identification, as the enemy was attempting to surround the party, [which] returned safely to Courselles at 5 a.m."

Many other small incidents which took place out of the line, and feature in Manning's narrative, are recorded in the battalion diary, not least including the departure of one CO with neurasthenia after only two months commanding the unit. In short, and scarcely surprisingly given the powerful sense of authenticity in Manning's writing, it is clear that the author has founded his story upon historical events much more precisely than do most novelists, even if he has shuffled the chronology. Though his own role in these actions remains conjectural, Manning's encounter with human experience of the most vivid and terrible kind prompted him to write a novel in a different class of literature from the fantasies to which he had devoted so many prewar years. He revealed gifts as a laconic observer of human tragedy that had remained entirely concealed in his earlier incarnation as an aspiring Thackeray.

Arnold Bennett asserted that Manning's book "is bound to survive as a major document in war literature." Ernest Hemingway claimed it as "the finest and noblest book of men in war that I have ever read." Herbert Read observed shrewdly that *Her Privates We* "avoided the hysterical morbidity of some [portraitists of the war], and the still more demoralising forced cheerfulness of others." Read suggested that Manning perceived war as "a God-determined scourge let loose among nations to purge them of their sins." Eric Partridge, himself a trench veteran, described the book as "uncontradictably the best English war novel." It was praised above all for its grasp of the speech and behaviour of the private soldier, which could only have been achieved by one who had shared the experience. Officers often record the words of their men, yet the snatches of dialogue captured by men set in authority must be untypical of the manner in which soldiers speak to each other when authority is absent.

The book constantly echoes and sometimes mocks Shakespeare, and most especially King Hal. Where Henry V wooed Katherine of France with courtly phrases, Manning's soldier of 1917 asks simply: *"Voulez-vous coucher avec moi, madame?"* An infantry attack carries men forward "on a wave of emotional excitement, transfiguring all the circumstances of their life so that these could only be expressed in terms of heroic tragedy." The writer perceived subtleties in his soldiers' behaviour that they themselves would have been wholly incapable of recognising. "The extreme of heroism," suggested Manning, "is indistinguishable from despair...Honour...is only an elaborate refinement of what are the decent instincts of the average man...civilised life...is after all only the organisation of man's appetites, for food or for women." His descriptive passages attain lyrical heights which dignify the most commonplace experience of the soldier of the Somme: "Bourne, floundering in the viscous mud, was at once the most abject and the most exalted of God's creatures. The effort and rage in him, the sense that others had left them to it, made him pant and sob, but there was a strange intoxication of joy in it, and again all his mind seemed focussed into one hard, bright point of action."

Her Privates We quickly sold fifteen thousand copies. Yet this was not enough to rescue Manning from chronic debt. He returned twice briefly to Australia. In April 1934 he sailed for the last time to England, where he died a few months later of double pneumonia, at the age of fifty-two. T. E. Lawrence wrote to a friend expressing pity for the manner of his passing: "Strange to think how Manning, sick, poor, fastidious, worked like a slave year after year...on stringing words together to shape his ideas and reasonings. That's what being a born writer means, I suppose. And today it is all over and nobody's ever heard of him...How I wish, for Manning's sake, that he hadn't slipped away in this fashion, but how like him."

In 1977 Manning's book was republished in its original unexpurgated form as *The Middle Parts of Fortune*. It is generally recognised as one of the outstanding literary achievements of the First World War, yet the author appears in no major British reference work. Frederic Manning was a failure in all his endeavours save one. His life suggests an unresolved confusion about his own identity. The doubtful good fortune of an income from his father spared him from being forced to make choices and to confront reality, as most people must. His career as a soldier was pathetic in its inadequacy. Yet he was redeemed first by the fact that, despite his temperamental unsuitability for military life, he served in France even though his social connections and medical record could have secured him exemption. He "did his bit," even if it was not of the kind that wins medals. In many respects, in life as in his fictional persona, the shortcomings and limitations he was forced to overcome make his achievement seem more worthy of respect than that of another, more coherent human being in uniform.

He came home to tell the tale of common men at war, of warriors inarticulate and stunted in their expressions of emotion amid shared tragedy. His book will retain its power to move the reader as long as tales of conflict command an audience. Frederic Manning chronicled the deeds of citizen soldiers in a fashion that made his own season among them uniquely serviceable.

CHAPTER EIGHT

THE KILLER

THE 1914–18 LAND WAR of which Frederic Manning wrote was so appalling an experience that the media and public of all the combatant nations sought elsewhere for such glamour as they might extract from the conflict. Above all, they looked to the sky. Air warfare was a new phenomenon which excited the curiosity and imagination of the world. To the uninitiated it offered a romance and even purity wholly absent from the slaughter taking place in the mud beneath, an opportunity to express individual identity denied to those serving with the armies. Many soldiers, despairing of trench life and death, volunteered for transfer to the flying corps of their respective nations, though relatively few such applications were accepted. By 1918, 3 per cent of combatant manpower was committed to air forces, against 58 per cent to infantry.

Cecil Lewis volunteered for the Royal Flying Corps, and was accepted, while still a seventeen-year-old schoolboy at Oundle. He wrote in *Sagittarius Rising* (1936), greatest of all 1914–18 pilots' autobiographies:

> From the first, the light fast single-seater scout was my ambition. To be alone, to have your life in your own hands, to use your own skill, single-handed, against the enemy. It was like the lists of the Middle Ages, the only sphere in modern warfare where a man saw his adversary and faced him in mortal combat, the only sphere where there was still chivalry and honour. If you won, it was your own bravery and skill: if you lost, it was because you had met a better man. You

did not sit in a muddy trench while someone who had no personal
enmity against you loosed off a gun, five miles away, and blew you to
smithereens—and did not know he had done it! That was not fighting; it was murder. Senseless, brutal, ignoble. We were spared that.

Many of those who became pilots achieved the personal fulfilment they
sought. Flying in that pioneer era was indeed an extraordinary experience. The canvas and wooden machines of the later part of the First
World War, flying at speeds no faster than a racing car covered a track,
more readily matched human physical capacity to manoeuvre them
than did their vastly more advanced successors. But soldiers who supposed they would improve their prospects of survival by taking to the
sky were disappointed. By late 1916, pilot wastage in the RFC was running at 25 per cent a month. The odds on death for a pilot were higher
than those facing an infantry officer. Even before the enemy became
involved, human error and structural failure killed airmen relentlessly,
many while still in training. In 1915, future air marshal John Slessor
smashed four aircraft during five weeks at flight school, and this was
deemed noteworthy only because he himself remained unscathed. Of
the RFC's total wartime pilot losses of 14,166, training in Britain
accounted for 8,000—significantly more than the Germans.

Even if a man escaped death, flying an aircraft with a cockpit
exposed to the elements induced in many airmen a wide range of physical disorders. The fumes of castor-oil lubricant inflicted chronic bowel
disorders on rotary-engine pilots, while the cold at high altitude
impaired the health of even the fittest young men. Their blood pressures
soared, and the g-forces of combat exercised strains on the human frame
that were as yet little understood. A dismaying number—including a
notable chronicler of the fighter pilot's experience, V. M. Yeates—
became infected by tuberculosis, "Flying Sickness D," which eventually
killed them. And then there were the consequences of enemy action.
Operational flying in France imposed appalling attrition, not least
because the Allies issued parachutes only to balloon observers. Pilots
sang:

> *Two valve springs you'll find in my stomach,*
> *Three spark plugs are safe in my lung,*

The prop is in splinters inside me,
To my fingers the joy stick has clung.

The "aces," fighter pilots who shot down large numbers of enemy air-craft, achieved a fame unique among the warriors of the era. Their achievement was perceived as representing a triumph of human endeav-our quite absent from the land war. Von Richthofen, Guynemer, Ball, Bishop, McCudden and the rest became celebrities to their respective nations. Cecil Lewis again: "Flying was still something of a miracle. We who practised it were thought very brave, very daring, very gallant: we belonged to a world apart. In certain respects it was true, and though I do not think we traded on this adulation, we could not but be conscious of it." As the pilots themselves readily recognised, however brief their exis-tences might be, they were sustained by comforts denied to the soldiers on the ground. After a few hours in the air they returned to airfields where they could enjoy baths, good food and warm beds. These things did not liberate them from strain. Indeed, many fliers in both world wars found the contrast between the tranquillity of their billets and the din of war to which they were exposed minutes after leaving the ground imposed greater psychological stresses than the even tenor of peril and discomfort in a trench or warship. But there were obvious compensa-tions about an airman's existence.

The aces were dedicated to their trade like successful fighters of all kinds. There was seldom anything chivalrous about the manner in which they achieved their "victories." The common characteristic of such men was not that they were virtuoso aviators—indeed, some of the most technically accomplished pilots failed to achieve high scores—but that they were killers. A psychological research adviser to the RFC who briefed medical examiners on the identification of potential impulsives, paranoids and psychopaths among recruits was obliged later to acknowl-edge that most aces were drawn from one of these categories. The per-sonal nature of war in the sky demanded from its successful practitioners an equally personal commitment to taking life which, in modern war-fare, was shared only by the infantry sniper. The objective of the air fighter throughout the twentieth century was to descend upon an enemy from behind and shoot him in the back. Ideally, an attacker inflicted mor-tal injury before the victim glimpsed his nemesis. The business of a successful fighter pilot was unpleasant and indeed brutal. It is fair to say that few aces were sympathetic human beings, whatever admiration their skills commanded.

A pilot who lived long enough to gain experience could survive for a remarkable length of time, but many of the great air fighters died in action sooner or later. Whatever pinnacles of proficiency a pilot scaled, these could not offer indefinite protection against the frailty of contemporary aircraft, a chance shell or bullet fired from the ground, a momentary misfortune in a dogfight. The German air force on the Western Front was actuarily more effective than its Allied counterparts. Canada, for some reason, produced an exceptional number of aces. It has been suggested that the dominion took far more trouble over pilot training than the British, whose approach remained frankly insouciant until a late stage of the war. "Parfait gentil knights," or even traditionally educated English gentlemen, seldom displayed the qualities to become outstanding fighter pilots, though one former Eton head boy—Arthur Rhys-Davies—achieved a substantial score before he was killed.

The most successful American scout pilot of the war was Eddie Rickenbacker. British and French sceptics remarked that he fought only in the last months of the conflict. Yet an airman's calling was little less dangerous in 1918 than at any other period. Among the famous aces, von Richthofen, McCudden and Mannock were all killed during Rickenbacker's time in the air. The American's score of twenty-five "victories" was not notable alongside those of the top French, German and British fliers, but he possessed another claim upon the attention of posterity. Most of the people described in this book emerged from obscurity to gain success as warriors. If they were fortunate enough to survive combat, their fame for the balance of their lives relied solely upon their battlefield achievements. Rickenbacker was different. Success in the sky over France was only one episode in a career that proved remarkable both before and after his days as a fighter pilot. An aptitude for killing Germans in the sky above the Western Front was only one among the gifts he displayed during his picaresque existence.

He was born Edward Rickenbacher—the spelling change came much later—in 1890, in a small house owned by his father's relations on one of the less sought-after back streets of Columbus, Ohio. His parents had migrated from Switzerland as newlyweds a few years earlier, passionately imbued with the New World ideal of which their son, third among eight children, was to prove one of the more prominent success stories. Although Eddie subsequently sought to improve on his family history in the recounting of it, in truth his father was a labourer. William Ricken-bacher graduated from working for the railroad to running his own little lumber construction business. He was poor, stern, heavy, ambitious and fiercely hardworking. The Rickenbacher family's life was almost a cari-cature of the nineteenth-century migrant experience. When Eddie was three, his mother browbeat his reluctant father into moving out of the relations' place into a tiny wooden house of their own. The Rickenbach-ers eked out a subsistence income by growing vegetables and rearing pigs in the backyard. Faith in God and an absolute devotion to the United States were bred into their children from the cradle, encouraged by frequent applications of the birch. The boy Eddie, with his strong German accent, was known in school as "Dutchy" or "Kraut." Street fighting was a way of life for him.

A fully fledged entrepreneur at ten, he became a part-time news-vendor and junk trader. He was fascinated by machinery of all kinds, in an age when his generation glimpsed all manner of innovations for the first time—the automobile and dirigible prominent among them. His father said: "Eddie, you're a lucky boy to be born when you were. There are a lot of new things in the making, and you ought to be ready to have a hand in them." One day in 1904, when Eddie was thirteen, his father was eating lunch with his work gang on the site where they were laying sidewalks for a city contractor. A hungry African-American named William Gaines asked for some food, was refused, and fell into a quarrel with Rickenbacher. Gaines hit him with a spirit level, inflicting injuries which killed him a few weeks later, after he developed an abscess in his fractured skull.

Eddie was ashamed of the manner of his father's end, as well as dis-traught about it, for he later invented an elaborate fiction about how William Rickenbacher had died in an industrial accident. In any case, the family was left almost destitute. To beat child labour laws, the boy claimed to be fourteen and took a job in a glass factory. He soon moved to a steel company to escape night shifts, and then to a brewery, work-ing from 7 a.m. to 6 p.m. for six dollars a week. Then he found a billet in the machine shops of the Pennsylvania Railroad, where he discovered a sympathy with technology that would persist throughout his life. At fifteen he took a pay cut to seventy-five cents a day to work in a former bicycle repair shop which had recently taken the big decision to branch out into automobiles. He learned to drive, to strip engines and to machine parts while taking a correspondence course in mechanical engineering. Within a few months he had promoted himself to the workshops of an embryo racing-car manufacturer named the Columbus Buggy Company. He rode as mechanic in one of the first Vanderbilt Cup contests, then became a test driver and engineer on the Firestone Columbus saloon car.

At nineteen the tall, thin, earnest young man was working in Dallas as part designer, part auto salesman, earning $125 a month, which seemed like riches. He sent most of the money home to his adored mother in Columbus. One of the most brilliant engineers of his era, Lee Frayer, designed a new sports car for Firestone, and Rickenbacher persuaded its bosses to let him earn publicity for the company by entering local automobile races, which had become a public passion across the United States. He drove to victory in contests all over Nebraska and Iowa. In 1911 and 1912 he performed at the Indianapolis Speedway. This experience convinced him that he was weary of selling cars. More than anything he wanted to drive, and to compete. He quit his job, and became once more a mechanic in the workshop of the legendary designer Fred Duesenburg at the Mason Company.

Every man working on the Mason racing car believed passionately in its potential, but the business was almost bankrupt, and most of young Rickenbacher's savings were committed to it. The team approached the $10,000 Sioux City three-hundred-mile race in 1914 faced with the need to win or go bust. When the boy told his mother his troubles, she recalled an old Swiss superstition about the merits of tying a bat's heart to one's finger for luck. At Sioux City, so broke that the crew had to garage the cars under the grandstand and eat on credit at a local greasy spoon, Rickenbacher persuaded the children of a local farmer to find him a dead bat. He performed a grisly feat of mammalian surgery, and started the race next day with the bat's heart tied to his finger, convinced that he was invincible. He won. He was launched upon a career as a driver that over the three years which followed made him famous and rich. In 1916, his last year as a racing driver, he earned $60,000. He closed his career on the track by winning the big race at Ascot Park, Los Angeles.

Rickenbacher experienced his first taste of flight that October, in California. He pulled off the road one day to inspect a flying machine standing in a nearby hangar. Its owner, designer and pilot recognised him from pictures in the paper. "Hi, Eddie, I'm glad to meet you. My name is Glenn Martin. Would you like to take a ride?" Martin, whose name later became famous in American aviation, took the young racing driver for a thirty-minute flip. This fascinated and exhilarated him. He was surprised to find that in the air, he suffered no fear of height. About the same time, he came across a plane standing immobilised in a field. The pilot, poking forlornly in its engine's entrails, introduced himself as Major Dodd of the U.S. Army Signal Corps, in those days overlords of American military aviation. Dodd asked if the passer-by knew anything about engines. Rickenbacher swiftly identified an ignition fault. The coupling had slipped off the magneto. Impressed and grateful, the major lifted away into the sky.

In the winter of 1916, somewhat bizarrely, Rickenbacher travelled to England, already more than two years into world war. The British Sunbeam company wanted to enlist his assistance with its racing-car programme. The American driver's Germanic name aroused immediate suspicion among the British authorities when he landed, and they subjected him to some hours of interrogation before he was freed to check into the Savoy Hotel in London, where Sunbeam had booked him a room. When he visited the famous Brooklands racing track to test cars, Rickenbacher found himself less interested in the Sunbeam than in the Royal Flying Corps pilots who were training on the field. He met combat veterans who were serving as instructors, and thrilled to their tales. For a moment, he was seized by an urge to join the RFC and fly in France against the Germans, whom he said his father had reared him to fear and hate.

Any dilemma was resolved a few days later, in April 1917, when the United States joined the war. Rickenbacher hastened home to stake his claim to a role with the embryo U.S. forces. The young celebrity racing driver became seized by the idea of forming a unit of American auto stars to fly in an air squadron. He persuaded several colleagues and rivals to join his scheme, but unsurprisingly this met summary rejection from the U.S. Signal Corps. In May, however, an army officer who was also a racing fan suddenly called Rickenbacher with a proposition: the first elements of the American Expeditionary Force were sailing immediately for Europe. Would Rickenbacher like to come with them, initially as a driver? He accepted at once, and a month later found himself a sergeant in France, often chauffeuring the great pioneer aviator Colonel "Billy" Mitchell—and sometimes a certain Colonel Dodd, the officer whose plane he had repaired a year earlier in a California field. In the topsy-turvy world created by America's hasty mobilisation, a New York banker named James Miller, translated into a captain's uniform, met Rickenbacher in Paris one day and said that he had been appointed to command the American advanced flying school at Issoudun. He wanted the racing star as his engineering officer. Rickenbacher responded that in order to do such a job, he first needed to learn to fly. Miller discussed the matter with Mitchell, who asked Rickenbacher if he really wanted to do this. Yes, he did. He was passed medically fit by a doctor who put him down as a twenty-five-year-old. The average age of pilots in a typical RFC squadron of the period was twenty. At twenty-seven, Rickenbacher's real age, he was technically overage for flight training. A few days later he was one of a class of a dozen Americans who reported to the French aviation school at Tours.

This turn of events roused some priggish disapproval. Here was a young sportsman, singled out for special treatment by his superiors because of his glamour and celebrity. Rickenbacher had started life the hard way, but had now become a favoured child of fortune. Success had caused him to shed the precocious gravity of his adolescence in favour of an extroverted, even bombastic personality. At six feet two inches he was too tall to fit comfortably into a cockpit, but he possessed an iron will and a natural way with machinery. The skills he had demonstrated driving automobiles—courage, spatial judgement, timing, rapid reflexes— were precisely those needed to fly an aircraft. If Rickenbacher's age cost him any physical edge alongside the teenagers who dominated flight schools, this was more than compensated for by the maturity and lightning coordination of hand and eye which he had displayed on the racetrack.

Most men who fought in France either on the ground or in the air found the experience harrowing to the limits of tolerance. Rickenbacher was among the few who embraced the war as a great adventure. He approached operational flying in a spirit little different from that in which he drove his big automobile races. At flight school he flew twice as a pupil passenger in a big, clumsy Caudron powered by an engine with a rear-facing propeller and a maximum speed of eighty miles per hour—slower than the cars he had raced. Then he went solo for the first time in a difficult crosswind which caused him to zig-zag dangerously across the grass field to take off. Once airborne, however, he began to enjoy himself, and continued to do so. After seventeen days of training and a total of twenty-five hours in the air, he passed out of the Tours school as a qualified pilot and first lieutenant in the U.S. Signal Corps. He fulfilled his bargain with Captain Miller by reporting to Issoudun late in September 1917 for duty as engineering officer. Soon afterwards Miller was replaced by Captain Carl Spaatz, who would later become leader of the U.S. air forces in Europe in the Second World War. Pupils who arrived at the new flight school, which was run by American officers named Spaatz, Wiedenbach, Tittel, Spiegel and Rickenbacher, christened them "the German spies."

The big, tough, direct Swiss-American engineering officer at first found it hard to rub along with the students, most of them smart young Ivy Leaguers whose experience of life was as remote as could be imagined from his own. Among all the warring nations, pilot training attracted men from the ambitious middle class, who possessed education though seldom aristocratic connections. Blue-blooded young European officers were prone to despise the air services. They regarded oil-smeared pilots as mere garage mechanics. Sons of the British peerage almost invariably opted for smart infantry regiments rather than the Royal Flying Corps. Yet Ivy Leaguers and English public-school boys in their turn looked askance at such a man as Rickenbacher, for whom modesty and social polish had never seemed important virtues. He had to rely upon deeds, not graces, to win his young comrades' respect.

Rickenbacher gained an important advantage during his months at Issoudun, frustrating as he found them when he yearned to get to the front. In off-duty hours he was able to gain additional flying experience of a kind denied to most graduate pilots, who were immediately committed to combat. In particular he practised recovery from tailspins, manoeuvres which killed novice fliers in scores. Designers had grasped the fact that successful fighter aircraft needed to be inherently unstable, to achieve responsiveness and tight turns, yet instability rendered them lethally dangerous to inexperienced pilots. In January 1918 Rickenbacher at last persuaded Spaatz to release him from his duties as engineering officer to attend the aerial gunnery school at Cazeau, as a preliminary to becoming a fighter pilot. He found himself standing in a bobbing boat on a lake, firing with a sporting rifle at targets towed behind another boat, an experience designed to introduce airmen to the difficulties of shooting from a moving aircraft. He graduated to attacking aerial targets from a Nieuport Scout. After qualification, in March 1918 he was posted to the 94th Pursuit Squadron, one of the first all-American units to be committed to the Western Front.

The 94th was commanded by Major John Huffer, who had spent most of his life in France, and was a veteran of the Lafayette Escadrille, the American volunteer squadron which had served with the French air force. Among its pilots was the first U.S. air ace of the war, Major Raoul Lufbery, who had shot down seventeen German aircraft. The squadron was based at Villeneuve, some fifteen miles behind the front, and equipped with French Nieuport 28 single-seaters. The Nieuport was aesthetically beautiful and responsive to handle, but was vulnerable to technical failures which troubled its pilots in a year of battle dominated by the French Spad, the English Sopwith Camel and SE5a, and the German Fokker D-VII, last words in the aeronautical technology of those days. To the chagrin of Americans, in 1917–18 their own nation's industries were slow to produce indigenous weapons and aircraft. The American Expeditionary Force in France was obliged to depend for almost all its fighting equipment upon the British or the French. Matériel reached American units only as the old Allies found convenient. When Rickenbacher arrived, the 94th was still waiting for its planes to be fitted with guns. Pilots passed their time flying a few unarmed familiarisation missions over the lines in company with French aircraft. A British pilot described the first Americans he met as "a strange, rough crowd," but applauded their "wild, keen spirit." This was soon to be displayed in the air.

Rickenbacher quizzed experienced pilots exhaustively about the techniques of air fighting. Their counsel was always the same. The advantage of height was decisive. The purpose of every fighter pilot was to attack his enemy from above and behind, and if possible out of the glare of the sun. It was important to get close—a hundred yards or less—before touching the triggers. To fire prematurely merely offered a warning to the intended victim, and was unlikely to inflict fatal damage. Absolute concentration was essential both to survival and to success in attack. Camel pilot V. M. Yeates explained the art:

> We had to train our senses of smell and hearing, for the continuous sound and smell of our own engines and exhaust filled all our immediate presence to the exclusion of more distant smells and sounds, except the dull whoof of an archie [antiaircraft] burst. It was the prehearing vision that meant so much, for it was the keenness of eyesight in spotting the Hun afar that enabled his eventual attack to be prepared for and met. The chief danger was to be surprised, to be shot down before one realised that an attack was in being.

In those days before two-way radio communication, a pilot in combat was a lonely man. Command could be exercised, warnings given, only by hand signal. The scale of a battlefield measured in three dimensions was awesome. Yeates again:

> Sometimes we played hide-and-seek with the enemy in and around large cloud formations towering in an otherwise clear sky, diving into the clouds when things got too hot while the enemy would do the same. For the first few seconds coming out of a cloud one was vulnerable, being blinded by the sudden light and having to pick one's bearings. It makes me shudder to think how gaily we flew into these clouds in formations, not thinking about chances of collision...We would also fly around the outside of a cloud formation, looking for enemy patrols, not knowing what we would come upon round the next corner where there might always be an enemy formation doing the same thing.

Armed at last, the 94th Squadron flew its first combat mission—and the first of the American air contingent's war—on 14 April 1918. The Nieuports of Rickenbacher and his two companions that morning were adorned, like many fighter aircraft of the period, with a distinguishing cartoon symbol. Recalling the old American custom of challenging a foe to combat by tossing a hat in the ring, they called themselves the "Hat in the Ring" squadron. They took off in thick fog, and one aircraft almost immediately returned home with engine trouble. Rickenbacher and his remaining companion for a time lost each other, and their course. Then they were pursued by two German aircraft which were rash enough to follow them back to their field. The American mission was retrieved by luck from fiasco. Two other 94th pilots took off to intercept the intruders, and shot them down. These first victories were ballyhooed across the United States with extravagant enthusiasm. The nation was eager for war heroes, and especially for "knights of the air."

In the days that followed, Rickenbacher learned a lot very quickly. He narrowly avoided a fatal confrontation with a French Spad, which at first he mistook for a German machine. He had several escapes from disaster after getting lost. One morning he glimpsed a lone German aircraft below him, and was preparing to attack when he remembered all the warnings he had received about decoys and traps. Sure enough, above and behind him he spotted two aircraft, closing fast. After a series of desperate manoeuvres to escape their attentions he reached the sheltering safety of cloud, returned to the airfield—and discovered that his pursuers had been Americans, bemused about why he broke off his attack on the lone German.

Rickenbacher was growing impatient about his failure to engage the enemy, but recognised that he was fortunate merely to stay alive to gain experience. The majority of every ace's victims were novices. The first priority of a successful combat pilot was to survive his own novitiate. Fliers who had carried out fewer than twenty combat missions accounted for 80 per cent of casualties. Some of the foremost aces flew for months before they acquired the skills which enabled them to shoot down their first enemy aircraft. The routine of aerial combat over the Western Front in 1918 was unique to its time and place. Allied and German aircraft had been contesting roughly the same airspace for almost four years. At the outset, rival commanders believed that aircraft should be employed solely for surveillance of the armies, and disdained the concept of aerial combat. Yet circumstances drastically amended this view. By 1918, the fighter dominated war in the sky—the RFC alone possessed thirty squadrons of pursuit planes—"scouts" in the parlance of the day. Their objective was to win freedom of operation for their own side's artillery observation, reconnaissance and strafing aircraft, while denying this to the other side. Distances from airfields to the front line were short. Most pilots carried out two or three missions a day, weather permitting, hunting the sky for quarry. One morning Rickenbacher and another pilot, James Norman Hall, were despatched to look for a German two-seater which had been reported in their sector. Hall, already a published writer, would later become famous as the author of *Mutiny on the Bounty*. For a time the two pilots saw nothing. Rickenbacher lost sight of his companion, then saw that he was playing a dangerous game over the lines, stunting to taunt the enemy's antiaircraft fire. Few sensible British or French combat veterans indulged themselves in such a rash fashion. The two Americans had just recognised each other when they glimpsed, a thousand feet below them, a lone Pfalz. Rickenbacher steered a course to cut off the German from flight homewards, while Hall attacked from behind.

One pilot likened the bunching of nerves as he entered combat to a plunge into a cold bath. Some men shivered involuntarily, others sensed a distinct metabolic change as the mouth dried, and sweat broke forth even at altitude. "The concentrated violence of aerial dogfights has to be experienced to be known," wrote Cecil Lewis. The Pfalz pilot saw both Americans just as Hall opened fire, and dived for home. Rickenbacher also fired. The Pfalz tilted askew, its pilot obviously dead, and crashed behind the German front. Rickenbacher had achieved his first "victory," and returned in ecstasy with Hall to their field: "It was one of the great moments...I experienced the greatest elation of my life. I had no regrets over killing a fellow human being. I do not believe that at that moment I even considered the matter. Like nearly all air fighters...I never thought of killing an individual but of shooting down an enemy plane." In truth, he confided to his diary that he believed Hall's guns had been responsible for bringing down the Pfalz. But, by the indulgent French rules governing pilots' scores, each of the two men involved in the action was credited with an enemy aircraft. What might have been a routine experience for war-weary British, French or German pilots made headlines back in America, hungry for news of its first combat airmen. Rickenbacher had taken a step towards national fame.

A few days later, some pilots of the 94th saw their admired veteran

Raoul Lufbery die a ghastly death almost over their field, when he was worsted in combat with an Albatros. His plane caught fire—the dread of every pilot in the days when the dope painted to tauten an aircraft's canvas wing and fuselage covering was lethally inflammable. Lufbery crawled out of his cockpit and clung straddling the fuselage for a few moments before the flames drove him to jump. One of the more vexed arguments among airmen of the period concerned the respective merits of hastening death in such a fashion, or clinging to the plane's controls in the hope of making a landing before fire engulfed the cockpit. Lufbery's comrades found his body impaled on a fence, which, they agreed, indicated a mercifully quick end. Sceptics might not have shared this view.

The loss of another pilot, Hall, who force-landed behind the German lines and was taken prisoner, prompted Rickenbacher's promotion to flight commander. He was hungry for glory. Within a few weeks he had accumulated more flying hours than any of his companions, chiefly operating alone over the lines in search of victims. This was a common practice among would-be "aces" of all the combatant nations. Their commanders acquiesced in freelance activity of a kind implausible in any later conflict. Some men who flew alone achieved impressive scores, while their comrades merely accepted the missions on which they were ordered, finding these sufficiently taxing for their nerves. Rickenbacher's score of "victories" began to creep upwards, driven by his "lone-wolf" tactics. Yet by 1918 there was already a growing belief, which later became standard doctrine, that properly directed air fighting should be a matter of teamwork, in which pilots worked at least in pairs, if not in larger flights.

Very early one May morning, Rickenbacher was patrolling the lines at eighteen thousand feet with a single companion, "looking for custom." They were dizzy with the altitude and numb with cold—which also made their guns more liable than usual to jam. Momentarily Rickenbacher lost his companion. Feeling secure from antiaircraft fire at such an altitude, he crossed the lines and wandered over the old fortress city of Metz. He glimpsed a German airfield below. Three Albatroses took off from it, and began to climb towards the front. Rickenbacher followed, hoping to remain unseen until he could make an attack on the Allied side of the front. Then black puffs of German "archie" began to dot the sky, as gunners who had seen the pursuer adopted the recognised tactic to warn their own men.

Rickenbacher was two hundred yards behind the nearest Albatros when its pilot turned his head, the American seeing sun glinting on the German's goggles. Though nervous of diving too fast, which was prone to cause a Nieuport's fabric to tear off the airframe, Rickenbacher pushed his aircraft downhill at 150 miles per hour, fired for ten seconds at a range of fifty yards, and saw his rounds strike the Albatros cockpit. Then the plane spiralled earthwards out of control. Suddenly, a terrifying crash shook his own aircraft. The entire upper-wing covering had ripped away amid the slipstream force of the dive. The Nieuport began to spin. The other two Albatroses circled, firing at the American whenever they could get a shot. Rickenbacher believed his plane must shake itself to pieces. At the last moment, inspiration prompted him to open his throttle. Increased speed stabilised the aircraft, enabling him to regain control. He flew the last miles towards the American lines amid a barrage of ground fire. He nursed the staggering Nieuport into his home field alternately praying to the Almighty and talking aloud to his plane. By a quirk, the stricken Albatros flew on until it crashed in American positions, though Rickenbacher was not officially credited with its destruction until after the war.

On 12 June 1918, his fifth "victory" was formally acknowledged. He received a Croix de Guerre from the French, and became an ace, the achievement of just one in five of all Western Front fliers. To the frustration of the eager hunter, however, he spent much of June grounded with fever. He was now a famous man in his own country—by another name. One day he wrote to a friend in Detroit, signing himself "Eddie Rickenbacker." Newspapers picked this up, and reported with the exuberant jingoism of the time: "Eddie Rickenbacker has taken the Hun out of his name!" Thereafter, he never called himself anything else. Early in July he flew back from convalescent leave to his squadron's new field at Touquin in a factory-fresh Spad. This aircraft, with its high speed and ceiling of twenty-two thousand feet, thrilled him, and seemed to offer all manner of opportunities. He was exasperated when an ear infection grounded him once more. Even when an abscess had been lanced, for some weeks the ear caused him excruciating pain in the air. Enthusiasm to rejoin the battle availed nothing. Luck seemed to have deserted his quest for glory. Finally Rickenbacker was passed fit to take to the air again. Hastening into a mêlée at the head of a formation of seven Spads one morning, his guns jammed. He was obliged to manoeuvre with his flight through some minutes of fierce action, the usual tangle of aircraft wheeling and diving across the sky, impotent and at the mercy of every attacker. A British pilot, Arthur Lee, vividly described the sensations amid such a mill of competing aircraft in the sky:

> We waltzed round one another as if in a vicious, unbreakable circle. First Giles, then Begbie, then a scarlet and black Hun would rush in mad confusion, each sweeping through the stringy mass of tracer bullets, making it curl up as if in a whirlpool. The barking of the machine guns was obliterated by imminence of a terrifying collision. It was an awe-inspiring sight of hurtling machines rushing through the sky at one another which developed into a game of snap-shooting. There was no time to take aim. Try as I would, I could not bring down a single bird...Suddenly I spotted a machine commencing to smoke, then burst into flames...I recognised by the marking that it was poor old Begbie. A sudden feeling of sickness overcame me. Fascinated with horror, I momentarily forgot to fight. Poor old Begbie had to leave us without a wave of farewell. I had a final peep at him as I flew nearby. Thank God he looked as if he were dead.

At last the Americans went home, Rickenbacker nursing his frustration: "I was furious. I had nearly been killed. Even worse, I had not killed any Germans, although they had been right there in front of me. And the whole right side of my head was one blinding mass of pain." After more weeks of medical problems, in September Rickenbacker renewed his contract with fortune. Two days running, flying alone, he shot down Fokker D-VIIs, the most potent German machines of the time. To his intense pride, with a score of seven victories, he became the American "ace of aces." His tally would not have impressed German, French or British pilots, many of whom had achieved as much, but in a few weeks of operational flying Rickenbacker had shown himself one of the most skilled and ruthless pilots on the Western Front. On 24 September he was named as commanding officer of the 94th Squadron. Dismayed that another unit, the 27th, had by now achieved a higher score of victories than his own pilots, Rickenbacker threw himself into regaining the ascendancy of the 94th.

To critics of another time and place, his attitude might seem selfish and childish. The manic egotism of the "victory chasers" made it appear that a world war was being treated merely as a quest for personal glory by a handful of indulged young men. Earlier in the war, sharing this view, the leaders of the Royal Flying Corps had strongly discouraged the glamorisation of British aces, or personal publicity for their achievements. Yet the generals had eventually been obliged to bow to the inevitable, and accept that personal competitiveness should be harnessed to the war effort. If the lionisation of star fliers irked some of their comrades, there was much to be said for cherishing young men who were impatient to kill Germans and highly proficient at it. Observers noted that most aces were loners. Ball was described as friendless, McCudden as ruthless and selfish, Mannock as aggressive and unpopular until the last weeks of his short life. A comrade wrote of the Canadian Billy Bishop: "There was something about him that left one feeling that he preferred to live as he fought, in a rather hard, brittle world of his own." This is a telling comment, which might be applied to many eager warriors. Although there is no such personal testimony about Rickenbacker, it is hard to believe that he was much different. Most young men in war are more readily motivated by a comprehensible and immediate personal objective than by appeals to great and remote national purposes. Without exception, the First World War aces shared Rickenbacker's fierce competitiveness. Billy Bishop recorded his sentiments at one moment in 1917:

> I began to feel that my list of victims was not climbing as steadily as I would have liked. Captain Ball was back from his winter rest in England and was adding constantly to his already big score. I felt I had to keep going to be second to him so I was over the enemy line from six to seven hours daily, praying for some easy victims to appear. I had had some pretty hard fighting. Now I wanted to shoot a rabbit or two.

Not much knight-of-the-air spirit is discernible there. On Rickenbacker's appointment to command, he summoned a meeting of his nineteen fliers at which he told them that henceforward he cared nothing about whether they saluted each other or observed other military formalities, but that they would abstain from alcohol every night before they were to operate, and must work much harder at nursing their engines. Failures were provoking a crippling unserviceability rate. The average American machine required a major overhaul for every fourteen hours airborne, while Rickenbacker was achieving a hundred hours for his own Spad. He concluded with a shamelessly patriotic appeal, of a kind that in some units would have evoked a cynical response: "Give your best for America, for the Allied cause and for the greatest squadron ever to take wing, the 94th." He wrote in his diary that night: "Just been promoted to command...I shall never ask a pilot to go on any mission I won't go on. I must work now harder than I did before." He underlined the last sentence, in the spirit of a student facing exams. Beneath Rickenbacker's superficial bonhomie, there was steely self-discipline.

Even as a squadron commander, Rickenbacker persisted with solo missions, often spending six or seven hours a day in the air. It was personal performance that overwhelmingly preoccupied him. The morning after his appointment, before breakfast he shot down a Fokker guarding two reconnaissance planes, and then one of the latter, an LVG. Back on the ground, he drove to the forward area to gain written confirmation from the local French commander of his "victories," a day's work for which he was later awarded the Congressional Medal of Honor. Next morning, 25 September, while his squadron was balloon-busting he destroyed another Fokker, although his own plane was almost shot to pieces in the process. The following day, a ground machine-gunner riddled the airframe around his cockpit, while leaving him unscathed. At such moments, luck was the sole factor in determining that Rickenbacker survived while so many others died. The evidence suggests that whatever physical toll combat flying imposed upon him, he bore the mental strain with little difficulty. He shared Bishop's view: "To me, it was not a business or profession but just a wonderful game. To bring down a machine did not seem to me like killing a man but more as if I was just destroying a mechanical target with no human being in it at all."

One of Rickenbacker's kills in those days, a Hanover bomber, glided down to a perfect landing two miles inside the Allied lines with a dead pilot at the controls. Rickenbacker had the aircraft hauled back to the 94th's field, a spectacular example of the mania for trophy-gathering among fighter pilots. Some would hang a dead German's boot on the mess wall if nothing larger and less pitiful was available. In the same dogfight, Rickenbacker shot down a Fokker and a third German aircraft which fell so far behind enemy lines that it was never confirmed, to the American's fury. By now it was plain to every combatant that the balance of advantage on the battlefield had swung dramatically in favour of the Allies, whose final triumph must soon be at hand. Rickenbacker wrote gleefully that his 94th Squadron had "pulled out well ahead of the 27th" in victories, "and after that our lead was never threatened." A manic urgency crept into his own performance, as he sought to amass the highest possible personal score before the end came.

One day while alone he was attacked by four Fokkers, of which he shot down two. During October 1918 he achieved 14 victories, and he ended the month—and the war—with an acknowledged grand total of 25. This represented a substantial proportion of his entire squadron's wartime total of 69 enemy aircraft destroyed, and was characteristic of air combat. Only a handful of fliers possessed the nerve and proficiency as marksmen to score. In the RFC's crack 56 Squadron, just two pilots were responsible for 94 of the unit's total wartime bag of 427, and ten men accounted for 246 enemy aircraft. On 11 November, Armistice Day, Rickenbacker calculated that he had taken part in a total of 134 air fights, though it seems more credible that this figure represents the total of combat missions he flew. When news came that the war was over, the "Hat in the Ring" squadron celebrated as exuberantly as any. One pilot displayed the triumph of his own ambitions, far more modest than those of Rickenbacker, by dancing round and round the unit's bonfire chanting happily: "I've lived through the war, I've lived through the war!" Their commander chose to spend the exact moment of the Armistice, the eleventh hour of the eleventh day of the eleventh month, flying alone over the front in defiance of orders which grounded all combat aircraft.

Rickenbacker, an authentic American hero, was swiftly conveyed home in January 1919 to assist in publicising a Liberty Bond drive. It is worth quoting the speech made by the U.S. secretary of war, Newton D. Baker, at one of the pilot's appearances, at the Waldorf Astoria Hotel in New York on 3 February 1919. "Captain Rickenbacker," said Baker, "is one of the real crusaders of America—one of the truest knights our country has ever known. He will find his greatest delight, when the evening of his life comes, in looking back on his experiences. He will never forget the thrill of combat in the clouds where it was his life or his adversary's. He will always know this thrill, even when he awakes from his deepest sleep. But his life will always be gladdened as he looks about him and sees men and women and children walking about free and unafraid and when he thinks that he has given his best and ventured his own life to bring this about."

Emotional civilians often lavish such sentiments upon uniformed men in the dark days of war, and amid the lingering gratitude which follows peace. There is truth in the words, insofar as victory would be unattainable without determined warriors like Eddie Rickenbacker. But the contrast is no less striking because it is a cliché, between the lofty phrases of the U.S. secretary of war and Eddie Rickenbacker's personal lust for glory. He was a great air fighter, but there was nothing selfless about his deeds, and nor did he ever claim that there was.

Rickenbacker's is one of the few biographies in this book to have a happy ending. He translated his wartime glamour and fame into a career as a businessman in which he made, lost and remade several fortunes. Only the coming of Charles Lindbergh eclipsed his celebrity as a flier. He became a prime mover in the growth of Eastern Airlines, and eventually the company's chairman. For a time he owned the Indianapolis Speedway. He married a wealthy divorcée named Adelaide whom he had met in California before the war. They adopted two sons, and remained a devoted couple for the balance of their long lives. Luck never deserted him. On 26 February 1941 he was a passenger on a scheduled Eastern Airlines DC-3 which crashed and somersaulted while approaching a landing at Atlanta, Georgia. Half the passengers and crew were killed. Rickenbacker himself almost died from appalling injuries, yet eventually made a full recovery. During World War II he carried out several inspection missions for the U.S. government and USAAF. On one of these, in October 1942, the B-17 in which he was a passenger became lost, and ditched in the Pacific. At the age of fifty-two, while others perished, he endured twenty-two days in a dinghy before being located and rescued by the U.S. Navy. He had lost fifty-four pounds.

His reputation was somewhat marred by political follies. Always a conservative, he became a violent opponent of Roosevelt's New Deal, and like Lindbergh a shameless isolationist in the approach to World

War II. In his last years he was also accused of racism for his public hostility to the Civil Rights movement. The moral, of course, is that men of action should not diminish themselves by political interventions. Sensible citizens take no heed of the philosophising of warriors, which is almost invariably ill-judged. Rickenbacker lingered too long at the helm of Eastern Airlines. He was eventually removed from its controls, most unwillingly, in 1963. He died at the age of eighty-three in 1973, full of honours, and has been the subject of several eulogistic studies, none more flattering to his memory than his own autobiography, published in 1968.

Yet for all the flights of fantasy in the accounts of his own life to which he put his name, there was nothing phoney about Eddie Rickenbacker. His achievements—the struggle out of poverty, the development of exceptional mechanical skills, success as racing driver, flying ace and then commercial aviation pioneer—were wholly real. He embraced war and fame with an ardour from which some men recoiled. It was his good fortune that his experience of combat lasted long enough to make his name, but ended before he fell victim to the most probable fate of any fighter pilot. Of the foremost aces, only the Canadian Billy Bishop and the German Ernst Udet—whose respective scores of seventy-two and sixty-two victories dwarfed that of Rickenbacker—survived the war. Posterity has a better understanding than the 1918 civilian world of the ruthless qualities which alone enabled a man to prosper in action above the Western Front. Rickenbacker was unusual among his kind for displaying skills which enabled him to prosper in peace as well as war. His life represented a triumph for the American dream which other nations, and other warriors, might justly envy.

CHAPTER NINE

AN INDIAN ODYSSEY

IN THE ANNALS of British military experience, for two and a half centuries India occupied a towering place. A host of famous soldiers served and fought there, from Robert Clive and the Duke of Wellington to Winston Churchill and Bill Slim. The Indian army, led by British officers immensely proud of their caste, dominated the raj legend. Generations of young imperialists grew up as familiar with Sikhs, Rajputs, Dogras and above all Gurkhas fighting under the Union flag as with the Grenadier Guards or Rifle Brigade.

John Masters represented the fifth generation of his family, and also the last, to serve in India. His own military career was notably colourful, but Masters's lasting achievement was to preserve it for posterity in a succession of books which became an elegy for Britain's experience in the subcontinent, and for the old Indian army. He joined its ranks as a twenty-year-old subaltern in 1935, served on and off the North-West Frontier until 1939, and afterwards commanded a brigade in one of the bloodiest and most painful nonsenses of the Second World War—the Chindit operation against the Japanese in Burma—all before he was thirty. His intelligence earned him respect. His ruthlessness and ready tongue made him enemies. He was always richly endowed with prickles, sharpened by malicious mess gossip that he was not really British but an Anglo-Indian, possessed of that gravest of all social embarrassments of the period, "a touch of the tarbrush." That he was anyway an outsider, quite unlike the run of professional soldiers of his day, was plain to all.

In his mid-thirties, Masters abandoned his military career. He moved to the United States, became a successful novelist and took up American citizenship. His most lasting memorial is his loving, exuberant memoir of service with the Gurkha Rifles, *Bugles and a Tiger* (1955), which ranks among the finest of all warriors' rhapsodies.

He was born in Calcutta in 1914, son of an Indian army colonel, and lived in the subcontinent until he was seven. By the time he went to Wellington College, and thence somewhat unenthusiastically to the army, his father was eking out an impoverished retirement. Young Jack's sensitivities were increased by consciousness of his own poverty and, in those class-conscious days, of his mother's Yorkshire accent and pedigree as a shopkeeper's daughter. At Sandhurst, the quick-witted young man prospered academically but not socially: "I knew what unpopularity was…I am good and bad, pleasant and unpleasant. The trouble in my case seemed to be that people first discovered all the good and then a little later, all the bad." Shrewd, ambitious, iconoclastic, sexually precocious and intolerant of fools, it was plain to his comrades that Jack Masters was interesting and clever, but he seemed to possess few of the qualities of a gentleman, as defined by professional soldiers of his generation. He, in his turn, found the Royal Military Academy a harsh, brutal place, though he acknowledged its virtues in training cadets to live with each other, and to fit themselves for war. Returning to India in October 1934, he was first posted to spend a year learning his business with the Duke of Cornwall's Light Infantry, one of the British army's forty-eight battalions stationed in the subcontinent. Then he went to the Gurkhas.

Like every regiment, the Prince of Wales's Own 4th Gurkha Rifles vetted every officer intended for its ranks, inviting the candidate to spend a ten-day leave at its home, the remote red-roofed Himalayan hill station of Bakloh. An American girl visiting the area a few years earlier had enquired who lived on this bleak summit. Told that it was the 4th Gurkhas, she demanded in horror: "What have *they* done?" Yet soldiers loved the place. Brash young Masters thought himself lucky that his own visit coincided with a sudden unit deployment to Lahore to deal with local riots, a situation in which he acquitted himself more creditably than he might have done in the mess: "I loved parties and I was wildly excited at the idea of joining this regiment. I was just getting teed up to

shine with an erratic brilliance my years were incapable of controlling."
Instead, able to display a cool head and willing heart amid the rocks and
bottles of Lahore, he was spared social disaster. In the winter of 1935 he
joined the lonely little community of British Gurkha officers at Bakloh,
blessed with names and nicknames that were to become intimately
familiar to him: James and John, Beetle, Midge and Moke, Bullet and
Boy, each one bearing the brand of his calling, the white impression of a
chinstrap on a deeply sunburnt head. He took up residence in the bach-
elors' bungalow, "the Rabbit Warren," and met his elderly Gurkha bearer
Biniram Thapa, who had charged the Prussian Guard with the bayonet
in Flanders in 1914. Masters wrote with deep emotion twenty years afterwards: "I had come to my home."

He spent the months that followed learning the language and ways of
the soldiers whom he was destined to command. The British had been
recruiting Nepalese tribesmen to their service since 1815, having discovered their remarkable martial virtues on punitive expeditions into their
native mountains abutting the Indian Empire. Gurkhas had become the
most esteemed soldiers in Britain's Indian army, above all since their
loyal service in the 1857 Mutiny. Generation after generation of British
officers who commanded Gurkha troops fell in love with them. Masters
himself wrote: "The distinguishing marks of the Gurkha are usually a
Mongolian appearance, short stature, a merry disposition, and an inde-
finable quality that is hard to pin down with one word. Straightness, honesty, naturalness, loyalty, courage—all these are near it, but none is quite
right, for the quality embraces all these. In a Gurkha regiment nothing
was ever stolen. Desertions were unheard of ... There were no intrigue,
no apple-polishing, and no servility." When the implacable mask of a
Gurkha face cracked into laughter, it came rich and strong, and often in
the most unpromising situations. Yet Masters also noted the Gurkha's
imperfections. He was slow to learn, resistant to innovation, naturally
unkempt in his own home, vulnerable to gambling, rum and women. He
then dismissed his own generalisations, for "the Gurkhas have the same-
ness and the uniqueness of a snowfield."

The young lieutenant learned the legends of Gurkha hardiness and
loyalty, the history of their regiments through wars innumerable, the
tales of heads severed with the kukri, of fortresses stormed or saved by
Gurkha courage. He perceived the infinite superiority of his own 4th

over lesser breeds such as the 1st, 2nd, 3rd and 5th. He was ceremonially "dined into" the regiment at a mess guest night, and then took command of the 120 men of A Company. At night he studied Gurkhali with a head clerk who read from a book of his people's fairy tales. Masters felt himself to be living in a world "where these gods and legends were as real as the unshaven topknot on the bugler's head."

On exercise in the cold season, the battalion marched for weeks from campsite to campsite, led by its pipe band and the colonel on a charger, baggage borne by a great train of camels, the dust of India thick upon the road and the trees. "We marched in the removed trance of the professional infantryman, our minds miles away from this business of moving, but linked to one another by unseen cords, the rhythm of the step, the sound of the bugles." Each afternoon around three they made camp. While the soldiers sang around their fires, officers wandered away to shoot snipe in the marshes. For a long time, both with officers and men, Masters felt himself to be among them, but not yet of them. In the mess, his British counterparts were irked by the fact that he talked too much and pontificated too often. With his company, Masters found that even when he had mastered Gurkhali, the men were slow to accept a new officer. He had been making jokes to his riflemen for two years before, at last, these provoked their laughter. Only then could he consider himself a full member of what he was proud to regard as his family.

Few writers have better expressed the ideal of the regiment, spiritual core of the British and Indian armies. "A small ideal," Masters called it, "because humanity cannot encompass a larger one... The spirit of the regiment took little heed of efficiency, discipline, or even loyalty. It had been built by generations of men... who all came to realise their continentality, one with the others, with those who had gone and those who had not yet come. It was for this spirit that we drilled together, got drunk together, hunted, danced, played, killed and saved life together. It was from this spirit that no man was alone, neither on the field of battle, which is a lonely place, nor in the chasm of death, nor in the dark places of life."

The supreme romantic experience of Indian service was action on the North-West Frontier against the Pathan tribesmen whose spasms of disorder provoked British retribution. Though Masters had never heard a shot fired in anger, he had gained experience of the harshness of the frontier, its extremes of weather and terrain, the regime of alternating boredom in barracks and peril in the hills, during his time with the Duke of Cornwall's. In the spring of 1937 he received a baptism of fire. The 4th Gurkhas were posted for service in Waziristan, where a local mullah, the Fakir of Ipi, was making trouble. One of the Fakir's people had abducted a Hindu girl, forcibly converted her to Islam, and refused demands for her return. The Fakir and his followers embarked upon a guerrilla campaign against the British, who were determined to rescue the girl and quash the mullah's pretensions. Masters's battalion found itself deployed amid the force hunting down the miscreants.

It was a war of skirmishes and ambushes. British columns marched stolidly through the mountain passes. Platoons panted up stony cliff faces to picket high ground. Mule batteries clattered through defiles in support. Bearers erected tents and messes protected by stone sangars wherever a battalion halted long enough to justify the labour. In those days before effective tactical radio, units communicated by heliograph mirror signals. War on the frontier was considered a nursery school for junior leaders, who found themselves thrust into hilltop scuffles in which the price of carelessness was death. It was a dirty conflict, with booby-trapped munitions being abandoned to maim careless Pathan hands. A soldier wounded and caught by the enemy was doomed to mutilation and death, perhaps at the hands of their women. Lumbering biplanes bombed recalcitrant villages without much diminishing the hostility of their inhabitants. The tribesmen hung on the heels of British columns, appearing over a summit to snap-shoot at a withdrawing picket, to strike at a carrying party or pick off an unwary scout.

For a soldier, the frontier offered an apprenticeship in war with only a fraction of the perils of the real thing. A Pathan with a rifle could kill a man surely enough, but he lacked the larger instruments of the modern orchestra of armies—machine guns, artillery, mines, mortars, aircraft. For the 4th Gurkhas and their kind, the experience offered the charms of big-game hunting: excitement and a modicum of risk, allied to an opportunity to exercise under fire. The frontier fittened and hardened all those deployed against the Fakir of Ipi, as it fittened and hardened Jack Masters. In his first months based at Miranshah, his unit suffered merely a few sniping incidents, and saw an aged Wapiti bomber blow up on the airstrip when it crashed on takeoff.

Then at dawn one morning, occupying a hilltop with his company, across the valley through his field glasses Masters glimpsed for the first time an enemy: a band of armed tribesmen moving along a riverbank, oblivious of the Gurkha presence. He gave the order to fire. His colonel later reproached him for failing to let the tribesmen close the range, but Masters's Gurkhas despatched eight among a party of twenty-seven Pathans. In the weeks that followed, the unit scoured the hills under spasmodic sniper fire. Jack wrote to his younger brother Alex, an officer with the 1st Gurkhas: "We've been shot at for twenty-three days continuously, and we had lice and worked nineteen hours a day for five days and I want a rest. One of these days I suppose they'll open leave, and then I'm off like shit from a duck." He experienced two months in the field before being posted back to Bakloh to command the regimental depot.

This was a lonely life in the absence of his battalion, with few other officers in the mess to provide social solace, and a host of unexpected responsibilities for a twenty-three-year-old lieutenant. He had to supervise the recruit intake, Gurkha wives, the administration of the rag-tag of men who staffed the depot. In his off-duty hours Masters read avidly, just as Winston Churchill had done during his days in India with the 4th Hussars forty years earlier: big, challenging books he had resisted in younger days—Gibbon, Machiavelli, Hakluyt's *Voyages*. An assertive womaniser since adolescence, Masters once fled Bakloh in quest of sexual release, which required a 140-mile pilgrimage to Lahore and cost him a painful encounter with venereal disease. He composed his first literary essay during those months, a forty-eight-page pamphlet in Gurkhali on the care of children, with an appendix about running a household. Here was a strange enough task for a warrior, but a not uncommon one for an officer of the Indian army, for whom benign paternalism was indispensable.

The highlight of Masters's Bakloh experience came one day in February 1938, when the depot was thrown into consternation by the almost unprecedented appearance, in scrub below the barracks squash court, of a tiger. The young officer seized a rifle and mustered a party of beaters, who set off to rouse the beast. They achieved swift and terrifying success. Suddenly, the great animal sprang from a tree at a Gurkha NCO, tearing open his face before bounding away. Masters, not a notable shot, succeeded only in putting a bullet through its forepaw before it disappeared back into cover. With an excited crowd of Gurkhas in attendance, the young officer followed the trail. He was lucky. He glimpsed the black and gold shape amid thick scrub, and dropped it dead with a round in the head before it could attack again. Amid riotous celebrations the carcass was slung on poles, carried to the mess and laid out in the guest room, while the triumphant hunter played "Tiger Rag" on the gramophone. He wrote an article about his experience which was published in *The Field* magazine in England, and found himself possessed of a stature among the Gurkhas which might otherwise have taken several campaigns to attain. Indeed, the most important achievement of his time at Bakloh was that it cemented his bond with the men whom he commanded, his love for an institution to which he felt that he could belong as he had never belonged before.

Masters spent much of his 1938 long leave travelling in the United States, a country for which he had already forged a long-range passion through his taste for its jazz and literature, and a subscription to the *New Yorker*. His months there proved among the happiest of his youth. He embraced everything about America—its sports, natural beauty, easy manners and an exuberance which matched his own zest for life. It was a paradox that Masters still cherished a romantic imperialism, a belief in Britain's destiny in India, while his imaginative and impulsive nature caused him to spend a lifetime pursuing new sensations. Such an outlook made him an unlikely inhabitant of an Indian army mess, where tradition and convention ruled. Senior officers respected Masters's brains and professional competence, but recoiled from his taste in music and mistrusted his curious enthusiasm for the society of women.

He returned to India via England and Paris in June 1939, after many new experiences and brief love affairs. His regiment had moved to Loralai, 120 miles east of Quetta, in Baluchistan. He was appointed the battalion's adjutant, a key administrative role which he enjoyed in all respects save the necessity to accompany the colonel onto the parade ground astride a charger. Ever since Sandhurst, Masters had nursed a keen dislike of horses. He was still at Loralai when the Second World War began. Like every professional soldier he was eager to play his part, and he was much frustrated when great events unfolded in Europe while the 4th Gurkhas languished, waiting for the call. To Masters's dismay, a new colonel assumed command who had disliked him since they met on the frontier in 1937: "Weallens kept persecuting me, as he thought I was a shit and kept needling me in order that I might cease to be a shit." Yet after this inauspicious start, the two men found themselves working surprisingly well together, though their idleness amid global conflict persisted. They felt "like firemen trying to find our shoes and socks while the alarm jangled ever louder and more hysterical in our ears." By a characteristic irony of war, the first member of the Masters family to suffer death at the enemy's hands was Jack's cousin Marjorie, killed with her fighter pilot fiancé by a Luftwaffe bomb as she danced at London's Café de Paris.

His own first battle experience was deferred until the spring of 1941, when the 2nd Battalion of the 4th Gurkhas Regiment landed in Iraq with 8th Indian Division and fought their way across the country amid desultory opposition. They were then launched against the Vichy French in Syria, an ugly little campaign. Masters much enjoyed watching his beloved Gurkhas in action, displaying the dogged resolution which the British always revered in them. He recorded the spectacle of two Bren-gunners amid a French strafing attack:

> The fighters screamed down on them—CRRRRRUMP. The bren began to fire back. I began to cry with pride. The earth boiled round and behind the two men, both nineteen years old, and they stood there, completely in the open, upright, and always sending that thin stream of fire back at the multi-gun monsters. This was what we were fighting with, and, by God, this was what we were fighting for, too—survival, and self respect, a refusal to be terrified by sheer force. The attacks continued for five minutes, and the last plane climbed away very slowly, black smoke pouring from its engine nacelle. Riflemen Deba and Ghanbahadur picked up the gun and tripod and marched on to their new position.

In February 1942, while the 2/4th Gurkhas departed for the war in the Western Desert, Masters was posted to the Indian Army Staff College amid the snow-clad mountains of Quetta, a vital preliminary to promotion. At twenty-eight, he was among the youngest of the ninety students on his course, a mark of professional promise. He threw himself into the energetic social life of the place, full of lonely wives, army nurses and daughters short of partners. On two counts Quetta proved a turning point for Masters. He fell in love with the wife of a brother Gurkha officer, Hugh Rose, with a passion that dominated his emotional life through the years which followed, and that enhanced his reputation as a cad. Second, he passed out of the staff college at the top of his course, and was posted as brigade-major of the 114th Indian Infantry Brigade, training in north-west India for the jungle campaign against the Japanese. His first thrill was to meet his new orderly—a rifleman of the 4/5th Gurkhas. As Daljit Thapa presented himself at attention before the young major, Masters felt that he wanted to embrace the man: "I had been too long away from him and his peerless like." Daljit served with Masters through many months that followed, and their mutual regard did not diminish with experience. Later, he portrayed the young Gurkha as a character in one of his novels.

In April 1943, just as the brigade was about to be committed to action in the Arakan offensive in Burma, to the fury of his brigade commander Masters was abruptly transferred to a new posting. Brigadier Joe Lentaigne had requested his services at 111th Indian Brigade, for a mission shrouded in secrecy and granted carte blanche for personnel and resources by Churchill himself. It was, apparently, "something about long-range penetration." Masters found himself committed to join one of the most famous—or to some, notorious—"private armies" of the war, the "Chindits," named for Burma's temple guardians and led by Orde Wingate.

In the early years after Dunkirk, when the British were unable effectively to challenge the main armies of the Axis, they encouraged or tolerated an extraordinary range of small striking forces, dominated by the personalities of their local leaders. These units achieved much publicity, irritated the enemy, delighted Winston Churchill, and contributed something to the morale of the British people, who might otherwise have despaired of victory. They included army and Royal Marine commandos, the Special Air Service, the Special Boat Service, Popski's Private Army, the Long Range Desert Group—and the Chindits. Their common function was to conduct raids behind enemy lines. In February 1943, three thousand Chindits had fought their way into Burma, cut the Mandalay-Myitkyina Railway in several places, and eventually returned to the British lines with the loss of a third of their strength. The ordeals which they had endured became a legend. Their exploits also provided a precious boost to a demoralised army in India, which had begun to doubt that British troops could ever engage the Japanese with conviction in the jungles of Asia.

Churchill thrilled to the Chindits' achievement. For a time he wished to appoint Wingate, their begetter and leader, commander of the entire British army on the Burma front. Dissuaded from this absurdity— Wingate was a wildly unstable personality, a mystic teetering on the edge of derangement—the prime minister nonetheless determined to support his new protégé in another dramatic venture behind the enemy's line, this time on a much larger scale. Here was the seed of many follies involving "private armies." The outcome of the war now hinged upon decisive battles fought by great hosts, Russian, American, British and German. Raids had become irrelevant. They represented, indeed, a rash diversion of resources from the main battlefields. It proved misguided to transform small guerrilla bodies into large forces.

Wingate, like the American "Vinegar Joe" Stilwell, who operated from China into Burma, was a powerful personality in whose makeup there was much of the charlatan. He decreed, for instance, that since normal military punishment was unenforceable in the jungle, Chindit malefactors would be flogged. This was occasionally done. The prime minister's extravagant personal support inspired in the Chindit leader a megalomania which persisted until his death. Wingate was now committed to lead into Burma a force of six brigades, more than twenty thousand men. As Stilwell pushed south into Burma with three halfhearted Chinese divisions and an American raiding force—"Merrill's Marauders"— the Chindits were tasked to dislocate the Japanese rear. Wingate set out to create and fortify a series of bases far behind the Japanese lines, supplied entirely from the air, then to sally forth from these and attack the enemy's supply lines. Joe Lentaigne was to command one such brigade, composed of Gurkhas, British infantry and several hundred mules. An Irishman, himself a former officer of the 4th Gurkhas, Lentaigne had known and admired Jack Masters since they met on the North-West Frontier. Masters found himself committed to a prominent role in the new Chindit operation, though from the outset both he and Lentaigne were uneasy about Wingate and his grandiose plan.

At the 111th Brigade, the new brigade-major inspired the same mixed sentiments that followed him through his army career. His energy and cleverness impressed his fellow officers. However, his egotism and relentless sexual banter irked them. During the force's long training in the jungle, Masters's attentions were distracted by his personal affairs, which had become tortuous. Barbara Rose, his lover, was pregnant, but her husband had not yet agreed to a divorce, and thus the new baby might not legally be Masters's. She had found a job with the Women's Army Auxiliary Corps in Quetta while tending two small children by her husband. As Masters prepared his brigade for battle, he knew that if he should die—which many people did, in Wingate's campaigns— Barbara would be left in an unenviable position.

On the night of 8 March 1944, the vanguard of the IIIth Brigade took off for Burma. Masters wrote: "I felt strong and alert. The long months of learning, of training and working towards an end, were over." He tucked a copy of Milton's *Paradise Lost* into his haversack among code-books, maps and message pads, then set off for the airfield in the gathering gloom. They landed by glider 150 miles behind the Japanese front in Burma at Chowringhee and "Broadway," two of a dozen designated landing sites for Wingate's little army. Over the three nights that followed, six hundred glider sorties brought in the rest of Lentaigne's men almost without loss, a remarkable achievement. Some other brigades suffered disastrously from crashes and aircraft lost in the jungle. "Our first task is fulfilled," Wingate exulted to his men. "All our columns are inserted in the enemy's guts. This is a moment to live in history." Masters's column set out to cover 130 miles from Chowringhee through dense jungle, their supplies carried by mule, to rendezvous with the rest of the brigade at Broadway. This phase of the operation was remarkably successful. The Japanese were unaware of what was happening. Supplies and mail were dropped by air every five days, so Masters learned at regular intervals of the progress of his new daughter, Susan.

Then things began to go wrong. They suffered a nightmare crossing of the Irrawaddy river, where many air-landed boats and outboard motors proved unserviceable. It proved necessary to divide the column, and to abandon much equipment and many heavy weapons. On 24 March, exhausted by the jungle march and its difficulties, Lentaigne, Masters and their men reached the Broadway rendezvous. That very night, however, startling news came. Orde Wingate had been killed in an air crash. Lentaigne—"the only one [of Wingate's officers] who was not mad," in the laconic opinion of General William Slim, the army commander—was appointed to overall leadership of the Chindits. To Masters's astonishment, though he was a mere major, Lentaigne placed him in command of the operations of the 111th Brigade. One of Masters's staff, Richard Rhodes James, wrote of his comrades' reactions: "The less charitable murmured: 'That's a gong for him,' while others said: 'I wonder if he'll be able to make it.'" Rhodes James observed that "with Wingate's death, our great hopes of the future disappeared. The sense of intoxication we had experienced while waiting to fly in was gone, and in its place was a resignation to do some rather ordinary and pointless soldiering."

To avoid embarrassing the unit's COs, who were lieutenant-colonels, Masters removed his own badges of rank. For the rest of the bloody business on which they now embarked he ranked himself simply as "the brigade commander." Curiously enough, though Masters was a vastly more rational personality than Wingate, some men detected the same spirit in him. During their jungle march Masters often read the Bible aloud to them, though not himself a believer. He sought to inspire the soldiers with his own fierce fighting spirit, just as the Chindits' creator would have done. They responded by christening him "Chota Wingate"— "little Wingate." Ordinary soldiers liked his coarse wit, as their officers did not. They also admired his lack of class or rank condescension.

Under Masters's command the column resumed a march northwards, skirmishing intermittently with the Japanese and destroying a big enemy supply dump which they encountered. One night, on impulse, to boost morale their commander decided to break the rules of operational silence and the ban on firelighting. He let his men shout, sing, relax, share a tot of rum apiece, while he strolled easily among them cracking jokes. It was a wise gamble. The enemy were too distant to interfere, and next day the column set off with renewed eagerness. Suddenly, new orders came. Stilwell was attacking the town of Mogaung, in the north of Burma. With Wingate's death, the American reached out to assume direct authority over Chindit operations. Everything was to be subordinated to Stilwell's Mogaung assault. Masters was instructed to establish a base at a new site twenty miles from the town, from which he could harass Japanese supply routes. He was dismayed: this location would be dangerously close to the main Japanese army. The Chindits would be challenging far stronger enemy forces than they were equipped to handle. Against Japanese troops with artillery support their prospects of survival would be slender, even by the standards set by Wingate. But this was their mission, and they set forth to accomplish it.

Masters marched along the Meza River with his headquarters, a battalion of the King's Own, and the 3/4th Gurkhas. As they approached their appointed location he left the Gurkhas to guard the rear, together with many of the column's mules, which could only become hapless targets in action. He sent his senior RAF officer, disguised as a Burmese villager, to reconnoitre ten miles forward, where the force would establish its designated "stronghold," and to choose an airfield site. Finding the coast clear, Masters signalled his troops forward. The position was code-named "Blackpool." Next day, gliders began to bring in bulldozers, wire and supplies. It was a messy business. American pilots displayed extraordinary courage and skill, but there were crashes, failures, losses of equipment. Masters himself watched one fatal glider pile-up: "I shall not forget the sudden lurch in my own stomach, and the bitten-off cry I gave as the tail went up and the nose straight down."

His column had already been in Burma forty-five days, and the men were tired even before they had accomplished anything significant, or suffered their first serious encounter with the Japanese. Officers became increasingly conscious that their long jungle training had wearied the soldiers even before they embarked on this operation. Worse, Wingate had explicitly promised that they would have to operate only for ninety days before being withdrawn. This "ninety-day contract" created a fatal mind-set among soldiers who, in reality, would find much more being asked of them. Stilwell cared nothing for Wingate's earlier assurances. Facing immense difficulties with his Chinese forces, he needed far more assistance from the British than they were fit to give.

The first enemy attacks, on the Chindits' second night at Blackpool, were pressed with much determination but no success. In the morning, Japanese dead lay strewn around the perimeter. Thereafter, shellfire began to harry the British position day and night. Again and again Japanese infantry threw themselves forward, sometimes gaining ground which had to be recaptured at painful cost. Attrition eroded the Chindit strength, and especially that of the King's Own battalion, which bore the brunt of the action. Men could take cover, but mules could not. Masters was as grieved as anyone by the sight of the hapless animals torn and bleeding around the positions. One in particular, Maggie, had become a favourite of brigade headquarters. It distressed them acutely when she was mangled by shrapnel, and stood in patient passivity until a soldier put her out of her misery. American aircraft provided superb close air support, but the burden of air-landing mortar and field artillery ammunition in quantities to sustain the Chindit defence proved first acute, then unsustainable.

Crisis came when the monsoon broke. Air resupply faltered. Heavy rain not only soaked men and filled trenches, but made the landing strip unusable for casualty evacuation. Masters's men became dependent upon parachuted supplies. Efforts to do the job for which they had been sent, to cut the railway to Mogaung, petered out. Every man was needed to guard the perimeter. Wingate's rash, extravagant plan had collapsed. Instead of exploiting mobility to harass the Japanese rear areas with small bodies of men, everywhere in the region Chindit units too big to hide were struggling to hold their own in static positions against superior Japanese forces. Some performed well, others did not. Wingate's "private army" had become much too large to be considered an elite, except in the degree of its sufferings.

This was the finest hour of Masters's career as a soldier. He showed himself an outstanding commander: clear, decisive, forceful, inspiring—and personally brave. Though he was never in doubt about the folly of the deployment to which his men had been committed, he fought his big battle with outstanding professionalism. Privately he railed against the predicament in which his superiors had placed the brigade, and their failure to provide adequate support. But in front of his men, his resolution never faltered. A fellow Chindit noted with admiration Masters's "complete confidence...he seemed to be on top of the world, thoroughly enjoying himself and ready to cope with anything." When it became plain that the King's Own were shattered, Masters sent forward the Cameronians to relieve them. He was shocked by the condition of the men pulling back, "their eyes wandered, their mouths drooped open...I wanted to cry, but dared not."

Two reinforcement battalions arrived, one of the Gurkhas and one of the King's. A newly arrived young British soldier was startled to be vis-

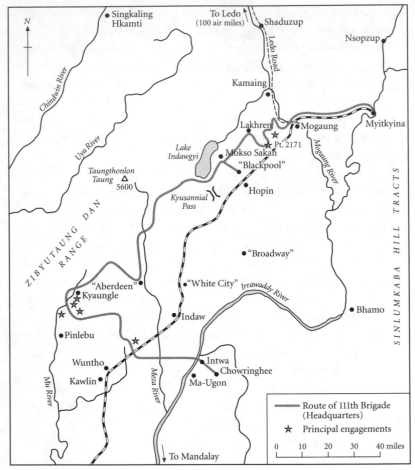

John Masters's Burma campaign with the Chindits, 1944.

ited in his position by "a rather gaunt looking individual, unkempt in appearance, with a minimum of clothing, but armed with carbine, revolver and grenades." Who was this shirtless, apparently rankless desperado, he asked. "Masters," answered his officer succinctly. The soldier was unimpressed by his new commander. There were critics at Blackpool who suggested both then and later that for all his showmanship, Masters commanded too much from his brigade headquarters, and not enough from the front, by example. There was no suggestion that he was cowardly, but rather that his approach was too cerebral for a real warrior possessed of a proper Chindit spirit.

This seems unjust. Many battles are lost because foolishly brave officers sacrifice themselves in the spearheads, instead of maintaining the "grip" from the rear which is their proper function. Masters behaved less like a hero than some men described in these pages, yet much more as a commander should do. His principal handicap, perhaps, was that he was too intelligent to suppose that the defence of Blackpool was either viable or worthwhile. As a serious professional soldier, unlike some stars of the stamp of "Mad Mike" Calvert, who was leading another Chindit column, he knew that he was attempting to make sense of a strategic nonsense. Yet in doing so he displayed remarkable competence. If the British or Indian armies had possessed a few more officers of the stamp of Jack Masters, and rather fewer in the mould of Calvert or Wingate, the British cause in Burma might have prospered much sooner than it did.

The men at Blackpool were appalled now to learn that Stilwell's attack on Mogaung had been delayed, meaning that the Chindits must continue to hold their positions if they were to accomplish their purpose of assisting the American-led operation. Masters flew in an L-5 light plane to meet Lentaigne and Stilwell. The American, notorious for his loathing of the British, merely asked him if the Chindits had cut the railway, and showed his contempt when told that they had not. Masters responded in kind, that his people would do their part when Stilwell's did theirs.

By 22 May, Japanese antiaircraft fire was rendering air resupply of Blackpool increasingly hazardous. Losses among the garrison mounted. On the night of the twenty-fourth the Japanese broke through the perimeter, and were then able to force the defenders to abandon most of their eastern flank positions. At this point Masters determined that the "stronghold" had become untenable. The survivors, short of ammunition and bereft of food, must withdraw. He signalled to Lentaigne for permission, but began the retreat before any answer was received. He directed the disengagement "by bounds," thinning each position in turn as his men pulled back, with considerable skill. There was one insoluble problem: what to do with nineteen men too badly wounded to be moved. "I don't want them to see any Japanese," he told the doctor with a mask of harshness that was far from his private sentiment at that moment. Each critically wounded man was shot. Given the unsparing brutality of the enemy, this was unquestionably a humane decision, but it cost Masters many traumatic memories in the years ahead.

He himself was the last to leave Blackpool, in heavy rain behind the Cameronians. To his immense relief the Japanese did not press the British retreat. It emerged later that many of the enemy's foot soldiers were reservists, who had suffered a thousand casualties against the Chindits' two hundred dead. Though the battle of Blackpool was a defeat, it was far from a dishonourable one. A British section lost its way during the withdrawal, and blundered into fierce Japanese fire. Masters personally led a reserve force to succour them, armed with his Gurkha kukri, pistol and carbine, and wearing a Japanese officer's sword. If his behaviour was theatrical, it was impressive theatre.

As the British column stumbled exhausted through the jungle, Masters himself was at the end of his tether, after weeks with little or no sleep. Resisting offers from his escort to carry him, he marched with the rearguard, behind the line of wounded men, including the blind whom the doctor had tied to each other with bandages. One Gurkha soldier carried another for three miles. After four days, they reached a rendezvous with other Chindit forces at Mokso San. Here, Masters exploded in rage when he learned that a British colonel was to supersede him in command of the remains of the 111th Brigade. The defender of Blackpool sent a furious signal to Lentaigne, which embraced all his bitterness about the lack of support he had received during the battle. Lentaigne apologised, and agreed that Masters should remain in command. By 28 May, the major signalled proudly that his force now comprised two thousand men armed, organised and fit to fight, along with 130 wounded. His success in getting his men back from Blackpool was one of the more notable achievements of the Chindit campaign, albeit a forlorn one.

Sunderland flying boats landed on Lake Indawgyi and evacuated the Chindit wounded. Hourly they expected an order for the fit survivors—all exhausted after eighty days in the jungle—to withdraw also. Masters's humour never deserted him. He sat on a splendid bamboo chair constructed for him by his Gurkhas and told his disconsolate officers: "Well, chaps, let's get this next phase over and then we can go back to

India for some proper peacetime soldiering." Some of his comrades admired such "bounce," others found the facetiousness tiresome. The sick list mounted, and so did the men's exhaustion and dismay.

It was a ghastly shock when, on 8 June, new orders came. Instead of being evacuated, Masters's weary force was required to march twenty-five miles eastward, across mosquito-infested swamps, to assist Stilwell's hesitant assault on Mogaung by attacking from the west. Their assault on Point 2171, a hilltop held by the Japanese and commanding rail and road links to Mogaung, occupied the attentions of the 111th Brigade for two weeks, between 20 June and 5 July. Losses were high, misery was unbroken. Base doctors signalled: "To prevent foot trouble essential troops use dry socks." The Chindits responded: "Please arrange for rain to decrease from ten hours a day and the mud from six inches. Then we will be able to follow your advice." Masters wrote of clashes with the equally weakened Japanese: "We were falling against each other, spent, drugged, crazed fighters, bare knuckles, pawing at each other, falling down." Some Chindits behaved bravely, others were simply exhausted, and had little left to give the battle. The 3rd Gurkhas finally captured the position, just before a belated order came for the brigade to withdraw. Masters was bitter. Most of his men were crippled by disease. Short rations together with their exertions had induced average weight losses of thirty to forty pounds. He told Lentaigne repeatedly that his men were capable of no more. When at last they were medically examined, it was found that just 118 out of 2,000 were fit for operations—Masters himself, 7 other officers, 20 British soldiers and 90 Gurkhas. Masters and this small group were ordered by Stilwell to join his own force and provide infantry protection for a Chinese artillery battery.

For all the American's braggadocio and his stubborn faith in the Chinese, throughout the campaign he proved unable to induce Chiang Kai-shek's troops to fight aggressively. In the end, it was "Mad Mike" Calvert's Chindit contingent which was obliged to storm Mogaung when it became plain that the Chinese were incapable of doing so. Stilwell caused a report to be broadcast to the world that Chiang Kai-shek's forces had taken the town. This prompted Calvert to signal: "Chinese take Mogaung. We take umbrage." On 1 August, with Stilwell's objective finally achieved, Masters's men were flown out from the town's airfield. The sick and wounded had already gone. The entire Chindit operation had achieved a marginal success by forcing the Japanese to divert a division to counter Wingate's men, which would otherwise have been committed to the decisive battles for Imphal and Kohima. But the cost had been high, command and control lamentable. Churchill's extravagant sponsorship of Wingate, like that of other private armies in the last two years of the war, was a costly folly. British propaganda made much of the Chindits' achievement, but their experience became a legend because of the sufferings they endured rather than the military successes they achieved. In January 1945 the Chindits were disbanded, their battalions posted to regular formations.

Masters received a DSO for his own part in the Blackpool operation, which some of his comrades resented but which posterity may think well-deserved. Resentment stemmed from a belief that Masters was too much concerned with self-advancement. Yet while his ambition was plain, it is hard to fault his performance as a commander upon whom great responsibilities were thrust. On emerging from Burma he travelled at once to join Barbara and their six-month-old daughter at a quiet hill station in Assam, where he succumbed to jaundice. Many times in the night he awoke shouting orders and reliving images of the battle, which had cost him intense emotional pain. For a few short weeks he achieved one of his life's ambitions by taking command of the 3/4th Gurkhas, with the rank of lieutenant-colonel. But to his mingled chagrin and satisfaction he was abruptly plucked from this role to become senior staff officer of the 19th Indian Division for the final drive into Burma.

Barbara at last gained her divorce. She married Masters during a brief leave, with two 111th Brigade battalion commanders as witnesses, and the Masters's tiny daughter in attendance. If this was unorthodox behaviour for a British officer even in the last years of the raj, it was entirely of a piece with Masters's career. He proved a brilliantly successful staff officer, planning the advance of his division to Mandalay and beyond with his usual flair and energy. He stood proudly on the route to Rangoon, watching the victorious army hasten by, a last great pageant of Britain's Indian legions.

The dust thickened under the trees lining the road until the column was motoring into a thunderous yellow tunnel, first the tanks, infantry all over them, then trucks filled with men, then more tanks going nose to tail, guns, more trucks, more guns—British, Sikhs, Gurkhas, Madrassis, Pathan, Americans, most of the soldiers were on their feet, cheering and yelling. The Gurkhas, of course, went by stiffly to attention, whole truckloads bouncing four feet in the air without change of expression... This was the old Indian Army going into attack for the last time in history, exactly two hundred and fifty years after the Honourable East India Company had enlisted its first ten sepoys on the Coromandel Coast... Certainly we had been masters, and imperialists, but we had not been afraid to die with these men and we had always loved them and their country, usually with an intense, blind passion which could ignore all theoretical considerations of right and wrong.

Astoundingly, at this moment a message arrived from the office of His Excellency the Commander-in-Chief of the Indian Army demanding to know why Lieutenant-Colonel Masters should not be required to resign his commission in accordance with army instruction, he having been involved in a divorce case involving a brother officer. His general sent a terse response, observing that Lieutenant-Colonel Masters could not be spared from military operations. To the offender's deep relief he was informed that his resignation would not be required. In May 1945, exhausted, Masters asked his general for leave. This was granted. Before he left, he was offered command of a parachute brigade. He refused—he was committed to finishing his war with the 19th Indian Division. He was walking with Barbara in the Indian hills he loved so well when they learned of the dropping of the atomic bomb on Hiroshima on 6 August.

With the war's ending, Masters was posted to a staff appointment at Indian army headquarters. It was in this role, during a visit to a unit in Persia, that he met an old friend from the Quetta staff college, and enlivened a unit mess night by dancing with an American major on a tabletop and delivering an exuberant solo rendering of "Who'll Take the Mail to Dead Man's Gulch?" The principal guest was the commander-in-chief of the Indian army, Field Marshal Sir Claude Auchinleck. "The Auk" watched Masters's performance with mixed feelings, then summoned him for a conversation about their common school, Wellington.

Finally the great man said: "You're the most extraordinary Old Welling-
tonian I've ever come across." This was intended as a mixed compliment.
Now, as ever, Lieutenant-Colonel John Masters, DSO, was still the outsider amid the caste with which he had fought and made his career.

In 1946 Masters returned to England with Barbara, their daughter
and a newborn son to take up a posting at the Camberley Staff College.
The following year, when India became independent, he was shocked to
hear that in the division of Gurkha units between the British and the
new Indian army, his own regiment, the 4th, was to become part of the
latter. It was a bitter blow. Through everything that had happened to him
in war and peace, he had always thought of the 4th Prince of Wales's
Gurkhas as his army family, Bakloh as a home he loved. He had expected
to return to both, and now they were gone. "I was cut adrift from my
past," he wrote sadly, and told a former Indian army officer whom he met
in London: "They've taken my India away from me." Masters made a
sudden, angry decision: "If they don't want the 4th, they won't get me."
He resolved to cut his ties with an England by which he felt betrayed,
and with a British army in which he believed that he could never feel at
home. In 1948 he resigned his commission and set off for America, where
Barbara and their two children later followed him.

It was a characteristically bold decision. He suffered a harsh initia-
tion in the United States before he began to make a life for himself as a
writer. By the mid-1950s, however, his novels—*Bhowani Junction, Coromandel, Nightrunners of Bengal* and others—had achieved extraordinary
success on both sides of the Atlantic. With some help from Hollywood
checks for film options, he became a modestly rich man. He spent the
later years of his life among the mountains of New Mexico, gregarious,
prickly and energetic as ever. Only in 1962 did he learn conclusively,
from a researcher investigating an 1830s Scottish forebear, that there was
indeed a Muslim strand in his own ancestry, though he had long guessed
at something of the kind from his father's swarthy appearance. One of
his early-nineteenth-century ancestors had fathered two children by his
Indian mistress, from whom Masters was descended. He wrote to his
brother Alex, on discovering that each of them was, as he put it, "1/32nd
Indian . . . I didn't comment on the news of Singhi Kaum because there
didn't seem much to say. It was always obvious that we were a 'country'
family . . . I am quite glad I did not know for sure until my attitudes on a

great many matters had hardened, as my feelings against race prejudice might have seemed to others and perhaps to me as a mere defence mechanism…On the whole I think the older generation probably did the right thing in burying the poor girl without trace, since they determined to…become pukka sahibs again."

Masters died in 1983, at the age of sixty-eight, from complications following emphysema. To the end, India coursed through his veins and through the pages of most of his books. Few writers have evoked with such verve and passion the sensations which the subcontinent inspired through the centuries in its British inhabitants. Masters was not destined to be a contented man, but his achievements as a soldier and as a chronicler of soldiers were alike remarkable. He never outgrew an adolescent attitude towards sex, which impaired his novels, but he carried the extraordinary energy of his life into everything he wrote. He was an instinctive warrior from the cradle to the grave, as often fighting himself as his country's enemies.

There is a wry postscript to his story. Barbara Masters's divorce from her husband, Hugh Rose, was exceptionally acrimonious. The two Rose children suffered childhoods turbulent and dislocated even by the standards of imperial offspring. They spent much time in children's homes and with friends in England while their father was serving abroad, Barbara being denied access to them. It was some years before an accommodation was achieved, and they were able to travel to America and see their mother and stepfather. Michael, the boy, joined the Coldstream Guards after Oxford, and was then seconded to the Special Air Service, which he commanded during the Falklands War, experiencing adventures which Jack Masters might have envied. Sir Michael Rose eventually retired from the army as a general, having commanded the United Nations peacekeepers in Bosnia during the bitter conflicts of the 1990s.

Before Jack died, he asked for his ashes to be scattered over the Pecos Wilderness, outside Santa Fe. Among his American friends was Bill Mauldin, the great GI cartoonist of World War II, and star of a host of U.S. newspapers thereafter. One morning Mauldin took off in his own plane with the Masters family and the ashes of the old Chindit. "I told you I'd get Jack up in this crate some day," he said to Barbara. Over the Pecos, the mortal remains of John Masters whipped away into the slipstream through the medium of the cardboard cylinder in which Michael

Rose had brought his duty-free malt whisky from Heathrow Airport. To depart this world through a Glenfiddich tube was a gesture which would surely have delighted the man himself. One of his obituaries observed that John Masters had been "an officer, but not quite a gentleman." That verdict, too, would not have troubled his free spirit.

CHAPTER TEN

THE DAM BUSTER

THE ALLIED BOMBER offensive in the Second World War became so steeped in controversy, strategic and moral, that this has clouded the reputations of most of those involved in it. There is a striking exception, however. Guy Gibson, the twenty-four-year-old RAF officer who led the May 1943 raid on the Ruhr dams, achieved an iconic status in his own time which has never faded. He was the archetype of the aerial warrior, entirely a figure of the mid-twentieth century in his mastery of technology, yet timeless in his courage and willingness for sacrifice. Posterity remembers Gibson as he was portrayed by Richard Todd in the stirring, indeed deeply moving, 1954 British feature film *The Dam Busters*. The reality, inevitably, was more complex, more melancholy, but certainly no less interesting.

Guy Gibson was born in the Punjab in 1918, third child of an unhappy alliance between a nineteen-year-old Englishwoman and her much older husband, a senior officer of the Indian Forestry Service. The boy spent his early years pampered by the large domestic staff common to imperial offspring of the day, and then at six sailed "home" for an English school. His mother travelled with him, having abandoned her marriage. Guy had little subsequent contact with his father, a remote and eccentric figure. His mother sought refuge in alcohol. If many imperial childhoods of that period were dysfunctional, Gibson's was exceptionally so. Coincidentally, it closely resembled that of the legless RAF fighter pilot Douglas Bader. If most men's ambition contains a strand of anger, it is easy to perceive the origins of Guy Gibson's.

He attended St. Edward's School, Oxford, without disgrace but without distinction. Like millions of young men of his time, "the Lindbergh generation," he formed an early passion to fly. A career in the air force offered the easiest path to achieve this. There was nothing smart about the prewar RAF—indeed, its snobbish sister services considered airmen incorrigibly vulgar. It simply provided, for a generation of mostly doomed young men, a path to the sky. Gibson's initial application to become a pilot was rejected, but after a few months the RAF relented. Aged just eighteen, in November 1936 he reported for training at Yatesbury in Wiltshire, three months after leaving school. He was a gauche young man, assertive and immodest, perhaps in compensation for a lack of physical stature. To use the adjective of the period, he was "bumptious." He was graded "average" as a pilot, but lower than that as a companion. In particular—and this vice never left him—he was sometimes rude and condescending to junior ranks, and especially to ground crew. Some comrades speculated that this was how he had learned to treat underlings in his Indian childhood. No one doubted Gibson's fierce ambition to get on, to make a mark, to earn renown. But few of those who encountered him cared for his manner of doing so in those early days.

When war came in September 1939, his squadron commander said wryly: "Now's your chance to be a hero, Gibbo." Gibson indeed welcomed the personal opportunity war offered, but also recognised his slender chances of survival in the front line of the greatest conflict in history. When his elder brother tried to buy him a wristwatch, Guy resisted his generosity. "Don't do it," he said. "I'm a dead man." In the first months of the conflict he saw little action, but committed a familiar folly for a very young warrior who perceives himself in the shadow of death: he married a chorus girl. He met Eve Moore in December 1939, at a Coventry theatre where she was performing. He was twenty-one. She was a worldly, somewhat coarse woman of twenty-eight, unable to bear children. Friends speculated that their relationship was overwhelmingly founded upon sexual compatibility. Both before and after they met, however, Gibson sustained a reputation as a compulsive sexual adventurer, scarcely able to help himself from propositioning any woman with whom he spent a few hours. His loneliness intensified when his mother allowed her clothes to catch fire in a sordid accident at her lodgings. On Christmas Eve 1939 she died from the burns she had received. This horror can scarcely have failed to inflict new emotional wounds on her son.

By September 1940, Gibson had flown thirty-seven bomber operations with 83 Squadron, a Hampden unit. These were neither especially hazardous nor very effective by the standards of what followed later in the war, but already Gibson had seen a fair number of friends and comrades "go for a Burton." Even at a time when Germany's defences were unimpressive, British bombers were uncomfortable for their crews and poorly provided with navigational aids. Merely to fly a mission and find a way home again was challenge enough for most pilots. Gibson earned a reputation as a "press-on type," volunteering for extra sorties, specialising in low flying, evidently keen to win a medal, and more than happy to accept the risks involved in doing so. He duly received a Distinguished Flying Cross in July 1940. He remained less than popular among his peers, but attracted the warm approval of his superiors. Here was a tough, simple, direct young man eager to do his share—and more than his share—to win the war. When so many pilots were relieved to see the weather clamp down, cancelling operations, Gibson fumed. He wanted to get on with it, to fly, to engage the enemy, to fight. What more could any commander desire from a young officer?

In that first winter of the Luftwaffe's blitz on Britain, there was a sudden demand for experienced pilots to man the RAF's night fighters. These assumed great importance in the defence of Britain. Gibson was one of the fliers who accepted a temporary transfer to Fighter Command, joining 29 Squadron to fly twin-engined Beaufighters. Fighter and bomber men formed separate castes, which seldom mixed much after their training was complete. Yet Gibson made the transition without fuss. He was simply impatient to confront the enemy, to deploy himself wherever the action was. He and Eve moved into a billet near his Lincolnshire airfield. Appointed a flight commander, he set about learning the new technique of engaging German aircraft with the primitive radar sets being installed in two-seat fighters. At first he found the limitations of radar-guided interception intensely frustrating, and was prone to vent his anger on whatever hapless NCO was manning the AI set behind him. At 29 Squadron as at 83, he earned a reputation for determination.

He was always willing to fly in marginal weather. On one alarming occasion his aircraft was shot up by a German intruder as he came in to land. In the course of a year of fighter operations he flew 101 sorties, shot down three German aircraft and received a second DFC. He seemed dissatisfied, however, that he had not become a high scorer like some of his comrades. If he could not make himself an ace fighter pilot, he would prefer to be somewhere else. Towards the end of 1941, when Luftwaffe activity over Britain declined, he asked to return to Bomber Command.

Gibson's quota of operational flying was already remarkable. In accordance with RAF practice, he was posted to a training unit as an instructor, to give him a break. This was not at all what he had in mind, and within weeks he requested a transfer back to operations. It was now, in the spring of 1942, that his wartime career began to accelerate. Air Chief Marshal Sir Arthur Harris had just assumed direction of the bomber offensive with which his name would be indelibly associated. He knew young Gibson, who represented all the virtues Harris sought in the human instruments to fulfil his vision for the destruction of Germany: courage, commitment, elemental passion. Gibson, like Harris, had no patience with shirkers or weaklings. He seemed to scorn introspection, perhaps because its fruits would have been so bitter for anyone from his troubled family background. He was a man of action who sought to imbue every flier he led with his own commitment to carry the war to the foe, to inflict retribution upon Nazi Germany in fire and rubble for the great evil which it had brought upon the world. Gibson possessed an attribute Harris esteemed, but which many mild-mannered young bomber pilots lacked: "Hun-hate."

On 12 March 1942, Bomber Command's C-in-C despatched Gibson to 5 Group, with a directive that he should be given a command. He was posted to 106 Squadron, then equipped with the twin-engined Avro Manchester, inadequate forerunner of the Lancaster. Gibson arrived at his new unit's base at Coningsby in Lincolnshire determined to impose his personality upon every one of the seven hundred men now under his orders. He himself was only twenty-three, yet when he summoned his NCO aircrew for a pep talk and they failed to stand up as he entered, he delivered a scorching rebuke and received a contemptuous nickname in return: "the boy emperor." His group commander once described Gibson to me as "the sort of boy who would have been head prefect in any school," though oddly enough he had not achieved that office at St. Edward's. In Bomber Command—a world in which those described as "men" indeed possessed the spirit of adolescents who still thought it the funniest thing in the world to pull off a comrade's trousers after dinner— Gibson displayed all the virtues and many of the vices of a punctilious, even officious, public-school head prefect.

He drove the squadron, in May reequipped with four-engined Avro Lancasters, as hard as himself. At least one of the crews with whom he flew was appalled by his insouciance in the face of mortal peril. He almost invariably flew low over Germany, once circling a thousand feet above a line of U-boats in Rostock harbour to collect information for the intelligence staff. His intolerance of others who failed to match his standards, to play the game, to pull their weight for the house, became notorious. He reserved special contempt for those who made "early returns," aborting a mission because of technical failure—or something worse. One night as a Lancaster was preparing to take off, the self-destruct device on its Gee radar-navigational aid exploded, filling the cockpit with smoke. The crew hastily evacuated the aircraft. Gibson, raging, raced to the scene in a Jeep. He made it plain that he suspected the crew of "lacking moral fibre," and said flatly: "You've got four good engines, you'll bloody well go and bomb Germany." Crews suspected of malingering were expelled from the squadron.

Gibson embraced to his bosom a tightly knit group of "press-on types" like himself, several of whom would later join him in the attack on the Ruhr dams. They were not unlike the gang which Sapper's fictional hero Bulldog Drummond mustered for his adventures. Outsiders who did not match up to Gibson's expectations for membership felt the chill of his disapproval. His marriage was already creaking, with both partners seeking consolation wherever they could find it. Gibson seemed, in the words of his best biographer, Richard Morris, "addicted to stress." He had become a monomaniac in the fashion of Harris, his mentor. He cared only for bombing Germany, and carried his commitment to the point of obsession.

It is easy to understand why some of his own men disliked Gibson. By the summer of 1942, aircrew who came to Bomber Command fully grasped the peril of the task they had undertaken. A man was required to fly thirty operations to earn a transfer to instructional or ground duties, which most gratefully embraced. But only one in four of all Bomber Command aircrew completed a tour, and more than half died. The vast majority of fliers did their duty as best they could. They showed great courage in overcoming fear, accepting the statistical likelihood that they would meet death. But fear was always there, from their first rising in the airfield huts on the flat, misty fields of Lincolnshire or Yorkshire, through the hours of briefing and preparation, to the trundling taxi around the perimeter track at dusk for takeoff towards the fury of searchlights, flak and fighters that awaited them across the Channel.

To many decent, conscientious, frightened young men who welcomed a night of heavy overcast which delayed their next dalliance with death for just a little longer, it seemed harsh to find themselves at the mercy of such a commander as Gibson. His brilliant smile indicated a man unlike themselves. If he suffered from fear, ambition and responsibility had driven it so deep underground that it did not trouble him. More than a few of Gibson's aircrew thought: "It's all right for *him* if he wants to be like this. But why should he expect it from *us*? We don't want gongs. We want to live." Gibson's harshness towards weaker vessels was by no means a universal characteristic of successful squadron commanders. Leonard Cheshire, for instance, at least as great a bomber leader as the dam buster, was famously sympathetic towards his men's frailties, and was repaid with an affection from subordinates which was seldom accorded to his counterpart.

Gibson seldom revealed chinks in his carapace, but he sometimes did so to girlfriends, notable among whom was a WAAF corporal named Margaret North. One night at Syerston, the Nottinghamshire airfield at which 106 Squadron was now based, the station commander, "Gus" Walker, was terribly injured when a Lancaster's bombload exploded at its dispersal. Gibson accompanied Walker in the ambulance to the nearby medical quarters. While doctors set to work on the injured man, the squadron commander fell into conversation with a nurse from the area's crash and burns unit. Next day he asked her out, brushing aside her murmurings that officers and NCOs were forbidden to fraternise off-duty. The couple began a relationship which became important to Gibson in the last two years of his life, though he was no more faithful to Margaret than to his wife. They rattled round the country lanes in Gibson's little black car, usually accompanied by his beloved black labradorish mongrel, Nigger. Margaret perceived the pilot's weariness and loneliness. He talked incessantly, mostly about bombing; and quizzed her intently about her work in the burns unit. One night while she was on duty, she heard that Gibson had suddenly appeared in the building and set himself down beside the bed of a young gunner swathed in bandages, who was dying of burns inflicted when a flare caught fire in his aircraft. Gibson simply said: "My name's Guy Gibson. Can I sit with you?" The injured airman was incapable of reply. His visitor remained in silence beside him, so that he should not be alone as he died.

This was a remarkable breach of Gibson's recognised customs and totems—a disdain for junior ranks, the restless impatience which characterised his life as a squadron commander. It suggests that beneath the protective armour in which he had encased himself, his imagination vividly comprehended his own likely end. In his book *Enemy Coast Ahead* (1946) there is a word portrait of what happens to a bomber and its crew after it is hit by enemy fire, falling steeply out of the sky for a terrible minute or two: "Then it is all over and you hit the ground. Petrol flames come soaring up into the sky, almost reaching to meet you as though to rocket your soul to heaven." He knew.

In March 1943, after a year with 106 Squadron Gibson relinquished command. He had now flown 72 bomber operations, vastly more than most pilots survived or were willing to endure, in addition to his 101 fighter sorties. During his time at 106, unlike some squadron COs who seldom flew, or at least chose easy targets for themselves, Gibson led from the front. Harris, whose personal interest in the young man's career continued, insisted that he should receive a second DSO in recognition of this extraordinary performance, and the decoration seemed richly justified. It was now time, and more than time, for Gibson to quit operational flying. Yet what would he do? What was he fit for? War had wound the mainspring of this vital, energetic, intensely focused youth to pursue a single purpose. Even Gibson's relationship with Margaret North seemed to depend, in some degree, on the fact that unlike his wife she was a member of the Bomber Command "family," part of the monotone existence which alone possessed meaning for him.

Despite all Gibson's ready laughter, there was no gaiety about him. He possessed no great private enthusiasms, save a certain liking for small boats and the sea. He had become merely a supremely effective instru-

ment of Harris's will, a young man who found a satisfaction in his role as
a bomber leader that was probably beyond his reach in any other, in the
world as it was in 1943. Gibson was due for a rest—overdue, in the eyes of
most of those who served with him. Strain and exhaustion were etched
into his features. Yet he himself possessed no notion of what to do with
leisure. When his commander, Sir Ralph Cochrane, summoned him to 5
Group headquarters and asked if, before taking leave, he would be willing to fly one more operation, for which he would have to form a special
unit, Gibson unhesitatingly accepted.

War compresses time. Guy Gibson spent just four months of his life
with 617 Squadron, yet his name would be indelibly coupled with its
experience. He arrived at Scampton in Lincolnshire in his Humber
shooting brake, accompanied by Nigger, on the afternoon of 21 March.
At once he threw all his energy and aggression into demanding,
haranguing, insisting upon everything needed to form his new squadron
in a hurry. He did not know his target, but he had been told that the mission would involve very low flying. Contrary to legend, not all his crews
were handpicked or experienced men. He knew several of the pilots,
including Hopgood and Shannon from 106 Squadron. Others came from
57 Squadron, others again from 50. Gibson specially requested Flight-
Lieutenant Harold "Micky" Martin, because the Australian was a celebrated low-flying expert. A surprising number of 617's aircrew, however,
had not completed even a single tour of operations. Several flight-
engineers had never flown a mission to Germany. Even Gibson's own
crew was almost unknown to him. He seems to have felt towards some of
its members the disdain and impatience characteristic of his attitude
towards junior ranks. Intensely egocentric, generosity in recognising
other men's contributions was never among Gibson's virtues. Fortunately for his posthumous reputation, some of his less charitable asides
on comrades were excised by an official hand from the published version
of *Enemy Coast Ahead*. Richard Morris observes in his penetrating biography of Gibson: "In the cockpit of Gibson's Lancaster there was a distinct
air of master and servant."

When twenty-year-old pilot David Shannon invited his own crew to
accompany him to Gibson's new unit, only one man accepted. The others, very reasonably, felt that after completing a tour of operations, they

had "done their bit" and were entitled to a break. The fliers who made up Gibson's embryo 617 Squadron were a not untypical mix for any Bomber Command unit of the period: some eager and practised, others green and hesitant. They were certainly not all volunteers, and could scarcely be called an elite. This makes all the more remarkable Gibson's achievement in preparing them for the dams raid, the war's supreme feat of precision flying, inside three months.

The squadron commander was relieved to be told on 29 March that 617's targets would not, as he had feared, be enemy warships, which were notoriously heavily defended. Instead he was to lead an assault on Germany's dams. The Mohne and Sorpe, in the midst of the Ruhr, had been identified as installations vital to Nazi war production. Without water, the Ruhr could not produce steel. The Ministry of Economic Warfare asserted that destruction of both dams would inflict more than twice the damage of breaking only either one. At the end of March, Gibson met for the first time Barnes Wallis, the scientist who was sole begetter of the dam-busting "bouncing bomb." An unusual and moving intimacy, founded upon mutual respect, developed between these two utterly different men, the middle-aged scientist and the young warrior. Through early April, Gibson led his crews on training exercises in low-level navigation, then began to practise attacks on English dams at the designated height, 150 feet. Several aircraft came home with tree foliage entangled in their fuselage projections.

On 24 April at a meeting at Weybridge, Wallis asked Gibson if his crews could drop their mines—for his projectiles were, indeed, cylindrical mines rather than bombs—not at 150 feet, but at 60. If released from any greater height, it seemed, the casings shattered. After three days of trials, Gibson telephoned to report that it was feasible to attack at 60 feet. It is hard to overstate the feat of flying which this required. Pilots, most of them with vastly less experience than Gibson himself, had to fly a heavy bomber straight and level for at least twenty seconds at a height above water less than the length of a cricket pitch, far lower than most treetops, amid enemy antiaircraft fire, and in darkness. This was an awesome challenge. Gibson drove his men fiercely, some said tyrannically. He sacked from the squadron three crews which failed to measure up. Working sixteen, eighteen, occasionally twenty hours a day, he raced between meetings with Wallis and the Air Ministry, training exercises and planning conferences, while coping with all the administrative duties inseparable from command of seven hundred men.

He found time for one desultory meeting with Margaret North, whom he took to see *Casablanca* in Grantham. Despairing that Gibson would ever be available to her, she had married another man. By now Gibson scarcely pretended that he loved Eve, but somehow the couple maintained the semblance of a marriage. Obsessively and justly concerned about security for the dams raid, he gave neither his wife nor Margaret any hint of what was coming, and exploded in rage when he discovered that the operation was being freely discussed among some Bomber Command staff officers who had no business to know about it. The squadron's only hope of success lay in achieving surprise. The operation order given to Gibson early in May emphasised that the Mohne and Sorpe dams were 617's key targets, while the Eder was of secondary importance. He is less than frank about this in his own account, which states that he allocated his best crews to the Mohne and Eder, and sent others to the Sorpe "really to act as a diversionary force." This was a post-facto rationalisation of events.

Final details of the attack were refined at a four-hour meeting, which Barnes Wallis and Gibson's two flight commanders attended, on the afternoon of Saturday, 15 May. When the session was over, Gibson was told that Nigger had been run over by a car and killed. He was terribly shocked, and fearful that his crews might think this a bad omen for Operation Chastise. He was already suffering severe pains in his feet from an attack of gout which must have been the product of exhaustion and stress. The symptoms worsened next day, 16 May, when he was destined to take off for the Ruhr. The station doctor did not dare to prescribe painkillers, lest these dull his senses. On that fine, sunny day at Scampton, feeling much less than his best, from midday onwards Gibson was engaged in briefing his crews. He warned them bleakly that if they failed to breach the dams they would have to return the following night—and everybody could guess what the Germans would then have waiting for them.

As the men of the squadron waited on the grass outside the hangar for trucks to take them to the dispersals, Hopgood confided to Shannon that he did not expect to come back. He was right. Indeed, for almost half the young men assembled on the Lincolnshire turf that Sunday afternoon, these were their last few hours on earth. The bomber offensive against Germany required terrible sacrifices from those who took part. The dams raid imposed risks far beyond the norm, in pursuit of a strategic objective which commanders deemed worthy of the price. Yet it was a measure of Gibson's driving confidence—his powers of leadership—that he had infused the 132 men who accompanied him into the sky that night with his own conviction that this extraordinary job might be done, that the dams could be breached, and that it was worth hazarding their lives to do so.

The aircraft of 617 Squadron left for Germany in waves, flying all the way to their objectives at low level. Gibson, Hopgood and Martin took off at 9:30 p.m. Less than three hours later, in bright moonlight, they began their attack on the Mohne. All of 617's craft had been specially equipped for the operation with VHF speech radios. With the assistance of these, Gibson was able to direct the Mohne attack personally, calling in his aircraft one by one. He himself flew a dummy bomb run "to look the place over," to which the German flak-gunners on the dam wall responded vigorously. After he had dropped his own mine, which failed to make a breach, in a gesture far beyond the call of duty he flew the bomb run twice more alongside other attacking Lancasters, to divert the fire of the flak gunners. The fifth mine, which appears to have been released with exceptional precision by Squadron Leader Melvin Young, broke the dam, which had already been cracked by the second. Tens of millions of gallons of water poured forth onto the German countryside. Gibson's wireless operator signalled the triumphant code word "Nigger" to 5 Group headquarters just before 1 a.m., prompting exuberant celebration among the assembled Bomber Command "brass." Gibson sent home the aircraft which had attacked, and led the three still carrying mines to the Eder. Here there was no German flak, but the approach over the reservoir required a dogleg course, and a terrifying feat of flying amid the surrounding high ground. David Shannon made five runs before he was satisfied that his aim was sure and dropped his mine, damaging the dam wall. The third and last mine caused the Eder to crack open. The exultant survivors turned for home. Shannon "found it almost impossible to describe the elation in success."

Only two aircraft of the designated five—the others were lost en route—attacked the Sorpe, an earth construction much less vulnerable to Wallis's projectiles. The dam suffered superficial damage, but was not breached. Of the nineteen Lancasters that set out for the Ruhr, ten are known to have dropped their mines, and eleven came home. Of the eight which failed to return, two were lost over the dams, while the other six were shot down or crashed during the low-level flights to or from the targets. This was a shocking casualty rate even by the standards of Bomber Command. Of fifty-six crewmen in the stricken aircraft, just three survived as prisoners. Wallis was deeply depressed, racked with self-reproach despite all the assurances offered to him by Gibson and others that this victory was worth the price. Most of the crews which survived celebrated extravagantly at Scampton. Two which had returned early were interrogated by Gibson, and acquitted of blame. One pilot who landed with his mine, having failed to find the Sorpe, was castigated by the squadron commander and told to expect posting out of 617.

The dams raid badly frightened the German high command, appalled by the vulnerability of the Ruhr water supply which it exposed. Even Goebbels paid private tribute to the effectiveness and technical ingenuity of the operation. It did not, however, inflict lasting damage on industrial production. First, British failure to break the Sorpe left the Germans with adequate supplies of water. Second, Bomber Command made no attempt to interfere with German repairs to the Mohne and Eder. Many years later, Wallis lamented this omission to me, asserting that the reconstruction programme could easily have been interdicted with conventional bombs. When I put this point to Sir Arthur Harris he responded with this gruff dictum: "Any action deserving of the Victoria Cross is, by its nature, unfit to be repeated as an operation of war." Harris did not believe any renewed bombing of the dams was feasible. One of his major errors throughout the campaign was to underrate the importance of returning again and again to key targets, to prevent the Germans restoring them to production.

Gibson was awarded the Victoria Cross for leading 617 Squadron's assault on the Ruhr dams. Before the operation was launched, commanders had intended to preserve secrecy about the special unit even after the event. Yet once the Mohne and Eder were breached, the Royal Air Force perceived an unprecedented propaganda opportunity. The first Eve knew of what her husband had done was the announcement to the world by the BBC of the dams attack, "led by Wing-Commander Guy Gibson, DSO, DFC." In the last days of May 1943 the crews of 617 Squadron became the most famous airmen in Britain. The nation thrilled to their astounding achievement. This was a time when the military and industrial might of the United States, together with the Red Army's millions, were driving the weary British surely and steadily from the centre of the stage, a source of deep chagrin to the nation which had suffered so much to defy the Nazis since 1939. Here, however, was a triumph of explicitly British guts, flying skill and scientific ingenuity. Churchill's people celebrated it wholeheartedly.

Ironically, the dams raid attracted such admiration partly because an attack on enemy industrial installations carried none of the moral baggage already associated with burning German cities. Yet the flooding which followed the breaching of the Mohne and the Eder killed 1,300 people, almost half of them slave labourers and prisoners-of-war. The dams operation thus inflicted more fatalities than the average city attack, in which civilians usually had time to reach a shelter before bombs fell. Yet no reasonable person, then or since, would allow this grim reality to diminish admiration for the aircrew of 617 Squadron. Nothing could tarnish the brilliance of their feat of arms, nor dim the lustre of their leader. King George VI visited Scampton, and there was an investiture at Buckingham Palace for Gibson and his men and a celebration dinner given by A. V. Roe, manufacturers of the Lancaster. For weeks it was hard for a man from the squadron to buy a drink or pay for a taxi. Overnight Gibson himself, at the age of twenty-four, became one of the most famous men in the country.

What could he do now? It was decided to keep 617 Squadron in being, as an elite unit for special operations. Yet it was unthinkable for Gibson to be allowed to fly with them. His death or capture would represent too great a propaganda coup for the enemy. For two months he remained at Scampton, a restless and discomfiting presence for all who had to serve with him. His obsession with bombing persisted, to the point that he might be seen in a pub flirting with a WAAF while simultaneously conducting a conversation about tactics with a fellow flier. His conceit was markedly not diminished by fame, yet his loneliness persisted. His marriage stumbled on, perhaps partly because it would have been so dismaying for the Air Ministry publicity machine to be asked to accommodate a Gibson divorce. He had little contact with his father, now remarried. One night he gave way to melancholy and lamented lost comrades who had perished at the dam, especially Hopgood and Henry Maudslay. Finally he added miserably: "My Niggy's dead."

Winston Churchill solved the immediate "Gibson problem." The prime minister liked to surround himself with young heroes, and especially to show them off to the Americans. He invited Gibson to a lunch at Chequers, and immediately warmed to "the dam buster," as he christened his guest. In the first days of August 1943, when the prime minister sailed for the Quadrant summit conference in Quebec, he took with him the Chindit leader Orde Wingate—and Guy Gibson. After being introduced to some of the greatest men in the Grand Alliance, and favourably impressing them, Gibson was despatched across North America on a propaganda tour, making speeches and giving interviews from coast to coast, including a fortnight being lionised in Hollywood. He was royally entertained, and proved surprisingly indiscreet about the means by which the dams operations had been carried out.

Four months later he returned to England weary and restless, hopeful of a return to operations over Germany, the only brand of reality he recognised. It was at this time, however, that a chill began to descend on Gibson's career which did not lift before his death. The RAF remained determined that he should not again fly over Germany. More than that, there was a widespread belief that fame had gone to his head. In the United States he was perceived by his RAF superiors to have grown too big for his boots. This was certainly the view of Harris, his mentor, who later ordered that another Bomber Command hero, Leonard Cheshire, should not be allowed to visit America "after our experience with the way they spoiled young Gibson." Gossip began to echo among RAF messes that the star of the dams raid now spent too much time in bed with fellow officers' wives. Even more serious from Sir Arthur Harris's viewpoint, the most famous bomber pilot in Britain appeared to harbour doubts, and to be expressing them publicly, about the "area" bombing of Germany.

Harris was, in Churchill's words, "a considerable commander." Yet in the last two years of the war, the C-in-C of Bomber Command's dedication to the destruction of Germany's cities became a personal fixation, to the exclusion of all rational debate about the role of bombing in the war effort. There is little doubt that Harris should have been sacked when his mania for sustaining urban carnage tipped over into open defiance of the opposing wishes of the Combined Chiefs of Staff. There was simply no place for debate or dissent in Harris's universe. The shock to him must have been profound when he learned that both in the United States and afterwards in England, his protégé Gibson had been publicly expressing reservations not about whether striking Germany was a valid activity, but about whether Bomber Command could alone bring about the collapse of Nazism. Gibson's disloyalty—for so Harris perceived it—was revealed at precisely the moment in the winter of 1943 when the C-in-C of Bomber Command was assuring Winston Churchill, in writing, that his squadrons could force the surrender of Germany by a specified date, 1 April 1944, without need for what he saw as the soldiers' extravagant plans to land in Normandy and fight the Germans all the way to Berlin.

By contrast, during a speech in Montreal Gibson had asserted that while there were those who believed that bombing alone could defeat Hitler, he himself was not one of them. "Of course, when I am at home I have to subscribe to that creed. But even if we cannot bomb Germany out of the war, we can soften up the country." On another occasion he said: "It would be foolish to expect our bombing, devastating though it is, to result in a German collapse." There was even a hint of conscience in a reference in his memoirs to those who drowned when the dams broke: "The fact that people were in the way was incidental. The fact that they might drown had not occurred to us. But we hoped that the dam wardens would warn those living below in time, even if they were Germans. No one likes mass slaughter and we did not like being the authors of it. Besides, it brought us in line with Himmler and his boys."

To many Allied war leaders, and to posterity, Gibson's remarks about the limitations of what he and his comrades were doing suggest a striking common sense. Yet to Harris they were a betrayal of everything Bomber Command was trying to achieve. Harris's anger does much to explain why Gibson died still in the rank of wing-commander, which he had held since the spring of 1942. Everything he now did reinforced the fears of his superiors that this formidable young warrior was ranging outside their control. He seemed guilty of at best presumption, at worst insubordination. He appeared to have developed political ambitions, together with some vague theories, which he also aired publicly, about the importance of ensuring that the young supplanted the old in charge of the postwar world. He spoke in the vein he later echoed in *Enemy Coast Ahead:* "If, by any chance, we had a hope of winning this war, and it seemed very remote, then in order to protect our children let the young men who have done the fighting have a say in the affairs of state." In a mad moment, encouraged by Churchill, who perceived in Gibson a useful man for his own party, the airman accepted an invitation to become Conservative parliamentary candidate for Macclesfield. A few months later he withdrew, saying that he realised he could not reconcile such a role with his RAF duties; but his flirtation with politics, and the inevitable publicity which it attracted, further alarmed his service masters.

Through the months that followed his return from America, Gibson continued to make public appearances and to receive media attention. He was interviewed for Roy Plomley's already famous BBC radio programme *Desert Island Discs,* and chose for one of his eight records Wagner's "Ride of the Valkyries." He said that it reminded him of a bombing raid—this, thirty years before film director Francis Ford Coppola chose the same theme for *Apocalypse Now.* At the beginning of January 1944 Gibson was posted to an absurdly unsuitable staff job in the Air Ministry's Accident Prevention Branch. Yet his real business was to write a book. Public relations was a skill in which the air force excelled. Some senior officer conceived the notion that for the RAF's foremost hero to write an account of his experiences as a bomber pilot must redound to the credit of the service—and of course whatever Gibson wrote would be subject to censorship. There could be no embarrassing indiscretions. Here was a young man who, more than any other, had made bombing seem respectable at a time when morally scrupulous critics were voicing doubts. Who, properly managed, was better able to silence sceptics than Guy Gibson?

Gibson wrote *Enemy Coast Ahead* in the space of two or three months early in 1944, when he and Eve were living in a London flat. Naturally he had no trouble finding a publisher. Michael Joseph promised a print run of fifty thousand copies. A draft was completed in March 1944, though in the event the book was only published in 1946, after the war ended. To many people who knew Gibson, he revealed himself in his writing as more sympathetic and sensitive than the somewhat unmannered, angry, cocky little man they met in the mess. The manuscript was significantly edited by the censor, by the publisher, by Gibson's wife, Eve, and perhaps also by expert literary hands in the Air Ministry to remove its indiscretions, soften its harshnesses and gaucheries, moderate its infelicities. Yet the original draft, as dictated by Gibson either to a Dictaphone or a typist, still exists. It suggests that the core of *Enemy Coast Ahead* is indeed an authentic expression of his personality, albeit uneven in quality and full of factual errors. It possesses all the breeziness of youth, in an age when the highest tribute Gibson could pay a comrade was to describe him as "a sportsman…white as a man can be." He describes a world in which alcohol equates with pleasure rather more convincingly than do girls, and in which to "shoot a line" was the greatest social crime, though Gibson himself was scarcely immune from it. After selling many hundreds of thousands of copies over half a century, it remains a moving self-portrait of one of the doomed young men of Bomber Command, who crowded what passed for a lifetime into just twenty-five years.

Gibson's last months were neither happy nor distinguished. The invasion of Normandy in June 1944 filled him with fears that the war would be won without any further assistance from himself. He called personally on Harris at his headquarters at High Wycombe, and pleaded for a return to an operational unit. Harris's residual patronage sufficed to gain him a posting four days later to a staff job back at 5 Group. In the weeks that followed, Gibson made few friends. Many men who did not know him were irked by his conceit and outbreaks of pomposity. Once after a typical mess shindig at Woodhall Spa, the "gallant Guy" suffered the removal of his trousers. He resented this indignity sufficiently to place one of those responsible on a charge. He did more work on the manuscript of *Enemy Coast Ahead,* which had been returned to him by the Air Ministry with a host of passages blue-pencilled by the censor— especially those in which he made personal or political comments which the service considered inappropriate for a young RAF hero. On a dank, wet afternoon he had a meeting with Margaret North, then living in Bognor Regis with her six-month-old baby, Guy's godson. They discussed the frustrations of their unhappy marriages, and he said: "Afterwards, I'm coming to find you." A few days later she received a note: "The day was perfect. I love you now and for ever." She never heard from him again.

On the afternoon of 19 September 1944, Mosquito crews preparing for the night's attack on the German city of Rheydt were amazed to hear that the raid controller would be Guy Gibson, the base air staff officer. Gibson had been an uncomfortable presence since June, visibly chafing at his nonoperational role. Yet it seemed extraordinary that he was now abruptly granted permission to fly again. First, he possessed negligible experience of flying the twin-engined Mosquito marker plane. Second, techniques of aerial bombardment had vastly advanced since his last operation, fifteen months earlier. The role of master bomber, directing attacking aircraft by VHF radio, was indeed one which he had pioneered over the dams, but it now played on a much larger and more sophisticated stage. Sir Ralph Cochrane, 5 Group's commander, never explained why he gave permission for Gibson to fly again. It is reasonable to assume that he had merely grown weary of being importuned by this angry young man, transformed from the greatest star of Bomber Command into something of an embarrassment.

Eve Gibson telephoned Guy that afternoon, and received a frosty and preoccupied reception. He asked her what was wrong. Nothing, said Eve, she merely wanted to talk. He promised to telephone her next morning, and hung up. Soon after 7:30 p.m., Gibson took off from Woodhall Spa, accompanied by the station navigation officer, James Warwick. By that stage of the war, attacking the Ruhr had become a much less hazardous affair than two years earlier. The officer who briefed Gibson for the raid told him that when he turned for home he could be back over the Allied lines in France within ten minutes, and should stay above ten thousand feet. No, said Gibson with his usual stubbornness, he intended to fly home low.

Bomber Command's attack on Rheydt was less than successful. Though Gibson maintained perfect calm over the target, several pilots asserted that his inexperience as a master bomber was plain. Half an hour after leaving the target around 10 p.m., Gibson's Mosquito crashed near the Dutch town of Steenbergen, for reasons and in circumstances that have never been resolved. Both in September 1944 and afterwards, airmen speculated that Gibson's inexperience as a Mosquito pilot, together with his long absence from operations, represented fatal hazards. It is hard to avoid sympathy for James Warwick, the hapless navigator who died with him. In the tough, brutal world of bomber operations in 1944, more than a few men at Coningsby suggested that Warwick was a victim not of the Germans but of Gibson, an egoist to the end. The remains of the two men were buried nearby. The only identifiable fragment of Gibson was a laundry mark on a sock. He left an estate of just £2,295, no will, and of course the manuscript of *Enemy Coast Ahead*. That book's appearance was followed by the immortalisation of 617 Squadron first in Paul Brickhill's romantic tale *The Dam Busters* (1952), then by the film of the same title. These ensured Guy Gibson's undying fame.

In the climactic final phase of a world war, Gibson's death caused surprisingly little stir. So many other people had died, so many more were yet to perish. The passing of one young flier, albeit a famous one, attracted respectful public regret, but no deep outpouring of grief. His memoir was still in the future. Much had happened since the dams raid. It is hard to imagine that, if Gibson had lived, his subsequent life would have been happy. The warriors who feature in the earlier part of this book were well-known among their own comrades, but little heard of in the world. Guy Gibson displayed talents, above all elemental determination, which were of priceless value to his nation at war, and made him a national hero, subject to more adulation even than modern football stars experience. He possessed a precocious maturity in the sphere of bomber operations, while remaining in the wider world a callow, awkward figure. Many young men who achieved celebrity in the war were obliged to spend the subsequent years of peace living off fading memories of the great deeds of their youth. Gibson's intolerance, his conceit and insensitivity in human relations, were not qualities that would have endeared him to a peacetime generation. Like many young flying stars, the gifts that enabled Gibson to achieve so much in his cockpit were not those which would have fitted him for high command.

Yet here was a young man who gave everything to the service of his country at war. The RAF used up Gibson long before his death, in the way that war uses up many young men, even those who are not maimed or killed. From Harris's viewpoint, "the dam buster" had served his turn. He had become redundant. The brilliant smile that captivated so many admirers of both sexes masked the tragedy of a man who lived his simple life in one dimension, that of battle. Where many warriors through the ages have discovered a consolation in comradeship, Gibson was a loner in a fashion unusual among bomber pilots, most of whom acknowledged dependence at least upon the other crew members of their own aircraft. Gibson did so much for the Royal Air Force and for his country that it is dismaying to acknowledge that he gained little happiness from the fame that followed. But for that foolish crash in Holland, actuarily he might still be alive today. Yet perhaps he gains greater satisfaction by viewing his own celebrity from some lofty vantage point as an eternally youthful hero of the skies, rather than as an arthritic, cross-grained old veteran, doomed to decades of reunions and memorial services.

CHAPTER ELEVEN

HOLLYWOOD HERO

IT IS A SCENE depicted in scores of low-budget movies produced during the twenty years after World War II ended: on a shell-torn hillside, a GI pokes up his head as a group of Germans offer surrender. He is shot. His body rolls back into the arms of his buddy, who stares at it for a few moments in shocked disbelief. Then, boyish features frozen into a mask of determination, the surviving soldier grasps his carbine and charges single-handed at the German machine-gun positions, shooting and grenading until every treacherous Kraut lies dead. Then he stands numb and drained amid the carnage as the rest of his platoon belatedly advance to join him. They stare warily at this lonely figure, half awed and half appalled by a display of suicidal courage they know they cannot match.

This is a Hollywood caricature of war, acted out many times by John Wayne and his kind. The scene features prominently in the 1955 movie *To Hell and Back,* with Audie Murphy playing the angry GI. The star was not much of an actor. His chief assets on screen were the baby-faced good looks of an all-American boy, which kept fans happy through his appearances in twenty-five years of cheap Westerns. His performance in *To Hell and Back* is wooden and one-dimensional. As the young soldier, he views shot-blasted battlefields with the sort of dismay a dutiful school-boy might show, gazing upon a classroom trashed by a cluster of delinquents. In scenes behind the lines, amid bar girls in seedy Italian clip joints, he looks as embarrassed as he deserves to be. Violins dominate the musical score. No cliché of soldiers' dialogue is omitted from the script. A film critic might say that Ronald Reagan could play this sort of corny stuff better than Murphy did.

Yet there is a profound pathos about Audie Murphy and the war film in which he starred. It was based upon his own experience of combat. When the Second World War ended, he was probably only nineteen, at most twenty—his birth date is uncertain, and seems to have been falsified to enable him to enlist underage. Yet he had become the most decorated American soldier of the conflict. Again and again in a succession of actions in Italy and France he displayed his courage in the face of the enemy. He possessed extraordinary qualities as a fighting infantryman, not least an eagerness to return to duty after being wounded three times. He cherished some notions of becoming a career soldier, but abandoned these when his fame attracted the attention of James Cagney, who was responsible for bringing him to Hollywood and launching him on a career in films. In 1948 the heavily ghosted memoir of his war experiences, *To Hell and Back,* became a best-seller, which led in turn to the film in which he so uncomfortably played himself. For all Murphy's celebrity, happiness and fulfilment eluded him. He was painfully conscious of his paucity of acting talent. It is difficult to be unmoved by the history of a man who contributed so much as a wartime soldier, yet found it impossible to parley military achievement into any rapprochement with himself.

Murphy was born into a dirt-poor sharecropper's family in Hunt County, Texas, probably in June 1925. One of twelve children of whom nine survived into adulthood, he gained little schooling before his despairing father abandoned their home. Audie's classmates mocked him as "short-breeches," because his only pair of trousers shrank with relentless washing. After the fifth grade he embarked on several teenage years of casual labour—cotton picking, selling newspapers, working in a gas station. His mother died of heart disease in 1941, and most of his siblings disappeared into orphanages. He himself had shown an early interest in the possibility of becoming a soldier. One of the few positive influences upon his childhood was a local World War I veteran who enthused the boy with his reminiscences. The U.S. Army was a familiar refuge for young southerners lacking money or education. When America entered the war in December 1941, Murphy sought to enlist. He was rejected by both the Marines and the paratroops. This was unsurprising, since he stood five feet five inches tall, and weighed just 112 pounds. The army eventually accepted him in June 1942, aged eighteen on his record, probably seventeen in reality. After training at Camp Wolters, Texas, "Baby," as he was initially nicknamed by comrades, was shipped overseas. In February 1943 he joined B Company of the 1/15th Infantry in North Africa as a replacement.

A reserved man all his life, beneath an iron mask of self-control it was plain that Murphy nursed a lot of anger, as well he might. From the outset of his military career he showed a determination to succeed as a soldier, and also a satisfaction in finding something he could belong to— the platoon. For the first and perhaps last time, here was a group amid which he felt at home. Loyalty to the handful of men among whom he served was among the most striking features of his wartime career. Again and again he refused opportunities and promotions that might cause him to be separated from them. Almost at the outset, an officer troubled by his slight figure and boyish features sought to make Murphy a headquarters runner rather than a rifleman, but the young soldier was having none of it. He remained in the same unit from beginning to end, until he became almost the sole survivor of the band which had mustered in North Africa.

Murphy had to wait some months before first experiencing action in July 1943, following the invasion of Sicily. Most soldiers in a theatre of war are willing to do what is asked of them, but are careful not to seek additional hazards. Murphy's eagerness to join patrols and take point during advances, together with an obvious dexterity with weapons, earned him a rapid promotion to corporal. He joined the Italian campaign with the U.S. 3rd Division, landing near Salerno, and was committed to a series of battles around the Volturno River. Encountering Germans on a night patrol, after a firefight he and his men took cover in a quarry. The enemy pursued them, but were halted by American fire which killed three men and caused the others to surrender. This action earned Murphy a sergeant's stripes.

A bout of malaria put him into hospital for the Anzio landing. Like many other infantrymen in the same predicament, when discharged he fiercely resisted efforts to send him as a replacement to a new regiment. He insisted upon rejoining the 15th Infantry, committed to heavy fighting in the beachhead. Murphy sought the front constantly, and became well-known for his enthusiasm for seeking out the enemy alone, stalking and killing Germans wherever he could find them. He earned his first Bronze Star for leading a night patrol to destroy with Molotov cocktails and rifle grenades a damaged tank which the Germans were striving to repair. Another attack of malaria sent him back to a field hospital for ten days, but he returned in time to join the advance on Rome late in May 1944. Offered a battlefield commission, he declined lest he should be obliged to leave his platoon, with whom he shared a disappointing leave in the Italian capital after its liberation: "We prowl through Rome like ghosts," he wrote later, "finding no satisfaction in anything we see or do. I feel like a man briefly reprieved from death; and there is no joy within me. We can have no hope until the war is ended. Thinking of the men on the fighting fronts, I grow lonely on the streets of Rome."

Murphy was a grave young man, who embraced responsibility and seemed happy to accept it on behalf of others less ardent. He fulfilled the hardest duty of a soldier in combat: he was willing to engage the enemy even when logic and instinct incited more normal men to seek shelter or to flee. Murphy claimed to be as vulnerable to fear as any of his comrades. This was patently untrue, though his excellent tactical judgement helped him to keep his nerve when others lost it. He demonstrated a gift for judging a combat situation, assessing whether holding a position or moving forward was in reality as perilous as the sound and fury of battle persuaded other men that it was: "Experience helps. You soon learn that a situation is seldom as black as the imagination paints it. Some always get through."

As an undersized boy, Murphy was a feisty classroom fighter who taught himself to repress visible emotion. "I'm not the crying kind," he told an army nurse, and there is no reason to disbelieve him. His loyalty to his platoon seemed almost obsessive: "As long as there's a man in the line, maybe I feel that my place is up there beside him." For all his unimpressive physique, he possessed a natural authority, enforced by cool, piercing eyes. Instinctively at home with weapons, he handled every kind of infantry small arm with assurance. He suffered not the slightest hesitation, such as was commonplace among citizen soldiers, about killing his fellow man. Most combatants seldom fired their rifles in action, and rarely hit anything when they did so. "Murph" always fired, often effectively. His platoon had the equivocal feelings about him which soldiers usually display towards zealous warriors—they respected his courage, but feared that it might prove excessively dangerous to the interests of others.

Murphy cut a lonely figure, a man who seldom received a letter from home at mail call, because he knew few people who might care to write. He was the sort of soldier whom commanding officers cherish, because they need them to win battles. A distinguished American World War II infantry officer wrote: "A few guys carry your attack, and the rest of the people sort of participate and arrive on the objective shortly after everybody else." This is an important truth. Likewise another veteran, Colonel William DePuy: "The average man, like nine out of ten, does not have an instinct for the battlefield, doesn't relish it, and will not act independently except under direct orders." Audie Murphy, it was plain to all those who observed him in action, was the one man in ten, indeed the one in a thousand, even if his exceptionality caused a 3rd Division officer later to observe enigmatically that the young hero "was not the most admired guy in the world." Such is usually the case with any soldier, sailor or airman vulnerable to the charge of being a "gong-chaser." Murphy's behaviour created some of the same discomfort among comrades as did that of Guy Gibson in the Royal Air Force.

The baby-faced sergeant won a Distinguished Service Cross during an advance up an enemy-held hillside near the town of Ramantuelle on 15 August 1944, the day of the Anvil landings in southern France. Three hours after crossing the beach south of St. Tropez, his battalion was driven to ground by German machine-gun fire as they neared a ridge crest. Murphy's platoon was moved forward from reserve to seek a new line of approach. Soon it too was pinned down. Perceiving that the enemy was out of range of carbines and grenades, on his own initiative Murphy crawled back downhill to the heavy-weapons platoon, borrowed a .30-calibre machine gun, returned with Private Lattie Tipton to find a firing position, and quickly killed two of the defending Germans. Having exhausted his single belt of .30-calibre ammunition, he and Tipton charged and overran one enemy trench with carbines and grenades. A German soldier in a nearby foxhole waved a white flag. Tipton rose to accept his surrender, and was at once shot dead. He was Murphy's closest friend in the army. Enraged, Murphy picked up a German MG42 machine gun lying at his feet and charged along the hillside, throwing grenades with his free hand. One by one, and entirely alone, he destroyed a succession of enemy positions, killing thirteen Germans. The rest of the unit, at whom he had been shouting vain curses and imprecations to follow him, then advanced to occupy the ridgeline.

After months of stagnation first in Italian mud and then dust, the American invaders of southern France exulted in the swift dash up the Rhône Valley. Murphy wrote: "We experience great exhilaration, for there is nothing so good for the morale of the footsoldier as progress." Late in August a shell fragment which nicked his heel cost Murphy two weeks in hospital. By now all the men of his platoon with whom he had found comradeship in North Africa and Italy were gone—wounded or dead. He forged no new close relationship with their successors. He was widely perceived as a soldier fighting a war of his own: "So many men have come and gone that I can no longer keep track of them...I have isolated myself as much as possible, desiring only to do my work and be left alone. I feel burnt out, emotionally and physically exhausted. Let the hill be strewn with corpses so long as I do not have to turn over the bodies and find the familiar face of a friend." Within days of returning to his unit from hospital Murphy led a patrol into a German ambush which pinned down his men. He crawled round to a flank, then charged alone with grenades and submachine gun, destroying the enemy ambush party. He received a Silver Star for this action. Three days later, several of his men were shot down in a similar surprise encounter. Murphy worked his way forward until he could see the German positions, then directed artillery and mortar fire by radio until the enemy retired with substantial casualties. This action, too, earned him a Silver Star.

A cynic might suggest that the U.S. Army had by now identified a story-book hero, and heaped decorations on him with extravagant enthusiasm. Other men did as much on the battlefield, yet their deeds went unremarked, or were rewarded with a single medal. The U.S. 3rd Division, a good formation which paid heavily in casualties for its repeated commitment to combat, was uncommonly generous in recommending awards—11.6 per cent of all the U.S. Army's wartime Medals of Honor were awarded to men from its ranks. Yet there is no reason to doubt the facts of each action for which Murphy was honoured. The American and British armies in northwest Europe suffered chronic difficulty because many of their infantry units were sluggish in attack. On encountering even small numbers of enemy, it was a habitual vice of Eisenhower's foot soldiers to halt and call down artillery and mortar fire, accepting a delay of hours or even days, rather than to launch a quick, bold infantry assault. By contrast, here was Sergeant Audie Murphy, again and again offering demonstrations straight out of the infantry manual which, had they been widely emulated, would have won the war months sooner. Who can be surprised that senior officers were eager to highlight such a man? And who can deny that Murphy's courage merited the applause which it received?

At last he accepted a battlefield commission, becoming commander of the platoon with which he had served since North Africa. On 26 October he was seriously wounded in the hip by a sniper's bullet. As is often the way in war, however skilful the soldier, Murphy suffered his most grievous injury when taken by surprise, in a situation in which his prowess counted for nothing. He merely overtaxed his luck. Many hours elapsed before he reached a field hospital. The wound turned gangrenous, and he was obliged to spend three dreary and often painful months enduring treatment and recuperation, his life saved by penicillin. "These Krauts are getting to be better shots than they used to be or else my luck's playing out on me," he wrote ruefully from his bed. "I guess some day they will tag me for keeps."

Had he wished, he could have gone home to the United States with his medals and his wounds. Instead, by January 1945 he was back with his battalion in Alsace, participating in the battle of the Colmar Pocket. On 26 January he was commanding his company, every other officer having been killed in unsuccessful attacks. The 15th Infantry were once again preparing to advance near the village of Holzwihr when the Germans launched a counterattack with tanks and foot soldiers. Murphy ordered his heavily outnumbered men to pull back, but himself remained in his position to direct artillery fire. As the Germans came on, the lieutenant noticed an American tank destroyer on fire nearby. The armoured M-10 had been abandoned by its crew after they rashly ignored Murphy's warning not to expose themselves, and suffered the consequences. A .50-calibre machine gun stood loaded and idle on the hull mounting. Murphy ran forward, seized the gun and began pouring fire into the approaching German infantry. Some attackers were later found dead within a few yards of his position. For an hour he maintained his defence despite a leg wound after two further German hits on the tank destroyer, and with flames surging around him. Only when his ammunition was exhausted did he slip back to rejoin the men of his company, who had been awed spectators of this performance from the comparative safety of a forest two hundred yards to the rear. He led them forward once more against the battered and dispirited Germans, who turned in retreat. Murphy then collapsed. For the Holzwihr episode he was awarded the Congressional Medal of Honor, together with the Legion of Merit for his achievements throughout the campaign.

This very young man was not unreasonably thrilled by his deluge of decorations. After hearing that he was to receive the Medal of Honor, he wrote to a friend: "Since that is all the Medals they have to offer I'll have to take it easy for a while." First Lieutenant Murphy was henceforward considered too precious a commodity to be allowed to continue in service with a rifle company. After a leave in Paris, somewhat to his dismay he spent the last weeks of the campaign as a liaison officer. Though he often found excuses to explore the forward areas, the war was almost won. He was denied any further authorised combat role.

Murphy had become the epitome of the American hero. In the aftermath of VE-Day, the army and his fellow countrymen hastened to celebrate his achievement. *Life* magazine featured him on its cover. Absurd calculations were made about the number of Germans this one-man task force had personally killed, wounded or captured. European governments added their own garlands to the symbolic liberator's collection— Lieutenant Murphy was finally entitled to wear twenty-eight medals. From Paris, on 10 June 1945, he was among the very first Americans to be flown home. Yet what was home? He had left the Lone Star State less than three years earlier as a nobody who knew almost no one. "Who would have expected Shorty to be anything more than another kid from Texas?" mused an old acquaintance. Murphy evinced a stab of disgust about the fashion in which both his local towns, McKinney and Greenville, which had treated the threadbare orphan with disdain three years earlier, now fought to claim him. Everybody wanted to meet and shower praise upon the absurdly handsome, apparently diffident hero. When he went to a barber's shop for a haircut a crowd gathered outside, peering fascinated through the window at the young god.

But here, once again, was a familiar problem for commanders: what was to be done with the successful warrior? He had no education, and indeed no great intellect. Most of the comrades whom he had known—in some cases loved—were dead. He appeared without vices, yet possessed only one demonstrable skill: he could fight. Continuing pain from his hip wound made it improbable that he should continue a combat career in the army, even if new enemies could be found for him to kill. He was too deficient in the qualities of a team player to seem a future general. On 21 September 1945, immensely famous yet with no fixed abode or future, Audie Murphy was discharged from military service.

It was a sight of the photograph on the *Life* cover which convinced the superstar James Cagney that this boy could make it in movies: "I saw that Audie could be photographed well from any angle, and I figured that a guy with drive enough to take him that far in the war had drive enough to become a star." Murphy at first ignored a cable from Cagney in Hollywood, seeking a meeting. When at last they got together, the star—who was exactly Murphy's height—enthused: "Dignity from within! Not the kind imposed upon you from without. Spiritual overtones. He looks like Huckleberry Finn grown up. No, not really grown up. There's something in those eyes that is as old as death and yet as young as springtime." Cagney put the grave young veteran on a salary and a personal contract, then spent some time studying his man to decide how best to make an actor of him. For a year Murphy lodged in Cagney's Beverley Hills poolhouse. The star decided against any formal training, but employed a dance instructor to teach the young war veteran to walk gracefully. He noted that Murphy had an excellent memory and remarkable powers of observation, but not much else. He persuaded him, somewhat unwillingly, to read aloud to an empty room, to strengthen his speaking voice.

The Texan farmboy found all this pretty dispiriting. Again and again he was tempted to throw in his hand. Acutely conscious of his disqualifications to become a public performer, he wrote to a friend: "James Cagney is trying to teach me show business, but I'm afraid he doesn't have much to work with." The star and his protégé eventually fell out and parted company, for reasons neither ever discussed and which remain a matter for speculation. It was widely acknowledged in Hollywood that Murphy travelled with demons, and it was generally assumed that these derived from his war experiences. There was much talk, as well there might be, about his insistence upon sleeping with a pistol under his pillow, sometimes waking from nightmares to fire it at an unoffending cupboard or mirror. That the demons existed is undoubted, but it seems reasonable to suppose that they predated Murphy's war experiences.

Resigned to attempting to make a success of Hollywood, for a time he attended drama classes, but quit disgusted by what he perceived as the left-wing attitudes he encountered there. Exponents of a wide range of political causes sought in vain to recruit the hero for their own purposes. Murphy found it impossible to take seriously drama exercises such as pretending to sew up an imaginary pair of gloves. He adopted the customary Beverly Hills panacea for trauma by visiting a psychiatrist. Asked how their meetings went, Murphy responded with laconic wit: "He went off to see *his* psychiatrist." The aspirant actor fell in with an alcoholic screenwriter of intellectual pretensions named David "Spec" McLure, who became his cultural mentor and launched him—with indifferent success—upon a programme of self-education.

It was plain to most people who encountered Audie that he was a psychological mess of epic proportions. He met and married a beautiful starlet named Wanda Hendrix, then lived with her through a few sad years in which his career prospered while hers sagged. She found it hard to live with his tensions, expressed in chronic stomach disorders. He once told her that in action he had seen the face of his own father in that of every German soldier he killed. She grew to perceive that he was a gloomy, tormented soul: "Audie's worst fault is his pessimism," she said. He had no sustaining core of values or self-belief, and as a result was fearful of dropping his defences in relationships with either sex. There was a chronic melancholy, apparent to all who knew him well. He lived on the shortest of fuses, once shooting a light switch amid his midnight torments, wading into fistfights with men rash enough to challenge him. He was sometimes seen by his wife holding a loaded gun to his own mouth. "He played with death as if it were a toy," Hendrix told Spec McLure. It surprised no one when the marriage ended in divorce in 1950.

Yet Murphy possessed two qualities that could, and did, carry him a long way in the Hollywood of the late 1940s and the 1950s: looks and charm. He swiftly graduated from a bit part in a 1948 West Point courtroom drama, *Beyond Glory*—"I had eight words in the script, seven more than I could handle"—to bigger things. In 1949 he starred as William Bonney, Billy the Kid, in *The Kid from Texas*. This part convinced him that his future lay in Westerns—"oaters" in the jargon of the trade. He had exactly the gifts to convince an audience that he was, indeed, the lonely gunfighter of legend. By a notable irony, however, in order to fulfil his screen destiny the kid from Texas had to acquire some essential skills, prominent among them that of riding a horse. There had been no money for horses in a Hunt County childhood. His war wounds troubled him constantly: he was in discomfort in the saddle, and in pain when he fell out of it. Yet here, true grit prevailed. He turned himself into a fine horseman. Filming as Billy the Kid, on the first day his stunt double broke a collarbone. Thereafter, Murphy did almost all his own stunt work on the picture.

Willard Willingham, who later took up a role as Murphy's stunt double when one was needed, also became his personal assistant and closest friend. Willingham later said: "He was pretty strange in those days. He was difficult for everyone." A man of natural good manners who recoiled from coarse behaviour, Murphy had no patience with people who offended his own sense of propriety, not least in their choice of language. He was sometimes heard to lacerate erring crew members on set. Those who worked with him learned to be wary of his notorious temper.

Murphy went on to make some forty Western pictures. For all his limitations, he became a star of his day. "Audie could learn the lines and hit his marks. Anything else about acting was a mystery to him," remarked a fellow performer. Critics noted that he could never be a convincing ensemble player, because on screen he always looked what he was—a man apart, a man alone. Even among a screen cluster of cowboys, never for a moment did Murphy seem a credible member of a gang. Yet none of this mattered to the public, who idolised the handsome kid with the steady, hurt eyes, whose wartime achievements they never forgot. Whatever Murphy's insecurities in other departments, he was sufficiently assured of his own courage to be unafraid sometimes to play cowards on celluloid. From 1949 onwards his celebrity was increased by the publication of his war memoir, ghosted by Spec McLure.

The battlefield feats recorded under Murphy's name in *To Hell and Back* are a matter of record. However, most of the book consists of reported dialogue between the soldier and his platoon. It will always be a matter for speculation how far these are fictionalised. The tone is half right, but the text sometimes attributes implausible reflective powers to Murphy the young infantryman. The book is laden with cliché, of a kind which suggests the voice of McLure rather than that of the nominal author. Here was no Frederic Manning—though both men fought, and lost, bitter battles with publishers whom they sought to convince that no soldiers' dialogue could be credible without its blasphemies and obscenities. Murphy himself never disowned the book—how could he?—but he was outspokenly critical of the subsequent film, which he considered a betrayal of the soldiers among whom he served. It is a preposterous notion that any man could convincingly reenact on celluloid feats which he himself had performed on the battlefield. Murphy cringed before the studio copy on the movie posters: "Just a kid too young to shave...but old enough to win every medal his country had to give."

In the Hollywood of that period men were expected to die apparently bloodlessly on screen. Murphy remembered all too vividly the reality of severed limbs, mangled torsos, bare bones and dangling intestines. He fought in vain to toughen the bowdlerised script dialogue. He understood, as the filmmakers had no desire to understand, that courage is displayed in war against a backdrop of almost unbridled squalor and sorrow. The detachment he displays on screen as the star of *To Hell and Back* hints at the disgust about the whole venture which he freely acknowledged off set.

The screen role of which he remained most proud was that of Fleming, another young soldier, in John Huston's 1951 film of Stephen Crane's *Red Badge of Courage*. Critics were unimpressed by the movie, yet Murphy—on whose casting Huston insisted, against the strong wishes of the studio, MGM—was able to play an infantryman of the American Civil War period suffering experiences at least as harrowing as his own with a conviction he could not bring to a portrayal of himself. Murphy's career as an actor, if not as a star, was fatally flawed by a resistance to masquerade or self-revelation. His own being was rooted in a painful, even exaggerated, sense of reality. He found it impossible to throw himself convincingly into the fantasies contrived by directors and screenwriters. He felt a disdain for actors who had not served in the wartime

One of the most celebrated images of the Second World War: the Ruhr's Mohne dam breached by pilots of the RAF's 617 Squadron in the May 1943 attack led by Guy Gibson. Like so many warriors, Gibson *(right)* found little contentment in his fame and decorations before his death in action in September 1944.

America's most decorated wartime soldier, Audie Murphy *(above)*, as a lieutenant in Paris after his battlefield exploits were over, and *(below)*, re-creating them for the 1955 movie *To Hell and Back*, in which he starred as himself. The little Texan forged a Hollywood career, chiefly in Westerns, but never shed the traumas of combat.

(Left) General Matthew Ridgway and his most famous subordinate, "Slim Jim" Gavin, commander of the 82nd Airborne Division, in Belgium in March 1945. Gavin was one of America's outstanding wartime soldiers, and its youngest general since Custer, but Ridgway was galled by his protégé's conceit.

One of the huge 1944 airborne landings in France in which Gavin participated. He was among the foremost advocates of the new science of parachute warfare.

The doughty Australian Nancy Wake, in the uniform of a captain in the First Aid Nursing Yeomanry, cover for her role as a British agent with the French resistance in 1944. She is captured more informally in the picture below, with her wireless operator Denis Rake and American OSS officer John Alsop *(top)*, gleefully exploring the wine cellar of a château their maquis group commandeered as a headquarters shortly before the liberation.

Colonel John Paul Vann, one of the most ardent and inspiring of U.S. officers who served in Vietnam, with Colonel Huynh Van Cao of the ARVN, to whom he served as chief adviser during his first posting to the country in 1962.

(Overleaf) Vann's hopes of promoting American victory in Vietnam would crumble to dust as the war dragged on. He died in a helicopter crash during bitter fighting around the Kontum province in June 1972.

Avigdor Kahalani sits bearded amid his tank crew on the Golan Heights at the end of the 1973 Yom Kippur War, where he made his name as one of the saviors of Israel.

The Golan battlefield where Kahalani and his comrades destroyed Syrian tanks in the hundreds during their epic battle of attrition, the greatest clash of armor since the Second World War.

armed forces, and showed it. Many of them responded in kind, by spurn-
ing Murphy. Kirk Douglas thought him "a vicious little guy." After a
serious falling out with Tony Curtis, Murphy never spoke to the star
again. He saved his admiration for the relatively few Hollywood figures
such as James Stewart, Lee Marvin and Clark Gable who had served
their country in uniform.

After his separation from Wanda Hendrix, Murphy told Spec
McLure that he would live a hermit's life: "I'll be the poor man's Howard
Hughes." Four days after he won his divorce decree, however, he married
a Texan girl named Pamela Archer, with whom he had two sons whom
he adored. The couple were soon living apart. Murphy embarked upon a
long succession of casual liaisons—a familiar pastime for Hollywood
stars, but one which he pursued with an almost inhuman detachment.
He spent many hours alone, even on movie sets. An actor who worked
with him on *Gunfight at Comanche Creek* (1963) and *Arizona Raiders* (1965)
said: "He always looked as if he'd rather be somewhere else." His contempt for his own thespian skills never diminished, but he developed
sufficient confidence in his powers as a box-office draw to impose his will
on set. He made himself seem foolish by declaring one day that he
wanted to raise his game, to play in screen adaptations of Ibsen and Dos-
toyevsky. The nearest he came to attempting such pinnacles was to play
the lead opposite Michael Redgrave in a disastrously misconceived 1957
production of Graham Greene's novel *The Quiet American*.

The film was chiefly shot on location in Vietnam, which was enjoying
an interval of relative tranquillity between the French war with the
Vietminh and the American war with the Vietcong. By now Murphy was
past thirty—far older than that in experience, still absurdly younger in
looks. Neither he nor Redgrave was first choice for their parts, which
were intended for Montgomery Clift and Laurence Olivier. Redgrave, a
veteran British actor who represented the highest standards of his profession on stage and screen, recoiled in disgust from Murphy's approach
to acting after hearing the Texan shrug, "It beats picking cotton." Murphy, in his turn, knew nothing of Redgrave's reputation, and plainly
cared little for the bisexual Englishman. He did not enjoy his weeks in
Saigon's thick, clammy, hundred-degree temperatures. He contracted
appendicitis and had to be rushed to hospital in Hong Kong, at vast cost
in delays to the production. One scene in the movie required him to

carry an injured Redgrave out of danger during a firefight in paddy fields. Redgrave was a big, heavy man. For Murphy, with his slight frame and war wounds, the experience of supporting him was an agony, intensified when a retake was needed.

During his convalescence from the appendix operation, Murphy made the grave mistake of reading Graham Greene's novel on which the film was based. Brooding about its contemptuous anti-Americanism, he was tempted to refuse to return to the set. Murphy the patriot was disgusted by the novelist's cynicism. "Greene never met a real American, I think. He believes a guy who goes to Harvard and lives in Boston is a real American. Did you ever meet anyone from Boston who went to Harvard? They all come from anyplace but…" In Saigon, Murphy was made deeply unhappy by the army of child street beggars. "There's always children," he told Spec McClure wearily, recalling Naples and Rome. "The children grow up and become soldiers. And somebody gets the soldiers together and declares a war. So the soldiers cripple and kill each other until one side hollers 'Uncle.' Then people ring bells, blow whistles and talk about how great peace is for a while. But new children come along, new soldiers, new wars." If these were banal sentiments, there is no reason to doubt their sincerity.

The film's interior sequences were shot in Rome, from which Murphy several times revisited Anzio, scene of some of his most brutal wartime experiences. His wife, Pamela, whom he seems to have made no effort to contact during his months in Asia, also made the Anzio trip with him. Shooting of *The Quiet American* was completed on 5 June 1957, thirteen years almost to the day since Murphy had first entered Rome as a young GI. He was thirty-two, or thirty-three according to army records. His movie career was already slipping downhill, though it would stumble on for a few more years. He appeared in forty-four films in all, and saved none of the money from them. He was chronically careless, indeed reckless, about his finances, a regular and unlucky gambler. He later went bankrupt when a business venture failed.

Murphy found himself wholly out of step with the new world of the 1960s, and above all with the protest movement against the war in Vietnam. He himself was a product of an earlier era and a different ethic, in which any decent man's actions were governed by loyalty to his country's chosen causes. He found his reputation borrowed in disturbing circumstances when Lieutenant William Calley of the Americal Division, the officer held responsible for the 1968 My Lai massacre, testified after his atrocities were exposed: "We thought we would go to Vietnam and be Audie Murphys. Kick in the door. Run in the hooch, give it a good burst—kill. And get a big kill ratio in Vietnam." To those who wished Murphy well, it was embarrassing enough that such a soldier as Calley should cite his example. Matters became worse, however, when Murphy himself observed staunchly that he thought Calley guilty of nothing worse than a military misjudgement. The star-hero's achievements of which 1945 America had been so proud, the killing of Germans in industrial quantities, for which he was rewarded with a chestful of decorations and the applause of the public, inspired much more equivocal responses from a new generation. What kind of man was this, who could have taken life so readily at his country's bidding, and who displayed no apparent misgivings about the murderous task of a soldier? Murphy faced further embarrassing publicity in 1970, when he was indicted for the attempted murder of a dog trainer at whom he had allegedly fired a pistol. He was acquitted for lack of evidence, but was quizzed outside the courtroom by reporters about whether he had indeed let off a gun at the man. "If I had," said Murphy defiantly, "do you think I would have missed?" Everyone knew that whatever the truth of this episode, the star possessed a dark and unhealthy obsession with firearms.

Murphy's relationships with studio executives, never cordial, were not assisted when word got around of a remark he made one day in the 1960s, when visiting the Universal lot to discuss a new movie. As he was gazing thoughtfully at a cluster of studio executives, somebody asked what was on his mind. He responded: "I was just thinking that with one hand grenade, a person could get rid of all those no-talent bastards at one stroke."

Murphy failed in his oft-expressed ambition to find some means of achieving financial security without continuing to make third-rate Westerns. By the end of the 1960s the third-rate Western era was about through, and so was Murphy's box-office appeal. He was killed in a light plane crash in fog at Roanoke, Virginia, on 28 May 1971, aged forty-five or forty-six. It is hard to feel that death deprived him of anything he valued. His lavish funeral at Arlington National Cemetery flouted the wishes expressed in his 1965 will that he should be buried without ceremony, and especially without any military presence. He wanted to lie anywhere save at Arlington, he said. Yet even if America's relationship with its former hero had grown uneasy, at his death the nation was determined to reclaim possession of Audie Murphy.

Spec McLure recorded a conversation with Murphy in the 1950s in which he said: "I have a deadly hatred of fear. It has me by the throat, and I have it by the throat. We have been struggling for many years. And I still don't know which will win the battle. But that very hatred of fear has driven me to do a lot of things which I have never bothered to explain and which nobody understands. Fear is the blot on the thinking process, crippling the individual's ability to act. I am not brave. I simply perform first and think later."

Making allowance for artistic licence in McLure's version of Murphy's words, the sentiment rings true. Most men who act bravely in war do so because they dread succumbing to fear more than they dread the risk of being killed. Like more than a few such men, in war as in peace Murphy fought as many battles with himself as with the enemy. If he lacked self-belief, he possessed willpower of an extraordinary kind, together with an anger that never left him. He was better at fighting than anything else, and when the fighting was over, he found himself at a loss. Captain Ian Fraser of the Royal Navy, who won a Victoria Cross in the Second World War, wisely observed: "A man is trained for the task that might win him a VC. He is not trained to cope with what follows."

There was no joy for Murphy in movie stardom. He seemed to hate himself for accepting the indignities of Hollywood life in return for fame, cash and an unlimited supply of pretty girls. He perceived himself as a one-man freak show, the war hero exhibited before a predatory and invasive public in a fashion little different from that of the Elephant Man almost a century earlier. Wretched though his childhood was, it seems likely that after the war he might have found repose more easily in a humbler role in the sort of town he first came from, rather than in Hollywood. James Cagney may have done Murphy no favours by his patronage in 1945. Other men honoured for notable battlefield feats somehow contrived to return to civilian life without pretension or trauma. The youngest British winner of the Victoria Cross in the First World War was a gardener who came home in 1918 to spend the rest of his life among flowers and fruits. By contrast, the experience of Hollywood stardom almost destroyed Audie Murphy's fragile self-esteem. He was a superb foot soldier and close-quarter fighter who deserved well of his country for his wartime service, but whom celebrity exposed as a tragic figure. It laid bare his lack of other gifts, indispensable to the conduct of a normal existence in time of peace. Murphy's history is a cautionary tale for any modern reader rash enough to envy those who experience the thrills and adventures offered by war.

CHAPTER TWELVE

SLIM JIM

PARATROOPS WERE among the most spectacular military innovations of the Second World War. Like everything else to do with the sky, they attracted some of the boldest spirits of the combatant nations. By 1945 many commanders had become doubtful whether airborne forces justified the resources, human and material, devoted to them first by the Germans, latterly by the Allies. While airborne soldiers proved their value in commando raids and coup de main operations, massed drops cost heavy casualties for limited returns. Paradoxically, however, even those sceptical about the value of dropping airborne armies onto the battlefield recognised that the men who embraced this kind of warfare made exceptional soldiers with or without their parachutes. To this day, therefore, most armies retain paratroops as elites, even if they seldom jump into battle. In World War II they achieved a glamour which they have never lost. The three most effective Allied airborne formation leaders—Matthew Ridgway, Maxwell Taylor and James Gavin—were all Americans. In any list of able corps and divisional commanders, Ridgway and Gavin figure close to the top. Gavin lacked the gifts which later made Ridgway a fine army commander in Korea, but he remains one of the most attractive and impressive soldiers America has produced, the model of a fighting formation leader.

Gavin's ascent to fame was as steep as any man's could be. In 1909, at the age of two, he was adopted out of a New York Catholic foundlings' hospital by a Pennsylvania couple, Martin and Mary Gavin. All subsequent efforts to discover his real parentage failed, save that there seems a possibility he was the son of a young Irish immigrant from County Clare named Katherine Ryan. He nursed a belief of his own that his mother was a nun, who conceived a child by a prominent priest. The Gavins were assuredly Irish—the husband a gentle, weak-natured coal miner, the wife a fierce, often drunken virago who took in boarders and beat her foster son. The boy James acquired more education on the streets, working a paper round, than he got from schools. He was impelled by a fierce determination not to spend his life down the mines, and to escape from the cruelties of Mary Gavin. At seventeen he took off for New York City. After a week, having failed to find work, he adopted a familiar resort of his kind and enlisted in the U.S. Army. He was promptly shipped out to serve with a coastal artillery unit in Panama.

Gavin's wretched childhood echoed that of Audie Murphy. Hereafter, however, the boy's life was transformed, not least because he possessed an intellect Murphy lacked. Gavin found in the army the happy home that had eluded him in childhood. A diligent recruit, he was quickly promoted to corporal. Panama seemed a great improvement on Pennsylvania. He began to study in his off-duty hours, to make up for the education he had missed. A small miracle followed. His first sergeant, a Native American, perceived Gavin's potential and drew his attention to the possibility of a vacancy at West Point. With a friendly lieutenant coaching him in subjects of which he knew nothing—algebra, geometry, history—he passed the vital exams, and in July 1925 was accepted as an officer cadet.

So much has been written about the unhappy experiences of some West Point cadets that it is noteworthy how easily James Gavin adapted to a life quite outside his previous experience. He encountered no snobbery from young men of grander origins, though he himself chose to box rather than play polo. He plunged into fierce efforts to learn all the things he had missed out on as a boy. His ambition and dedication might have roused resentment, yet he masked these qualities behind a protective reserve. Gavin was always a driven man, but the outside world saw a quiet, shy figure, who expressed his strongest feelings, especially on professional matters, in writing. His good looks made him attractive to women, and he soon learned to be vain about his clothes. He passed out of West Point in June 1929, in the middle of his class. The foundling from Brooklyn had become an officer and a gentleman. The two are not always synonymous, but soldiers later nicknamed Gavin "Gentleman Jim" or "Slim Jim," in deference to his perfect turnout and punctilious manners. He himself voiced some sadness about quitting West Point, "my Spartan mother," where he had found his first safe harbour. It is not surprising, given the loneliness of his circumstances, that he rushed into one misjudgement which cost pain later: marriage to Irma Baulsir, a Cornell student whose parents lived in upper-middle-class comfort in Washington, D.C., though no Baulsir money trickled down to the Gavins. The wedding took place in September 1929. He was a newly minted lieutenant, just twenty-two.

Gavin later declared that he chose to make himself a fighting infantryman in preference to any other arm of the service. "I went forth to seek the challenge," he wrote, in an uncharacteristically mawkish flourish, "to move towards the sounds of the guns, to go where danger was greatest, for there is where the issues would be resolved and the decisions made." This was disingenuous. In truth, he first attempted to become a pilot. To his chagrin he was washed out of flight school at Brooks Field, Texas. Only thereafter was he assigned as an infantry officer first to Arizona, then to Fort Benning under "Vinegar Joe" Stilwell, and afterwards to the Philippines. In his first seventeen years as a soldier he attained the rank of captain. Though he established his promise in the eyes of his superiors, promotion was painfully slow in that tiny, over-officered, underfunded prewar U.S. Army. He now had a daughter, Barbara, whom he adored. However, his relationship with Irma—whom he always knew as Peggy—soured quickly. Though the marriage struggled on, Gavin was seldom without some extramural interest.

In the spring of 1940 he was assigned to the Tactics Department at West Point. He threw himself energetically into the study of German airborne warfare, spectacularly demonstrated to the world in Hitler's blitzkriegs. Gavin was always an innovator. He did not doubt that America would soon join the war, and when it did so he was eager for the U.S. Army to create its own doctrine, methods, equipment and ideas, rather than merely to adopt those of the other combatants, as it had done in 1917. He became passionately committed to the vision of parachute war,

and moved heaven and earth to get himself made a part of it. After lobbying every Washington military friend he possessed, in August 1941 he
was sent to jump school at Fort Benning. On gaining his paratroop wings
he was posted as a company commander to the newly formed 503rd
Parachute Infantry Battalion. By October, as a major, he was drafting the
U.S. Army's first manual of airborne warfare. Its authorship focused a lot
of military attention where Gavin wanted it: on himself and the concept
of parachute soldiering. In February 1942 he attended an abbreviated
Command and General Staff course at Leavenworth, Kansas, to qualify
for more senior postings as the United States began the expansion of its
armed forces. By August he was a full colonel, commanding the 505th
Parachute Infantry Regiment.

In the course of the Second World War, like the British, the U.S. Army
experienced difficulty in producing infantrymen who could match those
of Hitler's Wehrmacht. On the battlefield, superb American artillery was
required to compensate for the shortcomings of many rifle regiments.
The best U.S. foot soldiers, however, had no superiors. Together with the
Marines, America's all-volunteer parachute formations proved the finest
fighting troops the nation sent overseas. Gavin quickly showed himself
an inspirational leader and trainer. He demanded that his officers should
be "first out of the airplane door and last in the chow line." He drove
them through endless exercises designed to make them not only physically fit, but mentally robust. The United States enjoyed the luxury of
being able to choose when to commit its ground forces to battle. The
nation had already been in the war for nineteen months when Ridgway's
82nd Airborne Division, of which Gavin's regiment was a part, was chosen to participate in the invasion of Sicily. Its men were as highly trained
as their leaders could make them, and hungry for glory. On the eve of
their drop at Gela, on the south coast, Gavin sent a personal message to
each man of his 505th:

> Tonight you embark upon a combat mission for which our people
> and the free people of the world have been waiting for two years. You
> will spearhead the landing of an American Force upon the island of
> SICILY. Every preparation has been made to eliminate the element
> of chance. You have been given the means to do the job and you are

backed by the largest assemblage of air power in the world's history. The eyes of the world are upon you. The hopes and prayers of every American go with you.

    James M. Gavin

Gavin's lofty phrases about the elimination of chance proved optimistic. Those who suggest that the Normandy invasion might have been launched in 1943, and the war ended a year sooner, neglect the painful educational process that preceded D-Day. In the Mediterranean, at shocking cost the Allies learned how not to conduct amphibious operations. The follies committed in Sicily and Italy were probably indispensable if they were to be avoided when the outcome mattered vastly more. In Sicily the Allies had an overwhelming superiority of men and matériel over the Germans—Italy's forces were almost moribund—yet the invaders made heavy weather of their campaign. The parachute landings were a fiasco. High winds and the incompetence of transport pilots, together with promiscuous gunfire from the Allied invasion armada on the sea below, wreaked havoc. Scores of planes were shot down by "friendly fire." American and British paratroopers fell to earth all over Sicily, usually far from their comrades, equipment and objectives.

    The colonel of the 505th Parachute Infantry badly bruised his knee as he landed on the unyielding Sicilian earth in the early hours of 10 July 1943. For a moment, Gavin exulted in the silence of the night after the roar of the aircraft, together with a sense that this was the fulfilling moment of his life: "Combat—at last. After a lifetime of preparation, I was on the threshold of battle." Reality swiftly intruded. He found two of his staff officers and a handful of men, but of the bulk of his regiment there was no sign. They could see distant gunfire, but it was plain that they had been dropped miles from the force's designated landing zone. Gavin later admitted to some doubt about whether he was in Sicily, Italy or the Balkans. At first light, he led his small party onto a hilltop to try to identify their position, and promptly came under fire. When they replied, within seconds most of their weapons jammed. Mortar bombs began to fall around them. Gavin told the others to pull back while he covered them, which would have been heroic conduct for a platoon sergeant, but was mildly absurd for a colonel. His group shrank to five men. He felt bitterly frustrated. Hearing spasmodic firing on all sides, he decided they would have to wait for dark before heading across country. This eager warrior was appalled by the notion of being taken prisoner before he had fought his first battle.

In the early hours of next day, 11 July, having collected a few more men along the way, Gavin led his party into the lines of the U.S. 45th Division, which had come ashore across the beaches. By midmorning he was in operational control of perhaps 250 paratroopers, less than 10 per cent of his regiment. They were advancing towards their original objective, Gela, with all the energy Gavin could infuse into his men, when they saw before them a hundred-foot-high ridge, its lower slopes studded with olive trees. Gavin ordered a platoon to secure the high ground, and himself made the climb with his men. As they reached the first crest, they met fierce fire from Germans deployed on the reverse slope. They were soon pinned down and taking casualties. Gavin crawled back to the main body to bring up reinforcements. He was angered by the discovery that the responsible battalion commander had disappeared in search of help from the 45th Division. He himself scarcely knew where he was, or that the disputed ground was named the Biazza Ridge. But it was a dominant feature, and plainly valued by the Germans. He led forward every available man in an attempt to secure it.

They scrambled up through the olive groves under desultory fire. Their troubles began in earnest when they breasted the crest and met German machine guns, supported by mortar and artillery fire. Here also, for the first time, they learned the hard way that American bazookas would not penetrate heavy tank armour. Gavin commandeered two 75mm pack howitzers and pushed them forward as antitank weapons. It proved a long afternoon for the Americans. Gavin's men exchanged fire with the Germans hour after hour on the further slope of the ridge, taking a steady stream of casualties. As they struggled to dig into the iron-hard ground, Gavin threw away his bent spade in disgust, and improvised with a helmet. He was appalled to meet a 505th battalion commander, who announced with tears streaming down his cheeks that the unit was finished. Gavin despatched the man to the rear, and continued himself to direct the battle. At last light, reinforcements arrived: some Sherman tanks, a naval gunfire support team, and several hundred assorted American soldiers. Gavin gathered his motley force and led them forward in an attack that swept through the German infantry and mortar lines, driving back the defenders in flight. After seeing his men dug in on the ground they had seized, at last Gavin retired to the olive grove below the ridge and established a regimental command post.

The Biazza Ridge action was an inspired act of initiative. The position had been held by Germans of the Hermann Goering Division. They were intended to deploy as one arm of a major counterattack against the invaders. Instead they found themselves frustrated by the paratroopers. Through the days that followed, the 505th's colonel continued as he had begun—urging on his men to engage the enemy wherever they chanced to meet resistance. Communications remained almost nonexistent. By 12 July, two days after the landing, Ridgway had to tell Patton, commander of the U.S. Seventh Army, that of the five thousand men of his division who had dropped into Sicily he was only in operational control of four hundred, not including Gavin. Over the five weeks that followed, the Allies stumbled and blundered their way towards completing the capture of the island. The final outcome could scarcely be called victory, since the Germans were able to evacuate 100,000 men with most of their equipment across the Straits of Messina. Thoughtful soldiers recognised that to win the war in Europe, from highest to lowest the Allies would need to perform a great deal more convincingly than they had done in July and August 1943.

Yet for a few men, the Sicilian campaign was a reputation-maker. Gavin was among these. He was awarded a Distinguished Service Cross for the Biazza Ridge action, and Ridgway told him he was marked for a general's star. At thirty-seven, he had shown himself one of the most effective combat leaders in Eisenhower's army. He commanded by example, and his grip on his men was never in doubt. He understood the fundamental principle that battle is about generating violence, that victory goes to whichever combatant is most successful in achieving this. A cynic might add that Gavin assiduously cultivated his own image. His turnout, even on the battlefield, was extravagantly perfect. He was eager to entertain reporters, and intensely conscious of how his actions should appear to others. "There is only one way to fight a battle or war, I am more than ever convinced," he wrote. "Fight intensely, smartly and tough. Take chances personally and in matters of decision... Most people become too mesmerised by the holocaust and the danger to be promptly and energetically decisive in a fight... Hit them quick and hit them hard."

This grave, impulsive young officer smiled often, but seldom made jokes. War was his trade. He was utterly committed to making a success of it. More than a few junior and middle-ranking American leaders in the Mediterranean were accused of lacking aggression. Gavin's attitude, by contrast, delighted his superiors. Here was an officer of courage and intelligence, who asked no man to do what he did not do himself. A few critics suggested that his eagerness to be at the front could be dangerous in battle, not for himself, but for his command. A colonel risked losing control of his regiment if he became personally engaged in firefights, if he sought the point in a fashion appropriate to a lieutenant. Fearless behaviour in a commander could reflect poor judgement. It is interesting that although Ridgway and Gavin held each other in high respect, there was no liking. Ridgway admired Gavin's fighting spirit, and strongly recommended his promotion. But he was exasperated by "Slim Jim's" casual attitude to communication with the rear, his tendency to carry initiative to the point of recklessness.

When a plan was mooted after Sicily to drop an Allied airborne division to seize Rome, Gavin was eager to lead the jump. He believed there was nothing determined men could not achieve, if the spirit was willing. It was left to Ridgway to squash this folly. The same happened when General Mark Clark proposed dropping airborne units forty miles north of the Salerno landing beaches at Capua, where they would have to hold the passes for five days until the amphibious force linked up with them. Gavin was happy to carry out such an operation—indeed, to do anything that was asked of him. Ridgway dismissed the Capua plan as "insane," which it was.

Sicily had demonstrated both the virtues and the limitations of airborne forces. Allied paratroopers had caused chaos behind the German front, and played a useful marginal role. But the plan for their organised deployment had failed. Parachuting might be glamorous—indeed, obviously was—but it was an art, not a science. It would be a rash commander who made the success of any future plan dependent upon paratroop action. Airborne soldiers without heavy weapons, tanks and artillery support were highly vulnerable to the enemy's heavy formations, and could move nowhere fast. Gavin's 505th fought as infantry through the first weeks of the Italian campaign, earning an outstanding combat reputation after dropping into the Salerno beachhead. On 10 October, at the age of thirty-six, their colonel received his stars as brigadier-general, the youngest since George Armstrong Custer in 1863.

A month later, Gavin left for England to become airborne adviser to the Normandy invasion planners, while the 82nd Airborne followed behind. In four months of combat he had formed strong opinions about tactics, which did not significantly alter for the rest of the war. He extolled the importance of closing quickly with the enemy, whereafter Germans often showed themselves willing to quit. Gavin thought little of the performance of U.S. line infantry, and fretted at the sluggishness of the British in assaults. He admired, however, what he perceived as British insouciance towards the business of fighting a war: "Some of them seem to enjoy it more than we do...They are reluctant to take losses, but when they do lose, they die well."

Gavin was thrilled by the experience of making his first visit to London as the youngest general in the U.S. Army, and certainly the most glamorous. His marriage to Peggy was over in all but name—he never wrote to her from Europe, though he corresponded eagerly with his teenage daughter Barbara. In Sicily there had been a succession of local girls. Now he forged a passionate relationship with his driver Valerie, a married Englishwoman with smart social connections, with whom for a time he thought seriously of making a new life. The world—his warrior's world—lay at his feet. Ridgway had told him that when, as expected, he himself moved to corps command, Gavin would take over the 82nd. The young star knew that he was about to play a key role in the greatest amphibious operation in history. After such painful rites of passage in his youth, who could grudge his exultation about reaching centre stage?

Gavin's experience at the headquarters of the Allied armies proved frustrating, however. He hated the interminable meetings, and was dismayed by the intrigues of the British general Sir Frederick Browning, who seemed eager to divert American transport aircraft to carry British paratroops. Many of the Allied D-Day commanders and staff officers were impressive men who thoroughly understood their business. Those charged with directing the airborne contribution were, however, among the least able. General Lewis Brereton was a short, vain, posturing officer whose chief wartime achievement was to get his entire B-17 force destroyed on the ground at Clark Field in the Philippines by Japanese aircraft in 1941. He had little interest in parachute operations, though Eisenhower soon afterwards made him responsible for all five Anglo-American airborne divisions. Air-Marshal Sir Trafford Leigh-Mallory was a skilful office politician, quickly perceived as a hollow man by those who had to work with him. From Gavin's viewpoint, the main achievement of those frustrating weeks as a planner was that General Omar Bradley agreed to an enlarged D-Day role for the 82nd and 101st Airborne, securing the American right flank behind Utah Beach.

Gavin was much relieved when he was allowed to abandon the conference rooms and return to the 82nd in mid-February 1944 as deputy divisional commander. He was even better pleased when Ridgway gave him an almost independent role for D-Day, leading all three parachute regiments of the formation into Normandy. Gavin was a soldiers' general. He believed that there were no bad units, only bad leaders. Before D-Day at the 82nd's camps in Leicestershire, he complained: "This fast-growing habit of officers putting their troops in tents, then getting themselves a fine house in a nearby village burns me up." He chafed because Ridgway would not allow him to relieve a regimental commander whom he thought incompetent. A trifle priggishly, he noted that the divisional commander, twelve years older than himself, seemed overtaxed by physical training: "General Ridgway was very badly stove up after our last jaunt. Sometimes it is difficult for a formerly active man to realise he is ageing." Yet if Gavin was in some respects youthfully intolerant, in others he was ahead of his time. He was disgusted that some white American soldiers—including men of the 82nd—reacted violently to the sight of black GIs consorting freely with Englishwomen.

For Gavin, the Normandy invasion began remarkably like the Sicilian one. He landed in darkness amid an orchard in the Cotentin Peninsula, and found himself on the edge of a marsh with some forty men, several miles beyond their designated dropping zone. They were two miles north of the La Fière bridge over the Merderet River. Once again, some troop-carrier pilots had offloaded their cargoes with criminal carelessness. Hundreds of American paratroopers drowned in waterlogged fields that night, without having fired a shot. The wild dispersal of air-landed forces caused confusion for the Germans all over western Normandy and into Brittany. But the paratroopers had to join battle by the crude expedient of engaging the enemy wherever they chanced to meet him. Only a fraction of the airborne contingent was immediately able to set about carrying out the painstaking plans to which Gavin and others had devoted so many hours.

Some of those who joined the brigadier-general were fresh to combat, and fell asleep in a Norman hedgerow after the trauma of the jump. Here was yet another hazard of airborne war: it was hard to condition men to recognise that their job as soldiers began only when they landed on the battlefield. It did not end, as many instinctively expected, when they stripped off their jump harness after the emotionally draining experience of the flight, followed by a descent from the sky into darkness and uncertainty. After advancing two miles under sporadic fire, to Gavin's huge relief he met 3/505th, apparently in good order and preparing to attack the La Fière bridge, as its orders demanded. He moved away to gather up other units and urge them on to assault the Germans. Most of the Wehrmacht's 91st Division was committed against the paratroopers, and a series of bitter local engagements developed. The open causeways approaching vital bridges and junctions amid the marshes were hard to negotiate under fire. The 3/505th was repulsed at La Fière, its colonel killed. A cautionary episode denied the Americans a quick victory on another causeway nearby. When some Germans tried to surrender, the paratroopers immediately shot them down. Not surprisingly, this provoked the remaining defenders to fight to the last. At one point in the afternoon Gavin was dismayed to meet some of his men retiring from La Fière, where they said the Germans had broken through. He checked their flight and was relieved to find the situation at the bridge stable. Bitter fighting persisted around the river crossings for days, as German and American counterattacks seesawed to and fro.

The brigadier finally established a command post late on the afternoon of D-Day between La Fière and St. Mère Église, the village his men had seized at heavy cost. He lay down for the night, shivering under a camouflage net in a hedgerow. After an hour or two, a runner interrupted his rest with word that Ridgway wanted him at divisional headquarters. Gavin trudged wearily into St. Mère Église and wakened his commander, who said angrily that he had sent no message, and resented being disturbed. The two generals parted in shared irritation. It may seem odd that intelligent men could fall out in this fashion, yet such pettinesses are inseparable from the strain of battle. Gavin once wrote in his diary of himself and Ridgway: "It is unfortunate in some respects that we are so goddamn much alike."

Through the days that followed, the 82nd defended its precarious bridgehead against repeated German counterattacks. Fortunately for the paratroopers, on this western flank the enemy could deploy only captured French tanks, whose light armour was susceptible to bazookas. However, the Germans inflicted savage punishment on glider-borne elements of the 82nd, which now began to land in the midst of the battlefield to reinforce the paratroopers. Radio communication with Bradley's divisions landing from the sea remained nonexistent: the arrival of a tank battalion provided Gavin's first assurance that the beaches were secure. Some unit commanders of the 82nd proved embarrassingly lacking in the determination displayed by both of their generals and most of their men. Gavin watched the start of a glider battalion's assault on one of the Merderet causeways. As the preliminary barrage died away, the attackers remained motionless. Gavin dashed across to the battalion commander, whom he found crouching by a wall. "Go! Go! Go!" he shouted urgently. The colonel shouted back: "I don't think I can do it."

"Why not?"

"Because I'm sick."

"OK, you're through."

The commanding officer was replaced, and the attack belatedly began. The first American attackers were shot down, but others pressed on, at last reaching and overrunning the German positions. Still many Americans hung back. Officers and NCOs ran among them kicking and dragging the prone figures into motion. Gavin urged men: "Son, you can do it." Ridgway arrived, and the frightened soldiers beheld the remarkable spectacle of their two generals running under fire across the causeway, goading riflemen into action. Later that afternoon, when the Germans counterattacked, some of the glider troops again broke and ran. Once more Gavin was obliged to rally them personally. A regimental commander collapsed—he was later diagnosed with cancer—and Gavin met his successor in the midst of the key village of Cauquigny, preparing to abandon his positions. "I can't hold," the unhappy officer told Gavin. The general responded ruthlessly: "We are going to counterattack with every resource we have—including you, regimental clerks, headquarters people and anyone else we can get our hands on with a weapon." So it went on, all that afternoon of D+1. Gavin seemed inexhaustible, trotting and crawling hither and thither around his patchwork perimeter, harassing, urging, goading men. It was a day when he sometimes seemed the only soldier in his line absolutely confident that it could be held.

Ridgway, Gavin and a small minority of like-minded soldiers did duty for hundreds of others whose confidence faltered on that critical 7 June. The 82nd's units had already lost more than 50 per cent of their strength, together with most of their heavy weapons and equipment. Yet somehow, together with the 101st they held the western Allied flank until they were relieved, utterly exhausted, by the 90th Infantry Division.

Once the initial bridgehead in Normandy was secure, the airborne formations expected to return to England to rest and prepare for further parachute operations. Instead, however, they were thrust into the line again and again through the fierce battles of June, to hold ground and make attacks. They proved capable of sustaining momentum in a way most line infantry units could not. Their performance caused some commanders to argue that paratroopers were far more useful fighting as elite infantry than making the "vertical envelopments" such airborne theorists as Gavin wanted. On D-Day, the American parachute and glider assault on Normandy had created immensely useful chaos behind the German front. But chaos the airborne landing was, nonetheless.

By the time the 82nd Airborne withdrew to England early in July 1944, sixteen of its original twenty-one regimental and battalion commanders had become casualties. Overall losses of 46 per cent among all ranks masked a much heavier toll in the rifle companies. It is hard to overstate the fundamental truth of war, that most of the bravest die. In a long campaign, the shortage of leaders becomes chronic. A Second World War British infantry battalion commander of great distinction and experience, Colonel Robin Hastings, wrote afterwards: "It was the best leaders with most initiative who were killed or wounded. That is the worst feature of the infantry battle, the levelling process, the continuous removal of the outstanding...in war the penalties for initiative are...great." Gavin's own survival was remarkable, given his practice of roaming the forward areas, making night inspections and repeatedly exposing himself to fire.

He returned from Normandy famous. The American press embraced him. This glamorous young general was a poor kid who had made very good indeed. He seemed to embody the ideal of the American fighting man. On 17 July Gavin was promoted major-general and took over the 82nd Airborne Division from Ridgway, who became corps commander. Through the weeks that followed he laboured at rebuilding the formation, incorporating fresh drafts, working on a succession of airborne plans that were prepared and then abandoned as they were overtaken by the speed of the Allied ground forces' breakout from Normandy. At last, early in September, the paratroopers were brought to readiness for an assault that would indeed take place. They were to stage the most ambitious operation in airborne history. Gavin's 82nd, Taylor's 101st and Roy Urquhart's British 1st Airborne were to land in Holland and seize and hold a long series of bridges between the British front and the Rhine at Arnhem. It is remarkable that the cautious Montgomery endorsed this attempt to break into Germany before winter, which most commanders recognised as bold to the point of recklessness. That the British field marshal did so reflected first his belief that the German army in the west was beaten, and second an obsessive ambition to retain for himself the leading role in the advance on Berlin.

Gavin hated everything about Operation Market Garden. It was to be commanded by Browning, whom he despised—for all their rivalry, Gavin would have much preferred Ridgway. Success required the British ground force to advance very fast up a single Dutch road to relieve Urquhart's "red berets" of the 1st Airborne Division, who should be holding the Rhine bridge at Arnhem. To achieve success, a great deal needed to go right for the Allies. Above all, the Germans must remain supine. Yet past experience showed that Hitler's soldiers were ruthlessly energetic in responding to Allied initiatives, and in punishing Allied mistakes. "The flak in the area is terrific, the Krauts many," Gavin wrote gloomily in his diary on 16 September. "It looks very rough. If I get through this one I will be very lucky. It will, I am afraid, do the Airborne cause a lot of harm." For Market Garden to work, another "organised shambles" would not suffice. The airborne divisions were required to mount a coordinated assault on a widely dispersed range of objectives. If any one of these was not quickly seized, the whole airborne operation would be set at nought. It was an absurdly optimistic plan.

They flew into Holland on the afternoon of 17 September. To avert the chaos of the night drops in Sicily and Normandy, this time the corps jumped in daylight. The initial landings worked perfectly. Thereafter, however, almost everything possible went wrong. Gavin had feared that his division was tasked to seize too many objectives, and so it proved. In the first hours, the 82nd secured all except the most vital—the bridge at Nijmegen. Afterwards their leader reproached himself for giving that assignment to the least effective of his regimental commanders, who, he said, approached the task sluggishly and unimaginatively. In truth, however, in Holland as often elsewhere, the paratroopers were hampered by the fact that once they landed, they depended for mobility on their own two feet. It took even the fittest men hours to reach their objectives from the landing zones. Meanwhile the Germans were rushing forward reinforcements by vehicle. At Nijmegen the Americans faced SS panzergrenadiers, among the best soldiers in Hitler's army. By the time Gavin's men at last paddled across the river and seized the bridge under heavy fire in one of the most brilliant and courageous actions of the war, on the afternoon of 21 September, it was too late. The Germans had destroyed the British bridgehead at Arnhem.

For the next two months, the 82nd and 101st were left to hold a salient across Holland that led to nowhere, feeling intense bitterness towards those they deemed responsible for the fiasco—the British in general and "Boy" Browning in particular. If there were any laurels to be garnered, however, they belonged to the American paratroopers, who had performed magnificently. They held open the long corridor to Nijmegen despite repeated German counterattacks. Gavin had broken two vertebrae in the initial jump, and was in constant pain thereafter. This did not prevent him from joining firefights in his usual fashion. He himself with his M-1 carbine killed a succession of elderly German reservists, herded into an assault in a fashion reminiscent of the earlier world war. "To cross an open field in the face of enemy known to be in the area was foolish," Gavin wrote laconically. He personally led a counterattack to clear a dropping zone ahead of glider landings.

Yet when it was all over, beyond depression about the failure of the operation, he suffered a hangover of his own. In the midst of the battle he had become embroiled in another spat with Ridgway. Once again the corps commander believed that Gavin treated him in a cavalier fashion, apparently ignoring his superior's presence at the 82nd's headquarters as he got on with his own war. Ridgway wrote Gavin a fierce personal letter. Gavin responded by offering his resignation. All this was foolish, and reflected the conceit of both men. Gavin's abilities were matched by his own consciousness of them. His offer of resignation was surely prompted by a conviction that it would never be accepted by Eisenhower, even if Ridgway was tiring of his young prima donna. In the event, Ridgway professed to regard Gavin's response to his letter as an apology. The issue was dropped, though tensions between the two generals persisted. Gavin remained at the head of his division in Holland for two wet, wretched months, chafing at what he perceived as an abuse of American elite formations to hold the British line.

While Gavin enjoyed his star status, he remained infinitely painstaking about his business, and especially about the welfare of his men. One incident in the 82nd that winter became famous. Gavin strictly enforced a prohibition upon looting. Out alone one morning he caught a young private soldier, Robert Beckman, rummaging on a Dutch civilian clothesline. Angrily asked to explain himself, Beckman pulled off a boot and revealed ragged, chafing socks. The only way he could get replacements was to steal them, he said. Gavin sent him back to his unit. Next morning a sergeant arrived from divisional headquarters with a pair of socks. Beckman was killed in the Bulge battle, but not a man of the 82nd forgot the story of the socks, which took its place in the Gavin legend. It never matters whether such stories are true or not: a commander's relationship with his men can be defined by the fact that they are happy to believe them. Jim Gavin's soldiers knew that if he asked much, he would move heaven and earth to serve their interests. He inspired absolute respect and loyalty. If some of his peers found him irksomely cocky, he and his men had much to be cocky about.

When the 82nd at last went into reserve at Sissonne, in France, between training new drafts Gavin amused himself in Paris and London: "A most enjoyable night with Valerie," he wrote in his diary, when he resumed the affair with his married English lover; "had a wonderful time, just what I needed." A few weeks earlier, before Market Garden, he had been eager to move to the Pacific, believing the European war almost wound up. Now, however, after four combat jumps and many weeks of battlefield service, he was increasingly anxious about the condition of the division's veterans, who were growing weary. They believed

that they would soon have to parachute across the Rhine, and many had
had enough. "It hardly seems right," Gavin wrote. "There should be
some way out other than being killed or wounded."

There was not. On the evening of 17 December 1944, Gavin was about
to go to dinner when U.S. First Army called to alert him to the breakthrough in the Ardennes. He had heard hints of the German attack the
previous day, but at first it did not seem serious. Now, Eisenhower was
sufficiently alarmed to commit his strategic reserve, the XVIII Airborne
Corps, to the battlefield. Both Ridgway and Taylor were away, in England and the United States respectively. Gavin was acting corps commander. His initial orders were to move both his divisions to Bastogne,
on the southern flank of the German penetration. Airborne soldiers
were hustled back from leave and overnight passes in Paris and even further afield. The 82nd moved out at dawn on the icy morning of 18
December, the 101st close behind, both divisions lamentably short of
equipment and even personal weapons. Gavin himself reached First
Army headquarters around 9 a.m., cold and wet after driving through
the night in a jeep with two aides and his familiar M-1 carbine. Now a
decision was taken—chiefly by Gavin, for First Army's senior officers
seemed reduced to paralysis by the crisis—to deploy only the 101st at
Bastogne, while the 82nd took up position around the Amblève River, at
the northern shoulder of what was already coming to be called "the
Bulge." When Ridgway later arrived, he expressed dismay that his corps
had been split. Gavin said he had simply sent the formations where they
seemed most urgently needed. He himself arranged the deployment of
the 82nd as its units arrived in the course of the night of the eighteenth,
then snatched a few hours' sleep on the floor of a farmhouse.

Next morning he walked his positions in an eerie silence which all his
instincts told him was the quiet of imminent action. Ridgway established his own headquarters nearby, and assumed responsibility for
holding the corridor between St. Vith and Butgenbach with the 82nd,
30th Infantry and 3rd Armored. Gavin set about moving his own division
onto strong defensive ground along the Salm River. Lightly equipped
airborne divisions were not well suited to defence, least of all against
German heavy armour. So much historical attention has focused upon
the stand of the 101st at Bastogne that the matching achievement of the
82nd in the north has received less notice than it deserves. The 504th

Infantry fought a fierce, costly battle around the bridge at Cheneux. Gavin believed that its commander, the combative Reuben Tucker, made a mistake by committing his battalions to a frontal counterattack. Tucker repulsed the Germans in bitter fighting, but lost 225 men. The 505th was obliged to give ground in an equally bitter struggle with 1st SS Panzer, but was able to hold the west bank of the Amblève until, on 23 December, the Germans finally fell back.

It was a source of bitter anger among GIs and their commanders that when Montgomery assumed command of the northern flank of the Bulge, on 22 December he insisted upon withdrawing the Americans from St. Vith, which they had defended so doggedly. The British field marshal was determined to shorten the Allied line and—in his provocative phrase—"tidy up the battlefield." Through the days that followed, Gavin and his men found themselves battling with elements of three panzer divisions. There was another undignified squabble at Ridgway's headquarters when Gavin demanded tank support for his battered front and was told that none was available. He exchanged harsh words with Ridgway's chief of staff, who blasted Gavin as "a goddamn Black Irishman, looking out for number one," and accused him of ingratitude to Ridgway, who had made his career. Gavin's anger was that of a commander fighting a dangerous battle in which his regiments were crumbling under superior enemy firepower. But in the long haul such scenes increased doubts about his fitness for higher command. He was a fighting soldier, at his worst in wrangles at the top. These made him enemies who did not forget.

Gavin resented being obliged to withdraw from positions which his units had lost many men to defend. Yet he was almost certainly wrong not to recognise that, in the big picture, such things had to be done. The twenty-third was an icy cold, moonlit night as he stood by the roadside watching the weary files of paratroopers march by. His rear guards fought some fierce little actions with Germans still showing aggression even though their forces had been disastrously depleted in the preceding week of battle. The Ardennes cost the 82nd Airborne 76 officers and 1,618 men. Gavin and his soldiers were irked that the 101st, together with Patton's Third Army, received most of the laurels of the battle. When the Allied counterattack began, he chafed when he perceived that this was designed to push the Germans methodically back the way they had come, rather than to strike at the base of the Bulge and cut off their retreat. Indeed, for the rest of the war he inveighed against the cautious strategy and tactics of the Allies. But Montgomery, Bradley and Eisenhower were as one in refusing to attempt bold manoeuvres against the Germans. It was enough to win, without taking risks. The 82nd played a prominent part in the new assault which began on 3 January 1945. Gavin, as usual, was up with his forward units, carbine in hand, chivvying and urging officers and men. He himself seemed oblivious to risk, even when his aide was wounded by his side.

Through the last months of the war, Gavin's impatience at the performance of Eisenhower's armies intensified. "If our infantry would fight," he confided to his diary, "this war would be over by now ... American infantry just simply will not fight. No one wants to get killed, not that anyone does, but at least others will take a chance now and then. Our artillery is wonderful and our air corps not bad. But the regular infantry—terrible. Everybody wants to live to a ripe old age. The sight of a few Germans drives them to their holes." Gavin was undoubtedly correct that the Western Allies took longer than should have been necessary to penetrate Germany, against vastly inferior forces. Yet he could not realistically expect the U.S. Army's line formations to match the performance of his own elite. He himself was an eager, ambitious professional, for whom the war represented the greatest opportunity of his career. He behaved on the battlefield with the insouciance of a soldier emboldened by the experience of being often fired upon without effect. Yet it was asking too much to expect many others to exhibit the same confidence in their own invulnerability. Most Allied soldiers were not professionals. They did not perceive the war in the way Gavin did, as a canvas on which to paint a reputation. They were amateurs whose overriding desire was to live to go home and resume their real lives.

It is not surprising that Gavin accrued enemies, that the conceit of the handsome young warrior prince irked peers and rivals. Though the 82nd took its part in the drive across Germany in the spring of 1945, it was committed to no more major actions, not least because the army wanted to keep elite formations intact for operations against Japan. Gavin's experience in the last months was anticlimactic, though enlivened by a fling with Marlene Dietrich and a more protracted affair with Ernest Hemingway's war-correspondent wife, Martha Gellhorn, which involved playing a lot of gin rummy in bed. Characteristically, the paratrooper was thrilled to learn of a plan to drop his division on Berlin. He did not share the relief of his comrades when this was abandoned.

When the war ended, Gavin went home to get divorced and marry the ex-wife of an army air corps officer, a happy union that produced three children. He commanded the 82nd Airborne until 1948, and later took over a corps in Germany. Thereafter, his peacetime career ran into the sand. To his disappointment he was not offered a combat role in Korea, perhaps because senior commanders such as Ridgway perceived him as the last man on earth to respect the disciplines of fighting a limited war. "Slim Jim" likewise proved quite unsuited to the serpentine politics of the Pentagon, where he found himself at odds with his old rival Maxwell Taylor, who had become army chief of staff. Early in 1958, at the age of fifty, Gavin resigned his commission and began a new career in business, interrupted by a spell as U.S. ambassador in Paris at the behest of President Kennedy. Kennedy was much attracted by the glamorous fighting Irishman, and overlooked Gavin's inability to speak more than restaurant French. The ambassador lasted eighteen months in France before returning, embarrassingly broke, to his business career. He died in 1990, aged eighty-three.

Jim Gavin was among the most inspirational field commanders of the Second World War. In his enthusiasm for the airborne cause, he overrated its potential. Like Patton, he was insensitive to the reality that other men were less willing than himself to allow ambition to suppress fear on the battlefield. His virtues were also the vices which disqualified him from the highest commands. The "can do" spirit is highly desirable in officers up to a certain ceiling. Thereafter, however, there is also merit in acknowledging arguments for "can't do." This was never in Gavin's nature. The reservations about him shared by Ridgway and Taylor may have owed something to personal rivalry, but they also reflected sound judgement. Gavin represented the ideal of the twentieth-century paratroop formation commander in combat. But it is the fate of most such men—the fighting men—to become redundant once the battle is over. Soldiers of duller metal take up the batons, and are better suited to carry them.

CHAPTER THIRTEEN

THE WHITE MOUSE

IN SOME SOCIETIES, women warriors have taken their place on the battlefield for centuries, even if the fifth-century B.C. Greek historian Herodotus's account of the Amazons is a fairy tale. Women fought for many twentieth-century communist and revolutionary movements. They played a substantial role in the 1941–45 Red Army, though the fame lavished on its all-female night-bomber squadron owed as much to the demands of propaganda as to military utility. Western armies have been reluctant to employ women in the front line, partly because to do so would infringe society's traditional view of their claims upon protection from the whitest heat of war, and partly because there are practical difficulties. Women cannot match the load-carrying ability of men. In some modern mixed-sex American units this reality has prompted male resentment of women soldiers' inability to bear their share of physical labour. The pragmatic argument carries more weight in contemporary society than the more traditionalist objection voiced by a modern British general: "You can't leave a woman behind on the battlefield."

Only naïve people, however, ignore the inescapable tensions created by sexual relationships between members of combat units, whether on land or at sea. When the British army was debating the rights of gay soldiers to fight in the front line a few years ago, a distinguished gay combat veteran observed, to the surprise of some, that he opposed the presence of actively gay men in the front line, for the same reason he opposed that of women: "There is no closer human relationship than that between men beside each other in battle. It is essential this should be uncompromised by sexual tensions." Contrary to a common misconception, women in the Israeli army have never assumed combat roles. Their performance of support tasks in forward areas causes significant disciplinary problems, prompted by sexual relationships. Arguments about the deployment of women in battle are complex, but there are good reasons for even enlightened societies to remain cautious.

In the Second World War, the Western Allies recruited millions of women as nurses and service auxiliaries, some of whom performed critical tasks, especially in communications and antiaircraft defence. Only one small female group, however, served actively in enemy-held territory. When Hitler occupied most of Europe in 1940, Winston Churchill committed himself to sponsor armed resistance among captive populations. He created a new secret organisation, the Special Operations Executive, charged not with espionage but with promoting guerrilla war. Although SOE was a military body whose members held ranks, only a handful of professional soldiers became involved. Most of its staff and all its agents were amateurs. In the Far East and the Balkans, from the outset SOE fulfilled a uniformed paramilitary role. In France, however, until 1944 agents posed as civilians, and potential recruits were required to display a grasp of the language and a knowledge of the country even before their fitness for clandestine warfare was assessed.

It was quickly apparent that women could play a vital part. Their role has attracted disproportionate attention from posterity, for obvious reasons. They were pioneers, the first of their sex to be offered such responsibilities by Western democracies. They lived dangerously, and if their role was indeed romantic, it was also lonely. If captured, almost invariably they faced a squalid death in a Nazi concentration camp. By the rules of war, the Germans were perfectly entitled to shoot British agents—a reality sometimes forgotten—yet the refinements of cruelty inflicted upon many captives before their execution have inspired the revulsion of history.

As well as the arts of covert warfare, all SOE's recruits were trained in basic military skills, notably the use of firearms. Their function was to organise, arm and train local resistance groups, almost all of which were commanded in action by Frenchmen, Yugoslavs, Greeks—not by Englishmen or Englishwomen. SOE's representatives had no authority to give orders, which was frequently a source of frustration; their influence derived from an ability to summon arms and cash from the sky, and from the force of their own personalities. Domestic rivalries dogged every national resistance movement. In France, supporters of General de Gaulle were at loggerheads with his political foes, especially the communist groups. De Gaulle bitterly resented SOE operations conducted outside his control.

Women agents who achieved postwar celebrity—several posthumously—were by no means those considered by their colleagues to have been the most successful. Because of the nature of their work, the published record of SOE's agents is overwhelmingly dependent on personal reminiscence rather than documentary evidence. In consequence, extravagant legends grew up after the war surrounding the activities of some French Section personnel, rather in the same fashion as those surrounding Lawrence of Arabia a generation before. Violette Szabo, widowed after a brief marriage to a French officer which left her with a small daughter, was working at the perfume counter of the Bon Marché store in Brixton when SOE recruited her. She was twenty-three years old, wonderfully pretty, much beloved, very brave, and later executed at Ravensbrück. In 1958 she became the subject of a romantic feature film, *Carve Her Name with Pride*, in which she was played by Virginia McKenna. Yet she worked in France for only a month before being captured in June 1944, on the second of two missions. Claims that she conducted a dramatic shoot-out with the Germans have been shown by modern research to be fanciful. Like Violette Szabo, Odette Sansom received a George Cross and also became the subject of a feature film— *Odette* (1950), starring Anna Neagle—but colleagues believed her capture was the result of carelessness, exemplified by a passionate affair with her fellow agent Peter Churchill, whom she subsequently married. Sexual relationships in the field handicapped the work of several SOE personnel.

None of this detracts in the smallest degree from the courage of those concerned, but there seems no reason why their deeds should forever be cloaked in sentiment. They chose to become warriors, in a struggle not new in kind—guerrilla warfare is as old as history—but revolutionised by the sponsorship of Allied governments, with all their resources of aircraft, communications and arms. A British agent's prospects of survival in occupied Europe were better than those of an infantry rifleman. Of 560 despatched, 133 died, a little more than one in five. Women were sent on fifty-three missions to France (sometimes the same agent more than once), and thirteen—about a quarter—lost their lives. The female agents of SOE were all exceptional, in that they embraced a role a long stride ahead of their sex in the Western world of the mid-twentieth century. Among SOE's personnel, Christina Granville, Pearl Witherington, Virginia Hall and Lise de Baissac—all much less famous than Szabo and Sansom—were outstanding intelligence operatives for any time and place. But like any other group in war or peace, some of SOE's women were successes and some were failures, some proved notably capable and some did not.

One of the most colourful of SOE's recruits was Nancy Wake. She was born in Wellington, New Zealand, in 1912. Two years later her parents settled in Sydney, Australia, where she grew up. Her childhood was tempestuous. She ran away from home twice, partly in disgust about being expected to do housework, which never appealed to her. At the age of eighteen she worked briefly as a nurse in a mental institution. At twenty she scraped together the money for a ticket around the world, to Europe by way of Vancouver and New York. A forceful, extravagantly extroverted personality with a sharp eye for comedy, from the outset she was eager for adventure, and a generation ahead of her time in sexual enlightenment. She took a journalism course in London, then found her way to Paris, where she rented an apartment. Through the years that followed she eked out a precarious living as a freelance reporter, travelling widely and partying enthusiastically. In 1939 she fell in love with a rich Marseilles businessman named Henri Fiocca. He was forty to her twenty-six, and introduced her to a sophisticated high life in the south of France such as she had never known. All her life she was heedless of money, but with Fiocca she briefly experienced the fun of having lots of it. Her last months before the war were a romantic idyll, generously garnished with fast cars and smart restaurants, fine food and clothes from the great designers.

Nancy became engaged to Henri Fiocca. They found an apartment overlooking the Old Port of Marseilles, which she staffed and furnished with exuberant enthusiasm. For the first time in her life she felt secure. She was visiting London, booked for a slimming course at Tring, when war broke out in September 1939. She at once offered her services to the British, who suggested that she might work in a NAAFI canteen. This was not at all what this tough, witty, strongly built young woman had in mind. She returned to France against the advice of a string of British officials from whom she was obliged to secure clearance: "You really sure you want to go, Miss? You, an Australian girl, to France?" "If you go, you'll never come back. You understand that, don't you?" She was wryly amused, on quitting blacked-out Britain, to find war-torn France ablaze with lights.

Nancy and Henri Fiocca were married in Marseilles on 30 November 1939, to the dismay of his Catholic family. The bride set about enjoying herself as much as possible before the war became serious. Black-marketeering on the streets of Marseilles, she acquired a formidable grasp of vernacular French which would later stand her in good stead. She consumed impressive quantities of champagne and caviar—not so much, she subsequently asserted, because she especially liked these things, as because she was thrilled to be able to afford them. Yet, knowing that her husband, who had served for a few months in the French army of 1918, would soon be mobilised, she hankered to play some part herself. She demanded to be taught to drive an ambulance, saying: "I want to go to the war. I'm sick of hearing how *you* won the last one! This one *I* shall win!" Soon afterwards, Henri was called up and posted to Belfort, near the German border. She took the ambulance which he had purchased for her to Alsace, terrorising the French by her insistence upon driving on the left. After each brush with disaster she would announce defiantly: *"Je suis Australienne. En Australie, on fait comme ça!"*

When the German onslaught came in May 1940, amid the shambles she transported refugees until it became plain that all was lost. She abandoned her vehicle when it broke down near Nîmes, and hitchhiked back to Marseilles, consumed with misery for the plight of France. For some weeks she was without news of her husband, then one morning without warning he walked through the door. Until November 1942 southern France would remain under the control of the puppet government of Vichy France rather than German occupation, but the Fioccas knew their world was shattered beyond repair.

One night in October 1940, dining at the Hôtel du Louvre, they had an encounter which changed their lives. Nancy saw a man alone in the lobby, reading an English book. Curious, she sent Henri to ask his identity. The man proved to be a British officer, on parole from Vichy captivity in the nearby barracks, Fort St. Jean. The Fioccas at once invited him to join them, and they arranged to meet again next day. This time the officer arrived with two comrades. Nancy provided them with as much food as they could carry, for the prisoners had no money and were very hungry. They returned to the fort with an invitation from the Fioccas to summon a succession of dinner guests from among the two hundred officer internees. They also discussed escape. The British could not decamp while they were on parole, but there was nothing to stop them exploiting this licence to make plans for regaining their freedom.

Henri Fiocca did not attempt to dissuade his wife from the course upon which she had embarked, but he pointed out its implications. Nancy was by temperament passionate and impulsive. A friend remarked of her: "She was one of those people who, whenever they walk into a room, without opening her mouth makes everyone in it look up." This is a notable quality, but one ill-suited to clandestine warfare. The best protection for an agent is to be unnoticeable. The Milice, the paramilitary police of Vichy France, were as hostile to the Allied cause and as brutal to its sympathisers as the Gestapo. Any course of action which focused official attention on the presence of an Australian woman in Marseilles could lead to trouble for Nancy—and also to grave complications for the Fiocca family, its property and business interests.

While it might seem cynical to suggest that it is easier to resist tyranny if one has little to lose, history suggests that this is the case. The French aristocracy, with only a few distinguished exceptions, collaborated wholesale with their 1940–45 occupiers. Most of the French bourgeoisie did likewise. Resistance, which anyway scarcely existed in the winter of 1940, depended overwhelmingly for its early recruits on little people—schoolteachers, peasants, trades unionists such as railway workers, socialists and—once the Soviet Union entered the war in June 1941—communists. They were drawn from circles which the more prosperous classes regarded as the "awkward squad" of French society, or less politely as communist terrorists. It was a reflection of Henri Fiocca's courage and loyalty to his wife, for which the price would eventually be paid, that he rejected the self-interest which guided the wartime behaviour of almost all his class, and acquiesced in her determination to assist the British internees of Fort St. Jean.

One day a very tall Scottish captain named Ian Garrow appeared among Nancy Fiocca's rota of guests. Garrow was impressed by what he had heard of his hostess's energy and sympathy. He was starting to organise an escape route to the Spanish frontier, and needed a lot of money. He asked Nancy for it, and she in turn asked Henri. Fiocca wrote the cheques uncomplainingly, though his resources were far from unlimited, and times were hard. Garrow then asked Nancy to take a step further. He needed a courier to carry messages along his "line," in particular to Toulon and Cannes. At once, she agreed to do this. She acquired new papers, which gave her identity as Nancy Fiocca, but omitted the fact that she was a British subject. This did not diminish the dangerous number of people along the coast who knew her as *'l'Australienne de Marseilles,"* but it did make her less vulnerable to immediate suspicion at checkpoints.

Through 1941 she kept up her work for Garrow's line, which was linked to the London-based MI9 organisation, dedicated to assisting escapers. As the war became global, German pressure on southern France grew. The Milice intensified its quest for enemies of the Axis. The greatest threat to resistance was always treachery, and one of the darkest aspects of wartime French society, riven by political divisions, was its propensity for betrayal and denunciation. An overwhelming proportion of Allied agents and sympathisers captured by the Germans were identified to the enemy by French people, motivated by ideological hostility, cash or mere spite. In the course of the conflict more Frenchmen bore arms in Vichy uniforms than in those of the Allies.

In the spring of 1942 Ian Garrow was caught, tried and sentenced by a Vichy court to ten years' imprisonment. He entered solitary confinement in Marseilles' Fort St. Nicolas. His escape network was taken over by one of the more remarkable figures of wartime resistance, an army doctor who variously claimed to be a Frenchman and a British naval officer named Patrick O'Leary, but who was in reality a Belgian army doctor named Albert Guérisse. O'Leary, who finished the war in a German concentration camp, was at that time thirty-one. He stands in the front rank of wartime heroes of the resistance, already in 1942 a veteran of secret war and a hundred hair's-breadth brushes with danger, running escape lines the length of France.

Nancy Fiocca had a serious argument with her husband when he learned that she had written to Ian Garrow in prison, claiming kinship and promising to visit him. This was risk-taking of an extraordinary kind. No professional intelligence organisation would have countenanced such a gesture for a moment, but at that time and place they were all amateurs, recognising few rules. Nancy was a woman of passionate loyalties, above all to friends in trouble. She held her ground against Henri, and braved the anger of O'Leary, who also thought her action rash. She began to visit Fort St. Nicolas three times a week to deliver food. She only saw Garrow himself three times during his incarceration, but she wrote constant letters to him. When her husband remonstrated again Nancy shrugged defiantly: "I know how much letters would mean to me, if I were in his position."

The only concession she made to security was to desist from having her own home as a rendezvous for escapers and their contacts. Instead, she leased another nearby apartment where illicit visitors could stay and where she could meet them. Yet she exposed herself again when, late in 1942, Garrow was moved from Fort St. Nicolas to the notorious Vichy camp at Meauzac. She and Henri went to see him off amid his guards at Marseilles station. Nancy then set off for Nice to escort three American aircrew to Perpignan, en route to the Spanish border. She was now travelling on identity papers showing her to be Lucienne Cartier. Wholly inappropriately for a character larger than most mammals, her local code name was "the White Mouse."

In November 1942, following the Allied invasion of North Africa, the Germans assumed control of Vichy France, which was henceforward occupied in the same fashion as the north. Nancy was paying regular visits to Ian Garrow in his camp at Meauzac. She was committed to securing his escape, and believed she was close to being able to bribe a guard to make this possible. One weekend she waited half the night by a nearby bridge to meet a man who did not appear. Next weekend she was there again—and the man came. In return for half a million francs—more than £2,500 in the currency of the day, a small fortune—he agreed to help Garrow gain freedom. Patrick O'Leary, with the aid of a large contribution from Henri Fiocca, provided the money. Two weekends later, dressed in a gendarme's uniform sent to the guard by O'Leary's people, on 8 December Garrow left Fort Meauzac among a guard detachment going off duty. He was met by O'Leary, who had concealed himself a short distance from the gates. After a fortnight in hiding to regain his strength, Garrow walked across the Pyrenees to freedom.

Henri Fiocca was increasingly convinced that his wife should travel the same route. Her behaviour was wonderfully gallant; indeed she sometimes seemed to regard the war as a game. But the eventual consequences were all but inevitable. For thirty months Nancy had lived a charmed life. All manner of warnings reached the Fioccas that the Germans were on the track of "the White Mouse." Having agreed to leave for England, Nancy took another bold step: she shipped all her clothes in a trunk from Marseilles to await her arrival at Thomas Cook's office in Madrid. As usual, she ignored warnings, remarking that no one any longer knew her as Nancy Wake. She said a hasty farewell to her husband, who told her that some £60,000 in cash and paper would be left in her safe deposit box in Marseilles, lest anything happen to him. Henri promised to follow her in flight, but it remains unclear why he supposed that his own liberty could outlast his wife's departure for even a few weeks. If Nancy was marked for arrest, so too, surely, must be her husband. Nonetheless he made the decision to remain, perhaps in the hope of protecting his commercial interests.

Nancy took a train to Toulouse, to hide until O'Leary's escape circuit was ready to get her to Spain. In that city, however, fate at last caught up with her. She was arrested by the Vichy police, and identified as Madame Fiocca. She spent several days in prison. One morning she was led into an office where she was astounded to see Patrick O'Leary. At first, assuming that he was also a captive, she pretended not to recognise him. Then he hissed: "Smile at me, you fool. You're supposed to be my mistress!" She was summoned into the police *commissaire*'s office, rebuked for having told a pack of lies, and released into O'Leary's hands. This was the fruit of a superb piece of bluff by the Belgian, who had risked everything to secure her freedom. He had presented himself at police headquarters carrying papers describing him as a member of the Milice, and claimed to be a personal friend of Vichy prime minister Pierre Laval. By sheer effrontery, he talked Nancy out of jail.

Brazen to the last, in February 1943 she travelled by train to Perpignan, en route for the Pyrenees, in silk stockings, Cuban-heeled shoes and a camel-hair coat, carrying her jewellery in a leather purse. She argued that thus attired, she scarcely looked a hunted woman. She travelled in company with O'Leary, a resistance wireless-operator, an ex-gendarme and a New Zealand airman, a not untypical party for an escape line of the period. Suddenly, a ticket collector warned them that the Germans were about to check the carriages. O'Leary told his charges they must jump. As the train slowed beside a vineyard, they threw themselves onto the track and stumbled away into the vines, pursued by desultory German rifle fire. The ex-gendarme disappeared, and later died in a concentration camp. Nancy found that she was free, but had lost her handbag, papers and jewels. Disconsolate, and walking only by night, she and the others made their way back to the safe house in Toulouse from which they had started.

On 2 March, in a café in the city, Patrick O'Leary was arrested by the Gestapo. When she heard the news Nancy at once quit her lodgings and briefly took refuge with a family who took pity on her plight. Then she set out for Marseilles. She did not dare visit Henri at their home, but instead called at their second flat, still a rendezvous for escapers. Taking two of these with her, she caught a train eastwards to hide with a resistance contact in Nice. There she remained for three weeks, acquiring new papers and clothes. She learned the whereabouts of guides who were taking parties over the Pyrenees, and caught a train to Perpignan—this time without incident.

The town was the French terminus of Europe's principal illegal escape route from Nazi tyranny between 1940 and 1944. The journey over the Pyrenees into neutral Spain was a punishing experience, even for a fit young man in summer. For older and weaker people, or in winter, it became a nightmare. Many of those who attempted it were captured by the guards and their dogs. More than a few collapsed and died of exposure. A large number of desperate pilgrims were already weakened by hunger or ill-health before they set out, and suffered terribly. The Germans had declared a twelve-mile stretch of French territory a forbidden zone, to bar the passage to Spain. On the Spanish side, a further thirty-mile zone was closed to travellers. Nancy and her small party travelled to the foothills of the Pyrenees hidden in the back of a coal lorry. As darkness fell, they were handed over to local guides—career smugglers who made fortunes from their wartime activities—for the long, pitiless march over the mountains. They were told to discard their shoes and put on rope-soled espadrilles. Then they set off on a trek that continued for the next forty-seven hours, the only interruptions being hourly ten-minute pauses. There was no purpose in halting for longer, since they were without access to food or shelter, and the cold was bitter.

Talking, smoking and coughing were forbidden, by day or night. Nancy's party all found themselves suffering from diarrhoea, after eating bad meat. They were thirsty as well as hungry, and Nancy ignored stern warnings against eating snow. Crawling and stumbling up the crags, despairing when each crest revealed another descent, another peak, they completed the journey in a snowstorm, reaching a hut where they lit a fire and waited for night. In darkness they forded a river and were led to a farmhouse where, in Spain at last, they were given their first food for thirty-six hours.

They were hiding in a haystack in broad daylight when Spanish police found them. The group was marched to the local town, and thrown into jail. After two nights they were taken to Gerona, to be told that they faced charges of illegal entry. In the event, however, after the usual bribes changed hands they were released into the hands of the British vice-consul, and taken to Barcelona. Thence, with money provided by the consulate, Nancy travelled to Madrid, where to her huge delight she found the trunk of clothes she had shipped from Marseilles. With her wardrobe as well as her spirits revived, she went on to Gibraltar, and ten days later gained passage on a convoy for England. It was June 1943. In London, having overcome some difficulties with the immigration authorities because of her lack of identity documents, she checked into a room which Ian Garrow had booked for her at the St. James's Hotel. After a dinner party at Quaglino's she fell into bed, exhausted but free.

Nancy suffered a period of deep depression after her escape, fuelled not least by concern for the welfare of her husband, about whose fate she could learn nothing. She herself was determined to work in France again. First she offered her services to de Gaulle's Free French. They unhesitatingly rejected her as a British "plant." She declined to work for MI9, the escape organisation run by the War Office, because she disliked one of its chiefs, whom she had met in Marseilles. She had never heard of Special Operations Executive, SOE, and got off to an inauspicious start when she was interviewed by one of French Section's officers, Major Gerry Morrell. He asked her: "Why do you want to go over to France? Is it because you think the job's glamorous?" She exploded: "For God's sake, if I want glamour I can get much more of it here in London than over in occupied France." When Morrell was asked afterwards why he had put such a silly question to her, he answered complacently: "Just wanted to see her reaction."

French Section seems to have had some hesitation about recruiting Nancy, perhaps based on doubts about her suitability for clandestine life. But eventually the section head, Colonel Maurice Buckmaster, intervened personally to invite her to train as an agent. As with almost all her female comrades, to provide a uniformed "cover" she was commissioned into the First Aid Nursing Yeomanry, the FANY, as Ensign Nancy Wake. She then began the round of paramilitary training to which all recruits were subjected. After her experience in France she found the play-acting aspects irksome, the assault courses unappetising, the psychiatric tests ridiculous. Her bluntness towards the officers in charge, which not infrequently tipped over into insubordination, roused unfavourable comment. She had always been an enthusiastic social drinker, which dismayed some of the staff. The most significant friendship she forged was with one of the instructors, a conspicuously gay little ex-actor named Denis Rake, who had enjoyed an extraordinary odyssey as a wireless-operator in France, and was now "resting." Rake, whose camp demeanour masked notable character and courage, was to play a substantial part in her career as an agent.

No lightweight in build, Nancy regarded the physical challenges of SOE training—cross-country runs and suchlike—with contempt, and remarked that she had never experienced any hazard in France to which an ability to scale walls and swing across chasms was relevant. In truth, of course, such training was designed to build confidence rather than to make the agent an alpinist. Nancy became an adequate shot, but like most of French Section's women, performed unconvincingly in unarmed combat training. She was bored by the Beaulieu security course, which included studying details of German army uniforms, aircraft identification and so on. When her class completed jump training at Ringway they hastened to London for a riotous night out, which ended with them performing parachute rolls on the dance floor of the Astor in the small hours of the morning. After a final course in explosives and demolitions, Ensign Wake's training was deemed complete.

What to do with her now? The formidable Vera Atkins, Buckmaster's personal assistant and perhaps the most influential force in the wartime French Section, had serious doubts about Nancy's suitability for employment in France. Her courage and irrepressible spirits commanded admiration and inspired gaiety everywhere. Her judgement and discretion, however, were much more open to question. The most difficult and dangerous SOE assignments throughout the war were in the big cities. There, German and Vichy surveillance was most thorough, and it was essential for an agent to live a convincing cover story. Most metropolitan-based SOE agents were caught sooner or later.

In the remoter rural areas of France, however, it was another story. The nature of resistance had been transformed by the Germans' 1943 introduction of massed deportation for forced labour, the hated Service de Travail Obligatoire. To escape STO, tens of thousands of young Frenchmen had taken to the countryside, living rough among the maquis, the guerrilla movement waging increasingly open war against the occupiers. The STO brought far more recruits to the French resistance than any political ideal. It was now 1944, and it had become plain that the Allies would win the war. All manner of French people who had been unwilling to lift a finger for the cause in 1941, 1942 or even 1943 were now calling themselves Gaullists. Resistance was strongest in the areas which strategically mattered least to the Germans, wildernesses which offered space to live, hide, train and receive arms drops. Dozens of SOE personnel were now working as weapons instructors among such groups. Discretion, an ability to blend into the landscape which is indispensable to any peacetime intelligence officer, was much less necessary for an SOE agent in rural France in 1944 than it had been in, say, Lyons in 1942. Nancy Wake's virtues were courage, wit, a fiercely combative spirit and a capacity to inspire others. French Section decided to send her as assistant to Captain John Farmer, code-named Hubert, in the Auvergne, the great tract of wooded highlands in south-central France, whose hub is the industrial city of Clermont-Ferrand.

Buckmaster presented her with a silver powder compact, a personal token of the kind he offered to every agent departing for the field. Then

Ensign Wake, codenamed "Witch" for the flight, was bundled into a Liberator bomber. "Say, are you really 'Witch'?" demanded the Texan despatcher. She assented. "Gee," he said, "a woman! We ain't never dropped a woman before." He gave her a cup of coffee and a Spam sandwich, which she ate, but which reappeared on the floor of the aircraft during subsequent violent manoeuvres in a flak zone. Shortly after 1 a.m. on 29 February 1944, Hubert and Andrée—her new code name in France—landed by parachute on a dropping zone near Montlucon, where they were greeted by an exuberant guerrilla who introduced himself as Tarvidat, leader of a prominent local resistance group. As she prepared to destroy her canopy in accordance with security procedure, the horrified Frenchman intervened: "No, no, Madame Andrée, such beautiful nylon is not to be destroyed." She was amazed to find herself conveyed away from the funfair exuberance of the drop zone by car—a mode of transport she had been warned was intolerably dangerous, yet which the Auvergne resistance employed everywhere.

In the village where she and Hubert were billeted above a radio shop, they were disconcerted to find themselves welcomed by locals who knew exactly who they were, and why they were there. It was impossible in tiny rural communities, where everyone knew each other, for any stranger to pass unnoticed. Here was the distinction between the ways of resistance in rural and urban areas—though also a reflection of the chronic insecurity of the maquis. The SOE pair's first encounters with local maquisards, led by a "colonel" named Gaspard, were unpromising. They appeared a dirty, disorderly, intransigent rabble, whose leaders seemed interested only in relieving the British woman of the million francs in cash which she was carrying.

Nancy gained some face among this gang of desperadoes by joining them in a raid on a sports store in St. Flour to remove its stocks of tents, blankets and boots. Nonetheless, after a few days the British agents and French maquisards had found nothing to say to each other. Nancy and Hubert could not contact London until their wireless operator joined them. The Frenchmen were determined to go about their business in their own fashion. They showed no interest in London's elaborate plans for pre-D-Day sabotage of transport links. All these were common problems among French resistance groups in 1944.

Gaspard's group was happy to provide a car to send the SOE pair to another maquis group, led by a balding little man named Fournier. He was civil enough, but suggested that they should retire to a remote hotel until their operator arrived. After two weeks in France, spent in idleness and impotence, Nancy was sitting listless on a cemetery wall, insouciantly ignoring the sound of an approaching car, when a well-known voice cried in English: "What are you doing here, ducky? Picking yourself a grave?" It was their wireless operator, the inimitable Denis Rake. She flung herself into his arms with a shriek of glee: "Den-Den, you darling! Where on *earth* have you been?" He answered: "My dear, *swarms* of Germans chasing me *everywhere!*" In truth, said Nancy after the war, Rake had resumed a brief dalliance with a lover he had met on an earlier assignment in France. In their gratitude at seeing him, however, this was forgiven. At last they could contact London. Watched by a cluster of entranced maquisards, Denis sat tapping out on his Morse key a coded message from Nancy and Hubert, summoning the magic harvest from the sky—guns, explosives, ammunition.

Once arms supplies began to reach the maquis, the prestige of the SOE agents soared. Every group in the region pleaded for their attentions, though not all were eager to accept instructions from London as the price. Gaspard paid heavily for his own intransigence. He and his men, some three thousand strong, were attacked at Mont Mouchet by German troops. They had few weapons, and no workable plan either for defence or escape. They were driven in headlong flight, with the loss of some 150 men. Many of the survivors trickled into Fournier's area north of Freydefont, where there were soon six thousand maquisards. The SOE team was thoroughly unhappy about such a concentration, and used all their powers of persuasion to urge them to disperse themselves. Such a mass was sure to become known to the Germans, and offered an irresistible target. Yet the British could not give orders. They could only argue and cajole, using their power to provide cash for the French groups' subsistence and arms for their self-respect. Nancy travelled constantly, driving fast by back roads, arranging parachutages, paying subsidies and urging cooperation with London's wishes.

Among the chronic problems of resistance was that for every man who had joined with a principled commitment to fight Germans, there were ten nominal maquisards whose only desire was to escape forced labour. Many made themselves unpopular with local people, living by banditry. Most lacked military training. Even those who boasted a Sten gun had only two or three magazines of ammunition apiece. They lacked heavy weapons and transport. For what military purpose could they credibly be employed? In large numbers, they could not engage German troops effectively. Their best course was to operate in small groups, utilising only a fraction of their available manpower, for local ambushes and demolitions.

All these limitations were thoroughly understood in London, and inspired scepticism about resistance among regular soldiers both during the war and afterwards. Yugoslavia was the only occupied country in which Allied guerrilla forces made a real impact on a key battlefield. In France, resistance lit a flame from which the self-respect of the nation could begin to be restored, but its military contribution was much more modest than legend has suggested. "Sometimes, the maquis could do wonderful things," said an American officer who served with them. "But other times, they just wouldn't turn up because somebody had forgotten to get the charcoal to fuel the *gazogène* lorry. You could never make any strategic plan depend on them." It remains a matter of fierce debate in France whether the military achievements of resistance justified the ghastly reprisals levied by the Germans upon the civilian population.

Yet for almost every SOE agent, service in the field with the resistance was the most powerful emotional experience of their lives. So it was for Nancy Wake. By the late spring of 1944, the British agents in the Auvergne felt that their grip on the four major groups in their area had become much more effective. Travelling remained a dangerous business, operationally essential yet often fatal to SOE officers. Nancy drove with heavy escorts of maquisards, and they were periodically required to shoot their way through German patrols and roadblocks. She was obliged sometimes to cycle alone into towns to meet contacts. Just before D-Day, she learned that a weapons instructor code-named Anselm had been dropped in her area, and must be collected from Montlucon, which was still strongly held by the Germans. She entered the town and eventually found her contact, a certain Madame Renard. "I believe you have a 'packet' for me," Nancy said. After some hesitation, Madame led the way into the kitchen, flung open a cupboard, and revealed "Anselm"—a moustachioed American named René Dusacq, looking extremely tense and clutching a pistol. Dusacq, a former Hollywood stuntman, had known Nancy in training. Like herself on first arrival, he was terrified to find himself being whisked across the Auvergne by car, his female companion sitting complacently in the front passenger seat with a Sten gun on her lap.

Dusacq set to work training maquisards in small arms handling. They christened him "Bazooka" because of his passionate enthusiasm for the weapon. Local groups had now begun attacks on the D-Day targets which London had designated, especially rail links, and power and telephone lines. It was remarkable that in mid-June 1944, as the decisive battle for Normandy raged, the Germans still deployed resources for counterattacks against the maquis. Logic decreed that if the Allies were beaten in Normandy, resistance could be suppressed at leisure. If Normandy was lost to Germany, then no local triumph against resistance could signify. Yet everywhere in France in the summer of 1944 the Nazis showed stubborn determination to retain every acre of their empire, and they used the most savage methods to try to do so.

On 20 June, Nancy was with a maquis group at Chaudes-Aigues, awaiting two arms drops scheduled within twenty-four hours. They received the first in darkness, and laboured for hours retrieving and stacking parachute containers. She had not long been in bed when, just before dawn next day, she heard gunfire. A powerful German force had been committed against the maquis on the plateau. At a hasty conference between the SOE team and the four local leaders, all agreed that they should withdraw and disperse under cover of darkness, except Gaspard, who insisted that he would stand and fight to the death. To the fury of the British, he refused to abandon this folly. As German shells began to fall around the village, Denis Rake hastily sent a coded message to London, cancelling their next parachutage and asking for a direct order to Gaspard to retreat. Denis said: "Gertie"—his pet name for Nancy—"I'm terrified." She gave him a quick kiss, and went out to begin unpacking the arms containers from the previous night's drop, to rush forward to the maquisards. Denis soon reported that their parachutage was cancelled, but that he was still awaiting London's order to Gaspard to withdraw. A German observation plane was directing artillery fire on the village, and to Denis's amazement, as shells continued to rain down around them, Nancy fell asleep. Fournier woke her and insisted furiously that she must move before she was hit. Complaining bitterly, she gathered her Sten gun, found some shade under a tree, and fell asleep once more. When she was woken again, it was to hear that General Koenig, head of de Gaulle's London headquarters, had sent a personal message ordering Gaspard to retreat. She drove forward alone to the maquis leader's position on a hillside, exchanging fire with the Germans, handed him the message, and was rewarded with a grudging nod of assent. Returning to Freydefont, her car was strafed and hit by German aircraft. She was forced to abandon the wreck, though not before rescuing her most cherished possessions—a jar of face cream, a packet of tea and a red satin cushion.

As darkness fell, in long files the maquisards began to fall back, threading paths through the woods and gorges to a rendezvous some sixty miles distant. It was a reflection of the improvement in their tactics and discipline that most of them made it. But Denis Rake was obliged to abandon his wireless set and destroy his codes. Their vital link with London was gone. Even when they reached St. Santin, without a set the SOE team was impotent. They had to find a means of contacting London. To provide perspective, it may be noted that at this time SOE's agents possessed fewer than fifty operational wireless sets across the whole of France.

They heard that there was a Gaullist operator across the mountains, and Nancy bicycled and walked many miles, alone, in vain pursuit of him. Learning that the man had been obliged to flee the district, she returned disconsolate to St. Santin. Then Rake remembered that he had heard of an operator 150 miles away at Châteauroux. Once again, Nancy set forth on her bicycle. Even the most reckless maquisards conceded that it was too dangerous to travel by car with the Germans active. First, in Aurillac, she visited a tailor to get some clothes, without which she could not travel to Châteauroux—she had lost all her own in the battle on the plateau. In a shoemaker's shop, she was warned to leave the town at once—Germans had been enquiring about the woman in military slacks who went into the tailor's house. She returned to St. Santin, where an elderly woman lent her an old peasant dress. Thus attired, she risked another visit to the tailor in Aurillac, from whom she collected her new clothes and set off alone to bicycle through the mountainous Puy-de-Dôme.

The journey was a formidable ordeal. At any time, she might encounter Germans or Vichy agents. She slept mostly in haystacks or in the open. She contacted one resistance group in vain, then heard of a Gaullist operator some twenty-five miles from Châteauroux, in the Creuse. At last, after many frustrations and delays, she found the man she sought, and asked him to transmit a signal for her. "I know there's a lot of friction between your headquarters in London and mine," she said, "but will you do it?" He agreed. Within hours, a message was on its way to London, requesting a new radio and codes for the maquis d'Auvergne. Her mission accomplished, a physically exhausted Nancy rode back to St. Santin. As she entered the village on the machine she had grown to detest, a crowd of cheering maquisards sprang up from their midday meal to surround her. To their astonishment, she burst into tears. She had bicycled more than three hundred miles in seventy-two hours. She said later: "When I'm asked what I'm most proud of doing during the war, I say: 'The bike ride.'" Copious quantities of brandy gradually restored her composure, but it took her several days to recover from her exertions.

Leaving René Dusacq with the group at St. Santin, Hubert and Nancy shifted their headquarters to the maquis of Tarvidat, whom they had met on first landing in France, in the Allier. Their next parachutage produced not only a new wireless set, but also an American Marine operator named Roger, who was henceforth deputed to work exclusively with Nancy, while Denis handled communications for Hubert. Nancy began to accompany Tarvidat on ambushes of German road convoys. "She is the most feminine woman I know—until the fighting starts!" exclaimed the Frenchman expansively. "Then, she is like five men!" She herself felt strongly that if she was to win and preserve the respect of the maquisards, she must show herself capable of doing anything that they did. And also, of course, she enjoyed it.

Nancy Wake was cast in the same metal as many of the men described in this book. They were stimulated by danger and largely indifferent to its potential consequences for themselves. She was an ardent warrior, possessed of a boundless appetite for sensation. In France in the summer of 1944 there was ample scope to satisfy this. Even at the last gasp of their occupation, the Germans somehow found energy for a new attack on Tarvidat's camp. This inflicted few casualties, but obliged the maquisards to move to another forest. Two more American weapons instructors were dropped to them, John Alsop—brother of

Stewart and Joseph, the famous newspaper columnists—and Reeve Schley. Both were in uniform, a welcome sign of the Allies' new self-confidence, but neither spoke much French. They were handed a bottle of champagne and driven to the maquis's forest headquarters, where there was more wine and food. Both Americans were members of the Office of Strategic Services—OSS, the American counterpart of SOE. They were profoundly impressed by the formidable "Gertie" and her guerrilla army, and touched, when shown to their mattresses, to find that she had set a jar of forest flowers between them. Likewise, whatever the hazards of the day, she invariably slept in a satin nightdress.

Next morning the Germans attacked again, supported by armoured cars. The two hundred maquisards in the immediate area began defending themselves, while Roger the wireless operator was hastily evacuated by truck with his set. Nancy, together with twenty men and the two Americans, advanced towards the sound of firing. After a few hundred yards, Schley suggested that they should exploit the cover of trees alongside the road. Thirteen of them, including Nancy, did so, while the remainder continued carelessly up the tarmac. Seconds later, a single burst of German machine-gun fire dropped all seven. The others, mostly teenagers, dropped their weapons and fled. Nancy amazed the Americans by a display of Marseilles street language which caused several of the fugitives to halt in shame. She and her little party advanced within bazooka range of the Germans. Schley and Alsop fired a succession of rockets before retiring to the forest clearing from which they had set out. Nancy sent for help from another nearby resistance group, lit a large Cuban cigar from a box which Schley had brought with him, and began firing enthusiastically in the direction of the enemy. Tarvidat's men then launched a diversionary attack on the German rear, to cover the maquis withdrawal.

Next day, Nancy returned to collect the bodies of the maquisards who had fallen on the road. The Germans had systematically shot each one, dead or alive, in the face. She herself washed the bodies and laid them in parachute silk. Then the whole party drove to a nearby cemetery and conducted a forty-five-minute funeral service, while maquisards stood guard around the walls. Schley and Alsop were appalled by the risk, but by now they were growing accustomed to the ways of the maquis d'Auvergne—and those of Nancy Wake. Her methods of man-

management were nothing if not direct. When a group of gendarmerie deserters joined the maquis, they announced that it was beneath their dignity to fetch water from the nearby lake. Madame Andrée drove her car to the lake, filled it with buckets of water, returned and deposited one on each gendarme. There were no further difficulties about water-carrying.

With more than seven thousand men in the region, the Americans were carrying out weapons-training classes almost around the clock. Parachutages had become routine. A personal escort of Spanish maquisards now accompanied Nancy on her journeys, car windscreens removed to make way for Bren guns. She herself insisted on travelling in the lead vehicle of her little convoy. When Denis Rake applauded her courage, she observed that it was simply that she could not bear the dust thrown up by cars ahead. This was the high season of resistance. The Germans were collapsing. Recruits eager to be identified with victory were hastening to every maquis. Targets could be attacked almost with impunity. Nancy lived in a bus in the forest of Troncais, where for relaxation British agents and maquisards swam in a nearby lake. She bought a horse for Schley, a cavalryman by training. One night the maquis held a banquet in the forest in honour of the Americans, cooked by a chef borrowed at gunpoint from a nearby hotel. The alfresco partying continued until the small hours, when it was broken up by a fierce thunderstorm.

It would be wrong to idealise the human relationships of those who lived among the maquis. Romantic their circumstances might have been, but they were also chronically tense and claustrophobic. Nancy never liked "Hubert"—John Farmer—and by 1945 avowed a hatred for him. She found the Americans who were parachuted to join them in the last phase green and naïve. She was much troubled that Denis Rake's sexual advances to young maquisards would precipitate some disastrous embarrassment, and she grew increasingly irked by his emotional protests about their privations. Her own beau ideal among the French was Henri Tarvidat, whom she perceived as brave, witty, handsome and—rarest of qualities among the resistance—highly disciplined. The truth was that groups of people who fight together develop likes and dislikes as strong as those which are commonplace in peacetime. In the maquis, these were intensified by the perils and discomforts of their existence, even if comradeship provided some alleviation.

In this last stage of their war there was less danger and more laughter, a reward for the appalling years through which occupied France and its people had passed. Nancy Wake had experienced the dark days of resistance, and now witnessed its weeks of triumph. The maquisards were undisciplined, impulsive, capable of fine things and also terrible ones. Respectable citizens in many parts of France, by no means all collaborators, deplored the pillage conducted by resistance groups. Nancy sought to make what amends she could after one of her groups raped a local girl. Another woman, who admitted spying for the Germans, was sentenced to death. When Nancy found that the traitor was first being tortured from mere spite, she insisted that the execution be carried out forthwith.

German garrisons now seemed more vulnerable, and Nancy took part in an attack on the enemy headquarters in Montlucon. After 15 August 1944, when the Allies landed in southern France, a wholesale German withdrawal began. Both Hubert and Nancy began openly to wear uniform and badges of rank. Overconfident, the maquisards launched a more ambitious attack on the Montlucon garrison, from which they were obliged to retreat after some hours of battle. Such actions, of which there were many all over France in July and August, were folly. They could serve no military purpose, and they engaged German troops on terms which suited the enemy. They brought misery, fear and often reprisals to the local civilian population. Recklessness of this kind did more than anything else to damage the credibility of the resistance in the eyes of serious soldiers. The resistance was at its best performing local acts of sabotage and ambush. Headlong military confrontation with the enemy almost invariably proved disastrous.

On 30 August 1944, Nancy's thirty-second birthday, the maquisards staged a grand review outside the château in which she and the rest of the Anglo-American team had now taken up residence. The French presented her with a dozen ice-cream spoons. Schley and Alsop gave her some etchings, and Denis a bottle of perfume. In the atmosphere of frenzied celebration which overtook France as everywhere the liberators assumed control, Nancy and her group drove into the enemy's French capital, Vichy, amid a great column of exultant resisters. The following afternoon, Nancy was attending a ceremony at the town's war memorial, being addressed by the mayor, when a woman edged through the crowd and began to whisper in her ear. Laughter froze on Nancy's face. She burst into tears. Denis Rake, appalled, took her aside. She wept helplessly until at last she said: "Den-Den—get me away from here." He led her gently out of the crowd, to a nearby hotel. There she said: "It's Henri. The Gestapo picked him up in our flat. He's dead."

Their job in the Auvergne was finished. Hubert, Alsop, Nancy and Denis took a big red Talbot car and set out for Marseilles. They found the city full of American troops, and sought lodgings with old friends of Nancy's. She pieced together what had happened. Henri had been arrested in May 1943, and tortured for news of his wife. His father once saw him, hideously maimed, before on 16 October Henri was taken out and shot. Nancy found that her safe deposit box had been emptied. Vichy or the Germans had seized everything pertaining to the Fioccas. She was penniless and without property, save for a little poodle named Picon, whom an old family friend had cherished through the occupation, and now surrendered to her. The dog was the only survival of her old life. Henri's family publicly accused Nancy of responsibility for Henri's death, by involving him in her resistance activities. There was nothing left for her in Marseilles. She left the city forever.

In 1945, Nancy Wake received the George Medal from the British. The French gave her two Croix de Guerres with Palm, a third with Star, together with the Resistance Medal, rarely awarded to foreigners. The United States added its Medal of Freedom. Her postwar life was a curious mixture of the tempestuous and the humdrum. She lived in Paris for two years, never losing her appetite for combat. One night at the British Officers' Club, she knocked out cold with a single punch a French waiter whom she considered to have insulted a fellow guest. She was posted for a time at the British Embassy in Czechoslovakia, and in 1948 she worked her passage back to Australia as a ship's nurse. The following year she made a brief but spectacular foray into politics, contesting for the Liberal Party the parliamentary seat of the Labour opposition deputy leader, Dr. Herbert Evatt, whose majority she reduced from 23,000 to 127. Jobless and forever restless, in 1951 she returned to London, where she spent an unlikely five years working in the offices of the Air Ministry. In 1957 she married a British officer stationed in Malta, and the couple eventually settled in Australia. Nancy never had any money. In old age she was awarded a pension by the Australian government, which in 2004 also made her, at the age of ninety-one, a Companion of the Order of Australia. After her husband's death, since 2001 she has lived in a retirement home at Richmond, Surrey.

Nancy Wake achieved an extraordinary personal fulfilment in France between 1940 and 1944. She herself said: "In those days we knew what we were fighting, and we had a job to do. We did it." The war offered many women of her generation their first opportunity to assume responsibility, and in many cases to perform work of critical importance. Yet only a tiny handful either sought or were offered the opportunity to serve in combat. Nancy's extravagantly powerful personality placed her among a host of Australians who, in the course of the twentieth century, proved exceptionally suited to waging war. Set in the context of SOE's operations in France, her personal role may have been a trifle more modest than some postwar eulogists suggested. Local legend exaggerated the exploits of the maquis d'Auvergne, like those of the resistance at large. Yet there is no debate about her personal impact. She was too incautious to be a natural secret agent, but she was a natural warrior. In spirit, she stood kin to Harry Smith and Marcellin Marbot. Had they met, they would have discovered many shared pleasures, above all the comradeship of the battlefield.

CHAPTER FOURTEEN

FREEDOM'S
YOUNG APOSTLE

THE COLD WAR made counterinsurgency a major preoccupation for the soldiers of the West. Between 1962 and 1975, Indochina provided the stage for a Herculean effort by the United States to reverse the tide of communist nationalism, which appeared to threaten to sweep Asia. The struggle was unlike anything in American military experience, and wholly unwelcome to conventional soldiers attuned to exploit the Second World War and Korean War doctrine of firepower. Thoughtful people perceived from an early stage that the struggle for "hearts and minds" among the Vietnamese people would be more important to the outcome than anything done on battlefields. Many senior U.S. officers, however, including successive Vietnam supremos Paul Harkins and William Westmoreland, were unable to accept this. It was left to Americans on the ground, "in the boonies," to discover the nature of the new war. It required thirteen years of agony, afflicting two nations, before the United States conceded that such a struggle could not be won on the terms it had chosen.

No man's experience more vividly reflected his country's eager hopes and bitter disillusionment in Vietnam than that of John Paul Vann. In the eyes of those who knew him—especially young U.S. reporters in Saigon—Vann's initial vision, energy, honesty and reckless courage epitomised the highest ideals in America's endeavour to "save Vietnam for freedom." Vann loved the country and its people in a fashion rare among his compatriots. He threw himself into the conflict with a single-mindedness which became obsessional. Afterwards, the way in which the experience corrupted him also seemed to symbolise the fate of his nation, lost in Vietnam.

Vann was born in Norfolk, Virginia, in 1924, a poor white southerner. His mother, Myrtle, was an eighteen-year-old of careless virtue, his father a trolley-car driver and occasional bootlegger named Johnny Spry, already possessed of a wife and two sons. The boy John Paul was therefore illegitimate, and never forgot it. When he was four, his mother married a city bus driver named Frank Vann, whose surname her son adopted as soon as he was old enough to make the wish stick. The family spent the Depression years in poverty, made more wretched by Myrtle Vann's drunkenness and brutality to her children—the youngest endured rickets in addition to her beatings.

At fourteen, John Paul Vann was salvaged from his home life by the friendship of a local Methodist minister named Garland Hopkins, who became a father substitute. Hopkins persuaded a rich local businessman to clothe the boy and pay fees for him to attend boarding schools in southwest Virginia. There he made friends and learned to laugh, was properly fed, housed and taught. In 1942, with America in the war, the handsome young man with the slick blond hair was eager to enlist, but Hopkins persuaded him that he had a better chance of fulfilling his ambition to become a fighter pilot if he completed junior college. It emerged much later that Hopkins's patronage was not entirely altruistic, and that he had sexually exploited Vann. In 1965 Hopkins killed himself when he was exposed as a paedophile. Here was a final twist in the horrors of Vann's adolescence.

In March 1943, Vann reported for military duty. His medical examiners noted that the Virginian stood five feet six and a half inches tall, and weighed 125 pounds. After a brief apprenticeship as a vehicle mechanic, in June he was accepted by the air corps. His college class yearbook for 1943 carried a quotation beside each leaving pupil's photograph. Vann's read:

> *Intelligent, clear-eyed—such as he*
> *Shall Freedom's young apostles be.*

He spent the next year in flight training, but his career as a pilot ended abruptly when he attempted forbidden stunt manoeuvres. Despite his dismissal, however, in recognition of an otherwise exemplary record he was sent to navigation school. By October 1945 he was a second lieutenant serving in a B-29 crew, still awaiting overseas posting. That month he married his girlfriend of two years' standing, Mary Jane Allen, who came from a home of picture-book middle-class respectability in Rochester, New York. She was eighteen, he was twenty-one. At last, in uniform, he felt that he had shaken off the horrors of his boyhood. Without consulting his new bride, who was soon pregnant, he applied for and was granted a regular army commission. In the fall of 1946, through the army he began a two-year economics course at Rutgers University in New Jersey. Yet the following summer he decided to abandon his studies and volunteer for infantry duty. With the separation of the U.S. Army and the air corps, he concluded that a navigator's career prospects would be less promising than those of a pilot's. He took the three-month junior leaders' training course at Fort Benning, and sought assignment to a paratroop unit. He wanted excitement, adventure, combat.

Instead, he was posted to Korea as a special services officer—responsible for soldiers' clubs and entertainments. After nine months in this dead-end role, he was nominated as purchasing and contracting officer at the headquarters of the 25th Infantry Division in Japan. What possessed the army to relegate such promising combatant material to an almost ignominious rear-area role is a mystery, but Vann was obliged to make the best of it. He summoned Mary Jane and her two small children to join him, and the family settled into the absurdly luxurious routine of American occupation forces in Osaka.

Their comfort and tranquillity were shattered in June 1950 by the communist invasion of South Korea. The 25th Division, along with every other American force in the hemisphere that could move and fight, was shipped to the peninsula. Vann was responsible for a supply line during the desperate battle of the Pusan Perimeter, though he made one notable contribution by flying repeated sorties in an L-5 observation plane, throwing out ammunition at low level to beleaguered American positions with a determination and daring that thoroughly frightened the pilots who carried him. In a just world he would probably have received a medal for these operations, but no official recognition was forthcoming.

Vann often told the story of how he commanded a Ranger company in one of the bloodiest Korean encounters. Many years later he described the action in a letter to President Nixon: "We had excellent artillery support and good fighting positions and killed them by hundreds. I realised however, after the third assault, that I was going to lose my company. On the sixth assault, just before dawn, I did lose my company. Myself and fifteen men, most of them wounded, were all that were left… on the way down the hill, I estimated that there were over five hundred dead Chinese soldiers in front of our positions."

Such an action indeed took place in Korea in November 1950, but Captain Vann had no part of it. The Ranger company was commanded by a young officer named Ralph Puckett. Only after Puckett was wounded did Vann persuade their divisional commander to allow him to take over the remains of the company. He held this job for just ten weeks, seeing no significant action, before being obliged to accept compassionate leave when one of his children in Japan contracted meningitis. Thereafter, he was posted away from the theatre of war to the Ranger Training School at Fort Benning. Not until reporter Neil Sheehan investigated Vann's career for a biography was this embellishment exposed. Vann was neither the first nor the last veteran to fantasise about his own war experiences, but here was an early example of a weakness for deceit which would dog his life, and stain the happiness of many people around him.

After a series of humdrum postings in the United States, in the autumn of 1954 Vann joined the 16th Infantry in Germany. There his commanding officer wrote on his final report: "one of the few highly outstanding officers I know… an officer with a bright future ahead of him." He gained equally glowing plaudits in his next posting, as a logistics specialist: "Major Vann is a virtual dynamo." In 1957 he attended the Command and General Staff College at Leavenworth. The following year he graduated eleventh out of 532 officers in his class, and went to Syracuse University to study for an MBA. He intended this as a preliminary to a career in logistics, the most promising promotion route open to an officer who had not attended West Point. He then spent eighteen months, bored to distraction, at the army's antiaircraft missile centre in El Paso, Texas.

Here was an officer deemed exceptional by all his superiors, who had now served in uniform for eighteen years without finding an opportunity to shine in war. Vann's experience of Korea did not amount to much in the brotherhood of warriors. Yet all this was about to change. The last decade of his life was crammed with incident of an extraordinary kind. Early in 1962 the thirty-seven-year-old lieutenant-colonel volunteered to join the newly created U.S. Military Assistance Command in Vietnam—MACV, as it was known—where 3,200 Americans were already serving alongside the South Vietnamese army in its struggle against communist insurgency. Late in March he reported for duty in Saigon, and was appointed senior adviser to the Vietnamese 7th Division, serving in the ricebowl of Indochina, the northern Mekong delta. He knew nothing of Vietnam or its language, nor about counterinsurgency. Yet he took with him to the riverside regional town of My Tho a boundless belief in his own abilities, and in the capacity of the United States to succeed in arresting the communist tide in Indochina where France, the former colonial power, had failed.

His first weeks infused him with clear ideas of what was needed. He was dismayed by the lethargy of the ARVN—the acronym by which the army of the Republic of Vietnam was always known. The 7th Division, commanded by thirty-four-year-old Colonel Huynh Van Cao, was content to man its garrisons and conduct occasional sweeps across the countryside. Most of the northern delta's six thousand square miles and two million people were left to the Vietcong, of whom two thousand regulars faced thirty-eight thousand government troops—ten thousand regulars and twenty-eight thousand provincial militia. Vann was determined to push the ARVN to take the initiative, to carry the fight to the enemy using the American helicopters and fighter-bombers committed in fulfilment of President Kennedy's mission to stem the communist tide. First, he sought to integrate his growing team of American advisers—two hundred of them by the end of 1962—into the ARVN planning structure at every level. Next, he sought to identify enemy concentrations for them to attack, and to train Vietnamese soldiers in tactics of fire and manoeuvre.

Colonel Cao assented willingly enough to Vann's proposals. He was less happy, however, when the American urged contesting control of the countryside with the Vietcong in the hours of darkness: "It is not safe to go out at night," said Cao uneasily. Vann, heedless, began himself to accompany squad-sized patrols. This troubled the colonel even more, because he was fearful of the embarrassment of losing his senior adviser. Yet at that time, when fewer than twenty Americans had died in Vietnam, among the MACV personnel a sense prevailed that they were participating in an exotic Asian adventure almost without risk. The Vietcong were still anxious to spare Americans, lest killing them provoke an escalation of the war. It was only during the months that followed, as the communists perceived escalation coming anyway, that American invulnerability began to be challenged.

In his jeep, Vann travelled the region unescorted by day and night with an insouciance which won the admiration of his subordinates. He overflew the countryside in an L-19 Bird Dog spotter plane. He learned to like, even to love, the Vietnamese soldiers, their small heads swallowed by American helmets, their rifles dwarfing the men who carried them. Vann yearned for action. He chafed as he began to perceive that the Vietnamese patrols which he accompanied possessed no desire to meet Vietcong, far less to surprise them. He was convinced that Saigon's cause could not prevail until the ARVN secured the countryside. This made it essential to kill Vietcong. He believed tactical success could be achieved in six months, while a longer-term pacification programme would require a decade. He was in a hurry to get started.

On the morning of 20 July 1962, sixteen U.S. Marine helicopters offloaded a striking force of two hundred Vietnamese troops in paddy fields near Moc Hoa, where Vann had planned an assault on the 504th Vietcong Battalion. Supported by strafing fighter-bombers, the Vietnamese began their attack, while another force landed to cut off the enemy's retreat. Then things started to go wrong. To the deep dismay of Vann, watching from a circling helicopter, he saw that the ARVN charged with cutting off the fleeing enemy had not advanced from their landing zone. When he urged their commander to move, the officer refused: Colonel Cao would not wish it, he said. Vann lost his temper. Here was his plan working perfectly, the enemy in flight, yet poised to escape because the ARVN would not engage. By the day's end, the only achievement of this elaborate operation was the killing of a handful of guerrillas and the capture of a few weapons. Vann fulminated in vain to Cao.

Two months after joining the 7th Division, the Virginian perceived that he and his comrades were attempting to direct a war in the hands of government troops with an institutionalised unwillingness to fight. In the eyes of the Saigon regime, its army represented simply a source of internal power and wealth, an enforcement arm for the vast edifice of corruption which dominated the country and enriched its rulers. While the United States was eager to assist the Vietnamese to fight communism, the ARVN had negligible interest in doing anything of the sort.

Yet if Vann began to understand the difficulties, his enthusiasm remained undiminished. Under his relentless urging, some of Colonel Cao's troops did kill Vietcong. In Vann's first four months, the division claimed as many enemy dead—4,056—as the rest of Saigon's forces combined. This figure, like most numbers in Vietnam, was a wild exaggeration. But Vann believed that if it was even half true, the Vietcong were facing a prohibitive rate of loss. He was heartened by another success in his area on 18 September, when a force of two hundred regular and local Vietcong was destroyed by ARVN troops manning amphibious M-113 armoured personnel carriers, which could roll across paddy fields impervious to small-arms fire.

In the space of a few months in country, Vann had made himself a showpiece U.S. adviser, the man whom generals in Saigon sent official visitors to see. He and Colonel Cao shared some overblown glory. Yet still Vann could not persuade the colonel to launch any operation which required his men to grapple the enemy. The dictatorship of President Diem in Saigon wanted victories, but victories without pain. If Vann pushed the little Vietnamese beyond a certain point, Cao would say stubbornly: "You are an adviser. I am the commander. I make the decision." Though Vann usually kept his temper in public, he vented his frustrations with increasing passion in private. He now saw clearly that the war would not be won by September, that under Saigon's rules it might not be won at all. He perceived the resilience of the Vietcong, rebuilding their forces after every encounter. He was increasingly appalled by the brutality of the ARVN towards the civilian population, which he recognised as politically disastrous. A Vietnamese officer was impressed by Vann's humanity when he summoned a helicopter to evacuate civilians wounded by an air strike, and personally carried an elderly woman aboard. "That American really cares," the ARVN spectator said to himself. "No Vietnamese officer would do that."

In vain, Vann urged Saigon's leaders to engage the enemy selectively, rather than to bomb and shell whole communities from which a few shots had come. He argued that a policy of terrorising the population into submission must fail, and that indiscriminate air and artillery bombardment was not only killing scores of innocents for every communist, but permanently alienating the population. Cruelties were appalling. One ARVN officer, a Captain Thuong, paraded a group of captured Vietcong and walked down the line, slashing the throats of three of them with a Bowie knife before Vann's eyes. "Hey, tell him to cut that shit out!" cried the American. The only consequence of his protests was that Cao's officers began to do these things beyond American view.

Vann tried to exploit his newly won prestige to pass tidings of such happenings, and to warn of their consequences, to the American command in Saigon. Yet senior officers, and above all the commanding general Paul Harkins, professed deafness. Washington wanted good news, and Harkins was bent upon providing it. The United States military was determined to use its greatest asset, firepower, to fight the war of its own choice in Vietnam, heedless of the implications for the Vietnamese people. Here was the fundamental betrayal: America committed itself to deny Vietnam to communism, but displayed from the outset a cynical indifference to the cost of such a policy for those whom it professed to wish to save. If this has become a familiar weakness of American foreign policy in modern times, Vietnam was its first manifestation. The tactics chosen, the pain inflicted, reflected the brutal truth that Vietnam was merely a battlefield upon which the United States was pursuing its own national interest, in a fashion convenient to its own military means. The welfare of those who chanced to inhabit the line of fire was of no interest to Harkins, nor to his successor Westmoreland, nor indeed to most of those who made American policy in Vietnam. Vietnamese of all hues were simply "gooks," "dinks"—scarcely real human beings.

All this John Paul Vann was growing to understand. His desire to defeat the communists was as passionate as ever. He believed, rightly, that the enemy was as ruthless as the Saigon regime. But the Vietcong appeared more intelligently and selectively brutal. Vann's concern for the Vietnamese people, together with his loathing for the systematic deceits practised by his superiors, increased daily. The 7th Division and Vann's aggressive tactics suffered a severe setback on 5 October 1962,

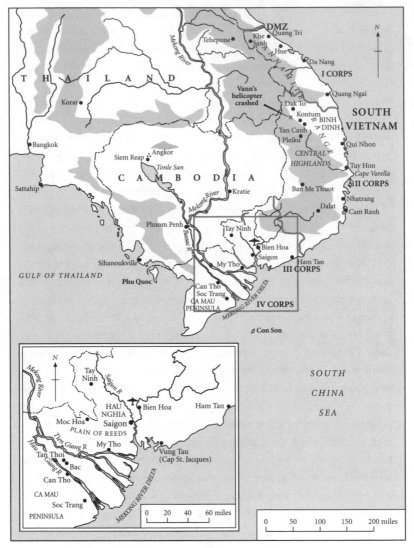

John Paul Vann's areas of operation in Vietnam, 1962–1972.

when a Ranger company attacking the Vietcong's 514th Regional Battalion suffered heavy casualties. Vann himself flew in with reinforcements. His helicopter was raked by communist machine-gun fire, which killed the American crew chief and hit most of the ARVN infantrymen aboard. Vann escaped unwounded, and shot it out with the guerrillas while he directed the evacuation of casualties. He was dismayed to perceive that the Vietcong performance, even under air attack, was vastly superior to that of the ARVN. President Ngo Dinh Diem was so disgusted by his army's losses that he ordered Colonel Cao to break off offensive operations, and to abandon joint planning with the Americans. All Vann's efforts to persuade the Vietnamese that passivity was military nonsense went unheeded. Diem's chosen policy was not to identify and seek out the communists, but instead to herd the entire peasant population into "strategic hamlets," where they could be quarantined—at the cost of losing their homes, their land, all that they held dear.

Yet on 2 January 1963, to Vann's delight the 7th Division was once more committed to an assault. Electronic eavesdroppers had pinpointed a Vietcong radio transmitter near a hamlet named Bac. Saigon ordered this to be seized. Here was another chance, Vann believed, to engage on terms which would enable the ARVN to concentrate firepower against the lightly armed guerrillas. He devised an elaborate plan, based again upon exploiting mobility, to hit the enemy simultaneously from three sides, with a unit of M-113 armoured carriers in support. As the first troop-carrying helicopters clattered away towards the landing zone, Vann circled in a spotter plane. He was to get his wish for a showdown with the Vietcong. There were more than three hundred guerrillas around the twin hamlets of Tan Thoi and Bac. Communist commanders were alarmed that local morale had been damaged by recent reverses. They believed the time had come to demonstrate that they could take on and defeat the ARVN, even with Americans in support. They were as eager to fight as John Paul Vann.

Fog delayed the second and third ARVN helicopter lifts of the morning for more than two hours, during which the initial landing force sat on its position and the Vietcong were granted ample time to ready themselves for battle. In consequence of the delays, civil guards approaching from the south were the first Saigon troops to meet the guerrillas, who opened a devastating fire, killing the senior attacking officers and driving their men to seek shelter behind a dike. Vann, flying low overhead in his L-19, could see even the bullet strikes of the battle below. When the next wave of helicopters approached the battlefield, rifle and machine-gun fire raked them. As ARVN soldiers threw themselves out of their helicopters into the paddies, instead of advancing to engage the enemy they lay prone. To the horror of the Americans, within seconds two helicopters smashed into the ground, riddled with fire. Every machine in the air was hit repeatedly. One, badly damaged, forced-landed a mile away. Yet another was downed as its pilot sought to rescue survivors of the earlier losses.

Vann found himself overseeing a disaster. The Vietnamese troops on the ground refused to move. Vietcong fire was still slashing across the paddies. Supporting artillery was so halfheartedly directed that it did little harm to the enemy. "Topper Six," the Virginian's call sign, tried to summon the supporting APCs to the aid of the men on the ground. He informed the American adviser with the armoured company that three choppers were down, and urged haste. He was enraged when the adviser radioed back: "I've got a problem, Topper Six. My counterpart won't move."

"Goddammit, doesn't he understand this is an emergency?" cried Vann.

"I described the situation to him exactly as you told me, Topper Six, but he says, 'I don't take orders from Americans.' "

Only after the intervention of the ARVN divisional commander did the APCs start to move. They soon halted at the edge of a canal. Another furious radio conversation followed, as Vann watched the drama from his L-19: "I told you people to do something and you're not doing it," he shouted to the American adviser. "Why can't you get the lead out of that son of a bitch's ass?" The Vietnamese commanding the APCs repeated the familiar excuses.

"Jesus Christ, this is intolerable," Vann shouted again. "That bastard has armored tracks and .50 cals and he's afraid of a bunch of VC with small arms. What's wrong with him?"

"We're doing the best we can, Topper Six," said the adviser apologetically.

"Your best isn't worth a shit, Walrus," responded Vann. "This is an emergency. These people are lying out there exposed ... Shoot that rotten, cowardly son of a bitch right now and move out." Vann's tantrum prompted the ARVN captain belatedly to order his vehicles to move. As the APCs began to advance, yet another critically damaged helicopter plunged onto the field beside them—the fifth such Vietcong triumph of the morning—after another failed attempt to rescue the downed crews. An ARVN infantry battalion now blundered into the Vietcong rear, and became locked in a firefight. This intervention denied the enemy any option of escape. Six hours after Vann had launched his operation, its principal achievement was to force the Vietcong to fight on until nightfall, dominating the battlefield against an ARVN and American foe superior in numbers, weapons and equipment.

As the first M-113s lumbered alongside the shot-down helicopters and began to take aboard survivors, communist machine-gun fire clattered on their hulls, killing one driver through his vision slit. Three American pilots were rescued, two crewmen were dead. ARVN infantry leapt down from two other APCs and began to advance on the enemy. Within seconds, men were falling. Contrary to all previous experience, the communists did not withdraw in the face of the armoured vehicles, but held their ground. The APC drivers began to back away. An American sergeant adviser who sprang forward crying "Attack!" ran twenty yards before finding himself alone. He hastily retired, while Vietcong fire picked off APC machine-gunners one by one. When M-113s attempted a headlong charge at the enemy positions, guerrillas surged out of their foxholes, hurling grenades at the leading carriers. Some of the communists were hit, but their boldness broke the spirit of the ARVN. The armoured vehicles hastily reversed, churning through the paddies.

Soon after 6 p.m. a battalion of Vietnamese paratroops was thrown into the battle, dropping from American aircraft. Vann had wanted them to land on the open eastern flank of the battlefield, trapping the guerrillas. Instead, Brigader Cao—he had been promoted to command the corps—insisted that they should drop on the west side, among the APCs, to support the struggling assault troops. Vann said in disgust afterwards: "They chose to reinforce defeat." The drop was a disaster. Nineteen paratroopers were killed and thirty-three wounded, including two American advisers. As evening fell, Vann urged dropping flares to sustain the battle through the night, preventing Vietcong disengagement. Cao would have none of it. He wanted the enemy to go. In darkness so they did, having won an extraordinary victory. Saigon's forces and their American advisers had suffered some two hundred casualties, against fifty-seven among the Vietcong.

For Vann, it was a personal catastrophe. This was a battle of his making, for which all the resources available to the ARVN and their American backers had been deployed, and were now confounded. In execution, the sophisticated, meticulous American plan became a shambles. The communists showed themselves much more skilful and determined than their opponents. To the disgust of the Americans, when helicopters returned to the battlefield next day to recover the dead, ARVN soldiers even proved reluctant to handle the corpses of their own men. The fiasco worsened when ARVN shells fell among the recovery party and its accompanying American officers and reporters. Four men were killed, twelve wounded. The Vietnamese infantry battalion commander, enraged and humiliated, drew a pistol and shot dead his own artillery forward observer.

In Saigon, General Harkins was equally furious when American media accounts of the battle were published. These quoted an anonymous American adviser as saying that the ARVN had put up "a miserable damn performance." Everyone knew that the words were those of Vann. He denied them, but only with difficulty was Harkins persuaded that sacking his most celebrated adviser would be a public relations catastrophe. The general appeased his own anger by portraying the battle at Bac to the Saigon press corps as a success story: "I consider it a victory. We took the objective." In such words lay the seeds of the notorious "credibility gap" which would play so large a part in America's Vietnam tragedy.

Despite Bac, Vann's personal standing remained high. He pursued and exploited celebrity, talking frankly about his hopes and fears to such young turks of the American media in Saigon as David Halberstam of the *New York Times* and Neil Sheehan of UPI. They repaid him with their respect and gratitude, and by projecting across America the story of what he was doing in Vietnam. While Harkins preached the doctrine of winning the war by "the three M's—men, money, matériel," Vann argued that only by making the ARVN a force capable of fighting for its own country, by defeating corruption and reaching out to the peasant population with sympathy, not bombardment, was victory achievable. One of his most famous remarks, often quoted by Saigon newsmen, was: "This is a political war and it calls for discrimination in killing. The best weapon for killing would be a knife, but I'm afraid we can't do it that way. The worst is an airplane. The next worst is artillery. Barring a knife, the best is a rifle—you know who you're killing."

Yet Vann, with his impassioned American faith in the attainability of objectives, resisted a fundamental truth: the regime and social structure of South Vietnam were so rotten that internal reform was impossible. The abuse of American might was hastening the work of the Vietcong, but it is doubtful that any plausible U.S. policy could have rendered the Saigon regime self-sustaining. An extraordinarily corrupt perversion of capitalism was incapable of defeating communist nationalism. For all Vann's clear-eyed analysis of the tactical issues, it was a bridge too far for him to acknowledge the fatal political flaws upon which the American presence in Vietnam was founded.

As it was, however, his briefings of the media were bold to the point of recklessness for an ambitious career officer. Even if Harkins did not sack him, in the eyes of his superiors Vann's name was increasingly identified with trouble. The young reporters who became his friends almost idolised him for what they perceived as his flinty integrity. He told David Halberstam that he always rejected the women whom province chiefs invariably offered him when they met: "It lowers our prestige in their eyes. Too damn many Americans in this country are sleeping with Vietnamese women. It's bad for our image. The Vietnamese don't like it. It arouses their resentment." Halberstam, then as committed as Vann to American victory in Vietnam, felt a stab of guilt about his own Vietnamese girlfriend in Saigon. He thought: "Jesus. Am I undermining the war effort?"

On 8 February 1963 Vann sent a three-page memorandum to his own chief, copied to the commanding general in Saigon, detailing both the extraordinary mastery achieved by the Vietcong in his zone, and the refusal of the ARVN to act effectively to challenge this. General Harkins, enraged, sent his chief of intelligence to investigate. This officer returned to Saigon to report: "The only thing wrong with what [Vann] wrote is that all of it is true." Harkins still declined to transmit tidings of such gloom to Washington. Vann refused to be stymied. He briefed Halberstam on what he had told Harkins. The story was prominently featured in the *New York Times.*

It was Vann's last shot. On 1 April, having completed his one-year posting, he relinquished command of his advisory team. He flew home to America after an emotional parting not only from his comrades, but from the American press correspondents in Saigon, who perceived him as a crusader in the cause of truth. It is hard to overstate Vann's significance in educating newsmen who became vocal critics of the war about the reality of what was being done in their country's name in Indochina. At that time they lacked influence to arrest their country's huge force buildup in Vietnam; but they began to understand the foundation of fallacies upon which this was undertaken.

Back in the United States, Vann pressed his views. He was dismayed to learn that, at the explicit behest of Harkins in Saigon, he would not be debriefed by the Pentagon. After relentless lobbying, he won a promise that he could meet the Joint Chiefs of Staff. He took immense pains about preparing a report for them, detailing the absurdly distorted "body counts," the slaughter of innocent civilians: "We never had intelligence good enough to justify prestrikes by air, artillery or mortars." He argued that if the Vietnamese army could be made to fight, victory was still attainable. However, he was convinced that American armed forces should not be committed to do the job in which the ARVN was failing.

This devastating verdict was never delivered. Vann's meeting with the chiefs did not take place. He spent the morning of 8 July 1963 waiting in an anteroom at the Pentagon, before being told by an aide: "Looks like you don't brief today, buddy." The chairman of the Joint Chiefs, General Maxwell Taylor, had decreed that Vann's report be deleted from the agenda. Vann learned shortly afterwards that he would be denied a further troop command assignment. He wrote to his friends among the correspondents in Saigon that he had decided to retire from the U.S. Army, to accept a civilian job as an aerospace executive.

What he did not tell them—and what became the source of a powerful sense of betrayal among his admirers—was that his military career was blighted not merely by his struggle for truth in Vietnam, but also by a charge of statutory rape that had followed the seduction of a fifteen-year-old girl while he was attending the Command and General Staff

College in 1957. The accusation was dropped after Vann persuaded his hapless wife to lie to save him. But the incident remained a shocking blot on his file, which he believed—surely rightly—must disqualify him from a general's stars. At that time only Mary Jane Vann was aware of his compulsively priapic nature, his affairs with American secretaries, Japanese housemaids and German babysitters. He was a man sexually obsessed. Although nothing of this was publicly known until after Vann's death, its shadow must have hung heavy upon him for many years.

A few weeks after Vann became a civilian, the commanding general of the 82nd Airborne, one of his foremost admirers, wrote to offer him command of a paratroop battalion if he would rejoin the army. The higher command, however, would not hear of this. The frustrations of holding a humdrum office job while his country embarked upon the fateful escalation of its war in Vietnam gnawed deep, and in the winter of 1964 Vann applied successfully for a civilian post as regional director of pacification for the Mekong delta. Maxwell Taylor, now America's ambassador in Vietnam, vetoed the appointment. Indeed, Taylor said flatly that Vann could not return in any capacity. In Denver, the retired colonel pined. A friend in Saigon interceded for him. Taylor grudgingly agreed that Vann would be acceptable in a junior role, as a province pacification officer. In March 1965, after a two-year absence, he landed once more at Tan Son Nhut.

He set out for Hau Nghia province, west of Saigon, just as American Marines waded ashore at Da Nang, first earnest of a huge U.S. troop commitment, and President Lyndon Johnson began his bombing campaign against North Vietnam. Vann's new job was supposed to mean supervising school-building, agricultural programmes and refugee relief. He set about making it something much more ambitious—a struggle for political control of the province. The ARVN had deteriorated dramatically since Vann left two years earlier. Within weeks of his arrival he was gazing on the ruins of a hamlet where a casual Vietcong mortar attack had almost annihilated a Vietnamese Ranger company. Drunken ARVN soldiers shot up villages, and even Vann's quarters, with impunity. The use of marijuana had become widespread among troops.

Vann wrote miserably to a friend in the United States: "We're going to lose because of the moral degeneration in South Vietnam coupled with the excellent discipline of the VC. This country has pissed away its opportunities so long it is now force of habit ... I'm bitter ... not at these ridiculous little Oriental play soldiers—but at our goddam military geniuses and politicians for refusing to admit and act on the obvious—to take over the command of this operation lock, stock and barrel—but maintain Vietnamese front men." He wrote to a senior general and former colleague: "If it were not for the fact that Vietnam is but a pawn in the larger East-West confrontation ... then it would be damned hard to justify our support of the existing government. There is a revolution going on in this country—and the principles, goals, and desires of the *other* side are much closer to what Americans believe in than those of the [Saigon government] ... If I were a lad of eighteen faced with the same choice—whether to support the GVN [government of Vietnam] or the NLF [Vietcong]—and a member of a rural community, I would surely choose the NLF."

"If this war is to be won," he had written to an American friend in Saigon a year earlier, "then it must be done by Vietnamese—nothing could be more foolhardy than the employment of U.S. (or any other foreign) troops in quantity. We could pour our entire Army into Vietnam—and accomplish nothing worthwhile." Now there were fifty thousand Americans in Vietnam, and many, many more coming. The enemy was escalating too. Vann found that travelling the province in his accustomed fashion—alone in a pickup truck—had become much more dangerous. Ambushes multiplied.

One day in June, a group of black-pyjama-clad figures waved him down on the road to Cu Chi. He accelerated past them, and survived the bursts of fire that riddled the vehicle's cab with only superficial wounds from glass splinters. Thereafter he travelled with a carbine and a clutch of grenades on the seat beside him. He and his assistant, a young Foreign Service officer named Doug Ramsey, were dismayed by their impotence to check the relentless bombing of civilians by the American command and the Saigon government. In a local dispensary they met a young woman being treated for napalm burns. She was the sole survivor of eight workers in a field. Eight months pregnant, she would never be able to nurse her child. Her nipples had been burnt away.

In September, Vann drafted a major paper entitled "Harnessing the Revolution in South Vietnam." This called for a twin-track strategy of defeating the Vietcong militarily, while replacing the Saigon regime with a government capable of addressing the needs of the Vietnamese people. He passionately opposed compulsory relocation of the peasantry through the Strategic Hamlet Programme, and was infuriated when parts of his own province were declared "free bombing zones," in which anything that moved was assumed to be communist. As a government helicopter overflew the countryside, ordering local people to pack and leave, Vann denounced the policy as "idiocy." He wrote: "A successful military venture will be negated by a continuing failure of GVN to win its own people." When he saw TV film of U.S. Marines torching Vietnamese homes near Da Nang, he wrote to a military friend: "If this is to be our policy, then I want no part of it." He had resumed a close and indiscreet relationship with the Saigon press corps who had made him famous. He gave Doug Ramsey a copy of an admiring profile of himself by David Halberstam in *Esquire* magazine. His celebrity—Ward Just of the *Washington Post* called him "one of the legendary Americans in Vietnam"—enfolded Vann in a protective aura when the U.S. military became exasperated by his refusal to toe the line of official policy. Vann sent Henry Cabot Lodge, now back for a second tour as American envoy, his "Harnessing the Revolution" paper. Lodge passed it to his Political Section, where it vanished without trace.

Yet some Americans did respond to Vann's imprecations. In October 1965 he was translated to a far more influential role as adviser on civilian affairs to the U.S. general commanding in the III Corps zone, covering southern South Vietnam. He had become a man obsessed with the war, "his" war. He talked about it relentlessly, compulsively, to anyone who would listen, from Saigon to Washington. In his way, he was as wrong about America's options as were Lodge, Secretary of Defense Robert McNamara, Lyndon Johnson and the generals in theirs. Vann believed that Americans could lead Vietnamese, as British officers such as Jack Masters had earlier led native troops across their empire for generations. His vision was essentially colonialist, founded upon a belief that the Vietnamese could be moulded to American ways. He supposed that American power could impose at will an acceptable, benign, honest, credible local government. Yet the redeeming merit of Vann's naïvety was its human sympathy for the Vietnamese people, a quality which seemed quite absent in his critics.

In January 1966 Vann's former assistant Doug Ramsey was captured by the Vietcong. Vann raced to the scene in his own car, a little Triumph saloon, and trawled the area offering a ransom for his friend's release. The Vietcong were uninterested: Ramsey remained a prisoner in the jungle for seven terrible years. Vann himself narrowly escaped death when he drove into another ambush. His companion in the passenger seat hurled a grenade from the car window to clear a path through the guerrillas. Vann's lifestyle was becoming increasingly frenzied. His marriage was over in all but name, and he established relationships with not one, but two Vietnamese mistresses. The first was Lee, who was twenty. Under pressure from her family he eventually went through a ceremony of engagement to her. The second, Annie, was a lycée school-girl of seventeen when they met. She eventually gave birth to a child by him. For several years he successfully concealed the existence of each woman from the other, and his manic pursuit of other girls from both.

Early in 1966 Vann was promoted to deputy director of pacification for III Corps, and then in November to the zone's top job, which made him one of the most important American civilians in Vietnam. Whatever the official doubts about his judgement and discretion, nobody could dispute his energy, intelligence and exceptional knowledge of the country and its people. He was now responsible for a staff of 330 Americans and more than 600 Vietnamese and other civilian staffers. At Christmas he wrote to a military friend: "I am still optimistic about what can be done in Vietnam, but I continue to be distressed at how little actually is being done." As the war escalated, so did the ghastly civilian toll—some twenty-five thousand dead and fifty thousand wounded every year. Neil Sheehan, now with the *New York Times*, asked General William Westmoreland in August 1966 if he was troubled by the non-combatant casualty roll. "Yes, Neil, it's a problem," acknowledged the general, "but it does deprive the enemy of the population, doesn't it?"

It was an irony, if not a paradox, that America's descent into a quag-mire in Vietnam during 1966 and 1967 witnessed a steady rise in John Paul Vann's influence and stature. The cocky, earnest little Virginian became a key figure behind Robert "Blowtorch" Komer, new chief of the country's pacification operations, through the CORDS—Civil Opera-tions and Revolutionary Development—programme. Komer, a formida-ble and ruthless operator, enjoyed the personal support of Lyndon Johnson. Vann, in turn, found himself profiting from the backing of

Komer, and of III Corps's new U.S. commanding general, Fred Weyand. Outside Vann's office at Bien Hoa airbase now stood a personal helicopter. By air and road he roamed restlessly across the country, gathering news, gossip, sensations, returning in the small hours to one of his two mistresses. He sent a circular to friends, exulting: "I am back in the military fold, and I am in command."

Yet by the summer of 1967, pessimism dogged him once more. He thought Komer obsessed with systems at the expense of reality. Reality was that the South Vietnamese army was no more capable than it had ever been of securing its own people from the Vietcong. The U.S. Army pursued its destructive path across the country, its troop numbers rising constantly. A great American carpet was laid across Vietnam as an infrastructure of bases, air-conditioning, cold beer, hot showers, cinemas and officers' clubs was created to sustain the military presence. "I think we are on the road to doom," Vann wrote to his friend Daniel Ellsberg, who in 1971 would become famous for leaking the Pentagon Papers, which exposed the squalid truth behind U.S. operations in southeast Asia, through Neil Sheehan. While Vann possessed in full measure the trappings of personal power and success, he was impotent to deflect the disastrous course on which his country was set. During an eight-week leave in Europe and the United States in the winter of 1967 he met Walt Rostow, national security adviser at the Johnson White House. Rostow listened to Vann for a while, then interrupted to ask whether he agreed that for all Vietnam's problems, the war should be past its worst in six months. Vann replied: "Oh hell no, Mr. Rostow. I'm a born optimist. I think we can hold out longer than that." Rostow, unamused, said that a man with such views should not be working for the United States in Vietnam.

Early in the morning of 31 January 1968, the second day of the Vietnamese Tet holiday, Vann was woken in his bed at Bien Hoa by the sound of Vietcong rockets exploding on the base. The Tet offensive, the most unwelcome shock of the war to Saigon and the government of the United States, had begun. For the first few hours he was engaged in contacting his CORDS teams around the provinces, as American troops fought Vietcong infiltrators inside the Bien Hoa perimeter. Then he took his helicopter to rescue his Vietnamese mistress Annie, together with their baby daughter. He found that Annie's parents had already retrieved her by car, though that did not prevent him from telling friends he had whisked her to safety in his Ranger. He could, however, claim credit for having urged General Weyand to refuse Westmoreland's demands to despatch most of his troops towards the Cambodian border. The Vietcong might have won Saigon had not Weyand's powerful forces been at hand to frustrate them.

Two weeks of desperate fighting throughout Vietnam followed the onset of Tet, in which at least 14,300 civilians died, 72,000 homes were destroyed, and 627,000 people were made homeless. The North Vietnamese army held out for twenty-six days in the citadel at Hué. At the end, America had achieved a decisive military victory over the Vietcong. Thereafter, Hanoi was obliged to depend overwhelmingly upon the regular North Vietnamese army to prosecute its war. Yet America's moral and political battle was equally decisively lost, when the world saw Vietcong guerrillas battling inside the compound of the United States Embassy in Saigon.

It was in the aftermath of Tet, in the eyes of men who were formerly Vann's foremost admirers, such as his biographer Neil Sheehan, that their hero lost his way in Vietnam, never to regain it. He parted company with reality, because he could not see Tet for the turning point it was. Though the war had seven years yet to run, the American people had lost the will to seek victory. The balance of Vann's life was devoted to pursuing a campaign that flew in the face of everything he himself had said about Vietnam since 1962. He succumbed to delusions about American rightness and mightiness, as surely as Washington and the generals had done. In the weeks that followed Tet, Vann hastened across his region, urging, inciting, pleading—and promising that victory was still attainable. In February 1968 he sent a circular to his CORDS teams: "Now is the time, quite literally, to separate the men from the boys. I have been disappointed in several instances to find advisers who are obviously feeling very sorry for themselves and mentally wringing their hands...Get your counterparts and their troops out from behind their barbed wire and aggressively on the offensive, both day and night..." One night in May, he buckled under the strain. His mistress Lee found him unconscious on the floor of their house, vomiting blood. He was rushed to hospital, and almost died before the doctors diagnosed him with a rare condition called Mallory-Weiss syndrome, and successfully treated him.

Vann's optimism put heart into some Americans who were close to losing theirs—as they had every reason to do. He was promoted again. Just as U.S. defeat became inevitable for those with eyes to see, John Paul Vann's power and influence reached a high point. He devised a plan for transferring the burden of combat from American soldiers to the very ARVN whom he acknowledged as unwilling to fight. He was quoted by name in an Associated Press despatch, citing hundreds of thousands of American support personnel who, he said, could be sent home "for free," with no negative military consequences.

Vann later claimed to have thought that he was talking to a reporter off the record, but that did not stem the bitter row which followed. For the new commanding general in Vietnam, Creighton Abrams, here was one Vann indiscretion too many. Abrams demanded that the III Corps pacification chief must be sacked. Yet the support of Robert Komer saved Vann, and somebody much more important than Komer was impressed by what Vann said: the newly elected president, Richard Nixon. When Nixon, after his inauguration, unveiled the strategy of "Vietnamisation," his national security adviser, Dr. Henry Kissinger, told Vann flatteringly: "It's your policy." Although to his disappointment he was not offered the Nixon administration job which he now craved to implement his strategy, he felt that at last he had achieved influence at the highest level in the United States.

This was reflected most vividly by an invitation to meet Nixon and Kissinger at the White House on 22 December 1969. The tone of the encounter was set by Vann's new optimism. The previous autumn he had told columnist Joseph Alsop, who spent a week touring the Mekong delta, that he believed the Saigon government was close to controlling 90 per cent of the delta population. Alsop, in his writing, praised Vann as "an infinitely patriotic, intelligent, and courageous and magnificent leader." He said that if this man, "in the long past... Vietnam's super-pessimist," now believed America was winning, then it must be true. At the White House, Nixon welcomed Vann's rosy vision for Vietnam's future—not least because Vann was convinced that it could be achieved with a minimum of American soldiers. He returned to Saigon in January 1970 bolstered by the endorsement of Nixon, who gave him an auto-graphed pen and golf ball as souvenirs of his visit. Daniel Ellsberg taunted his old friend: "You finally had some good news to give the president, John."

What caused the extraordinary change in Vann's attitude? Neil Sheehan wrote twenty years later: "The John Vann his old friends had known
disappeared into the war. Each year South Vietnam had become a more
perfect place for him. The war satisfied him so completely that he could
no longer look at it as something separate from himself. He had finally
bent the truth about the war as he had bent other and lesser truths in the
past." Vann's optimism was surely founded more than anything upon the
fact that he now possessed a very large personal stake in the conflict. He
had achieved the status and influence he had always craved, together
with a lifestyle which perfectly suited his extravagant temperament. If
Vietnam could be "saved," Vann would be an American hero. If he conceded his country's failure, then he could expect only relegation to an
obscure existence as a civilian corporate executive. There would be no
more personal helicopters, command status, Vietnamese mistresses.

As Vann's power grew in the Vietnam of the early 1970s, he was able
to initiate and direct military operations on a spectacular scale. All his
old scepticism about the ARVN, his contempt for the abuse of firepower,
vanished as he became the architect of ground assaults on communist
strongholds, as well as overlord of B-52 strike programmes. In May 1971
he became director of the Second Regional Assistance Command, covering the entire II Corps area of Vietnam, the Central Highlands and
much of the central coast. Though still a nominal civilian, he held effective ranking as a major-general, with a subordinate American brigadier
to serve as his military executive officer. When his old friend Ellsberg
leaked the Pentagon Papers to the world in May 1971, exposing the follies
and deceits of American Vietnam policy for a decade, Vann was disgusted. He urged that Ellsberg should be jailed for treason.

In the last months of Vann's career in Vietnam, the winter of 1971 and
spring of 1972, his life assumed an almost hysterical character. Now
divorced from Mary Jane, he maintained a household with his Vietnamese "wife" Annie and their daughter, while continuing the relationship with his lover Lee. In his new military role he not only planned
battles, but threw himself into combat. During fierce fighting in April
1972 for the ARVN's Firebase Delta, one of the government's fortified
hilltop bases, he flew his Ranger helicopter through the mountains to
rescue the crew of a shot-down Chinook. He roamed the sky above the
battlefield, calling in air strikes and watching the ebb and flow of action

below—the explosions, the running figures and the dying ones. When the Vietnamese commander of Delta asserted that without immediate resupply he was doomed, Vann responded that he would fly the mission himself. His officers told him not to be a fool. Vann replied: "I'm experienced at this." He may have been remembering his exploits in Korea. To the awe and disbelief of Vietnamese and Americans alike, that afternoon of 3 April he flew six supply sorties into Firebase Delta under fire. Next day, a relief force broke the North Vietnamese siege.

This experience seemed to lift Vann into a condition of euphoria. His faith in the South Vietnamese capacity for victory, and in his own invulnerability, had become messianic: "A lot of soldiers are yet to die," he wrote, but "we expect to hold our major positions." Within days, his prediction was rendered risible. In Binh Dinh, a large province on the central coast, on 10 April a fire-support base known as Pony was lost when local South Vietnamese forces collapsed in the face of communist attack. Vann landed under mortar fire in the positions of the ARVN 40th Regiment, to stiffen resistance. He failed. On 19 April he was obliged to order an evacuation of South Vietnamese troops in the area by M-113 armoured vehicles.

This movement disintegrated into bloody chaos amid North Vietnamese assaults. Over the days that followed, ARVN forces crumbled across the whole of northern Binh Dinh province. Thousands of government troops threw away their uniforms and deserted. South Vietnamese helicopter crews sold seats on their Hueys to deserters paying cash, while wounded men died untended. On 21 April, Firebase Delta was overrun. In a score of places, entire Vietnamese formations faced disaster as the communists mercilessly tightened the screw. Saigon's generals seemed seized by paralysis, incapable of manoeuvre or effective military response of any kind. This was not merely a defeat, it was an experience that laid bare the moral, social and military bankruptcy of the Saigon regime and its servants. When the North Vietnamese began to deploy T-54 tanks, Vann refused to accept reports of their sighting. He was in denial about what was happening to "his" war.

He was sufficient of a realist, however, about his own mortality to scribble a will as he flew in his Jet Ranger to the beleaguered ARVN headquarters at Tan Canh in the mountains of northern Kontum province, under heavy North Vietnamese assault on the morning of 24 April 1972.

He timed and dated the page of his spiral notepad, and requested that his "wife" Annie and their Vietnamese daughter should "share equally in his estate," and receive the proceeds of the sale of his property in Vietnam, though there was precious little of it. Since he had never signed any valid marriage agreement relating to Annie, his American will, leaving everything to Mary Jane and their children, was the only document possessed of legal force. Yet perhaps the gesture persuaded him that he was honourably acquitting his responsibilities.

He spoke by radio to the Tan Canh command group's American advisers. They had been forced to abandon an ARVN divisional headquarters under heavy fire and seek refuge in a minefield outside the perimeter, in which many Vietnamese fugitives had already blown themselves up. Vann and his pilot, a warrant officer named Bob Richards whose nerve had been drained to the dregs by almost two years of flying the Virginian, descended with another Ranger to rescue the Americans. Richards was appalled to glimpse a communist T-54 tank a bare two hundred yards distant, its 100mm gun trained on them. The helicopters lingered a few seconds above the ground as three American advisers scrambled aboard. Then they swung up and away—with four Vietnamese soldiers clinging to the helicopters' skids. For some reason, the T-54 did not fire on them. They landed safely at nearby Dak To, offloaded their human cargo, and went back for more.

Richards and Vann were contour-chasing to avoid low cloud and communist antiaircraft fire when a burst of AK-47 fire struck the cockpit and fuselage, wrecking the radio and holing the fuel tanks. Several rounds impacted under Vann's seat. Richards reared the Ranger up, round and away. They landed at Pleiku. The pilot was understandably traumatised by the experience, and declined to fly again. Vann simply ran across to another helicopter as soon as it had retrieved the remaining advisers from Tan Canh. He flew to another stricken position to rescue another American. As they touched down, Vann used the butt of his M-16 rifle to beat off ARVN fugitives seeking to scramble aboard. Yet so many others seized the skids on the pilot's side that as the Ranger lifted off, it lurched askew until the flailing rotor struck the ground. The machine somersaulted twice, then collapsed. Vann pulled his Vietnamese aide Lieutenant Huynh Van Cai from under the wreckage, then summoned assistance by radio. A Huey rescued the American party at the cost of multiple hits. Back in safety, Vann paused only long enough to get an American officer to witness his will and accept custody of the flimsy scribble before setting out once more for Tan Canh.

All that day he directed air strikes against the attacking communist formations, and sought to destroy munitions dumps before they fell into enemy hands. He seemed incapable of pausing for a moment from his frenzied personal struggle to arrest the catastrophe to which his own delusions had contributed. Yet he also arranged for personal effects from his quarters at Pleiku to be discreetly flown out. His action acknowledged awareness that the town could not hold. Everywhere in the Central Highlands the communists were triumphant.

Logic suggested that Kontum town, the provincial capital, was also indefensible, but Vann took personal control of operations to save the place. He entrusted command to—of all people—the same Captain Ba, now a colonel commanding a division, who had led the M-113 company to such sorry effect during the 1963 battle at Bac. Over the weeks that followed, the defence of Kontum became Vann's obsession. Bypassing normal air control procedures, he overflew the battlefield in his Ranger, marshalling and often personally directing almost three hundred strikes by giant B-52s between mid-May and early June. After the aircraft had bombed, he sometimes circled at low level, firing at communist survivors with his M-16. On one mission he assured two accompanying reporters that this was not a dangerous practice, since anyone alive below would be too shocked to touch a trigger for at least half an hour after the bombers had gone. He told a *Washington Post* reporter with apparent satisfaction: "You can tell from the battlefield stench that the strikes are effective." Vietnamese staff at his headquarters nicknamed him "Mr. B-52." On 30 May he personally flew South Vietnam's President Thieu into Kontum on a morale-boosting visit. The politician pinned brigadier's stars on Ba's fatigues, yet everyone involved, American and Vietnamese, knew that the defence of the town was Vann's achievement. Had he not willed it, no one else would have accomplished it. He was wildly throwing up sand to halt the march of the tide.

On 9 June, Vann flew to Saigon. In the morning he took time off to make love first to Lee, afterwards to two other women, before attending an afternoon strategy conference. He determined thereafter to visit Kontum, as he had done every day since its battle began. A little past

9 p.m. on a relatively clear night, he reported himself by radio to be fifteen minutes from the landing zone. Shortly afterwards, ARVN soldiers
observed a sudden fireball in a grove of trees a few hundred yards from
their position. Vann's Ranger was in inexperienced hands. His former
pilot Bob Richards had suffered a nervous collapse after his experiences
at Tan Canh, and disappeared absent without leave in Bangkok. On the
night of 9 June, pilot error rather than enemy action precipitated the
fatal crash of Vann's Ranger.

American helicopters were easily guided to the scene by lingering
flames. A searchlight illuminated the scene. Vann's body had been
thrown clear of the crash, but broken by the impact. An ARVN patrol
which had been first to reach the spot extorted a cash handout from the
Americans for having ventured out of their positions in darkness,
despite having exploited the opportunity to steal rings and watches from
the dead. The American pilot who took the crash victims' bodies aboard
a Huey said: "I hate to be the guy to give John Vann his last ride." Yet it is
hard to believe that the man who lay dead on the helicopter floor would
have nursed regrets. No one who behaved as did Vann in those last
weeks can have cared whether he lived or died. At the moment of his
death, however, he cherished a fantasy of personal success. He retained
an extraordinary optimism that his defence of Kontum had turned the
tide of the war, and cherished a delusion that he, John Paul Vann, had
transformed his country's prospects in Vietnam, averting defeat. In reality, of course, though it would be three more years before the last act
came, by 1972 few knowledgeable observers doubted what the end
would be.

Vann's death made front-page news in the United States, where he
was mourned as one of his country's Indochina legends. He was buried
at Arlington National Cemetery on 16 June amid a great gathering of
generals and politicians. Daniel Ellsberg attended, along with Senator
Edward Kennedy and the long-suffering Mary Jane Vann, who despite
their divorce had never renounced her husband. General Westmoreland,
now army chief of staff, was there, along with William Rogers, the secretary of state, and Melvin Laird, the secretary of defense. Robert
Komer delivered the eulogy. At the graveside, Vann's sixteen-year-old
son, Peter, received the coffin flag from the honour guard. His eldest son,
John Allen, now twenty-four, preferred to be a passive witness. He bore

considerable bitterness towards some of the great men present, who he believed had forced his father out of the army. Likewise, Vann's twenty-one-year-old second son, Jesse, was only with difficulty dissuaded from handing Richard Nixon his torn-up draft card at the family's meeting with the president in the White House after the ceremony.

Nixon told them that he regretted being unable to award the fallen hero a Congressional Medal of Honor, because Vann was technically a civilian at the time of his death. Instead, he could offer only the Presidential Medal of Freedom. The family was dismayed by the notion that Vann was getting second-best. Nixon proclaimed sonorously: "Soldier of peace and patriot of two nations, the name of John Paul Vann will be honoured as long as free men remember the struggle to preserve the independence of South Vietnam...A truly noble American, a superb leader, he stands with Lafayette in that gallery of heroes who have made another brave people's cause their own."

Even by the standards of graveyard hyperbole, this was extravagant. Vann's behaviour in the last phase of his life was little short of deranged, not unworthy of a character in Stanley Kubrick's *Dr. Strangelove*. The pomp of the Arlington funeral reflected the political requirements of a beleaguered administration, searching for honour where there was none to be found. In Vann's first tour in Vietnam, and even during the early years after his return, he had seemed a beacon of truth, humanity and integrity. Afterwards, however, the pursuit of personal fulfilment and vainglory eclipsed all these things. At his death, Vann's political and military masters sought to exploit the tatters of his earlier reputation in their quest for a fig leaf of justification to sustain a struggle whose futility had become plain to all those capable of thinking for themselves. Neil Sheehan, the young *New York Times* reporter who had been captivated by Vann a decade earlier, was prominent among those who felt betrayed by his apostasy. In 1988 Sheehan published his monumental work *A Bright Shining Lie*, which adopted Vann as the symbol of America's failure in Vietnam, and of the massive deceits entwined with it.

Vann's energy and courage enthralled many of those who met him, before they learned to fear the manifestations of these qualities. He was a driven, obsessive figure, who bore his demons unexorcised from the cradle to the grave. A fundamental selfishness dominated his conduct, which brought grief to many of those who fell beneath his influence. He embodied the American spirit of "can do," but misapplied it to tragic effect in Vietnam from the late 1960s until his death. He clung to a stubborn faith in the doctrine of American universalism, of exactly the kind that guided Washington's neoconservatives to their blunderings in Iraq in 2003 and 2004. Vann wanted to persuade the Vietnamese to become Asian Americans. When they declined to do so, he lost his compass. He became too incontinent a human being to deserve command in a war of others who valued their lives more highly than he did his own.

CHAPTER FIFTEEN

EPIC ON THE GOLAN

NO PORTRAIT of the modern warrior would be complete which omitted the experience of the Israelis in arms. Until 1948, while educated people knew that many fine soldiers throughout history had been Jewish, the world did not perceive the Jews as a warlike race. Indeed, among the ignorant their martial qualities were despised. Yet following the foundation of Israel, all this changed. National survival demanded the application of the Jewish genius to military affairs, with extraordinary results. First, in Israel's war of independence (1948–49), the Palmach—little more than a guerrilla force—repelled every Arab army deployed to crush the fledgling state. In 1956 the Israelis' lightning dash across Sinai astonished the world. In 1967 it was widely expected that the Arabs' overwhelming superiority of numbers must prevail, as Egypt's President Nasser persuaded Syria and Jordan to join his country's mobilisation against Israel. Instead, of course, the Israelis struck first, and achieved one of the most brilliant victories in modern warfare, reaching the Suez Canal and capturing Jerusalem and the Golan Heights in six days. This achievement provoked a surge of hubris in Israel, a conviction among its people that they could defeat any Arab army on any terms, which almost proved their undoing. In October 1973, when the Egyptians and Syrians struck with overwhelming force and a formidable array of new Soviet technology, they gained surprise and came close to breakthrough. For the first four days of the war an Arab victory seemed possible. Every Israeli learns to recite from the cradle: "Israel can win wars again and again and there are only more Arabs; but if the Arabs win just once, there is no more Israel."

Students of military history regard the 1973 Yom Kippur War (named for the Jewish Day of Atonement on which it began) as the greatest achievement of the IDF—the Israel Defence Force, as the army is always known. Its soldiers sustained their initial resistance with tiny numbers, under the most unfavourable circumstances. Then they turned the tables and counterattacked, inflicting a crushing defeat on the Syrians and Egyptians, which must have ended in the annihilation of the Arab armies had not political imperatives prompted a cease-fire. I was a witness to some of those dramatic events, as a war correspondent first on the Golan Heights and then in Sinai. It was deeply moving to behold the spectacle of these haggard, unshaven, exhausted men, members of an army unlike any other in the world, fighting their tanks and guns in the knowledge that failure might precipitate the destruction of their nation. One of these was a thirty-one-year-old tank officer named Avigdor Kahalani. Neither I nor the world had ever heard of him. Kahalani was not Israel's most brilliant soldier. He was only one among several thousand men who held the line through the first critical days of the war. Many Israelis apportion chief credit for directing the defence of the northern Golan to the dour, taciturn "Raful," Brigadier Rafael Eitan. They argue that Kahalani, a mere lieutenant-colonel in 1973, did not prove a success in subsequent higher command postings, and he later became a controversial figure in Israeli politics.

Yet none of this matters in rehearsing the man's experience as leader of a Centurion battalion in 1973. Kahalani embodied most of the virtues and vices of his nation, conceit not least among the latter. Beyond peradventure, he was a superb tank soldier in an army which has exploited armour more skilfully and imaginatively than any since—ironically— Hitler's Wehrmacht. So much political controversy has fallen upon Israel and its army over the past generation, first with the 1982 invasion of Lebanon and then with the IDF's ruthless stewardship of its occupied territories, that even today many Israelis feel a stab of nostalgia for the simple certainties of 1973. If their nation then faced mortal peril, none doubted the justice of its cause nor the achievement of its soldiers at a decisive moment in their national history.

Avigdor Kahalani was born in 1944, eldest son of parents who met in

Israel after emigrating from Yemen. Their origins placed them at the bottom of the social pile among the rival castes of their new homeland. Israelis often referred to Yemenites as "blacks," sometimes in jest and sometimes in real contempt. Kahalani grew up in Nes Ziona, then a rural suburb of Tel Aviv, in a house which his father built with his own hands. The family worked in the nearby citrus groves. After elementary school, in deference to his father's wish that he should learn a trade, he studied mechanics at a vocational school rather than seeking higher education. When the time came for his induction for military service, he was among the May 1962 intake to the army's conscript processing unit, the Kelet. May recruits were always dismissively known to their contemporaries as "the Mau-Mau," because they were supposed to include the stupidest and least promising of the four annual crops. The short, stocky Kahalani was rejected for flight training because of partial deafness, and for the paratroops because of flat feet. Most unwillingly, he found himself despatched to the armoured corps, the boys of lowest academic attainment. "Avi," his father had said, "use your head and do what you want. But one thing I ask: do everything not to be a tankist!" In 1948 and 1956 his father had been among those responsible for recovering wrecked tanks from the battlefield. He had seen what men looked like who crewed a vehicle which "brewed up." His son hated the notion of being shut into a stinking steel box. Yet now, this was to be his fate. He set about making the most of it.

In training, Kahalani often felt that as a Yemenite, he drew the short straw. When he reported sick with stomach cramps, he was accused of malingering. That suspicion was not dispelled even when he was diagnosed with a burst appendix. He was initially rejected for the tank commanders' course, and only scraped in because of a shortfall of candidates. He passed out top, was named "outstanding trainee" and given a sergeant's stripes. These in turn gained him passage to officer school. To his bitter disappointment, however, after a few weeks he was expelled with a damning report: "Poor familiarity with the subject matter. No command and leadership ability. Unfit to be an officer in the IDF." He returned to his unit nursing despondency, convinced that crude caste or racial prejudice had been responsible for his disgrace. The battalion sympathised, and so did some senior officers. He was given command of a reconnaissance platoon, and soon afterwards received a lieutenant's bars, even though he never completed the officers' training course.

Kahalani still intended to quit the army when his conscript service was up in 1964. His father had started a garage in Nes Ziona and called the place "Avi's," intending its stewardship for his eldest son. The young officer was persuaded to extend his term in uniform only by the promise of an assignment to Germany, whence he accompanied a team secretly despatched to train on the American Patton tank, which was being sold to Israel. The swarthy appearance of Kahalani and another Yemenite officer caused their comrades to refer to them as "the niggers." They shrugged this off, just as they accepted orders not to date German girls, lest it cause trouble with the locals. Kahalani returned to Israel in 1966 committed to stay in the army and help form its first Patton battalion. He had come to love soldiering, and tanks. By the time the Six-Day War began in June 1967 he was a company commander, responsible for fourteen Pattons of the 79th Battalion, deployed on the frontier with Egypt, facing the Sinai desert. To make sense of Kahalani's experience in the 1973 war of Yom Kippur, it is necessary to describe what happened to him in 1967.

On 4 June their brigade commander addressed the tank men in language that electrified them: "Tomorrow is war. I want you to empty your machine-guns on them. Leave no one alive. Run 'em over with your tank treads. Don't hesitate! If you want to live, wipe 'em out. They're your enemy—you're not gonna be shooting at barrels any more. If you don't fire at them, they're gonna hit you! They hate us. We should have gone into Egypt long ago and given 'em the smashing they deserve! It's a historical moment—let's exploit it!" Military leaders often find it hard to motivate their soldiers for campaigns. Most Americans in Europe in the Second World War, for instance, felt little or no hatred for their enemy, except insofar as Germans represented a threat to their personal welfare. Among Israelis in their wars of survival, motivation has never been a problem. Every soldier has known, in each of his nation's major conflicts save the 1982 invasion of Lebanon, that the country's very existence was at stake. This helps to explain the paradox that while Israel is a notoriously undisciplined society, its citizens instinctively reluctant to obey, this intransigence is shed like an outer garment when its people deploy on a battlefield. Israel is a small country, in which almost everyone seems to know everyone else. At war, it becomes a village in arms. The best Israeli soldiers and commanders display extraordinary personal initiative, indeed sometimes an excess of this. There is an intimacy, as well as a deadly intensity of purpose, about the Israeli army at war that creates a mood unique to the nation—or at least did so in all the conflicts of the twentieth century in which Israel fought the Arab states.

At 8 a.m. on 5 June 1967, Israel's armies began to move. Kahalani led his company of Pattons, in which not a man among the crews was more than twenty years of age, through a cluster of eucalyptus groves, heading west. Excited foot soldiers along the road cheered and clapped as the armoured columns powered past, throwing up their great clouds of dust. Young officers asked impatiently over the radio: "Can we load the guns?" Forty-eight minutes later, they smashed through the Egyptian border fence. As Kahalani's tank plunged into a cactus thicket, he was momentarily bemused by the chips flying off his tank's paintwork, which he thought must be a natural phenomenon until he realised that he was under Arab machine-gun fire. The roar of an armoured vehicle drowns out every lesser sound, even if a crewman is not wearing headphones. To Kahalani's frustration and embarrassment, in the rough going his Patton threw a track. Hastily he switched tanks. They pressed on towards their first objective, Khan Yunis, at the southern end of the Gaza strip. Two Pattons struck mines and stopped. Kahalani told the rest to follow his own path in a single column. Suddenly glimpsing another tank in front, he traversed his gun before identifying it as one of his own battalion. On and on they drove, answering sporadic Egyptian machine-gun fire with bursts from their own turrets, wreaking havoc among a jumble of military vehicles outside a police station with 90mm shells, meeting no serious opposition.

A grenade thudded onto Kahalani's turret top, and lodged there. He ducked and huddled below the hatch lid for what seemed an eternity, before an explosion came. He and his crew were unhurt. Minutes later, without warning a United Nations truck loomed headlong into their path. The Patton's gun barrel smashed into the vehicle, destroying everything above its own height. Kahalani's tank lumbered on, but its gun-firing mechanism was damaged beyond repair. Feeling, the young officer wrote, "like a hunter without a rifle," he and his company hastened into Rafah, their next objective, amid a crackle of machine-gun fire, both incoming and outgoing. Kahalani kept inside the turret until the shooting faded. In defiance of all the rules of armoured warfare, the Israeli tanks were accompanied by no supporting infantry to deal with the enemy's foot soldiers. Against a more energetic foe than the Egyptians, this would have left them dangerously exposed. As it was, the Israelis relied upon the momentum of their armoured spearheads to shatter the enemy's formations. Their gamble was triumphantly successful.

Kahalani's tank came under fire from an Egyptian T-34. With his gun disabled, he called urgently to a neighbouring Patton to reply. Within seconds the Arab tank was burning. As they began to pass Egyptian trenches, the Israelis tossed down grenades from their turrets. Kahalani's command cupola machine gun jammed, leaving only the coaxial machine gun operational. On and on they went, shooting up trucks, antiaircraft guns, tanks wherever they met them. Most often, however, they saw scurrying Egyptian infantrymen, many throwing away their boots to hasten their flight.

Early afternoon found the regiment nine miles southwest of Rafah, in the midst of the sands of Sinai. They halted to check their tanks and discuss their progress in terse, tense shorthand. They knew they had a long way still to roll and fight. Kahalani switched to yet another tank, which had a functioning weapons system. His men clambered back into their turrets and set off again. Forward they went, past scores of blackened and burnt-out Egyptian vehicles, destroyed by Israel's air force.

Late in the afternoon they were heading south towards El Arish in a long column behind the brigade commander's tactical headquarters group when Kahalani was ordered to overtake and assume the lead. He had no idea what might be ahead, and nor did anyone else. As he sped along, to his surprise he was waved down by three Israeli soldiers: "Watch out! Egyptian tanks nearby!" they shouted. The Patton crept cautiously forward, past a burnt-out Israeli personnel carrier. Then they halted on a low ridge. Kahalani scanned the western horizon through binoculars. The sinking sun dazzled him. He asked whether his gunner could glimpse any enemy. "All I see are trenches. No tanks," came the response. Suddenly there was an explosion, and Kahalani felt a savage pain. After a moment of paralysis, he fell back into the turret and shouted: "We've been hit. Bail out!"

The Israeli army never liked the Patton, because when struck by an incoming projectile the American tank burned fast. Armoured soldiers called it the *"guanikim"*—Hebrew slang for a flare. Kahalani's tank dissolved into a blazing shambles. He collapsed on the turret floor amid the flames, thinking: "That's that, my life is over." He surprised himself, however, by mustering sufficient will and strength to climb onto his seat and hang out of the turret, shouting: "Mother, I'm burning, I'm burning, I'm burning…" He ripped away his radio lead, lurched off the turret onto the hull, and rolled in flames to the ground, throwing himself frantically hither and thither in the sand, seeking to put out the fires enveloping his body, while tanks manoeuvred around him and more shells exploded overhead. He crawled frantically out of the path of an oncoming tank. The rags of his charred clothes had fallen off. He saw commanders peering down aghast at his tortured figure, almost naked save for boots. The battalion commander's tank stopped beside him. The colonel leaned out: "Kahalani, what's happened?" Kahalani shrugged: "Watch out. Enemy tanks there." In his agony he started to run, shreds of charred skin dangling from his hands and body. Seeing the tank of a comrade, a young lieutenant, he clambered onto the hull, crawled into the turret and pleaded: "Ilan, get me out of here fast." As the tank lurched towards the rear, the loader helped Kahalani remove the tatters of his clothing, including boots that were still smouldering. He was left wearing only a wristwatch. Ilan stopped by a brigade headquarters jeep and urged its driver to take the wounded man to the rear. Officers gazed in mute dismay at this roasted figure. It was an agony to Kahalani to use his ruined hands to hold on to the vehicle as it bumped over the sand, wisps of skin flapping in the breeze.

A helicopter finally deposited Kahalani at Beersheba Hospital among a load of casualties from Sinai at 1 a.m. on 6 June. Burns, mostly third-degree, covered 60 per cent of his body. His father, hastily summoned from home, burst into tears at the first sight of him. The young tank officer was not expected to survive. He slipped away into a drugged, hallucinating world in which sometimes he was back commanding his company, shouting orders through a 105-degree fever. For weeks he lay on his stomach while inch by inch the stripped flesh of his back was repaired. He endured twelve rounds of plastic surgery in all, as skin was transplanted. The stench of his own rotting body became for the suffering soldier the most repulsive sensation of all. While he was being treated, in the same hospital his first child, a boy named Dror, was born. At last, half-healed, he was discharged.

After many months of passivity, Kahalani emerged desperate to play some role, to feel himself again of value. While still in bandages he persuaded the army to let him become an instructor at the Armoured Corps School once he was fit. Yet it was plain that he would require a long recuperation before there was any prospect that he might return to duty. For a year he studied at the army high school for his matriculation. Then he reported to the Armoured Corps training centre as a gunnery group commander. After two years there, he was sent to the Command and Staff College, to qualify him for higher rank. On completing the course in 1971 he was posted as deputy commander of the 77th Tank Battalion. He was twenty-seven. Brigadier Musa Peled, commander of the college, told him: "Kahalani, you're a nice guy and your soldiers will love you. Lieutenant-colonel—I think you'll make the grade."

Kahalani was grieved by this interview, because he perceived that Peled considered a lieutenant-colonelcy to be his ceiling. The Israeli army did not rate him as a high flier. At this stage there must have been an element of embarrassment about its dealings with him. Here was an officer to whom the IDF owed a debt, because he had suffered so much. Yet his superiors were unconvinced that he possessed the stuff of higher command. That he was tough was not in doubt, but he was not deemed very clever. He seemed a chippy, prickly, aggressive little figure. In those days, few of the best brains in the Israeli army were posted to armour. They became paratroopers, served in staff posts or special forces. Tanks were big, blunt instruments, acknowledged to be of vital importance on the battlefield. But manning them was not perceived as a task for the army's brightest and best. As for Kahalani himself, there must always be an enigma about a man who endures what he had on the battlefield, yet shows himself willing to go back for more. James Gavin could delude himself that he was invulnerable, because he was never hit, and thus was never forced to acknowledge his own mortality. By contrast, Avigdor Kahalani had learned through the most ghastly personal experience that he was vulnerable to the enemy's fire, and what were its consequences.

How could he have brought himself voluntarily to expose himself to the same horrors again? In part, perhaps, a man may delude himself that what has happened once will not happen again. More plausibly, for over a decade Kahalani had made a life as a soldier, liked it, and knew no other. It was less alarming to persevere in uniform than to hazard himself upon the uncertainties of the civilian world. The difference between the army of Israel and most of its counterparts around the world is that it fights with remarkable frequency. Any realistic assessment would have told Kahalani that Israel's wars had not ended in 1967, that the perils he had faced in the desert were likely to recur. Yet he accepted this prospect, and returned to an operational tank unit. Whatever he lacked in imagination, he made up in iron toughness.

He spent almost two years as deputy commander of the 77th Battalion, a dreary existence deep in Sinai, before early in 1973 the unit's colonel was promoted, and he himself took over. Late that summer Yanosh, their brigade commander, had a premonition that his men, so familiar with the desert, might instead have to fight on the Golan Heights, the northern cease-fire line with Syria. He took his officers for several days' study of the area, examining operational plans, comparing maps with reality on the barren rocks around Kuneitra. At that time, two battalions of the Barak Brigade represented Israel's only armoured force on the Golan. Just three days later, on 26 September, Kahalani was on leave at home at Nes Ziona for the Jewish New Year, Rosh Hashana, when he was called down from the roof, where he was fixing shingles, to take a call from brigade headquarters. There was uneasiness about a possible Syrian initiative on the Golan front, he was told. He was to take his battalion's crews up north, report to the Barak Brigade which would supply tanks, and remain there until further notice. His wife, Dalia, received the news in stony silence. She had endured so many of these sudden alerts, separations, family disappointments.

Arrived at the Barak Brigade, Kahalani was told that his unit was to become the local counterattack force. Crews from Sinai were flown north to join them, while those on leave drove from their homes. They worked into the night arming and preparing the twenty-two Centurions which they were allocated, then spent the days that followed testing equipment and reconnoitring their new sector. At this stage the Israelis anticipated only the possibility of a limited Syrian strike on the Golan. They dismissed any notion of an all-out assault.

In 1973 Israel paid the price for reckless overconfidence created by victory in 1967. First, the country now possessed a deep buffer zone between its homeland and an attacker. Second, the Six-Day War appeared to show that Israel could defeat any combination of Arab armies. Among the most important consequences of 1967 was that Israelis reposed almost unlimited faith in the power of their intelligence, air force and armoured corps. In Sinai, Israel's tanks had broken every rule of tactics about the need for infantry to operate in close support of tanks. They had got away with it. Armoured units must anyway be the weapon of choice for a small nation, because they require less manpower than infantry formations. In 1973 Israel's tank forces were quite inadequately supported by foot soldiers and mortars. On the Golan, their only important advantage was that engineers had created hundreds of purpose-built "ramps"—essentially customised firing positions for tanks, sheltered by reverse slopes. A defending tank force could manoeuvre between these ramps to great effect. Yet when the war of Yom Kippur came, Israel had few troops and tanks on the Golan. The Syrians had many—very many.

Kahalani suffered disciplinary problems in his battalion through the days that followed. To some officers and men, the alert was no more than a ridiculous official panic that had dragged them from their homes at holiday time. Some crews went about their tasks with a visible lack of urgency. On 29 September their colonel himself went home for the weekend. He arrived at his parents' house to be smartly saluted by his brother Emanuel, less than a week married and rather drunk. "Sir," he said, "you're late." Then, more seriously: "Avi, what's all this about you being on alert on the Golan?"

"It's hot up there, and somebody has to defend you."

"Do the Syrians want another war?"

"Nothing's clear yet. How was the honeymoon?"

Next day, Kahalani returned to his battalion in the north. Tension and uncertainty persisted. General Hofi, commanding the northern sector of Israel, warned his tank commanders that they should keep to dirt tracks as far as possible, rather than ruin asphalt surfaces. There had been too many crashes between tanks and civilian vehicles. Commanders were told that they must manoeuvre carefully, to avoid damaging the irrigation pipes of kibbutz farmland. Kahalani suggested acidly that if they had to fight, there would be more important things to worry about. At noon on 4 October the battalion moved into Nafah camp, the big Israeli base behind the frontier. Then, because distances in Israel are short—and so, too, is the divide between war and peace—Kahalani slipped away to attend a friend's wedding, still in army fatigues. He returned to Nafah in the middle of the morning of 5 October, to be told that the whole of the 7th Brigade, his battalion's parent unit, was moving north from Beersheba and would take up positions in the line before nightfall. He discussed deployments with the brigade commander, then visited the tank crews. He offered the traditional Yom Kippur greeting, wishing them "well over the fast." Many of his men were attending the camp synagogue even as Kahalani briefed his officers on arrangements, when the 7th Brigade arrived. Crews were ordered to draw battle rations, to check radio frequencies and call signs for each company: "Vespa," "Zechar," "Houmus," "Mattress," "Tiger." The battalion's collective call sign was "Shoter." At midnight Kahalani was wakened, and drove himself to brigade headquarters. Yanosh, his commander, said: "Kahalani, are you completely ready? We're going to have a serious war here." The colonel was chilled to hear, for the first time, that war was a real possibility.

"Are you afraid?" one of the girls in the battalion operations section blurted to him as she packed her kit before evacuation. "Afraid? I don't know," he answered. "You fear the unknown, but I know what we can expect and I don't need to be afraid. I haven't fought since I was wounded in the Six-Day War, and I don't know how I will react to be in a war again. I would say I am excited, in a way, about what will happen…In any event, if the Syrians open fire we will lay into them hard. We have a battalion of lions."

Early next morning, as tanks and vehicles of the 7th Brigade continued to stream into Nafah, Kahalani worked at organising beds, blankets, showers and all the wherewithal for a protracted stay in the camp, which was what they expected. So often, these long, dreary alerts ended in anti-climax. The men of the 77th Battalion checked their Centurions, originally British tanks almost wholly rebuilt by the Israelis. Their commander met for the first time the crew that was to be his own in battle: Yuval Ben-Ner, the driver, who seemed bewildered by the crisis; David Kilyon, the gunner, a confident kibbutznik; the loader–radio operator, another kibbutznik named Gideon Shemesh, improbably fair-haired for a Jew. "Nobody gave me permission to die at my age," Kahalani told them jovially, "so you gotta take care of me and wipe out anyone who goes for my neck!"

Most of the men on the Golan that day shared with the colonel and the rest of Israel an instinctive confidence in the nation's political and military leadership. They possessed a belief, founded in past experience, that those in charge knew what they were doing. This was now to be tested to the limit. On the morning of 6 October, the soldiers were told that war would almost certainly break out by six o'clock that evening. A few minutes before noon, a flight of Syrian MiGs streaked over Nafah, dropping bombs. Kahalani raced his jeep from the camp to his tanks' rendezvous a few kilometres away. Their engines were already roaring. Most of the 77th Battalion was despatched to the northern sector allocated to the 7th Brigade, near the town of Kuneitra. They took up position on the five-foot-high earthen ramps surmounting a ridge known as Booster. Lit by the sinking sun, with artillery fire already falling around them, tank commanders scanned the eastern horizon through binoculars, searching for a first glimpse of the Syrians.

Kahalani heard a voice on his radio: "This is Zilia." The colonel was disbelieving. "Zilia" was the old call sign of Lieutenant Efraim Laor, who had been a company commander until he disappeared from the battalion three months earlier to serve a prison sentence for crashing a jeep, injuring its passengers, while driving without a licence. Kahalani said: "You're nuts! What are you doing here?"

"I came to fight. I want to join you. Where are you?"

"On Booster Ridge. There's a war here. Hold on."

"OK. I'm looking for a tank."

Somebody found a tank for Laor, and he was soon hastening into action. Night was falling as the first Arab armoured columns approached their positions. The Syrians were equipped with Soviet infrared nightfighting equipment. The Israelis were not. They were chiefly dependent on their own lights to illuminate the battlefield, at mortal risk to themselves. All through the hours of darkness, in the first utterly unwelcome shock of the assault, the enemy pushed forward among the confused defenders, who soon exhausted their small supply of flares. Desperately, they pleaded for more. Kahalani stood beside his tank in the blackness, trying to use his infrascope to pick out infrared beams on Syrian tanks.

The Israelis were soon suffering losses. They could hit the enemy's Soviet-built T-55s and T-62s only when these came very close, and they could spot the attackers' dim shadows in the blackness. Matters became a little better as the flames of both sides' blazing tanks began to cast a fierce, brutal light across the battlefield. Within hours of the end of peace, the men on the Golan found themselves plunged into the utmost intensity of combat against overwhelming odds—sometimes and in some places twenty to one.

All through those terrible hours, Kahalani thought simply: if we can only hold on until daylight, we can beat them. Again and again he pleaded with his artillery forward observation officer to produce star shells: "Yell at them," he said. "I want illumination! My friend, I ask nothing else of you—just light up the area." But there were no more star shells that night, for ready-use supplies were exhausted. When word came of the first of his men to die, Kahalani felt a stab of recollection. A few hours earlier that same young soldier had proclaimed his eagerness to fight, saying: "I'm sick of shooting at barrels."

Suddenly Kahalani, in the turret peering through his infrascope, realised that they were caught in the full glare of a Syrian infrared gunsight. "Driver! Back up! Quickly! Move!" he cried. It seemed to take an eternity to engage the gears. The Centurion roared into reverse, lurching downhill over rocks and terracing. Belatedly there was a moment for him to explain to the crew: "We were being set up. A tank had his projector on us. We had more luck than sense." They took up a new position, then glimpsed a taillight in the darkness. Kahalani called over the radio to his tanks to ensure that all their lights were off and their engines silenced. They were. Yet fifty yards away stood a vehicle with a light showing and its engine running. It must be Syrian. Kahalani told one of his commanders to switch on a searchlight. It blazed out, revealing a Syrian T-55 at point-blank range. Kahalani fired a single shell and the enemy tank caught fire. The flames revealed a second intruder, absurdly close. An Israeli gunner fired, destroying this one too. Yet many, many more were coming.

Dawn on Sunday, 7 October, revealed some eighty enemy tanks advancing in a dense mass towards the 77th Battalion, a spectacle matched up and down the Golan and Suez fronts, as Israel's leaders found that they faced the entire might of Egypt and Syria. Israeli tank gunners were shooting as fast as they could load and aim. As the light improved on the Golan they were hitting attackers again and again, yet still the Syrians came on. Attrition was hurting the enemy badly, but was also taking a desperate toll of the defenders. Commanders, especially, paid a high price for the Israeli practice of fighting with their heads exposed above the turret cupolas, to see the battlefield. Periscopes are no substitute for eyesight. Poor visibility is a chronic weakness of all closed-down armoured vehicles. Yet for a man to expose his head on a shell-torn battlefield poses a mortal risk. Several of Kahalani's best men were already wounded or dead. Ammunition was running low. Daniel, the driver of a crippled tank, forced open his jammed steel hatch flaps as flames licked around him and scrambled to the ground, where he lay sheltering from intense Syrian artillery fire. Yair, the company commander, drove his tank alongside and leaned out to help Daniel climb its hull. A Syrian shell landed between the two, killing Yair instantly. Daniel ran away westwards towards the rear, screaming. Yair's gunner and loader, both wounded, fled after him. Kahalani ordered another officer to assume command of the company.

Amid the sound and fury of relentless gunfire, Kahalani found it hard to balance his responsibility to direct the battalion with the need to fight his own tank, engaging attacking armour wherever it appeared. The chief advantage the Israelis possessed was that their tanks were stationary, while those of the Syrians were moving. Even in the era of gyro-stabilised gunsights, it is far easier for a tank gunner to hit a mark from a stable platform. On the debit side, however, the Syrians had now seized Mount Hermon, north of the Booster Ridge. From its nine-thousand-foot summit, the enemy's gunnery observers possessed a commanding view over the battlefield. They used it well. Artillery fire poses little threat to tanks unless it is very accurate indeed. This it now became. Shell fragments took a terrible toll of tank crewmen who exposed themselves, and of some soldiers even behind armoured hulls.

Every Israeli on the Golan knew that if the battle was not yet lost, the issue—an Arab breakthrough from the heights into the green fields of Israel a few miles beyond—hung in the balance. The defenders, accustomed to command of the air, were dismayed to find themselves strafed by MiGs without interference from their own fighters or antiaircraft guns, which were either in action elsewhere, or not yet deployed. Seven of Kahalani's tank commanders were already dead. His battalion medical teams raced forward in armoured carriers, evacuating wounded under fire. The ordnance crews struggled to repair damaged tanks and return them to action. Half the Golan Heights were now in Syrian hands, including for a time Nafah camp. Much of the Barak Brigade had been destroyed. The defenders had only limited artillery support, and lacked the armoured infantry essential in modern war, especially to repel foot soldiers with handheld antitank missiles. These were now revealed as an alarming novelty on the Middle East battlefield, a critical element of the Arab assault. A tank is a woefully clumsy weapon with which to stop a man dashing across open ground.

On Monday, 8 October, Kahalani was ordered to lead his battalion to recapture the valley below their positions. They surged forward, weaving their steel monsters through the mass of wreckage clogging the battlefield. It was hard to distinguish between enemy tanks that were abandoned hulks, and others that still stood manned and dangerous. The enemy's Sagger handheld missiles began to take a serious toll, alongside Syrian artillery and tank gunfire. One by one Centurions fell out of line and halted, disabled. Kahalani concluded that the counterattack was hopeless. He requested and received permission to pull back to the start line. His men were exhausted and depressed, fighting to stay awake in their turrets. "Sleeplessness is more powerful than any fear," he wrote. "An exhausted body does not function." In all their earlier wars, the Israelis had been able to exploit lulls in the fighting during the hours of darkness, to make some rest possible. Now, instead, they found themselves in action without pause around the clock. The strain on the dwindling force of defenders was appalling, as they fought to stay awake amid the stink of sweat, cordite, fumes and fear in their steel boxes. When they withdrew briefly to load fuel and ammunition, the maintenance crews were alarmed by their weariness. Yet the battle was nowhere near done. It was the iron toughness of such men as Kahalani, their ability to endure and continue to fight almost robotically, that enabled Israel in those days to hold the line against overwhelming odds.

That evening, Kahalani was ordered to shift position to cover the northern side of Kuneitra. At daybreak on Tuesday he moved again, taking eight tanks to a kibbutz on the edge of the escarpment from which they watched passively, almost despairingly, as another Centurion bat-

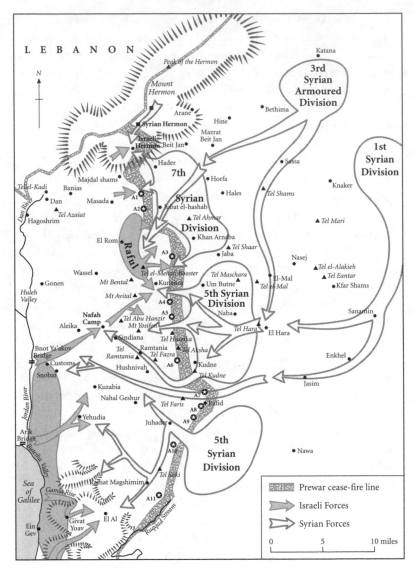

The Golan Heights, midnight, Sunday, 7 October 1973.

talion was shattered by a fresh Syrian assault. Kahalani, intent on watching the battle, responded impatiently when his hungry crew asked permission to open battle rations. "Are you crazy?" he said. "We may have to move at any minute. Stay in firing positions." The crew said: "We don't want to fight on empty stomachs." Their commander responded: "We'll find time for it." Through that early morning he chafed as he watched the carnage before him, finding it unbearable temporarily to be a mere spectator. Suddenly there was a new sensation: six big helicopters laden with Syrian commandos swept over their heads and landed in the rear, pursued by ineffectual machine-gun fire from the tank gunners, though Israeli defenders brought down one helicopter. The tank crews felt a surge of despondency at the knowledge that the enemy was behind them. It seemed that the 77th Battalion's lifeline to fuel and casualty evacuation was cut off. In reality the Syrians were swiftly destroyed by Israeli special forces, but no one gave that reassuring news to Kahalani.

Later that day the battalion's seven surviving tanks moved to new positions amid a chaos of vehicles and blackened foot soldiers scurrying to and fro in search of safety or tactical advantage. Suddenly the smoke and dust which rose in clouds and eddied around the advancing Centurions blew aside. Kahalani saw fifty yards to his front a terrifying sight: three Syrian tanks, two stationary and one moving. "Stop!" he shouted to his driver. Ducking into the turret and grabbing the traverse handle, he roared at the gunner: "Fire fast!" Kilyon asked innocently: "What's the range?" Kahalani was almost hysterical. Kicking out at the gunner, he cried: "It doesn't matter. Fire already!" The recoil rocked the tank. The Syrian T-62 did not brew up, but its crew bailed out. Kahalani traversed again. "See it?" he demanded. "Yes!" said Kilyon, and fired again, opening a great hole in the Syrian's turret. The third Arab tank's gun was already trained directly on their own. Kahalani crouched, ready to leap out and run for his life, rather than face again the blazing horror he had experienced in 1967. There was a heart-stopping moment. As the Israeli commander shouted furiously: "Fire, fire!" Kilyon said: "It doesn't work!" The shellcase of their previous round was jammed in the breech. Gideon the loader tugged with all his might. Somehow they pulled the case free, and rammed home a fresh charge. There was an explosion. Mercifully, it was the detonation of their own gun. The target burst into flames. A fourth Syrian tank ground into view. This too was despatched, by a neighbouring Centurion. After those seconds of crisis, Kahalani found himself dripping with the sweat of fear. That morning, on his battalion's front alone some sixty Syrian tanks were destroyed.

It was through such startling rates of attrition, commonplace in the 1973 conflict, that the defence of Israel was narrowly sustained. At no time after the first day did the 7th Brigade muster more than forty tanks, while the Syrians committed five hundred. As so often in war, the quality and training of the men manning the weapons proved decisive, even against overwhelming numbers and superior enemy technology. The 77th Battalion moved forward to its new positions, Kahalani as usual straining his ears to identify on his radio headset messages destined for his own unit, amid the babble of brigade and divisional traffic.

That Tuesday morning, a new force of some forty Syrian tanks took up position 1,500 yards east of Kahalani's position, along the fence that marked the prewar boundary of Syria and Israeli-occupied Golan. He was deputed by his brigade commander to take control of the whole sector's defence. Every tank that could be spared was sent to his aid. There were perilously few of them. And even as the reinforcements deployed, they took more losses. A frightened voice announced over the air: "The battalion commander is dead!" Kahalani interrupted quickly: "This is the battalion commander. I'm alive. They don't kill me that quickly." But Ratess, another colonel, was indeed dead, hit as he led his Centurions to cover Kahalani's flank. Several other tanks of Ratess's unit were destroyed. The remainder fell back. Kahalani was convinced that unless the Israelis could regain control of the low ridge ahead of them, they were lost. Everywhere around him he saw Israeli tanks halting, considering retreat. Syrian tank fire began to fall among them. He sensed that his force was on the verge of panic.

Urgently, he called the Centurions on his radio: "Shoter stations, this is Shoter. Look at the enemy's guts! He takes his positions and looks us in the eye. What about us? What the hell's happening to us? Who's stronger, we or these Arabs? Start advancing and line up with me. I'm waving the flag. Go!" The heads of commanders poked from cupolas up and down the hill, looking for their leader. Some newly arrived Centurions from another battalion were operating on a different radio frequency, to Kahalani's frustration, and appeared not to hear his commands. Yet most of the tanks surged obediently forward. The colonel urged on those who hung back: "Don't stop, don't stop."

One company commander, Amnon, had lost his traversing mechanism and was now aiming by wrenching his entire tank right or left to engage targets. He did not even feel a Syrian shell strike his turret. It penetrated, pulverising his loader. The ghastly sight caused the gunner to throw up. Then the surviving crew members bailed out, and a second lieutenant took over the company. The rest of the Centurions reached the crest of the ridge, and were rewarded with a panoramic vision of Syrian tanks crossing the valley below them. "Shoot only at the moving ones," Kahalani urged his crews. He was desperate to avoid wasting precious ammunition on the abandoned vehicles which lay everywhere across the battlefield. He wrote later: "We kept firing like maniacs, every man fighting for his life." They noticed enviously that Syrian shellcases were spewing from the T-62 turrets by automatic ejection, which significantly speeded the enemy's rate of fire. In every way, it seemed, the Arab equipment was superior to their own. Only the men were different. The brigade's leader, Yanosh, told his divisional commander, Raful: "Still holding the ridge, but the pressure is heavy, very heavy. It's all very close range." The rocklike Raful said doggedly: "We're better than them." So they were. Kahalani told Yanosh on the radio, proudly asserting his Yemenite heritage: "Don't worry! I'm a black panther! They won't get past me." Yet some Syrian tanks had already crossed his line. The Israelis were engaging targets at every point of the compass.

On Kahalani's right flank, the Centurions had taken heavy losses. He was relieved to see a small reinforcement of eight tanks moving up to fill the gap. These just sufficed to stem the tide. Every gunner was firing as fast as he could load and aim. Burning vehicles crowded the rockscape. Bailed-out Syrian crewmen scuttled for safety amid the shambles in the valley below. Suddenly, the Israelis perceived that the balance had shifted. Arab tanks were pulling back eastwards. Incoming gunfire was falling away. Israeli aircraft appeared—at last reaching the battlefield in strength—and swooped to destroy the bridges laid by the enemy across the old prewar antitank ditch. The Syrian assault was petering out. The 7th Brigade was reduced to twenty operational tanks. Hardly a single Israeli Centurion was without battle damage. The survivors had expended almost all their ammunition. But they had held their hill, and named the valley below "The Vale of Tears." Syrian losses were devastating. Some 260 wrecked or abandoned Arab tanks, together with hundreds of other armoured vehicles, lay amid the barren rocks in front of the victors.

By sections, the Israelis withdrew to refuel and rearm. Blackened and filthy, as he stood by the hull of his tank Kahalani saw his brother Amon, a mechanic. The two men embraced. The support teams clustered around the tank crews, offering congratulations. They knew what the Centurions had achieved. By the narrowest of margins, the Barak Brigade and the 7th Brigade had saved the people of Israel. Tuesday, 9 October, saw the frustration of the last big Syrian offensive effort. Israeli reinforcements were now pouring to the front, as mobilised reservists reached Golan and Sinai. The tide of the war had turned decisively. The brigade intelligence officer told a disbelieving Kahalani: "Tomorrow you go into Syria." Israel was poised to launch the great counteroffensive that would sweep her forces into the enemy's land, until they halted within artillery range of Damascus. Weary days and hard fighting lay ahead, but every man on the Golan knew that the crisis was over, their country was once more secure.

After the briefing for the drive into Syria, the 7th Brigade's commander, Yanosh, called: "Kahalani, come here a minute." He took the colonel aside and put his arm around his shoulder. "Listen," he said, "I met with the chief of the General Staff...I wanted you to know...I spoke with him about you, told him how you stopped the Syrians. I told him you're a hero of Israel." Yanosh shook Kahalani's hand, and the two men parted: "It'll be OK. See you."

They did not meet again until 24 October. It was the last day of the war, and they were deep inside Syria. Kahalani was summoned by jeep to brigade headquarters. He had no idea why. Yanosh took him for a drive. They proceeded for some distance in silence, then Yanosh said: "Your brother's been killed." Kahalani asked: "Which one?" It was Emanuel, whose wedding he had attended only days before. He had met his fate in Sinai some days earlier, but the decision was made to keep the news from the tank colonel until his own battle was done. There was more bad news yet: his brother-in-law Ilan, brother of Avigdor's wife, Dalia, and a communications officer with a tank brigade at Suez, had also died. He too was newly married, his wife five months pregnant. Israel is a family. Almost every home in the nation had a loved one to mourn after Yom Kippur. "Go home," said Yanosh to Kahalani. And so he did.

After Yom Kippur, Israel made eleven awards of its highest military honour, the Medal of Valour, of which three were posthumous. One of the eight decorations conferred on living soldiers went to Avigdor Kahalani. His dead brother was awarded the Distinguished Service Medal. Kahalani went on to become one of Israel's most famous soldiers—a general, a divisional commander in the 1982 invasion of Lebanon, and later like so many Israeli military leaders, a controversial politician. Some critics continued to harbour doubts about his character and abilities. They disliked what they considered the vainglory of the book, *The Heights of Courage* (1997), he wrote about his experiences in 1973, and suggested that Israel's eagerness to discover heroes among her unfashionable minorities, the Yemenites prominent among them, had caused the army to overpromote Kahalani.

Avigdor Kahalani was certainly not an intellectual soldier, yet his vanity has been shared by many successful warriors. His deeds on the Golan Heights, which were surely remarkable by any standard, should perhaps be regarded as an example of the achievement of the entire Israeli tank corps in 1973, rather than of any one man. Other officers also fought bravely against overwhelming odds, several of them on the Syrian front. Yet nothing can detract from the fact that Kahalani showed himself an exceptionally determined and courageous commander, worthy of Yanosh's accolade as "a hero of Israel." For so many years Israel's tank units had been the army's Cinderellas, forced to seek recruits among those whom the elite arms rejected. Yet after Yom Kippur, every Israeli knew that it was the tank crews which had saved their people. To an extraordinary degree, probably never again to be repeated in war, 1973 was a clash of massed armour, in which victory was attained by those soldiers who proved supreme exponents of the tank fighter's art, Avigdor Kahalani prominent among them.

Today, the reputation of the Israeli army has been sadly tarnished by its commitment as an army of occupation, its units chiefly committed to the repression of Palestinians. Most students of war prefer to remember the Israel Defence Force as it was in 1973, when its citizen soldiers fought magnificently in an epic defence. Kahalani was no Marlborough or Patton, no Sherman or Wellington. He was not even made of the stuff of Dayan, Rafael Eitan and other great Israeli commanders. But he was the sort of soldier who made Israel's historic victories possible, and who saved the Jewish nation at Yom Kippur.

AFTERWORD

When I started to write this book, I chose its subjects to reflect a range of military experience in the nineteenth and twentieth centuries, rather than because I perceived common personal characteristics. Baron Marbot, Harry Smith, John Masters and Nancy Wake might be described as joyous warriors. Lieutenant Chard was thrust into remarkable circumstances, which caused him to be rewarded in a remarkable way. Frederic Manning was a bard of soldiers, rather than being himself a notable example of the breed.

Yet among the others, and especially those of the twentieth century, when war ceased to be considered a legitimate entertainment for the leisured classes, similarities are striking. Most were products of bleak childhoods. Ruthlessness of purpose was indispensable to them, and many were fired by a measure of anger. Few stars of the battlefield have been popular comrades. Like Achilles they command admiration, but are also feared and sometimes resented by those among whom they serve. Soldiers, and especially conscript citizen soldiers, prefer to share a foxhole with men whom they recognise as being made of the same frail stuff as themselves. Most are willing—often movingly so—to do their duty. But among normal men, the urge for self-preservation is stronger than any impulse to perform heroic deeds.

Most successful warriors are powerfully influenced by personal ambition. Why should they not be? They discover that they are good at fighting, better able than their comrades to subordinate fear to the pur-

poses of battle. Few have been without vanity about their achievements, any more than were the gods and heroes of Greek myth. Having
achieved celebrity, however, many have been handicapped by immatu-
rity. Men and women who achieve fame and success in politics, the pro-
fessions or commerce are almost invariably approaching middle age.
Warriors, like sports and movie stars, often achieve their triumphs very
young, and suffer in consequence. Moreover, the skills of a successful
warrior are those least suited for adaptation to a subsequent peacetime
career in which incoming fire is verbal rather than explosive. To a businessman or politician, judgement is a more useful virtue than courage.
Dexterity in handling weapons of war is valueless except on the battlefield. Even within a nation's armed forces, men who show themselves
able fighters are seldom fitted for the highest commands. Not since the
Hundred Years' War has prowess in the physical act of killing proved a
valid criterion for appointing a general. Modern attempts to reward
heroes by promotion have usually proved ill-starred.

The professional soldier Edmund Verney wrote gleefully to his
brother from the war in Flanders in 1639: "'Twere sport to hear that all
the World were in combustion, for then we could not want work. 'Tis a
blessed trade." Verney was twenty-three at the time he penned these
words, a fine age for a warrior. He did not live long enough—he was
killed in Ireland in 1649—to experience the disillusionment of a veteran's existence in times of peace. Many warriors who achieve great
things as young men avow later in life that nothing remotely as stimulat-
ing or interesting happened to them afterwards, which is usually cause
for melancholy. Once they have achieved fame—sometimes together
with authority and responsibility—at an age when most people in
peacetime are mere students or apprentices, the passage of years offers
soldiers sour fruits. Every schoolboy used to learn the words Shakespeare wrote for Henry V on the morning of Agincourt in 1415:

> *He that shall live this day, and see old age,*
> *Will yearly on the vigil feast his neighbours,*
> *And say, "Tomorrow is Saint Crispian":*
> *Then will he strip his sleeve and show his scars,*
> *And say, "These wounds I had on Crispin's day."*

Old men forget; yet all shall be forgot,
But he'll remember with advantages
What feats he did that day.

Contrast that glorious prophecy with the petition of an authentic Agincourt veteran to the authentic Henry VI in 1429:

> To the King, our sovereign lord,
>
> Beseecheth meekly your poor liegeman and humble petitioner Thomas Hostelle...that in consideration of his service done to your noble progenitors of full blessed memory, King Henry IV and King Henry V (whose souls God assoile), being at the siege of Harfleur there smitten with a springbolt through the head, losing his one eye and his cheek bone broken; also at the battle of Agincourt, and afore at the taking of the carracks on the sea, there with a gadde of iron his plates smitten into his body and his hand smitten in sunder, and sore hurt, maimed and wounded, by means whereof he being sore feebled and bruised, now fall to great age and poverty, greatly indebted, and may not help himself... and being for his said service never yet recompensed nor rewarded, it please your high and excellent grace...of your benign pity and grace to relieve and refresh your said petitioner as it shall please you...

History does not record the fate of Hostelle's petition, but it is hard to be optimistic. Harry Smith died in genteel poverty, his repeated solicitations for a peerage or pension denied by the governments of the day. Joshua Lawrence Chamberlain and James Gavin, remarkable warriors both, were disappointed in many of their later ambitions. The sorry circumstances of John Paul Vann's passing speak for themselves. More than a few holders of the Victoria Cross have been driven to sell their medals. Kipling wrote in 1891:

> *There were thirty million English who talked of England's might,*
> *There were twenty broken troopers who lacked a bed for the night.*
> *They had neither food nor money, they had neither service nor trade;*
> *They were only shiftless soldiers, the last of the Light Brigade.*

Service to one's country in war has seldom been a profitable affair since plunder and the award of prize money to naval officers went out of fashion. The commanding officer of the British battalion in which Sergeant-Major Stan Hollis served on D-Day wrote sadly: "I am afraid it was easier to get him a VC in the war than a decent job after it." Most warriors must be content with their medals and memories, even if some find it hard to live with the latter. It has been calculated that of III British VC winners in the nineteenth century, seven subsequently committed suicide—almost a hundred times the average for the population at large—while many more lived out unsatisfactory existences. In modern times war is no longer viewed, as once it was, as a golden gateway through which bold spirits may journey to adventure and glory. Overwhelmingly influenced as we are by the horrors of the twentieth century's two world wars, together with the intimate awareness of conflict's horrors which television brings into every home, mankind's descents into violence are now perceived with revulsion—and no civilised person can regret this.

The only professional soldiers to enjoy widespread fame and regard in the twenty-first century are Western special forces in the vanguard of the struggle against terrorism, prominent among them America's Delta Force and Britain's Special Air Service. The 1981 pictures of the SAS abseiling into the Iranian Embassy in Kensington to rescue innocent hostages from terrorists are the most sympathetic warrior images of modern times. No tank commander, pilot or infantryman, however decorated, can match the glamour conferred upon special forces, not least by Hollywood. Their men appear to keep alive the concepts of personal initiative and individual heroism, in an age when warfare is dominated by technology.

Amid cruise missiles, Stealth Bombers and computer-driven battlefield operations, their doings seem reassuringly human. They inspire myths and legends as fanciful as any featured in the mediaeval chronicles of Froissart. The qualities demonstrated by special forces are perceived by a twenty-first-century generation as deserving of adulation, in a fashion in which pilots dropping cluster bombs or tank crews firing depleted uranium shells are not. The distinction is fanciful, of course. The business of any warrior today is what it has always been: to kill the enemy. Special forces display greater ruthlessness than most in doing so.

Yet the public cherishes its illusions, together with its nostalgia for the old-fashioned superman.

Such figures as Guy Gibson and Audie Murphy were indeed supermen, in that they showed themselves capable of repeatedly performing feats in the cause of freedom which few others would have attempted. They slew dragons not once, but again and again. It is melancholy to observe how little happiness their achievements brought them. Yet we should continue to honour their memories, along with those of others of their kind. Whatever their vanities and blemishes, they did great service to their countries, of a kind which few are capable of rendering. It may be pleasant to dream of a future in which warriors will become redundant, but it is foolish to suppose that this will come. Even the most civilised societies should take pride in the military heritage which has secured their prosperity, and sometimes their survival, through the centuries.

There is a famous, if sadly apocryphal, story of two RAF fighter pilots who, at the height of the Second World War, were invited back to their former Oxford college to dine. After an evening amid the professors and tutors at High Table, the young fliers became drunk. One of them taunted the complacent old men, demanding what contribution they were making to the war effort. "Young man," answered a sage magisterially, "*we* are the culture *you* are fighting to defend." Warriors might today turn this tale on its head, asserting to a modern generation: "We are those who have fought to defend the culture of peace which you perceive as your entitlement."

Kipling again:

> *We aren't no thin red heroes, nor we aren't no blackguards too,*
> *But single men in barricks, most remarkable like you;*
> *An' if sometimes our conduck isn't all your fancy paints,*
> *Why, single men in barricks don't grow into plaster saints;*
> *While it's Tommy this, an' Tommy that, an' "Tommy, fall be'ind,"*
> *But it's "Please to walk in front, sir," when there's trouble in the wind.*

I have aspired to tell the tales of some warriors who walked in front when there was trouble in the wind.

SOURCES AND REFERENCES

This book is intended as an entertainment rather than an academic study, and I have thus adopted a more cavalier attitude to references than in my other works based upon original research. I learned something about some of my subjects from following in their footsteps. I retraced the path of the Gordon relief expedition across the Bayuda Desert for a television documentary, and have visited the lonely and inhospitable battlefield where Fred Burnaby died. I spent some time as a correspondent in Vietnam in the 1970s, and so became familiar with most of the places where John Paul Vann worked and fought. As mentioned above, I was a spectator on the Golan Heights with the Israeli army in October 1973 when Avigdor Kahalani was fighting his epic battle. I met Jim Gavin and John Masten.

The book is otherwise almost entirely based upon published material. There seems no purpose in cataloguing background reading about each of the conflicts concerned, which is prodigious. I have here confined myself to listing my principal sources, together with works from which I have quoted. Dates of publication refer to the editions which I have used, rather than to dates of first appearances.

CHAPTER ONE: BONAPARTE'S BLESSED FOOL

The Memoirs of Baron Marbot (Greenhill Books, 1988).

CHAPTER TWO: HARRY AND JUANA

Memoirs of Lieutenant-General Sir Harry Smith edited by J. C. Mooresmith (John Murray, 1902); *Remember You Are an Englishman* by Joseph H. Lehmann (Jonathan Cape, 1977); *Adventures in the Rifle Brigade* by J. Kincaid (Spellmount, 1996); *Random Shots from a Rifleman* by J. Kincaid (Spellmount, 1998).

337

CHAPTER THREE: PROFESSOR OF ARMS

In the Hands of Providence by Alice Rains Trulock (University of North Carolina Press, 1992); *Blood and Fire at Gettysburg* by Joshua Lawrence Chamberlain (Stan Clark Military Books, 1994); *The Passing of the Armies* by Joshua Lawrence Chamberlain (Bantam, New York, 1993); *Bayonet! Forward!* by Joshua Lawrence Chamberlain (Stan Clark Military Books, 1994); *Soul of the Lion* by Willard M. Wallace (Stan Clark Military Books, 1995).

CHAPTER FOUR: THE LAZY ENGINEER

The Washing of the Spears by Donald R. Morris (Jonathan Cape, 1965); *Rorke's Drift* by Michael Glover (Leo Cooper, 1975); unpublished material in the Royal Engineers Museum, Chatham; *Zulu* by Saul David (Penguin, 2004).

CHAPTER FIVE: COLONEL FRED

True Blue by Michael Alexander (Hart Davis, 1957).

CHAPTER SIX: GENTLEMAN-OF-WAR

The Last Corsair by Dan van der Vat (Birlinn, 2002).

CHAPTER SEVEN: MOST PRIVATE SOLDIER

Frederic Manning: An Unfinished Life by Jonathan Marwil (Duke University, 1988); *The Middle Parts of Fortune* by Frederic Manning (Peter Davies, 1978); the MS War Diary of 7th KSLI 1916, in the British National Archive; *A Schoolboy Goes to War* by H.E.L. Mellersh (London, 1978).

CHAPTER EIGHT: THE KILLER

Fighting the Flying Circus by E. V. Rickenbacker (Stokes, 1919); *Rickenbacker: An Autobiography* (Hutchinson, 1968); *Eddie Rickenbacker* by Hans Christian Adamson (Macmillan, New York, 1946); *Ace of Aces: The Life of Captain Eddie Rickenbacker* by H. Paul Jeffers (Ballantine, 2004); *The First of the Few* by Denis Winter (Penguin, 1981); *Sagittarius Rising* by Cecil Lewis (Peter Davies, 1936); *Winged Victory* by V. M. Yeates (Mayflower, 1972). Professor W. David Lewis, the distinguished American aviation historian and author of a forthcoming biography of Rickenbacker, read my draft chapter, corrected some errors and drew my attention to some issues, for which I am most grateful.

CHAPTER NINE: AN INDIAN ODYSSEY

John Masters: A Regimented Life by John Clay (Michael Joseph, 1992); *Bugles and a Tiger* by John Masters (Michael Joseph, 1955); *The Road Past Mandalay* by John

Masters (Michael Joseph, 1961); *Chindit* by Robert Rhodes James (John Murray, 1980); *The Chindit War* by Shelford Bidwell (Hodder and Stoughton, 1979).

CHAPTER TEN: THE DAM BUSTER

Guy Gibson by Richard Morris with Colin Dobinson (Penguin, 1995); *Enemy Coast Ahead* by Guy Gibson (Michael Joseph, 1946). I am indebted to Richard Morris for reading and commenting upon the draft of this chapter, though of course he bears no responsibility for my judgements, and indeed would himself qualify some of them.

CHAPTER ELEVEN: HOLLYWOOD HERO

To Hell and Back by Audie Murphy (Henry Holt and Co., 1948); *A Thinker's Damn* by William Russo (William Russo, 2001); publications of the Audie Murphy Foundation; "The Price of Valor" by Roger Spiller (*Military History Quarterly*, spring 1993).

CHAPTER TWELVE: SLIM JIM

Paratrooper by T. Michael Booth and Duncan Spencer (Simon and Schuster, 1994); *On to Berlin* by James Gavin (Viking, 1978); *Airborne Warfare* by James Gavin (Infantry Journal Press, Washington, D.C., 1947).

CHAPTER THIRTEEN: THE WHITE MOUSE

Nancy Wake by Russell Braddon (Cassell, 1957); *The White Mouse* by Nancy Wake (Macmillan Australia, 1997).

CHAPTER FOURTEEN: FREEDOM'S YOUNG APOSTLE

A Bright Shining Lie by Neil Sheehan (Random House, 1988). Neil Sheehan was generous enough to read and comment upon the draft of this chapter, for which I am warmly grateful.

CHAPTER FIFTEEN: EPIC ON THE GOLAN

The Heights of Courage by Avigdor Kahalani (Steimatzky, 1997); *A Warrior's Way* by Avigdor Kahalani (Steimatzky, 1999).

INDEX

Ranks and titles given are those held at the time of the events described.

ILLUSTRATION CREDITS

ALSO BY MAX HASTINGS

OVERLORD

D-Day and the Battle for Normandy

On June 6, 1944, American and British troops staged the greatest amphibious landing in history to begin Operation Overlord, the battle to liberate Europe from the scourge of the Third Reich. With gut-wrenching realism and immediacy, Hastings reveals the terrible human cost that this battle exacted. Uncompromising and powerful in its depiction of wartime, this is the definitive book on D-Day and the Battle of Normandy.

Military History/World War II/978-0-307-27571-4

ARMAGEDDON

The Battle for Germany, 1944–1945

In September 1944, the Allies believed that Hitler's army was beaten and expected the bloodshed to end by Christmas. Yet a series of mistakes and setbacks, drastically altered this timetable and led to eight more months of brutal fighting. With *Armageddon*, the eminent military historian Max Hastings gives us memorable accounts of the great battles and captures their human impact on soldiers and civilians. This rousing chronicle brings to life the crucial final months of the twentieth century's greatest global conflict.

Military History/World War II/978-0-375-71422-1

VINTAGE BOOKS
Available at your local bookstore, or call toll-free to order:
1-800-793-2665 (credit cards only).